THE HINGE OF HISTORY

by
Charlotte Waterlow

Charlotte Waterlow

CHARLOTTE WATERLOW was born in England, the daughter of a diplomat, in 1915. She studied history at Cambridge University. From 1940 until 1953 she was a temporary administrative grade civil servant, during the War in the Ministry of War Transport, and from 1945 to 1953 in the Foreign Office, where she worked on the economic and social development of the Middle East and the problems of the Palestinian refugees, and was awarded the M.B.E. This experience gave her an insight into the inner workings of government and diplomacy. From 1954 until her retirement in 1982 she taught modern world history at the senior level, first in a girls' State High School (Grammar School) at Guildford in England, and from 1972 to 1982 at a private co-educational High School in Cambridge, Massachusetts, USA. She is the author of four text books in this field, on comparative government and justice (Methuen, London, 1964): India in the 20th century (Ginn, London, 1967); Europe 1945 to 1970 (Methuen, London, 1972), and "Superpowers and Victims" – the rich and the poor nations (Prentice-Hall, USA, 1974). Since she retired she has been active in the United Nations' Association (UK) and the World Federalist Movement, and written a number of books and pamphlets for them. Her travels include visits to India, USSR, China, Australia, New Zealand, Canada and many countries of West and East Europe.

A One World Trust Book
First published in Great Britain in 1995 by The One World Trust.
Copyright © 1995 by Charlotte Waterlow
The moral right of the author has been asserted.

A British Library Cataloguing in Publication Data
catalogue record for this book is available from the British Library.

ISBN No. 0 9504434 5 X

Printed in England by ESG London.

DEDICATED TO:

The memory of my father, Sydney Waterlow, who sowed the seeds of the theme of this book in my mind when I was seventeen; and to my friend Mary Holdstock.

ACKNOWLEDGEMENTS:

I should like to express my deep thanks to: Dr. Douglas Holdstock, who, together with Mary Holdstock, has given me invaluable help in editing the book and checking the references; to Mary Holdstock and Rosemary Douglas for typing much of it; to Duncan Smith, trustee of the New Economics Foundation, for reading and commenting on the whole text; to Professor Klaus Trott and Uta Trott for commenting on the chapters on art and science; to Professor Emeritus Paul Lawrence of Harvard University for reading the text and writing the Preface; to Philip Harmsworth for contributing a section on the Baha'i faith in Chapter 16; to Alison Van Dyk and Juliette Hollister of the Temple of Understanding in New York for their enthusiastic support; to all my friends and colleagues in the World Federalist Movement throughout the world and in particular to Archibald Evans, former senior official in the International Labour Organisation and to John Roberts, Chairman of the Association of World Federalists in Britain, for all I have learnt from them in 20 years comradely association; and to Jon Skinner and Pete Rowe for their extreme friendliness in the work of printing the book.

Finally, I owe an incalculable debt of gratitude to the girls and boys of Guildford Girls' Grammar School in England and Buckingham, Browne and Nichols School in Cambridge, Massachusette, USA, for the interest and enthusiasm with which they worked with me in the study of modern world history.

CONTENTS

PART I. TRADITIONAL CIVILISATIONS

PART II. THE MODERN CIVILISATION

PREFACE

By Paul R. Lawrence, Professor Emeritus at the Graduate School of Business Administration, Harvard University.

THIS is a book of unusual originality. After working for thirteen years in the British Civil Service, including eight years in the Foreign Office, and then teaching history for thirty years in Britain and the United States, Charlotte Waterlow has turned a perceptive eye on the whole development of humanity, from 3000 B.C. to what it could become in the future. In this era of specialisation a wide-angle appraisal of this kind can be very helpful - particularly for younger people, many of whom are distressed by the ideological uncertainty in which they live.

This work is divided clearly into two parts. Part I discusses traditional civilisations, in the plural, as they flourished during the period 3000 B.C. to 1800 A.D. - the beginning of the "modern" age. The author shows that all these civilisations or "cultures" had basic features in common. They were all essentially static, with the partial exception of Western Europe, where the enzymes of Greek philosophy and Roman law and the separation of church and state helped catalyse the Renaissance, the Reformation, the scientific revolution of the 17th century and the "enlightenment" of the 18th century.

And then, with the French and American Revolutions, a new kind of consciousness dawned - the very hinge of history. Part II deals with the modern civilisation, in the singular, which has burst forth in the part 200 years, grounded on two tremendous developments - science, both pure and applied, and the concept of human rights. The latter is based on the affirmation that every individual is a unique person, who has the right to the conditions of life needed to enable him or her to fulfil his inherent creative potential. In the past 200 years the application of this principle has begun to release human energies. Part II discusses the ethics, philosophy and implementation of human rights.

It outlines the enormous problem which now confronts humanity as the clash between modernity and tradition releases the pent-up emotions and aspirations of centuries. It ends with an account of concrete factors such as the creation of the United Nations and the European Community, the development of international law and the proliferation of non-governmental organisations, which are promoting world community at various levels of action.

Some readers may be critical of an attempt to cover so much historical ground in a single account. In my view, the author is to be praised for her courage in seeking out major themes in the course of human civilisation.

The long term view of history presented in this book should give encouragement and hope to those who are troubled by the upheavals and the horrors of the present day. It offers readers, especially younger people, a perspective that can help them develop their own philosophies and belief systems.

Cambridge, Massachusetts, USA
September 1994

FOREWORD

WHO IS A PERSON ?

A RTICLE 26 of the United Nations' Universal Declaration of Human Rights of 1948 asserts that: "Everyone has the right to education . . . Education shall be directed to the full development of the human personality . . ."

This is perhaps the most important sentence in the modern world. Who is a person? What is his or her "personality"?

We all know that we humans are a species of animal, distinguished from other animals by possessing not merely consciousness but self-consciousness: the ability to think, reason, calculate, love, hate, respond to and create beauty and ugliness, experience courage and fear. Our creative potential is involved with values and ideas of a kind not displayed by animals. We also know that every individual person is expressed in his or her genetic code and fingerprints. His psychological uniqueness is inexpressible. It is not fundamentally affected by gender, colour, race or other factors which may condition his membership of a group. "Personhood" may be a more appropriate word than "personality", which is sometimes used today to imply the *persona,* the Latin word for "mask" which masks the true person. A teacher may adopt a persona in the class room, a business man in the office, or a politician at the podium. A fundamental attribute of personhood is the capacity for growth. Abram Maslow, in his seminal book *Towards a Psychology of Being,* talks of "self-actualising persons".

Are these statements an adequate definition of you or me or John or Mary? Surely not! There must be some factor which provides a person's imprimatur, which expresses itself in his or her unique style, which impels the inherent direction of his unfolding creativity. Let us call it the psyche, the Greek word for soul, the word on which that exploding modern phenomenon, psychology, is based. We may then say that personhood is the actualisation of the soul, and personality its expression. What is the soul? In religious terms it is a divine spark; it stems from God, and therefore embodies god-like qualities: immortality, perfectibility, and timelessness.

In the present age humanity is responding to a fundamental urge to grow into the realisation of personhood. This is the deeper meaning of the "universal" doctrine of human rights. It is small wonder that those who cannot cope with this urge, or who deflect it to express their hubris, are dehumanising, torturing and killing their fellow persons on a massive scale. Love and hate are polarised in the world as never before.

If the soul is the citadel of the person, and the soul is immortal, "death" is simply a change in the soul's garment or "body". The universe is therefore full of discarnate persons, who have lived on this earth, or else on other planets not yet discovered by us earthlings. This opens up vistas of love, joy and creative unfoldment of personhood beyond our wildest imagining. We are members of a vast celestial family of persons! The only other logical conclusion is that our personhood is simply the emanation of the chemicals of which our bodies are made, and goes out of existence when the physical body dies.

The purpose of this book is to suggest that history shows that in traditional societies the significance of personhood was not understood. Culture and civilisation were collective, set within the context of a universe which was regarded as divine. In the modern age a supreme leap forward is being taken into the understanding and expression of personhood; but there is great confusion about its divine context. The resolution of this confusion in the next century many see the human race move forward into what Churchill called the "broad, sun-lit uplands" of an order of civilisation not yet dreamed of.

PART I

TRADITIONAL CIVILISATIONS 3000 B.C. TO 1800 A.D.

Chapter 1

THE DISCOVERY OF THE PAST

ALL through the centuries the mighty ruins of ancient civilisations lay forgotten, covered over by tropical forests in Central America, or buried under soil or sand, or like the pyramids of Egypt, the temples of Greece and the sarsen stones of Stonehenge in England, simply ignored. Tombs were plundered by robbers; monuments were dismantled so that their stones could be used for contemporary construction (as at Avebury in England); documents were burnt (the fate of half a million scrolls in the great library of Greek manuscripts at Alexandria); and temples and statues dedicated to "idols" were smashed by fanatics.

In 529 A.D. the Emperor Justinian closed the Schools of Philosophy which Plato and Aristotle had founded in Athens. Centuries later, in the 12th and 13th centuries, universities arose in West Europe - in Salerno, Bologna, Paris, Oxford and Cambridge. The manuscripts of Aristotle's works (brought by Arabs) and the legal codes of Rome turned up in these new places of learning, and interest in the classical past was born. The dawn of the Renaissance in the 15th century brought a flood of oriental manuscripts into West Europe, and scholars began to master oriental languages, such as Arabic, Syriac, Aramaic, Coptic, Farsi and Turkish, as well, of course, as Greek and Hebrew.

In the 17th and 18th centuries the modern science of archaeology was born in Western Europe. The urge to explore, excavate, interpret and understand ancient civilisations began to seize the European imagination. Who really were the men and women of myth and legend, of Scripture stories and epic poems? "At the start of the 19th century such questions could be asked in the perfect assurance that nobody knew the answers", writes a scholar. "Myth and fact met at some undefined point and became one" (1). For centuries people everywhere, from scholars to peasants, accepted myth as fact.

By the beginning of the 19th century this cloud of oblivion had begun to lift. Travellers, scholars, soldiers, diplomats, clerics and art thieves, travelling on horseback or by foot, began to nose around the ruins, to start digging, and often to carry off the artefacts. The archaeology of Western Europe, Greece, Egypt and Mesopotamia was opened up in the 19th century, and of Mexico, South America, India, China and other Oriental regions in the 20th century. It was accompanied by the creation of art galleries and museums (the British Museum was founded by Act of Parliament in 1752), the establishment of learned societies, the founding of Chairs of Archaeology at the universities which were springing up all over the Western world, and the setting up of local Schools of Archaeology. At the beginning of this great surge of activity the Westerners just took away or bought what they fancied. In 1803 Lord Elgin, British Ambassador in Turkey (which then ruled Greece), sent the Parthenon friezes to England in 200 cases; the British Government bought these marvellous carvings from him for £35,000 and housed them in the British Museum, where they still are. When, however, on 17 February 1923 two British archaeologists broke into the inmost chamber of Tutankhamun's tomb, the only pharonic tomb which had not been robbed in past ages, the amazing treasures which they found were housed in the Egyptian National Museum in Cairo. The age of archaeological imperialism is largely over. A main motive of many of the 17th and 18th century antiquarians was to verify the myths recounted in the Bible from the evidence of the past. One of the most famous of such efforts was that of Archbishop Ussher of Armagh, who in 1650 calculated from his study of the Bible that the earth was created in 4004 B.C.

In the 19th century two fundamental developments struck at the foundations of the mythological approach to the past. The first was the discovery of fossils, tools and bones of great antiquity by scientists working in the new discipline of geology. Sir Charles Lyell's seminal book, *Principles of Geology,* published in 1830, produced irrefutable evidence that man and his antecedents were far older than 4004 B.C., and that hypotheses of floods were not necessary to explain his origin. At the same time, archaeologists were working out the theories of prehistory, the era before writing was invented.

The second development was the formulation of Charles Darwin's theory of biological evolution, proclaimed to the world in his books *The Origin of Species* (1859) and *The Descent of Man* (1871). This theory,

4

deduced from irrefutable facts, shows that *Homo sapiens* has evolved, through the process of "natural selection", over a period of some two million years. Henceforth legends which did not fit in with the facts revealed by geology and biology have had to be accepted simply as "myths" - symbolic stories - or fantasies.

In the second half of this century the archaeologists have been preoccupied with classifying and describing the vast collections of artefacts which are being discovered all the time all over the world. They have deciphered most of the ancient scripts, but the Etruscan, the Dravidian, the Mayan and one of the Minoan scripts, Linear A, remain elusive. New techniques invented since 1945 - radiocarbon technology and dendrochronology - have made it possible to establish the dates of many of these artefacts and thus to place their cultures in historical context. By 1980 about 50,000 dates had been determined in over 80 laboratories around the world.

For the first time in history, therefore, as a result of the work of the archaeologists, collaborating with the historians, anthropologists, biologists, geologists and astronomers (for the Ancients were very interested in the stars - see Chapter 3) humans are able to see their place in the whole world's long past, as well as in the whole world's wide present. For the first time in history, information is available to everybody about everybody else's ancients. An accurate map or model, though necessarily as yet far from complete, has replaced a collection of fantastic myths and legends as the source of "hard" information.

According to today's anthropologists, modern man emerged some 100,000 years ago from primitive man, who had been in existence for over two million years. Colin Renfrew, Professor of Archaeology at Cambridge University, points out that "Genetically, so far as we can tell . . . modern man is identical in terms of his physical constitution and abilities to his Stone Age predecessor in the last Ice Age . . . Today's new born child and the baby of a palaeolithic cave man cannot be distinguished". It is, he asserts, the effects of history and culture which differentiates them (2).

This 100,000 years of the historical life of our human species can be divided into three segments. The first is "prehistory", mentioned above. The people of prehistoric times were, and are, wandering hunter-gatherers, living in caves, huts, tents, wigwams or igloos in small settlements, socially egalitarian, building no great monuments or cities, developing no scripts, and showing a strong sense of affinity with animals and with the whole natural world.

The second segment is called "civilisation" by Colin Renfrew, and "traditional civilisations", in the plural, by me - so I will use my own term. Professor Renfrew supports "a simple, rather unsophisticated but eminently usable definition" made by anthropologist Clyde Kluckhohn. "His definition of 'city dweller' and 'urban' (*urbs,* town) loosely designates societies characterised by at least two of the following features: towns of upwards of, say, 5,000 inhabitants, a written language and monumental ceremonial centres" (3). He lists "the great civilisations which appeared early on", in which these criteria are found, together with the approximate date of origin; Egypt: c. 3000 B.C.; the Sumerians of Mesopotamia: c.3000 B.C.; the Indus Valley civilisation: c.2700 B.C.; Shang China: before c.1500 B.C.; Minoan Crete: c.2000 B.C.; the Olmecs of Mexico: c.1000 B.C.; and the Chavins of Peru: c.900 B.C. (4). To these I would add a galaxy of later "civilisations", including those of Greece and Rome, Assyria, Persia, Japan, Hindu and Buddhist India and South East Asia; the Mayas, Toltecs and Aztecs in Central America and Mexico, the Incas in Peru, the Byzantine, the Arab-Islamic civilisation, and our own medieval European Christendom.

Professor Renfrew attacks the "diffusion theory", according to which the civilisation which arose in the Near East, or more specifically in Egypt, was then diffused around the globe, sparking off the emergence of the phenomenon of civilisation elsewhere. Evidence from the new dating techniques undermines this hypothesis. In any case, the nature of these civilisations, each similar in structure but unique in style, suggests that they were a spontaneous phenomenon. In the first half of this book the main features of these traditional civilisations will be discussed.

I will call the third segment "the modern civilisation", in the singular. It has two basic features which are absent from all traditional civilisations, and which are not included in Dr. Kluckhohn's list: the urge to implement human rights, in order that every person should have a chance to fulfil his or her psychological and spiritual potential; and the urge to develop science and technology. And it does not have

6

Dr. Kluckhohn's third feature, the construction of "monumental ceremonial centres". I shall discuss in Part II of the book how the secularisation of modern society is an inevitable contemporary result of the development of human rights and of science, and consider the spiritualisation of these great developments in the future.

This leads to a crucial question. Why is modern man, who is such a secular, scientific animal, so avidly studying the Ancients, who were fundamentally concerned with religion? The Ancients themselves, while clinging hard to the hand of tradition, made no effort to examine their own traditions objectively, far less those of other contemporary civilisations - of which they were essentially completely ignorant. The modern urge to look at the past objectively is, surely, a symptom of psychological maturity: a truly mature person is one who is able to examine him or herself as if he were someone else, in order to see clearly how to change and improve his behaviour and his circumstances. He is concerned with growth, development, change - concepts which were alien to the Ancients.

Here we reach a paradox. What are the goals of the process of development and growth which modern man is consciously seeking to promote? Can the archaeologists assume that, because the Ancients did not see the world through the eyes of modern scientists, the religious beliefs which inspired them to worship God, or "the gods" in "monumental ceremonial centres" were delusions? The Ancients' great bequest to modern humanity is the vast corpus of their art. "Why is some of it (early art) so beautiful. Or more correctly, why is some of it so beautiful to us?" asks Professor Renfrew in what sounds like a *cri de coeur (5)*. These great works of beauty represented visions of celestial forms. Plato declared that "in the Mysteries men commune with the gods". The archaeologists rightly tell us of the dark and diabolic practices inspired by much ancient religion - the human and animal sacrifices, the taboos, the obsession with burial. But they seem in general to ignore the reverse side of the coin, the spiritual implications of that glorious art, the message that not only do "the gods" consort with and care for us humans as we walk the paths of earth, but that after death we shall consort with them. Why else was it more important to build huge temples than office blocks or factories? (see Chapter 11).

We may put the situation in another way. Modern people are

unconsciously attracted to the study of the ancient past because there is magic in it. Science has taken the magic out of modern life. This is a great gain because it has liberated millions from the bondage of superstition and sinister forces and practices - black magic. But it is a great loss because it has cut spiritual seekers off from white magic - "communion with the gods", and left them in a spiritual vacuum. We shall discuss the modern relevance of the principles of spiritual philosophy which underlay their ceremonies and teachings in Part II.

Meanwhile we must add a postscript about those societies in the modern world which seem to have remained in the stage of prehistory, bypassing the stage of traditional civilisation. Most of these societies consist of small groups of so-called "indigenous peoples", who are threatened with destruction by the modern conditions on whose frontiers they live: Eskimos, Australian Aborigines, North American Indians, indigenous tribes in the tropical forests of Asia and South America. An American professor of anthropology recently married a girl from a tribe in the Amazonian forest. When she first arrived in a modern town and saw cars with their lights on, she thought that they were animals with huge eyes! There is, however, one continent, with a population of 647 million people in 1990, which is essentially in this situation: Africa. During this century Africa has suffered profoundly from the confrontation of its prehistoric culture with some of the worst aspects of modern civilisation. But the continent is too huge, too vibrant, too rich in resources, to experience the debilitating fate of the small prehistoric groups elsewhere. It is possible that in the next century the absence of what might be called the cultural baggage of a traditional civilisation may enable Africa to develop a particularly creative version of modern civilisation. This will be discussed in Chapter 12.

Chapter 2

LANGUAGES AND SCRIPTS

L ANGUAGE is as old as *Homo sapiens;* he is "a language-having animal". It is the medium of thought and of communication between persons, human and divine. There may be from 2,500 to 5,000 languages today. Some spread far and wide, often being transformed in the process. Some, such as Greek, Latin, Arabic, Mandarin Chinese and after 1500 A.D., French, English, Russian, Spanish, Portuguese and German, became *linguae francae,* spoken over a wide area by the aristocracy, officials, scholars, tradesmen, soldiers - by educated people and travellers generally. Others remained to this day the mother-tongue of a few hundred or thousand remote tribesmen in the forests or mountains of South America, Africa, Asia, Australia and Polynesia. India, with a population of 853 million people in 1990, has 14 official national languages, all with their own scripts (see below), and some 500 spoken languages. Papua New Guinea, with a population of 4 million people in 1990, has 696 languages! There are some 90 languages spoken in Mexico. It is estimated that in Africa south of the Sahara, some 730 languages were spoken by 150 million people at the beginning of the 20th century. 250 are spoken in Nigeria today. Some ancient languages have disappeared. The language of Ancient Egypt was spoken there for about 4000 years; today we have no knowledge of what it sounded like. The last person to speak Cornish, a Celtic language which lingered on in the county of Cornwall in England, died in the 18th century.

In due course writing was invented. It took two forms: pictograms and alphabets. Pictograms - a symbol or a sign for each word - first appeared in Egypt and Mesopotamia around 3500 B.C. The Egyptian hieroglyphs were written on stone and on papyrus made from reeds, and the Mesopotamian cuneiforn (wedge-shaped) writing on clay tablets. Pictographic writing was adopted by the Cretans (3-2000 B.C.); the Indus Valley civilisation (from c.2500 B.C.); the Chinese (from c. 1700 B.C.); the Hittites in Asia Minor (c. 1400 - 1200 B.C.); the Japanese, who after the sixth century A.D. began to adopt Chinese characters for their very different language; and the Mayas and Aztecs in Central America (c. 0 - 450 A.D. and c. 1100 - 1500 A.D.). And pictographic writing, incised with shark's teeth on wooden tablets, has been found in Easter Island; it is unique in Polynesia and has been assigned by experts to c. 1500 A.D. Only one of these ancient pictographic scripts is still in use, the Chinese in China and Japan. In the third century B.C. the first Emperor of China ordered the standardisation of the writing system; and the invention of paper in 105 A.D., and of printing in the tenth century, enormously facilitated the use of writing for the government of a huge empire. By 100 A.D. "some 10,000 characters were being used for literary works and administrative documents". By the 17th century there were 49,000 characters listed in an imperial dictionary. But, nevertheless, despite its difficulty, "until the 18th century nearly half the world's books had been written in Chinese, including works of speculative thought, historical writings and novels, along with writings on government and law" - and, we should add, a vast amount of poetry. Despite extensive use for 4000 years, "the internal development of Chinese writing has been almost imperceptible . . . The writing has never reached even the syllabic stage" (1).

The second form of writing is the alphabetic, the formation of words from a fixed number of letters - most alphabets contain 20 - 30. The researches of modern scholars suggest that the concept of the alphabet originated with Semitic peoples in Western Asia sometime between 1800 and 1300 B.C. The idea spread west and east.

In the west the first alphabet was devised by the Phoenicians who lived in Asia Minor (modern Lebanon) and Carthage (modern Tunisia) 1,000 B.C. It was copied by the Greeks, who added letters for vowels as well as consonants. The Roman alphabet devised for Latin is based on a mixture of Etruscan and Greek letters. The Roman armies and officials, and later the Roman Catholic Church, spread its use throughout Western Europe, which thus gained a common written language. The medieval monks who for 1000 years copied Latin scripts (slaves did much of the copying under the Romans), did not significantly change it. And the invention of printing in the 15th century gave it a permanent form. The main text copied all over Europe was, of course, the Bible, "Holy Writ", which was translated into Latin by 800 A.D.

Meanwhile the Byzantine Empire and the Greek Orthodox Church, which split definitively from the Roman Church in 1054, adopted the Greek script as the script of Church and State. In the 9th century St Cyril and other Greek Orthodox missionaries converted the illiterate Slav tribes of Eastern Europe and Russia to Christianity. But they did not impose the Greek alphabet on them. They invented the Cyrillic alphabet, composed of Greek letters where the sounds were relevant to the Russian language and new letters for sounds in the rich Russian language which were unknown in Greek. By the modern age, therefore, Europe had but three alphabets in general use, the Latin, the Cyrillic and the Greek - the latter used today only by the inhabitants of Greece.

As the concept of the alphabet spread east it branched into hundreds of scripts, which included Hebrew, whose first known use dates from 1000 B.C., and the scripts of the Kurds, the Iranians, the Indians and the Arabs. Numerous alphabets appeared in India from about 500 B.C., of which the most important was the Deva-nagari script, the writing employed for the Sanskrit language of the Hindu scriptures, which today is the official script of India's main language, Hindi. Buddhist monks, meanwhile, took the Buddhist scriptures, written in the Pali language and script, throughout south and east Asia. "A unique empire was built up - based not on political and military unity, but on the common culture and spiritual life of politically more or less independent people. Buddhism played in south-eastern Asia a part similar to that of Roman Christianity in western and central Europe in the Middle Ages" (2). The influx of Hinduism and Buddhism inspired the development of many local scripts throughout the region, such as the Korean alphabet, the On - mun, the only native alphabet of the Far East.

Later, in the fourth century A.D., the Arabic script appeared. The first book to be written in Arabic was the *Koran,* the basis of the religion of Islam founded by the Prophet Muhammad (see Chapter 3). After the Prophet's death Islam spread far and wide, to Africa and Spain in the west, to Asia Minor and southern Russia in the north, to Indonesia and China in the east, and with it went the Arabic language and script, which in its first four formative centuries was written in Arabic. There are a billion Muslims in the world today, and Arabic is thus a major world language.

11

Today there are about 50 alphabets in use in the world, most of them in Asia. The motto: "alphabet follows religion" is applicable to ancient scripts generally. Scripts were essential for scriptures, and writing was a form of religious art - as a glance at a Chinese picture, an ancient Egyptian wall engraving or the inside decoration of a Muslim mosque will show. The sense that their pictographic writing has a sacred quality is of particular significance for the Chinese and Japanese today. Were they to adopt an alphabetic script, they would save themselves from the heavy task of having to memorise some 2,400 characters in order to be literate and to use a typewriter, and some 8,500 in order to be a scholar (there are 8,500 characters in a popular Chinese dictionary today). But they would cut themselves off, not only from a knowledge of their past, but from the stream of spiritual vision and energy embodied in it. This problem will be further discussed in Part II.

Some traditional cultures did not develop or adopt scripts - notably those of non-Muslim Africa, North and South America, Polynesia, apart from Easter Island, and Australia. The knotted cord was used for messages in the Inca civilisation of South America, and in Africa the memory stick or drum signals were used as memory devices or for communication.

Where writing did exist, only a small minority of people, scribes, priests, government officials and perhaps some nobles, almost all male, were literate (see Chapter 8).

Before the modern age, therefore, the vast majority of human beings could only communicate verbally, and with those who belonged to their own language group, whether large or tiny. This limitation was generally acceptable because the immersion of the individual's identity in the group identity was taken for granted. One felt comfortable in one's own language group, presided over by one's gods, kings and priests who knew the revealed truth. Different groups, with different languages and revelations, were threatening. In any case, poor communications meant that most linguistic groups were physically isolated. Such was the situation when the modern age dawned in the 19th century. The acute problems presented by the multiplicity of languages and scripts in the world today will be discussed in Part II.

Chapter 3

RELIGION AND PHILOSOPHY

Reason and Imagination

LL traditional civilisations were grounded on religion. The modern civilisation is the first in history which is generally secular. With the exception of a handful of crank intellectuals in Ancient Greece, it was universally assumed that "spirit" is the creator, mover and transformer of "matter" - of the visible universe and all things in it. An assessment of religion is therefore essential to an interpretation of history. This will take us into matters debated for centuries by thousands of learned scholars. Our assumptions and our definitions will be challenged. No matter! In the modern world the humblest amateur historian is free to formulate his or her definitions and hypotheses.

First, then, we will distinguish between two basic human faculties, that of reason and that of imagination. The rational faculty is concerned with deducing logical conclusions from the observation of facts. These conclusions are always hypotheses: if new facts emerge which do not fit into the previous conclusions, the conclusions must be changed. The rationalist - today, we would call him the scientist - is open-minded and humble before the facts. The facts may be of any nature, from the behaviour of cells of living matter magnified 100,000 times by the electron microscope to the moods of women writing books on word-processors! Rational knowledge is concerned, therefore, with the general, the repeatable and the impersonal. Imaginative knowledge, by contrast, is concerned with the kind of experience expressed in such words as vision, insight, intuition, reflection, illumination, with the particular, the unspeakable and the personal: with feeling rather than with thinking. The distinction between the two faculties was summed up by the poet William Blake:

How do you know that every bird that wings the airy way
is but a whole world of delight, enclosed by your senses five?
What is the "truth" about the bird? Is it that it is a material body

13

with wings and blood and bones and beak, or is it that it is a "world of delight?" Or is it both?

We shall see in Part II that one of the fundamental features of the modern civilisation is that it gives primacy to the rational faculty, to scientific knowledge. Imaginative vision may or may not "reveal" truth; but it is of secondary significance. The Ancients looked at truth from the other way around. Knowledge was acquired through the visionary faculty, and reason was brought in, if at all, simply to support such knowledge. The significance of this fact cannot be exaggerated.

The modern attitude that assertions contrary to rational evidence cannot be accepted as "true" was unthinkable. There was one long period when this fundamental attitude was rudely shaken, the thousand year period - 500 B.C. till 500 A.D. - when Greek philosophy flourished in intellectual circles in the Eastern Mediterranean. The Greeks examined, questioned and argued in an atmosphere of intellectual freedom; and their mighty mental achievement, embodied in hundreds of thousands of books (most, alas, lost!) prepared the ground for the emergence of the modern age 1,500 years later.

God, gods and spirits

Throughout history and pre-history, therefore, everyone, everywhere, with the exception of a small number of Graeco-Roman intellectuals in the period 500 B.C. to 500 A.D., regarded the material world as an embodiment or projection of the spiritual world. Mind conditioned matter; psychic energy motivated physical energy. (In this context I use the words psyche and psychic, spirit and spiritual, in the most general sense, as denoting that which is not material, or "matter"). Mind and psyche embody consciousness.

The often-made assertion by scholars and others that certain religions are "monotheistic", believing in "One God", and the rest "polytheistic", believing in many "gods", seems to be misleading. All traditional religions, with one major exception, affirmed that a supreme spiritual force or consciousness created and pervades the universe. He/She/It is both transcendent - beyond Its' creations - and immanent - within Its' creations. It is called by many names: JHVH by the Jews; God/Christ by the Christians; Allah by the Muslims; Heaven or Tao by

14

the Chinese; Brahma by the Hindus; Quetzalcoatl by the Aztecs; the "Great White Spirit" by the North American Indians; God (Theos) or Cosmos by the Ancient Greeks; God (Deus) by the Romans; and so on. The one exception is found in Buddhism. According to tradition, the Buddha refused to affirm or deny the existence of God, asserting that it was a matter beyond human conception. I shall suggest below that the antithesis drawn by moderns between monotheism and polytheism is based on a concern with ethics.

Who, then, were - and are - "the gods"? Every traditional civilisation believed, or felt, that the universe was full of "spirits" , a "cosmopolis", a "City of men and gods", as the Greek philosophers called it, a mighty family of which humans were one component. Others included plants, animals, ancestral spirits, nature spirits, dragons, demons, fairies, imps, jinns, devils, saints and angels.

All over the world , woods, glades, rivers, mountains, fields, homes, villages, towns, crafts and individuals - every place, activity and person were believed to have their guardian spirits. The following account from Japan, written by the American scholar Lafcardio Hearn, who lived there at the beginning of the 20th century, describes the general situation: "It was necessary that the carpenter should so perform his work as to honour the deity of the carpenters - that the farmer should never fail to respect the earth god, and the food god, and the scare-crow god, and the spirits of the trees about his habitation . . . The scholar could not dare to treat his writing implements with disrespect; such conduct would offend the god of calligraphy. The warrior was commanded to consider his weapons and armour as holy things . . . Gardens, too, were holy, and there were rules to be observed in their management, lest offence be given to the gods of trees and flowers. Carefulness, cleanliness and dustlessness were everywhere enforced as religious obligations".

Psychic Energies

Let us now attempt to look at the structure of the universe through the eyes of the Ancients.

First, all material forms and objects were held to be interrelated to each other in a fundamental way, since all embody the psychic magnetism which pervades the universe. True, modern science has proved that all material substances are linked together by the physical energy contained in the atoms. This physical energy may be the complement of psychic energy, but it is not the same thing. (See below). Sir Walter Raleigh, an intellectual of 16th century Tudor England , summed up this outlook as follows: "Seeing that they (the stars) are many in number and of eminent beauty and magnitude, we may not think that in the treasury of his wisdom who is infinite there can be wanting, even for every star, a peculiar virtue and operation; as every herb plant fruit and flower adorning the face of the earth hath the like". All things were linked in terms of value. What were the stars but potent entities in this cosmic system, of which the earth was assumed to be the centre? In the new academic subject of archaeo-astronomy, certain modern scholars are seeking to show how some of the most mysterious monuments of the Ancients, such as Stonehenge, the Great Pyramid and the Maya temples, were constructed as observatories as well as places of worship, for since the stars were divine, exact observation of their behaviour promoted the evocation of their power. In the Middle Ages the Roman Catholic Church incorporated the complex mathematical calculations of the Greeks, systematised by the Alexandrian Ptolemy in the 2nd century A.D., into its theological geography. Immediately round the Earth was the "sublunary sphere", the realm of change, growth and decay, of evil, Purgatory and Hell. Beyond the Moon was the locus of Heaven, where the Sun and the five known planets rotated in their perfect orbits, incorruptible and eternal, populated by angels. Beyond this zone was the sphere of the "fixed stars", and beyond that "the last heaven", where the throne of God was situated. "Below the Moon all is mortal and transitory, with the exception of the souls bestowed upon the human race by the benevolence of the gods. Above the Moon all things are eternal", wrote Cicero (106 - 43 B.C.), summing up the conventional astronomical wisdom. "It was an age when almost all men of learning believed in the causation of events on Earth through the medium of the stars", writes the British scholar J. D. North of 13th century Europe, a thousand years after Ptolemy had summed up the situation (1).

The psychic energies emanating from the stars and the gods and spirits whom they inspired penetrated into the material world at the lowliest level. For the energies at this level anthropologists often use the Polynesian word, *mana.* (It is fashionable now to talk about "vibes" - psychic vibrations). A king, a priest, a sage, a holy person was supposed to emanate good *mana,* so that their voice, their touch, even their age-old bones could bless and heal through the overshadowing of exalted spirits. Certain substances were widely supposed to emanate bad *mana,* so that contacting these substances became a channel for evil spirits to infect the person concerned. Such substances include dead bodies, excreta (which had to be dealt with manually - the first water closet in Europe was invented in Tudor England), menstrual and child-birth fluid, and in some cases those who dealt with the slaughter of animals, leather works and executions. All these activities were polluting, producing "ritual impurity". In many societies this attitude caused much undeserved suffering; and in Hindu India and in Japan it produced a caste of "Untouchables" who were almost totally cut off from the rest of society by the stigma of ritual pollution. Their situation will be discussed in Chapter 4.

At the end of her long life Mahatma Gandhi's elder sister cursed her brother to an English visitor "in toothless anger and tears". Gandhi's insistence on mixing with "unclean" people, on being his own sweeper (of excreta), his trips overseas, had led to the excommunication of the whole family. This meant a lifetime of ostracism and humiliation by the people about whom she minded: the orthodox of her sub-caste (see Chapter 4) and neighbourhood.

A particularly hideous application of the concept of dark *mana* inherent in material objects was the burning of people regarded as heretics or witches in medieval Europe and in 17th century America. This is well put by the author of a book about the legendary English King Arthur and his unfaithful wife Guinevere. The king condemned her to be burnt "because a queen who was guilty of treachery could die in no other way, given that she was sacred . . ." The logic of burning a sacred queen to death seems to have been to destroy her body. Otherwise it would have to be buried and the magic force inherent in it might contaminate the earth" (2).

Another dark aspect of the concept of *mana* was the almost universal practice of ritual blood sacrifices. In many civilisations, notably those of Egypt, Mesopotamia, Greece, China, Japan, Peru, Mexico, the Celts and the Minoans, humans were originally sacrificed. The horror of the Spaniards when they arrived in Mexico at the beginning of the 16th century A.D. and witnessed the ritual sacrifices of young men and women by the Aztec priests is well known. Accustomed though they were to the slaughter of Christian heretics (see below), they did not attempt to find out the rationale for this different system of religious killing, which has been described by a French scholar as follows: "To keep the sun moving in its course, so that the darkness would not overwhelm the world forever, it was necessary to feed it every day with its food . . . human blood. Sacrifice was a sacred duty towards the sun and a necessity for the welfare of men, without it the very life of the world would stop. Every time that a priest on the top of a pyramid held up the bleeding heart of a man and then placed it in the sacred chalice *(quauhxicalli)* the disaster that perpetually threatened to fall on the world was postponed once more" (3).

In due course human sacrifices were replaced by animal sacrifices; but the principle was the same: the gods needed the magnetism of blood in order to play their part in planetary and human affairs. When those great inventors of democracy, the Athenian Greeks, held their Assembly sessions, priests sacrificed pigs on the altar and traced a sacred circle round the Assembly with their blood. The town crier then addressed a prayer to the gods. There was an altar at the centre of every town assembly place, and it had to be spattered with blood. Sometimes the god was given a little of the meat and the rest was eaten by the gathering. Sometimes the victim was completely consumed by fire in a "holocaust".

But not all religious practices concerned with psychic magnetism were cruel, death-dealing or otherwise malign. Pilgrimages to places where saints had lived and imparted their charisma; climbs up sacred mountains; bathing in sacred rivers; performance in the Olympic Games dedicated to Zeus, the father of the gods - all these were healthy activities. Above all, psychic energies were expressed in healing, and in the performance of miracles. Every Christian knows how Jesus used divine power to heal. Here is a very humble example of the use of this power in modern times. I was told many years ago by a friend who had been an officer in the British Army in India in the 1930s of an Indian station master at a remote railway station in the countryside

18

who could cure snake bite by talking to the patient on the telephone. He was so successful that the British authorities installed a telephone at the station for this purpose.

Temples, Churches, Mosques, Palaces and Tombs

If we were to survey the world from a spaceship during the period 3000 B.C. to 1500 A.D., we would note a startling fact: that many regions were dotted with enormous and marvellous temples, churches, mosques, palaces and tombs, while the great majority of people lived in huts and hovels, often with little or no furniture - their life-style barely different from that of their animals. Economic activities were carried out by hand or with primitive tools, in equally modest workshops and sheds. The creation of these amazing religious edifices by small communities of people who had no modern machinery and knew no modern mathematics is one of the mysteries of history. For example, the Great Pyramid in Egypt, the largest of some 80 pyramids, built 4,000 years ago, had as its base an almost perfect square with sides of 230 metres and a height of 147 metres. Its sides were covered in pure white stone and it was crowned with a golden tip. It contained some 6 million tons of masonry. Salisbury Cathedral, built in 96 years in the 13th and 14th centuries A.D. in England, contains 50,000 tons of stone, 15,000 tons of marble, 3,500 tons of oak and 400 tons of lead. On the other side of the world, in remote Easter Island in the Pacific Ocean, are 200 colossal statues with strange faces, seated on raised burial platforms, carved from local stone quarries. The Romans were the first to invent the dome, and that of the Emperor Hadrian's Pantheon (2nd century A.D.) in Rome is 130 feet across, larger than the dome of St Paul's Cathedral in London. That great Indian tomb, the Taj Mahal, built in the 17th century A.D., covers an area of two and a half acres. Some 2,000 years earlier the Emperor of China, Han Lin Sheng, built separate tombs for himself and his wife, each large enough to hold 1,000 bodies of retainers and other objects thought necessary for the next life (see below).

Thousands of other examples could be cited from all over the world. Let us just add the proud boast of the first Roman Emperor, Augustus (27 B.C. to 14 A.D.), which he inscribed on bronze and stone and circulated throughout the Empire: "I built the Senate House and the Chalcidicum next to it, the temple of Apollo on the Palatine . . . the temple to the deified Julius, the Pupercal, the portico at the Circule Falaminius . . . the temples of the Capitol of Jupiter Feretrius and Jupiter the Thunderer, the temple of Quirinus, and on the Aventine the temples of Minerva, Queen Juno, and Jupiter Libertas, the temple of the Lares at the top of the Sacred Way, the temple of the Di Penates on the Velia, the temple of Youth and the temple of the Great Mother on the Palatine. . ." and more! (4)

I have included tombs and palaces in this brief account because in all traditional civilisations except one, government, burial and all life's activities were ordered and controlled by religion. The one exception was the culture of Greece and Rome. The secular buildings which they built - theatres, museums, libraries, sports stadia, circuses, civic forums - remain part of our glorious heritage. The great art embodied in all these buildings, sacred and secular, will be discussed in Chapter 11. Here I am essentially concerned with their purpose.

The temples, the churches, the palaces - for they were in a sense extensions of the temples - and in some cases the tombs - were the "Houses of God" or the gods, places where divine energies could be focused and concentrated through ritual and then used for many purposes - to bring well-being to the king and the people, to help the dead, and so on. "In the Mysteries", said Plato, referring to the Eleusinian Mysteries held in the temple at Eleusis near Athens, "men commune with the gods". Traditional ritual involved in some sense a personal communion between human and God, or a God, such as Jesus Christ or the Buddha, or the gods. There were only three major religions which rejected this approach, and concentrated their religious observances on the recitation and study of their scriptures (see below): Judaism, Islam and most sects of Protestant Christianity. We will leave these aside for the moment.

The following remark is attributed to Hermes Trismegistus, a legendary Graeco-Egyptian sage: "Do you not know, O Asclepius, that Egypt is the copy of Heaven, or rather, the place where here below are mediated and directed all operations which govern and activate the heavenly forces? Even more than that, if the truth is to be told, our land is the temple of the entire world" (5). Here is a similar interpretation of the essential purpose of the great Church of St. Sophia in Istanbul. Originally built by the Emperor Constantine when he founded the city in 325 A.D., later it became a mosque and is now a museum. "Almost all elements of the Byzantine architecture are concentrated in the internal space of the building. This space does not belong to the material world, but is rather the embodiment of a transubstantial space. The large central dome . . . represents the holy firmament as if with the intention of supporting it. The figures decorating the walls are naturally arranged in a symbolic order, and thus it is Christ, the Almighty God, who appears in the centre of the firmament. His image symbolises the Sun as a ruler of the Heavens . . . Angels, apostles and prophets are grouped around the image of Christ according to their spiritual rank, appearing suspended in an expanse of pure sky blue or gold which is the embodiment of celestial glory" (6).

Utterly different though the religious buildings of each culture were, they expressed a common idea: the reflection of celestial archetypes, forms or models which emanated from Heaven. We shall see that Plato was the first great thinker to express this idea in philosophical terms.

And it was because they believed that they were building for the gods that the work of these ancient craftsmen has a quality of excellence. "The Greeks aimed at perfection when building this temple", said our guide at Delphi when I was there in 1990, "in order to please the god" (Apollo). A thousand years later an Englishman said of the Taj Mahal in India: "They built like giants but with the precision of jewellers". The stones of the Great Pyramid, built about 2500 B.C., are so well cut that it would be impossible to insert a piece of paper between them. This was the work of idealists.

There were three main ways in which these great buildings were used. One was to provide an enclosed shrine in which the god or gods could enter into the material statue or tomb and from this base, as it were, radiate their influence over the land, since all material success and prosperity depended on them. The second was to provide a setting in which the masses could commune collectively with the power of the gods evoked by the priests and project it over the land. The third eschewed the magical energies evoked by ritual - incense, chanting, glorious vestments and symbols, evocations of the gods - and concentrated on scriptural instruction and personal prayer.

The first mode was prevalent in Egypt, Greece, Mesopotamia and Mexico and elsewhere. Here is an account of the kind of worship for which the temples of ancient Egypt, the mightiest in the world, were built. "Three times a day . . . the priests would carry dishes of prepared food and drink into the temple. The high priest, or the king if he were present, would walk through the temple into the sanctuary. There he would draw back the bolts on the door and enter it alone, taking a portion of the food and drink with him . . . The figure of the god, cast in gold or silver . . . would be revealed, and the spirit body, or *ka*, of the god was summoned to eat and drink. Before the meal the high priest would remove the clothing wrapped around the statue and cleanse it with water and natron . . . and then reclothe it in layers of fresh linen. Using the correct spoken formulae, he would then present the figure with jewellery and royal regalia, before finally offering up the food and drink for the divine repast.. . . In the major temples, once the god's meal was ended, a procession of food and drink bearers would move into a side corridor at the rear of the temple, where one wall was carved with a list of the ancient kings' names. By uttering the names of all the kings who had ever ruled Egypt (omitting those likely to offend the gods, such as the female king Hatshesut and the 'Great Enemy' Akhenaten), the *kas* of these pharaohs would also be summoned to partake of the essence of the food offered. On several special feast days each year the god would be carried by the priests round the perimeter of the temple in a gilded wooden boat, so that the people could contact his aura and put questions to him through the priests. Otherwise the ordinary people would have little contact with the temple, and would never be permitted to go beyond the front open courtyards" (7). In Greek temples the statue stood or sat in the innermost sanctuary, hidden from the eyes of the worshippers, who remained outside, performing sacrifices. Thus was Pheidias's 40-foot gold and ivory statue of the goddess Athena, who presided over what was perhaps the greatest cultural city in the world, enclosed from public sight. One of the most extraordinary examples of the urge to conceal the god has been found in the Olmec culture of Mexico, which appeared about 1000 B.C. Huge stone heads, weighing about 20 tons, constructed from blocks dragged by hand and foot over long distances, were buried in deep pits! They were not intended for public view! Since no bones were found in the pits, they were not connected with graves. Some were deliberately defaced and even decapitated. Some solemn, secret ritual had been performed; magical energies stored up (8). The most ancient versions of Christianity embody the same idea in their ritual. The priests, dressed in magnificent vestments and capes, mitres and crowns, perform the most sacred part of the central Christian ritual, the infusion of spirited powers into bread and water, behind screens, before emerging into the body of the church to administer the sacraments to the laity.

The second form of ritual was a great public gathering in which the whole community was drawn into the sacred building and its precincts to commune together with the divine. A striking example is the great traditional ritual which was performed in "The Temple of Heaven" in Peking - "a space large enough for a city of 50,000 inhabitants" - on the night before the winter solstice. "The Emperor, followed by the eldest in the imperial family, ministers and high officials, moved in solemn procession up the steps from one great marble terrace to the other until he reached the Altar of Heaven", which was open to the sky. After offering sacrifices of silks, precious stones and food, he recited prayers, accompanied by choral and orchestral music. Here is part of the prayer which he made on 22 December 1539 A.D. " 'O thou great God . . . I thine unworthy servant come before thee with worship and present this precious cup (lifting it) to him whose years have no end. Men and all creation are enclosed in thy love as in a garden, O God. All that lives is beholden to thee for thy goodness . . . Thou alone, O Lord, art father and mother of all things . . . As a potter thou hast formed all things . . . and the great are wrapped up in thee as in a garment . . .' The immense park-like enclosure was lighted with all the oriental splendour of colour that could be achieved, and a gripping solemnity rested upon the mighty gathering. He who was head of one third of the earth's inhabitants drew near to the Eternal God with confession and worship, for himself and for the people" (9).

And here is an account from Europe of the same phenomenon, the union of all members of a hierarchical society through the experience of a public ritual. "I can see even today a Sunday morning in Cejkovice", wrote Thomas Masaryk (1850-1937), the first President of Czechoslovakia, who was the son of a Slovakian serf. "The whole village comes together, acquaintances greet each other, boys and girls pass in couples, all dressed in their Sunday best; the scent of incense rises, music plays, the whole village sings, they all stand up together, kneel down together, squire and groom: you have the whole drama at the altar; you have the sermon which you can understand and the mysterious Latin which you cannot. Think what a Sunday like that gives to a man, and how it makes him one with his fellows! . . . The Church presides over a man's whole life, his birth, coming of age, marriage and death: it is all ordained and systematised to the highest degree. You must remember that the folk in a small village had nothing else, and that it made a very strong bond" (10).

In the Jewish synagogue, which is a gathering in a private building of ten or more male Jews for prayer and study (the only temple which the Jews have ever had was the Temple in Jerusalem which the Romans destroyed) and in the Muslim mosque, there is no ritual and there are no priests. All men are equal as they recite their prayers or listen to their chosen teacher - rabbi or imam. Only women are unequal - absent from the mosque or in a separate compartment of the synagogue. The element of magic, of evoking the presence of the gods, the Saviour, the saints, the dead, the charisma of the relics, is absent. The magic is concentrated in the Book, the Scriptures - see below.

The Scriptures

In certain civilisations which developed scripts, "scriptures" were produced, writings setting out religious revelations embodying teachings, doctrines, moral precepts, social instructions, myths, poems, etc. In due course these writings, many of which represented very ancient oral traditions, were organised and edited by priests and scholars; they received the blessing of kings, and came to be regarded as "the canon", the revealed and unalterable truth.

Certain of the great civilisations which produced scripts did *not* produce scriptures. The Egyptian *Book of the Dead* and other sacred books were collections of prayers and spells for ensuring the persistence of the personality after death, or its assimilation in the demi-urge. The Mesopotamians, Greeks and Romans all produced epics. The Gilgamesh epic and Hammurabi's Code are the key texts of

Mesopotamia; Homer's poems of Greece; Virgil's epic and Justinian's Code, of Rome. The Greeks and Romans also produced drama and poetry which belong to the corpus of the world's great literature. But these were of lesser significance for humanity than the achievement of the Greeks who produced *philosophy* rather than scriptures. This will be discussed below.

Let us first outline the emergence of the great Scriptures, and then note how they became "canon" for the civilisations concerned.

A few of the scriptures were written or dictated by the founders of the religions themselves. In China, Confucius (his Chinese name was Kung-fu-tze: the Jesuits gave him the latinised version by which he is known world-wide) (551-479 B.C.) edited a number of ancient texts which had been written down on bamboo strips, and some of his own sayings were committed to writing by his disciples. His contemporary, the sage Lao Tzu, wrote a 5,000 word book, *the Tao te-Ching*, at the instigation of the warden at a frontier post, as he journeyed to Tibet on a water buffalo to end his days in the mountains. Centuries later the Prophet Muhammad (570-632 A.D.), an illiterate Arabian camel merchant, had a series of visions as he slept in the desert. He dictated these visions to his disciples, who wrote them down on potsherds, sheep's shoulder blades and palm leaves, and thus produced the *Koran* or "Recitation", on which the religion of Islam - "Submission to God" - is based. The teachings of the founders of the other great religions were memorised by their followers and written down decades or centuries after their deaths. The major Hindu scriptures, composed by anonymous *rishis* or "seers" between about 1500 and 800 B.C., were the *Vedas*, which were written down in Sanskrit after about 150 B.C. They include the *Bhagavad Gita*, a philosophical poem, "the New Testament of Hinduism", which has inspired many modern Indian leaders and Western thinkers; and an epic poem called the *Mahabharata*, which has now been dramatised as a sort of ancient soap opera on Indian and British television! The Hindu scriptures also include the *Code of Manu*, a legal and social code attributed to a legendary sage, Manu. Buddhist scriptures were developed in much the same way. Buddhism was founded by an Indian prince, Siddhartha Guatama, (563-483 B.C.), whose disciples called him the Buddha or "Enlightened One" after he had experienced a spiritual revelation when sitting under a bodhi tree. After his death his teachings were handed down orally for some six centuries. By the 7th century A.D. Buddhism had begun to die out in India. But it was introduced by Buddhist monks into Sri Lanka (Ceylon) in the third century B.C., whence it spread to Burma, Thailand and Indochina. By 75 A.D. the Buddhist scriptures, consisting of the Buddha's sermons and sayings, had been written down in Sri Lanka in the Pali language, on large strips of palm leaf parchment stored in baskets. The Buddhist monks also travelled north, penetrating through the Himalayas into China and Tibet; and from China, in the 6th and 7th centuries A.D., they were taken to Korea and Japan. By the 10th century the Chinese had produced 1,076 texts in Chinese print, while by the 14th century 333 volumes of Buddhist scriptures had appeared in the Tibetan language and script.

There is no hard evidence for the existence of Moses, the founder of the Judaic religion, but the circumstantial evidence for the great story of his life and achievements, which probably occurred around 1300 B.C., is generally accepted by scholars. Divine revelations received by Moses form the basis of the *Torah*, (the Hebrew word for "teaching") the first five books of the Old Testament, the basic scripture of Judaism. These revelations were handed down orally by the leaders of the little tribe of Hebrews, estimated to have numbered some 125,000 when they were taken into exile in Babylon in 586 B.C. When they returned about 50 years later, the scribes and teachers (*Rabbi* means "my teacher") who were attached to the Temple began to write down the oral scriptures which had been handed down for centuries - the teachings of the Prophets who followed Moses, the Psalms, the Proverbs and the Book of Job: the Old Testament, written in Hebrew, were completed about 100 B.C. A Greek translation of the *Torah* was made in Alexandria about 250 B.C.

Jesus (c.6. B.C. to 29 A.D.) the Jewish carpenter, spoke Aramaic, the colloquial version of classical Hebrew. He does not appear to have been literate, although he is recorded as having written some letters with his finger in the sand. The four "Gospels" (Gospel means "good news") which tell the story of his life and report his sayings were written in Greek by unidentified authors, the earliest, the Gospel of Mark, probably about 30 years after his death, and the latest, the Gospel of

John, about a generation later. " 'The bottom line', says Jerome Neyrey of the Weston School of Theology in Cambridge, Massachusetts, USA, 'is that we really don't know for sure who wrote the Gospels.' " These Gospels, together with a book called "The Acts of the Apostles", which tells the exciting story of the founding of the early Christian churches; 21 epistles, letters of these churches, probably written by St. Paul, and a visionary book, "The Revelation of St John", constitute the "New Testament", the specific Christian scripture.

The fundamental revelation was often sealed by signs of divine glory. When Moses came down from his encounter with God on Mount Sinai bearing the Ten Commandments, the central ethical code of Judaism, his face is said to have shone so brightly that his followers were afraid to come near him. When Prince Siddhartha Gautama in India attained "Enlightenment" under the bodhi tree, "the earth quaked six times, and the whole universe was illumined by the supernatural splendour of the sixfold rays that proceeded from the body of the seated Buddha. Resentment faded from the hearts of all men, all want was supplied, the sick were healed, the chains of hell were loosened, and every creature . . . found peace and rest". When Jesus, towards the end of his ministry, went with his disciples up a mountain, "he was transfigured before them, and his face did shine as the sun, and his raiment was white as light". When the Prophet Muhammad was sleeping in a grotto near Mecca, the Angel Gabriel appeared and "infused" the Holy Book into his heart. The scriptures were given the imprimatur of a celestial origin.

The Canon. When the scholars compiled the scriptures they had therefore, in most cases, to sort out from the mass of fragmentary material those texts which were to be regarded as components of the infallible revelation, and those to be regarded as more indirectly revealed and therefore less authoritative. The first group of material was called the canon. At a certain point in time it would be defined, fixed and "closed" by the scholars. In some cases this presented no great problem. As noted, the *Koran,* a fairly short book (431 pages in the English Penguin version) was dictated by the Prophet Muhammad himself. Within 50 years of his death its canonical version had been completed and supplemented by the *Sunna* or "Tradition", composed of some 3,000 *Haditha,* contemporary statements about his words and deeds. The *Koran* and the *Sunna* thus constitute the Muslim canon. The Hindus also had little difficulty in fixing their canon. The Vedas were established as a major canon around the sixth century B.C., and the other texts referred to above were later incorporated as lesser canon. The Pali canon of southern Buddhism was crystallised into 332 texts at a series of great councils: four were held around the dawn of the Christian era, and the sixth in 1954-56! The Jewish Rabbis decided at a council held in the first century A.D. that the *Torah,* the Old Testament, constituted the approved canon. But by now the little Hebrew tribe had grown to about 6 million (equivalent to nearly half of the Jews in the world today), many scattered around the Eastern Mediterranean, and, after the Emperor Titus had destroyed Jerusalem in A.D. 70, they gradually "dispersed" around the world (the Great Dispersion). During the three centuries after the Dispersion the Rabbis, working mainly in Babylon, composed the Talmud, an immense commentary of the *Torah* which, according to a modern Jewish scholar, was accepted by all Jews of the time as "the first and final revelation of God's Will and Command . . .eternally relevant and everlastingly binding . . . the source of all truth and wisdom" (11). Although the *Talmud* is held to be derived from revelation rather than revealed, the Rabbis regarded it - and still do - as canonical.

It was not until A.D. 367 that the Fathers of the early Christian Churches finally selected those written records of the oral traditions of the apostolic age which they regarded as sacrosanct, and thus, by consensus, put together the 27 books of the New Testament. The great Alexandrian theologian Athanasius "declared [this] to be the canonical collection, to which nothing is to be added, from which nothing may be taken away". The discovery, in 1945, of a pot buried in the sand near an Egyptian village containing the texts of the contemporaneous "Gnostic Gospels", which the theologians had declared heretical, suggests that their selection may have been influenced by the desire to build up a dogmatic and authoritarian church (12). In 404 A.D. St. Jerome, a Roman Scholar, produced the *Vulgate,* a Latin translation of a Greek translation of the Old Testament and of the Greek New Testament, which has been used by the Roman Catholic Church ever since. Thus the Old and New Testaments together, whether in Hebrew, Greek or Latin, constitute the Christian canon, which was adopted by the Orthodox Church in the Byzantine Empire as well as by the Roman Catholic Church in the West.

The Christian "Church" was, however, a unique institution, with no parallel in other religions. It was based on the principle of "apostolic succession", the idea that the bishops, who were originally members of congregations elected to perform the key Christian rite, the Eucharist, were invested with a spiritual authority derived directly from the apostles. On the basis of this doctrine the Roman Catholic Church claimed to be a source of continuous revelation, so that the canon was never completely closed. In the first centuries of the Christian era the Church held a series of great councils to affirm its canonical authority. A thousand years later, when the Protestant Movement arose, all the Protestant sects except the Episcopalians rejected the concept of the apostolic succession, and of the Church's right to receive continuous revelation, and most of them turned back to the Bible as the sole source of spiritual authority. An American Bible Encyclopaedia sums up the situation of Christian canon as follows: "The apostolicity of the New Testament canon in its entirety cannot be historically proved. The Christian can only believe that this history, set in motion by the earthly Lord, has been superintended by the risen Lord, who will not lead His Church into error. We believe that he has built His Church upon this Scripture, and that all future development must spring from the grateful obedience exercised by a Church that may hear its Lord speak in the OT and the NT canon" (13).

The Chinese canon was unique in two ways. First, Confucius never claimed that his teachings were "revealed"; and secondly, for over two thousand years, 136 B.C. to 1906 A.D., they were fixed as canon, not by theologians, but by imperial decree, to form the basis for selecting civil servants by examination. This will be discussed in Chapters 4 and 8.

The Teachings of the Scriptures. The contents of the scriptures may be divided broadly into three categories:

(a) **Social codes,** laying down rules for behaviour in all contingencies of life, in particular marriage, sex, bequests, the paying of interest ("usury", forbidden by the early Christian Church and by the *Koran),* clothes, food and alcohol. Examples of some of these social

29

customs have been given in other chapters. Here suffice it to note that the imposition of conformity in all the small details of life has a stifling effect on the development of personality. It inhibits creativity and initiative, and fosters fear and intolerance of what is different. Lafcardio Hearn wrote of traditional Japan in 1905: "Everywhere the customs and laws . . . exact the most humble and implicit obedience, and regulate every detail of public and private life. Personality is wholly suppressed by coercion; and the coercion is chiefly from within, not from without, the life of every individual being so ordered by the will of the rest as to render free action, free speaking or free thinking out of the question . . . The individual did not legally exist - except for punishment; and from the whole of the producing classes, whether serfs or freemen, the most servile submission was ruthlessly exacted." All over the world, centuries of the imposition of social codes by priests and religious teachers have built a vast neurosis in the collective psyche of humanity, so that today, when freedom is often coming very suddenly (see Part II), vast forces of rage, resentment and fear are unleashed.

(b) **Ethical Codes.** What are "ethics" or "morals"? It is interesting to see how difficult the authors of Webster's Dictionary find it to define these two words. "Ethics" are referred to as "the science of ideal human character", and "morals" as "concerned with establishing principles of right and wrong behaviour, ethical". Modern ideas about ethics are essentially determined by the answer given to a question which did not trouble the Ancients: are values "absolute", i.e. derived from some eternal and universal authority such as "God"; or are they "relative", i.e. derived from humans and their rulers? In the latter case, it would be "wrong" to declare Aztec cannibalistic rituals "wrong", and Jesus's forgiveness of his crucifiers "right". The English phrase: "My country, right or wrong", illustrates the dilemma. Every modern person is free to have his or her own opinion about the nature of ethics (see Part II). However, in traditional societies the scriptures, or where they were lacking, "tradition", laid down ethical codes which had canonical authority.

It was inevitable that teachings transmitted, often orally, over such long periods of time by different personalities and in different circumstances should be full of contradictions and confusions. However, it is possible to distil from all the scriptures statements which, to the

30

modern mind, are the noblest which can be conceived. Here is a short list:

"But the truly wise know all men are one, and return with gladness good for evil one". (Hindu scriptures). "Repay evil with good, . . . For love is virtuous in attack, and invulnerable in defence. Heaven arms with love those whom it would not see destroyed". (Lao Tzu) "Never do to others what you would not wish them to do to you". (Confucius). "Hatred does not cease by hatred, hatred ceases by love". (The Buddha). "Love your neighbour as yourself", and "Thou shalt not kill" (Jewish scriptures). "Forgive seventy times seven". "Turn the other cheek" (Jesus). Every one of the 114 *Suras* or chapters of the *Koran* starts with the phrase: "In the Name of Allah [God], the Compassionate, the Merciful".

But mixed up with these lofty statements of love and compassion are statements which the modern mind would regard as unethical. When the Hebrew tribe took over the "Promised Land", inhabited by the Canaanites, which God had promised to their ancestor Abraham, they were told: "But of the cities of these people, which the Lord thy God doth give thee for an inheritance, thou shalt save nothing that breatheth; but thou shalt utterly destroy them". Jesus said: "As the tares are gathered and burned in the fire, so it shall be in the end of this world. And the Son of Man shall send forth his angels, and they shall gather out of his kingdom all things that offend, and them which do iniquity; and shall cast them into a furnace of fire; there shall be wailing and gnashing of teeth". According to the *Koran* "The faithful and the unbeliever contend about their Lord. Garments of fire have been prepared for the unbelievers. Scalding water shall be poured upon their heads, melting their skins and that which is in their bellies. They shall be lashed with rods or iron. Whenever, in their anguish, they try to escape from Hell, the angels will drag them back saying: 'Taste the torment of Hell-fire!' " And these statements are canonical too!

(c) **Doctrines and Dogmas.** A doctrine may be thought of as a guide to thinking about religion. It becomes a dogma when it is regarded as canonical and its criticism or rejection as heresy. I shall suggest - non-dogmatically! - that there is an essential difference between the two great religions of the Orient, Hinduism and Buddhism, and the two great religions of the Occident, Christianity and Islam. I will call the former "mystical", in the sense in which the word is used today. The mystic is one who by his or her own efforts seeks to develop the powers of the spiritual personality, the soul, so that "Enlightenment" - the light of Heaven - may flow into the heart and mind, and guide his or her actions. Mystics, like weeds, may crop up anywhere. Mahatma Gandhi, Mother Teresa and the Dalai Lama are examples of modern mystics. The mystic treads "the Path", following his own "inner light" and intuition, towards what the American psychologist, Abram Maslow has called "self-actualisation", striving to become who he or she truly is, and to do what God has called him to do. The Eastern religions are therefore essentially religions of method, inculcating meditation, yoga practices and good works. The great Hindu gods, and the Buddha, are held up as *models*. A major teaching is that of reincarnation. Everyone is responsible for his/her own deeds and development - this is the doctrine of *karma*. But one short human life is not normally sufficient for the necessary experiences for personal growth or for the putting right of wrongs done. Only when, after a series of incarnations, perhaps over a period of centuries, has the individual gained enlightenment, is he or she free from "the wheel of rebirth" and able to dwell in states of glory. He may then return to earth as an Enlightened One, a Hindu *Avatar,* or a Buddha, to help to redeem and uplift humankind. To me, the weakness of this doctrine, as it applies to ordinary people here and now, is its narcissism. It does not provide for redemption by love in ordinary life. If I, a modern high school teacher, *am* the Pharaoh Akhenaten, the latter has not progressed very far since he died over 3,000 years ago! But if I - and probably many others - are "overshadowed" by Akhenaten, now a god-like soul, the situation is very different. For love flows between the overshadower and the overshadowee - however unconscious the latter may be of the fact; and this love, expressed in unions of groups as well as of individuals, transmutes the evil deeds of the past and provides the spiritual energies to build the future. "Bearing each the others' burdens, sharing each the others' joys", between souls incarnate and discarnate, is the heretical Waterlow version of the doctrines of reincarnation and of *karma.*

Traditional Christianity and Islam have a much starker doctrinal approach. The wicked and the infidels will experience the torments of Hell - some say eternally; the Roman Catholics provide for a state of Purgatory for the lesser sinners. The good and the believers will soar away to Heaven. "Belief" for Christians is summed up in acceptance of the canon as infallible and affirmation of the New Testament doctrine that Jesus Christ, the "Only-Begotten Son of God" by the Virgin Mary, was born into the world as a human man in order to redeem it by his love and suffering, through death by crucifixion. For example, the World Council of Churches was founded in 1948 as "a fellowship of Churches which confess the Lord Jesus Christ as God and Saviour according to the Scriptures". Belief for Muslims is summed up in acceptance of the *Koran* as infallible and of its author, Muhammad, as God's last and greatest Prophet.

Religious Tolerance, Persecution and War

In the Orient, as a result of the attitudes described above, religious toleration generally prevailed. Hindu India simply treated each new sect as a sub-caste, a new section of the hive. The small minorities of Christians (e.g. in Portuguese-conquered Goa) and of Jews were easily assimilated. The Hindus and the Buddhists never fought each other. In Buddhist countries, as in India, sects proliferated because, as a modern Japanese professor has remarked, "the diversity of teachings is due to the variety of the dispositions of the learners". In the Far East Buddhism, Confucianism, Taoism and Japanese Shintoism (spirit worship) often flourished side by side; an individual worshipper would fulfil different personal needs in the shrines of different cults. A Japanese would be married in a Shinto shrine and have his funeral service conducted in a Buddhist temple. In traditional China and Japan religious persecution occurred only when Jesuit missionaries tried to replace allegiance to the Emperor by allegiance to the Pope.

By the same token the exclusive nature of their doctrines, and the dogmatic attitude of their canon, fostered intolerance, authoritarianism, aggression and cruelty in the leaders of Christianity and Islam. The Christians themselves were savagely persecuted by the pagan Roman authorities until the Emperor Constantine announced his conversion to Christianity in 313 A.D., thinking that

33

the Christian God would bring him success in battle. But thereafter, for some 1300 years, the Christians were the aggressors and the persecutors. They smashed up many marvellous Greek and Roman temples. They invaded Muslim Palestine for two centuries (1095 - 1291 A.D.) in the Crusades. They fought each other in Western Europe in the 16th and 17th centuries in wars of religion inspired by the Reformation. Up till the end of the 17th century the Roman Catholic Church dealt with Christian heretics with systematic cruelty. In 1233 A.D. the Papacy set up a system of special law courts, the Inquisition, to root out heresy. "The inquisitors tried to secure a confession of guilt from the heretic by alternating blandishments and intimidation, solitary confinement and torture. If he recanted, he might be committed to life-long imprisonment enchained in a dungeon (the fate offered to Joan of Arc) or he might be granted the mercy of being strangled before being burnt at the stake" (14). The Jews dispersed over Europe after the destruction of Jerusalem by the Romans in 70 A..D. were from time to time massacred ("pogrom", the Russian word for "devastation", was the term given to the officially condoned mob attacks on Jewish communities in Russia between 1881 and 1921); or they were expelled from the countries where they lived, as from England between 1290 and the rule of Cromwell (1649 - 60), and from Spain in the 16th century. Although the underlying motive may have been economic - the Jews were the merchants of the feudal age, and their religion did not forbid them from practising "usury" - taking interest - the ostensible motive was the terrible accusation of deicide - killing God, which the Roman Catholic Church did not finally revoke until the Second Vatican Council of 1962 - 65.

The Jews themselves, although not in a position to attack other religions, were not tolerant of their own heretics. This is what Bertrand Russell writes of Spinoza, whose family had emigrated from Spain or Portugal to Holland to escape the Inquisition: "Spinoza (1634 - 77) is the noblest and most loveable of the great philosophers . . . ethically he is supreme. As a natural consequence, he was considered, during his lifetime and for a century after his death, a man of appalling wickedness. He was born a Jew, but the Jews excommunicated him. Christians abhorred him equally; although his whole philosophy is dominated by the idea of God the orthodox accused him of atheism".

34

However, he was not burned at the stake, but lived quietly in Holland earning his living by polishing lenses (15).

Muslim policy towards non-Muslims under their rule was to treat adherents of the Semitic scriptures, that is, Jews and Christians, and also Zoroastrians, as second-class citizens. In return for paying a poll tax, they were allowed to practise their religion and to govern their communities by their own religious law. But Muslim heretics had short shrift. In 922 A.D. Mansur al Hallaj, an Iraqi wool-carder of the Sufi or mystical sect of Islam, was crucified for heresy because he claimed "to be God". He was in fact seeking Enlightenment, or infusion with the Light of God, the goal of Hindus and Buddhists described above. "When he saw the cross and nails he turned to the people and uttered a prayer . . . 'And these Thy servants who are gathered to slay me in zeal for Thy religion and in desire to win Thy favour, forgive them, O Lord . . . For verily if Thou hadst revealed to them that which Thou hast revealed to me, they would not have done what they have done; and if Thou hadst hidden from me that which Thou hast hidden from them, I should not have suffered this tribulation' " (16). Some years ago, in the 1970s, an Iranian scholar at Harvard talked to my 12th grade class in a high school in Cambridge, Massachusetts. He said: "the different religions of the world are like people who are climbing up a mountain by different paths; they find that they all meet at the top". The wool-carder's cry was uttered from the top of the mountain.

Spirtual Philosophy

When the climbers have reached the top of the mountain by their different paths - what do they see? Let us call their vision *spirtual philosophy*.

In the pagan world it was accepted, in general, that each city, each tribe, each kingdom had its own gods, and this led to a general atmosphere of religious toleration. The conquerors who came and went made due obeisance to the local gods. In Alexandria, in the 4th century A.D., there were 2,478 temples devoted to a wide variety of gods, Egyptian, Greek, Roman, Persian, etc. This atmosphere of tolerance made it possible for a unique phenomenon, the democratic Greek city-state, the *polis*, to emerge in the 5th century B.C.; and the *polis*, in turn, provided the conditions for the flowering of another unique phenomenon, Greek philosophy. This was produced by no revelation from on high, but by a group of ordinary men (not women) - Socrates (469 - 399 B.C.) was the son of a stone carver - talking, joking and arguing as they reclined on their dining couches, attended by slaves and flute playing maidens, or sitting on the grass outside the great public buildings. They discussed science, mathematics, aesthetics, political theory and metaphysics - ideas about the nature of God and man. There were no scriptures to serve as the yardsticks of orthodoxy or heresy; no caste of priests and scholars to impose such scriptures. The only religious crime, for which Socrates was put to death - was impiety - "not recognising the gods that the city recognises" - and he could have saved his life by accepting a few years of exile. Thus many schools of thought flourished, including sceptics, atheists, agnostics, cynics, sophists, Epicureans - all words which are used in our language today. Although the leading philosophers took their stand on spiritual idealism, this was the first time in history when cultured men freely discussed such modern attitudes as atheism,reductionism, materialism and relativism. "Man is the measure of all things", said Protagoras.

Out of this welter of ideas emerged the corpus of concepts associated with the names of Socrates, Plato and Aristotle. Socrates went round asking questions about the nature of goodness, beauty and happiness. Plato (c.427 - 347 B.C.), his young disciple at the time of his execution in 399 B.C., wrote books in the form of dialogues between Socrates and his friends; and Aristotle, (384 - 322 B.C.), Plato's disciple, wrote a large number of books which were a development of and complement to Plato's ideas. One of the most distinguished modern English philosophers, Alfred North Whitehead, has described all Western philosophy as a footnote to Plato.

It is difficult for a student of history to sum up one of the most important and widely studied subjects in world history. But four features of the philosophy which centred round Socrates, Plato and Aristotle are essential to my theme. (Since Socrates wrote nothing, scholars are uncertain how much of the thought which Plato puts into Socrates' conversation actually derives from Socrates or from his own thinking).

First, these philosophers were fundamentally concerned with the question of morality briefly discussed above. Socrates talked about the nature of ethics. He held that happiness was to be found in what he called, "the perfection of the soul", writes Professor Cornford of Cambridge University. "He meant, I believe, what we might call spiritual perfection. In this he saw man's proper concern . . . a direct insight (of which every man was capable) into the value of the various things which we desire. This is the knowledge which Socrates identified with goodness . . . It may also be called 'self-knowledge' - the recognition of that self or soul in each of us whose perfection is the true end of life. Socrates' claim to rank among the greatest of philosophers rests upon his discovery of this soul and of a morality of spiritual aspiration, to take the place of the current morality of social constraint" (17). To give point to Cornford's meaning, here is a statement about the "morality of social constraint", of what I call the "social ethic", which despite the noblest precepts scattered like jewels in the Scriptures (see above), prevailed almost everywhere in traditional societies. "It should be noted that what would be regarded in modern times as morality was not the same as that understood by the vast majority of the Egyptians. For them there was no clear-cut distinction between intellectual and moral qualities, such as good behaviour and virtue, respect for outward practices of religion and genuine piety, or unquestioning obedience to the king and submission to the divine will" (18).

It was because he rejected the "morality of social constraint" and "corrupted the young" by not worshipping the gods of the state, that Socrates was put to death. The Greek philosophers therefore gave moral values a metaphysical framework. They pervaded the universe, which is perfect and eternal, a cosmos, an "ordered harmony"; they were present in the soul of each person, creature and citizen of this universe; and as he develops them, the light of heaven illuminates his mind and irradiates his heart, as the sun illuminates and irradiates the earth. The Socratic doctrine of the soul has much in common with Hindu spirituality - and in fact is embodied in the mystical - and often secret - teachings of many religions. The Hindus emphasised meditation and yoga practices as a means for developing the powers of the soul, while Plato emphasised mathematics and music. Above the porch of the Academy which Plato founded in Athens - the first university in Europe - were the words: "Let no-one enter who does not know geometry".

Secondly, this philosophy, whose simplicity is perhaps an expression of its truth, implies the phenomenon of personhood set out in the Foreword to this book. The Socratic-Platonic doctrine of the soul points to the modern concept of Human Rights, based on the right of persons to fulfil their potential - see Part II.

Thirdly, the soul, whether or not it is in the sheath of the body, is not floating around in the universe as in a vacuum. The values which pervade the cosmos are not mere essences. A basic tenet of Greek philosophy is the concept of archetypal forms or models, a doctrine generally attributed to Plato rather than to Socrates. Every content has a form. Every phenomenon is an expression of a Perfect Form or archetype in heaven - though it may be warped by the time it is "earthed". Goethe expressed this doctrine in the last verse of *Faust* Part II; *Alles Vergängliche ist nur ein Gleichnis* - "All phenomena are but symbols". Wordsworth proclaimed it in one of his most famous poems:

> *Our birth is but a sleep and a forgetting;*
> *The Soul that riseth with us, our life's Star,*
> *Hath had elsewhere its setting,*
> *And cometh from afar: Not in entire forgetfulness,*
> *And not in utter nakedness,*
> *But trailing clouds of glory do we come*
> *From God, who is our home.*

Fourthly, Greek philosophy introduced the concept of *hypothesis* - a Greek word, a theory offered to explain a set of facts; if the facts do not logically fit into the hypothesis, it is the hypothesis, not the facts, which must be changed. This idea of hypothesis had two implications for religion. First, the concept is basic to scientific thinking, and the Greeks were the first culture in the world to initiate abstract scientific thought (see Chapter 10). Second, the concept therefore undermines the authority of revelation; if revealed facts do not fit into logical hypotheses, they must be discarded or adjusted. It was not until the 19th century A.D., in Western Europe that a beginning was made in applying this Greek attitude to some of the facts described in the Christian scriptures, and the emotional shock was intense.

Plato's mystical teachings about the origin and nature of the soul were elaborated centuries later by Plotinus (203 - 270 A.D.), a Roman, who after studying for eleven years in the Greek schools in Alexandria and visiting Persia, founded his own School in Rome. In his cosmogony, based on his personal mystical experiences as well as on his studies of Greek philosophy, he developed the concept of the *emanations* of archetypal forms from God into states of denser and denser matter, like the ripples in a pool emanating from a pulse at the centre. The early Christian Fathers, notably St. Augustine, absorbed Platonic ideas from Plotinus.

Just because Plato believed in the distinction between soul and body, between "knowledge" and "opinion", he was impelled to act in the world in order to transform it. His book *The Republic* is perhaps the most famous work on political theory ever written. His essential idea is that the best form of government would be to entrust power to an elite class of "philosopher-kings" (note the combination of thought and action in the phrase) those in whom, by appropriate training in mathematics, music etc., the powers of the soul have been awakened. These "Guardians", as he called them, would include women, who would be equal in all things with men; they would own no property, and would live and marry communally (though not promiscuously), bringing up their children in crèches. Plato spent several years trying unsuccessfully to educate a Sicilian tyrant to be a philosopher-king. At his Academy he taught jurisprudence "of which he is the real founder" as well as philosophy, and his last book, *The Laws,* the work of a somewhat disillusioned man, lays down detailed and severe rules for government, on the assumption that it may not after all be possible to train philosophers to rule. *"The Laws",* writes a scholar, "formed the basis of Hellenistic, and through that of Roman Law . . . There is no more useful corrective to the popular notion of Plato as an unpractical visionary than the careful study of the dullest and most technical parts of *The Laws* in the light of the *Institutes"* (of the Roman Emperor Justinian) (19).

Aristotle, who was an ardent biologist, rejected Plato's concept of the transcendental archetypal forms, but added to Platonism the teleological concept of potentiality, of the *evolution* of every organism, while alive, towards the expression of the *end (telos)* inherent in itself - the acorn into the oak, the baby into the man. It is as if Aristotle anticipated the concept of the structure of the genetic code, while Plato conceived the Mind which supplies the contents of the code. Aristotle did not reject the Platonic idea of God as the Eternal Unmoved Mover, "which moves", he said, "like a thing beloved", but he detached Him from His Creation. "As a man of science he had (so to say) no business to believe in such a spirit, distinct from the vital principle, or soul, which he declares to be inseparable from the matter of the mortal body it informs, and therefore itself mortal. The separable immortal spirit is an article of faith, inherited from Socrates and Plato" (20). Aristotle, like Plato, was anxious to see philosophy applied to government, and his *Politics* is a treatise about how man, the "political animal", can achieve self-development in the *polis.*

Plato and Aristotle were writing when the Athenian *polis* was in decline. They saw democracy degenerating into corruption and dissension under the impact of the Peloponnesian Wars. They thought that government by a few who were wise and virtuous was better than government by the many who were foolish and wicked. "Mankind will find no cessation from evil until either the real philosophers gain political control or else the politicians become by some miracle real philosophers", wrote Plato in one of his letters. They therefore in effect revived, in their writings, the traditional concept of class, discussed in Chapter 4. This is why some modern political theorists have called Plato a fascist. Yet it was because the Athenians had already partially solved the problem which Plato and Aristotle considered insoluble - the problem of combining political freedom with the achievement of virtue or excellence - that these philosophers were able to flourish: to teach and write and experiment in politics and science. In Plato's and Aristotle's time the very idea of working out a blueprint for the organisation of society and the government of the state was utterly new. In other civilisations the *status quo* was taken for granted as part of the divine order, and even in Greece change was conceived mainly as local readjustment. Today we expect "political scientists", sociologists, economists and others to analyse all institutions and make proposals for their improvement. It has been pointed out that Plato produced the first *Utopia*, the vision of an ideal state towards which man should strive. Plato and Aristotle therefore have a message for the modern world in its almost universal striving to transform its social, political and economic structures: they affirm the need to recognise teleological goals and to establish archetypal ideals.

Plato and Aristotle thus injected into Europe the spiritual idea of rule by the good and the wise. Christianity, by institutionalising the good and the wise in a "Church" separate from the "State", ensured a long drawn-out struggle for political power between the classes of warriors and clergy. The battle finally destroyed the political power of the Church; and when the ground was thus at last cleared again for democratic ideas to flourish, in the 18th century, Rousseau was able to hint at the logical conclusion to Platonic and Aristotelian political theory: the ideal state is one in which *all* are wise and good! (see Chapter 13).

The impact of Greek philosophy upon the theology of Judaism and Islam, carved in stone in their canonical scriptures, was traumatic. "The turmoil set up in the religious mind as it caught some of the spirit of free rational enquiry cannot be over-emphasised", writes a Jewish scholar (21). Professor Wilfred Cantwell-Smith of Harvard has noted that "Some Muslims have seen the introduction of Greek thought into the Islamic world as a greater threat to their religion than the Crusades or the Mongol invasions. Even theology was suspect" (22).

In the atmosphere of religious toleration established throughout the Roman Empire until the conversion of the Emperor Constantine to Christianity in 313 A.D., Greek philosophy and science continued to flourish. (Christians and Jews were persecuted because they would not tolerate other sects, nor perform the political act of obeisance to the Emperor). Wealth amassed under the aegis of the Pax Romana was poured into the building of universities, academies, libraries and museums, employing hosts of scholars to collect, edit and codify data, which in turn enabled knowledge to become standardised and diffused as never before. Greek scholarship was enriched by the intermingling of scholars from many cultures within the Roman orbit: Persians, Jews, Egyptians, West Europeans, even Welsh (Pelagius), North Africans - reminiscent of the "melting pot" situation in modern America. The ferment of thought in the Eastern Mediterranean, from the time of

Alexander until the Emperor Justinian closed the Schools of Philosophy in 529 A.D., has had no counterpart until modern times.

The advent of Macedonian and Roman rule put an end to the possibility that Greek philosophers could find a little *polis* or city state to use as a laboratory for the practical application of their ideas. The divorce of philosophy from politics contributed, of course, to the debasement of politics. But it stimulated philosophy to become *cosmopolitan.* Socrates had described himself as a *Kosmios,* a "citizen of the world". Many of Plato's successors realised that if the purpose of life is to find union with God by developing the powers of the soul, then all men and women must be members of *one* society created by God; and if one believes that "gods" or discarnate souls exist, then, of course, they are members too. For example, Posidonius of Apamea was an hellenized Syrian philosopher who taught in the university of Rhodes in the first century B.C. Cicero was his pupil, and it is likely that Caesar was acquainted with his ideas. Posidonius declared that it was his aim "to make men at home in the Universe", which was "one great city, of which gods and men were citizens". Marcus Aurelius, the Stoic Emperor (121 - 161 A.D.) (The Stoics were a Greek philosophic sect), summed up the simple Stoic creed as follows: "If the power of thought is universal among mankind, so likewise is the possession of reason, making us rational creatures. It follows, therefore, that this reason speaks no less universally to us all with its 'thou shalt' or 'thou shalt not'. So then there is a world-law; which in turn means that we are all fellow-citizens and share a common citizenship, and that the world is a single city . . . And it is from this world-polity that mind, reason and law themselves derive . . . As the earthy portion of me has its origin from earth . . . so too there must be an origin for the mind". Thus was born the conception of the world as a *cosmopolis:* the little *polis* was universalised. Stoicism preached the equality of all men and women, including slaves. The universal dimension which Stoicism gave to Greek philosophy spilled over, as it were, into the non-Greek religions which it was now encountering. "The religious movement of the latter centuries before Christ", writes Professor Barker, "was towards a fusion of cults and a general belief in a single God of the Universe" (23).

Thus the seeds were sown for the concept of the brotherhood of man, transcending barriers of race, creed and sex, which has come into its own in the Human Rights doctrines of the modern age. But the Romans did more than disseminate Greek philosophical ideas, which were soon to be swept aside by the tidal waves of the dogmatic creeds of Christianity and Islam - although Christianity absorbed enough Greek thought to undermine its dogmatism 1,500 years later. They "earthed" these ideas by embodying them in Roman law - their great heritage to mankind. Inspired by Greek philosophy, the Romans developed secular Natural Law. This will be discussed in Chapter 13.

Conclusion

The first section of this chapter sought to show that in traditional societies imagination or "vision" was the dominant faculty, taking precedence over reason; and that religion therefore determined government, social life, art and every other aspect of society. In Part II it will be shown that in the last two centuries - the modern age - there has been a fundamental reversal and reason now reigns supreme. So we have to ask: were "the gods" a fantasy? Is the concept of psychic energy a delusion? Were the marvellous temples and tombs simply built to satisfy the whims of kings?

The modern age is built on two foundation stones: the concept of Human Rights and the theory and practice of science. For the first time in history people in general are free to think as they like; for the first time in history secularity and agnosticism or atheism pervade society. For the first time in history man has acquired the capacity to change the world as he likes. How will he conceive his goals? How will he discover his values? This Chapter suggests that he has three alternatives: (i) To be an agnostic or an atheist. (ii) To follow and practise one of the traditional religions; or (iii) To tread the path of spiritual philosophy, seeking his goals and values in the vision of the celestial archetypes which the Greek philosophers expounded.

Chapter 4

GOVERNMENT AND SOCIETY: KINGSHIP AND CLASS

Introduction: the Need for "Order" in Society

IN almost every traditional civilisation we find three central concepts of social structure. First, society is an "organism", in which each social group has its allotted place or "station" according to its function. In medieval Europe the "body politic" was often compared to the physical body, each organ in its appropriate place. Second, at its head is the ruler - king or emperor - through whom divine power flows into the state, maintaining the harmonious relationship and functioning of all things, human and natural. On him (or occasionally her) depends not only the peace and productivity of men and women, but the beneficence of nature. He is just as responsible for the richness of the crops and the avoidance of droughts and floods as he is for good government. Third, in most of these civilisations it was taken for granted, as mentioned in Chapter 3, that the rulers represented the world order. Other cultures on the fringes were "barbarians", as the Greeks called them, to be repelled or ignored.

Everything therefore depended on the ruler. From the Hindu Vedic epic the *Ramayana,* dated about 300 B.C., to Shakespeare writing nearly 2,000 years later, echoes the same cry: a dread of anarchy and a call for order in the cosmos - the word meaning "ordered harmony", the opposite of "chaos" - which the Greeks applied to the universe. Here is Shakespeare's famous statement in *Troilus and Cressida:*

> *The heavens themselves, the plants and this centre*
> *Observe degree, priority and place,*
> *Insisture, course, proportion, season, form,*
> *Office and custom, all in line of order:*
> *And therefore is the glorious planet Sol*
> *In noble eminence enthron'd and sphere'd*

44

Amidst the other . . . But when the planets
In evil mixture, to disorder wander,
What plagues and what portents! What mutiny!
What raging of the sea! Shaking of earth!
Commotion in the winds! Frights, changes, horrors,
Divert and crack, rend and deracinate
The unity and married calm of states
Quite from their fixture.

The Divinity of the Ruler

Everything depended, therefore, on the king. He was regarded either as himself a god, as in Ancient Egypt and in Japan, or else as the channel for the divine power which ensured the cosmic order. We shall see in Chapter 10 that not only did most civilisations regard themselves as the centre of the earth, but all regarded the earth as the centre of the universe. A comparison of the coronation ceremonies of the only two ancient monarchies still in existence, those of England and of Japan, with the Inauguration ceremony of the American President, may illustrate the ancient attitude.

Queen Elizabeth II of Great Britain and Northern Ireland was crowned on 2 June 1953. "For the last 900 years this ancient ceremony has taken place in Westminster Abbey . . . The starting point is Buckingham Palace. The Sovereign sets out in the Gold State Coach, escorted by the Yeomen of the Guard, the Household Cavalry and the Royal Burgomaster. The procession, as it enters the Abbey, is some 200 strong, with traditional representatives from 'Crown, Church and State'. Three bishops carry the paten [dish for the holy bread], the chalice and the Bible; selected peers [lords] bear the Crown Jewels, and the Lord High Steward carries St Edward's Crown" - the Crown of Edward the Confessor, who ruled from 1042 - 1066 . . . " The Queen is presented to the people. She then takes the coronation oath, promising to exercise justice with mercy - promises symbolised by four swords in the regalia - and to maintain the Church of England. "For the anointing, the central act of the religious ceremony, the Sovereign removes the crimson robe worn till now and sits in King Edward's Chair under a canopy of gold held by four Knights of the Garter. She is then 'anointed, blessed and consecrated' by the Archbishop, using the 12th century anointing spoon . . . Meanwhile the choir sings the anthem 'Zadok the priest . . . anointed Solomon King', set to music by Handel for the coronation of George II on October 11 1727 . . . Every Sovereign since 1626, with the exception of King Edward VIII, who was never crowned, has sat on that same chair, under which rests the Stone of Scone, captured from the Scots in 1296. The Sovereign is then invested with the ornaments which are 'the outward sign of an inward and spiritual grace'. First, she puts on a sleeveless white garment, and then a robe of cloth of gold. The Lord Great Chamberlain presents the golden spurs, the symbol of chivalry, and the Archbishop of Canterbury a jewelled sword, and the golden bracelets of sincerity and wisdom. Finally, the Sovereign puts on the stole and cloth of gold Robe Royal (Imperial Mantle), and receives the orb (the globe dominated by the cross), the coronation ring, the glove, the sceptre with the cross and the rod or sceptre with the dove. There follows the actual moment of crowning. The entire assembly stands as the Archbishop raises on high St Edward's Crown, which is then 'reverently put . . . upon the Sovereign's head'. Then all the princes and princesses, peers [lords] and peeresses put on their coronets, and the kings of arms put on their crowns. A great shout goes up: 'God Save the Queen'" (1).

The present Emperor of Japan was consecrated in November 1990 in a ceremony called the *Daijosai,* which is at least as old as the 7th century A.D. and probably has prehistoric origins. It lasts for four days, and takes place in two wooden halls of archaic design, erected in seven days for the purpose and surrounded by a brushwood fence. On the first day, in the rite of "pacifying the soul", the Emperor is equipped with symbolic clothes, treated as a symbol of himself. On the second day he partakes of "the Festival of the Great Eating", consisting of two ritual meals, one in each hall. The meal consists essentially of sacred rice, grown some months beforehand in fields whose location is decided by divination from turtle shell cracks, under conditions of ritual purity (see Chapter 3). The Emperor's food consists of steamed rice and millet moulded into small dumplings. "The ceremony begins on the evening of the second day, when the Emperor takes a ritual bath of hot water . . . He wears meanwhile a hempen garment [called] the heavenly feather robe. After his bath he puts on another garment of white silk. He then walks in solemn procession . . . into the enclosure and the first hall. As he walks, a mat is unrolled before him, and rolled up immediately, so that no feet save his own shall touch it . . . Before him are carried two of the three imperial regalia, the Sword and the Jewels. He enters the outer chamber of the hall, and there waits while certain magic music is performed. . . Then he is summoned to the meal. In front of him are the two food mats, one for the *kami* (ancestral gods) and one for himself. He then offers the *kami* the special food prepared for them, and himself consumes three of the dumplings . . . The same ceremony is repeated in the other hall, and the buildings are dismantled the same day. The following two days are spent in human feasting . . . All scholars who have sought to interpret the general symbolic action of the *Daijosai* agree that the ritual sequence enables the future emperor to pass from a human to a divine condition." In 1946, after World War II, in *The Declaration of Humanity,* the Emperor renounced all claims to divinity. Why, then, was it revived for the consecration of the present Emperor in 1990? Dr Carmen Blacker, Professor Emeritus of Japanese at Cambridge University, offers the following answer. "In the *Daijosai* . . . we have marvellously preserved like a kind of spiritual fossil, one of the most complex and mysterious rituals for the consecration of a king to survive from the ancient world . . . Its antiquity and its astonishing powers of survival are enough to remind us that traditional symbols carry knowledge that we ourselves have temporarily forgotten" (2).

Finally, we may note the ritual laid down for the consecration of Indian kings (Rajahs) laid down in the Vedic scriptures of the 7th or 8th century B.C. (see Chapter 3). The Rajah held his office by the appointment of the gods, consummated in the royal consecration, "which in its full form comprised a series of sacrifices lasting for over a year", imbuing the king with divine power. "He took three steps on a tiger skin, which was thus magically identified with the god Vishnu, whose three paces covered earth and heaven. The chief priest addressed the gods with the words: 'Of mighty power is he who has been consecrated; now he has become one of yours; you must protect him'. The king was evidently the fellow of the gods, if not God himself". Further rites held during his reign "ensured the prosperity and fertility of the kingdom" (3).

47

Similar accounts could be given of the consecration of the rulers of almost all other traditional states from China, Peru and Mexico, through Ancient Egypt and medieval Europe to Buddhist kings of south east Asia and the Byzantine Empire, - with the major exceptions of Greece, Rome and the Islamic states - which will be discussed below.

Compare these solemn ceremonies, designed to initiate the ruler as the channel for divine power, if not to deify him, with the Inauguration of the American President, the head of the first country to be founded *ab initio* as a modern state. On 20 January, 1993 Bill Clinton, bareheaded and dressed in a dark business suit similar to the suits worn by the great majority of his countrymen, stood on a podium in front of the Capitol (the U.S. Legislature), faced the chairman of the Supreme Court of Justice, raised his right hand and said: "I do solemnly swear that I will faithfully execute the office of the President of the United States, and will to the best of my ability preserve, protect and defend the Constitution of the United States". No mention of God, though an unofficial clergyman made a couple of impromptu Christian prayers. In five minutes it was over.

These ancient ceremonies illustrate the fact that the ruler was generally regarded as the channel for divine power to enter the body politic. There are no written records of Japanese history before the 5th century A.D., when writing in Chinese characters was introduced. So in the 9th century A.D. Japanese historians invented an ancient past: the Japanese Empire was founded in 660 B.C. by Jimmu, the great grandson of the Sun Goddess Amaterasu Omikan, whose grandson had descended from Heaven for this purpose. His successors, the Yamoto rulers, have ruled Japan to this day, and today still maintain an aura of divine authority. The ancient Egyptians believed that the Pharaoh was the offspring of the god Osiris and a human mother; therefore he acted as mediator between gods and men. In the Old Kingdom (c.2800 - 2100 B.C.) it was thought that the Pharoah had personal immortality, and his subjects achieved it through his bounty. Hence the shock of the heresy of the Pharaoh Akhenaten (c.1379 - 62 B.C.), who proclaimed that Pharaohs were but men, and that all should worship the spiritual Creator, symbolised by the physical sun. No wonder his name was deleted from all future records of the Pharaohs.

The following account creates vividly the atmosphere of ancient kingship and its connection with ancient religion: "Consider these temples of the Nile . . . where kings living in mud brick rooms attended gods in huge chambers made of fine hard stone. These temples were the conduit between heaven and earth, they were the lenses pulling the universe into focus, the guy ropes of heaven, and they studded the capital with mystic interconnections. At Thebes there were two types of temple, . . . separated by the vast river. On the east bank . . . were the vast houses of the state gods, still among the largest religious buildings in the world. On the west bank, stretching in a single row along the edge of the fields, were the temples of the kings, gods among these other gods. As their priests were numbered in thousands, so the temples' servants were numbered in tens of thousands and their high priests ranked among the most powerful people in the state. All the temples had straight processional ways marching through their centres, through successive pairs of high gateways and sun bright courts, their pylons, monumental gateways, holding high pinewood masts, tips sheathed in gold and silver alloys, their doors as elephantine as an aircraft hanger's . . . [This was the area of the temple for the public. C.W.]. At the temples' centres stood airless complexes of sunless rooms, chambers that only the ritually pure could enter, surrounding the small central shrines. In these dark sanctuaries elaborate rituals were celebrated through days and nights, rites that spanned years, decades and centuries, communions with eternity, the designs of numberless lives absorbed in deep pieties . . . " (4). The Egyptian empire lasted thus, unchanging in style of rulership and cult, from 3000 B.C. to 30 B.C., when it became a Roman province.

The Chinese Empire, like the Egyptian, also lasted for some 3000 years, though it was born in 221 B.C. just before the Egyptian Empire ended. In that year the Emperor Qin unified the huge country of "warring feudal states", within which a great language, literature, art and philosophy already flourished. Qin adopted the title of "First Sovereign Emperor", and added the concept that he was the "Son of Heaven", titles which remained in use until the Empire collapsed in 1911 A.D. He claimed that he would emulate the "Yellow Emperor" of ancient days, who rose to heaven as an immortal figure. From this time the Emperor was the source of all political and administrative authority. "He acted as a visible figurehead, recognised at all levels.

His approval of edicts and commands, and the nomination of senior officials, was essential. He was the final arbiter of justice, and the source of bounties, punishments and amnesties. His word reigned supreme". But he was not regarded as either divine or infallible. He ruled under the "Mandate of Heaven", and could in principle be deposed by rebellion if he violated this Mandate. He was expected to rule in accordance with the principles of moral conduct laid down by Confucius and Lao Tzu, summed up in the concept of *li*, "the acceptance of forms of behaviour that were appropriate to the station in life to which a man or a woman had been called . . . The dignity and majesty of his court must, thanks to *li*, provide an example of civilised behaviour"(5).

Buddhist as well as Hindu kings were also regarded as semi-divine. In India Asoka, the great ruler (273 - 232 B.C.) who united the subcontinent for the first time, became converted to Buddhism and took the title "Beloved of the Gods". The universal Buddha was complemented by the universal Emperor. Buddhism largely faded out in India, but was adopted throughout South East Asia, as well as in Tibet, Korea and Japan. By about 600 A.D. the status of *Bodhisattva* "the reincarnation of the Buddha" - had been formally accorded to kings by the monks who were the leaders of the cult and the interpreters of its canon (see Chapter 3). This was promoted by the generous donations which the kings made to the monasteries. Images began to appear of the Buddha crowned with royal jewels. This stimulated the doctrine that "the Buddha nature, one and indivisible, was also capable of manifesting itself as a vast infinity of individual Buddhas" (6) . In Japan the Emperor considered that it was not incompatible with the doctrine of his divine descent from the Sun Goddess to declare both Buddhism and Confucianism state religions.

In the Byzantine Empire, which consisted essentially, after the Arab conquests of the Near East in the 7th century, of the Balkans and Asia Minor, the Roman Imperial system lasted a thousand years, until the Turks conquered Constantinople in 1453 A.D. The basic structure of the Christian Church remained unchanged - as we have seen in Chapter 3, the Roman Empire was converted to Christianity by the Emperor Constantine in 313 A.D. It was divided into self-governing "patriarchates" ("bishoprics" in the West) to which were added later the self-governing churches founded in Russia and south east Europe.

This "family" of Churches is collectively called the "Orthodox Church". (In the Balkans Poland, Hungary and Croatia became Roman Catholic - see below - and Greece, Bulgaria, Serbia, Macedonia and Romania Orthodox - a fact which is relevant to the situation there in the 1990s). In 1054 the Pope (see below) broke the final link which bound the Bishopric of Rome to the Patriarchate of Constantinople. Meanwhile the Byzantine Empire was increasingly on the defensive against the onslaughts of barbarians from the north and west and Muslims from the south and east. These circumstances cemented the fusion of Church and State in the Empire. The Emperor absorbed into his office the holy charisma which, as we have seen, was attributed to kings in more ancient societies. He was dressed like an icon; his garments were said to be divine, a gift from the angels to the Emperor Constantine. "His receptions were not audiences, but revelations. Since his meals were rituals, decapitation awaited him who dropped a plate, while the guests who had witnessed such a sacrilege must have their eyes put out. His subjects were, in theory, his slaves. In him all powers were concentrated: executive, legislative, judicial and religious. He appointed and dismissed ministers, fixed taxation, commanded the armies, pronounced supreme judgement, made and repealed laws, appointed or dismissed the Patriarch" (7). When the Byzantine Empire finally fell to the Turks in the 15th century Ivan the Great (1462 - 1505) of Russia arrogated to himself the title Czar or Caesar and the semi-divine attributes associated with it, and Moscow was dubbed the "Third Rome". Church and state were essentially fused in Russia until the Communist Revolution of 1917; Russia experienced no movements equivalent to the Renaissance, the Reformation, the Scientific Revolution of the 17th century or the "Enlightenment" of the 18th century, although Catherine the Great (1683 - 1727), a German, scratched the surface of introducing its ideas into Russia.

Kingship in Western Europe

The rulers of all the empires and countries which we have discussed, except for those of Greece, Rome and Islam (see below) were king-priests. Religious and civil authority were fused, placing in the ruler's hands an almost impregnable power - for rebellion spelt heresy; and heretical ideas were an attack on the state - *vide* the fate of the Pharaoh Akhenaten. This is a basic reason why these empires remained essentially unchanged for hundred of years. In Western Europe an entirely different situation arose: the religious and the secular establishments were separate. In the chaos of the barbarian invasions the Bishop of Rome began to assert his authority over the whole Church, claiming that Christ had given its keys to St. Peter, the first Bishop of Rome, describing it as "the Apostolic See", and by the 6th century calling himself not brother but Papa - Pope - "Father" in Greek. Meanwhile secular governments were carved out by tribal rulers, who, when they were converted to Christianity, were crowned by the Church in ceremonies which were the origin of the coronation ceremony of Queen Elizabeth II of England described above. Various German and Austrian monarchs claimed the title of Kaiser (Caesar), and called themselves "the Holy Roman Emperor". For centuries Pope and Emperor quarrelled over who should dictate to the other. Anathemas and excommunications were hurled by the Popes at Kings and Emperors, and Popes were invaded, deposed and exiled. Civil law was made and administered separately from religious or canon law - a situation unknown elsewhere. (The Greeks and Romans did not have canon law because they had no scriptures and therefore no canon; see Chapter 3). After the Reformation - a development which occurred in no other civilisation - the Protestant kings dominated or ignored the local churches, while the Catholic kings, such as those of France, Austria and Spain, developed the doctrine of "the divine right of kings", and tended to treat the Pope with contempt. The way was opened, by the 15th century, for the development of individual enterprise and self-expression as in no other culture.

Caste and Class

It is difficult to distinguish between the concepts of class and caste. The term "caste" derives from the Portuguese *casta* - "race" - and is normally applied specifically to the caste structure of ancient Hindu society, which was laid down in the Scriptures (see Chapter 3), and still profoundly conditions Indian social life today - although most caste practices have been illegal since Indian independence in 1947. The

Hindu caste system was an extreme form of the class system which prevailed in all traditional societies, except for the special cases of Greece, Rome and Islam - see below. It was based on the idea of functions assigned by Heaven, an idea summed up in the little rhyme: "God bless the squire and His relations and keep us in our proper stations". In general there were four basic classes: the warriors; the priest - scribes; the artisans and merchants; and the peasants. A fifth class, the Untouchables, was unique to India and to a small community in Japan, the *Eta*.

First we must look at the way the class system was organised. Naturally, in huge empires where transport was never quicker than the speed of a horse's gallop (see Chapter 9) administration was extremely localised. But essentially there were two kinds of administrative structure. One was feudalism, described by the Encyclopaedia Britannica as "a social system of rights and duties based on land tenure and personal relationships in which the land is held in fief by vassals for lords to whom they owe specific services and with whom they are bound by personal loyalty" (8). This was not service to the king but to the lord. Public functions were associated with the fief; authority was decentralised. In West Europe Church lands were distributed in this way; the Church was also feudalised. The other system was essentially centralised; the ruler ruled through his officials - which at senior level might well be also landowners, nobles or clergy - but the contractual element which was the essence of feudalism was lacking. The first Chinese Emperor abolished feudalism in B.C. 221. It is considered that Hindu India never had a true feudal system; the relationship between vassal and overlord was based not on contract, but on conquest. Egypt was administered by government officials. Feudalism prevailed essentially in Japan, Byzantium and West Europe. In a feudal society the warrior class was likely to be more powerful than the priestly or scholar class, or the merchant/artisan class. The peasants owed their first loyalty to their lords. When the king needed an armed force, or a labour gang, he called on his nobles. The response from both noble and peasant was often unpredictable or negative. The feudal system has been described as "organised anarchy". In Western Europe it was dying out by the 14th century. The nobles were living in elegant country houses surrounded by gardens instead of massive stone castles surrounded by moats and were wearing gorgeous clothes of velvet, silk, fur and feathers instead of thick slabs of iron armour. In earlier times "the medieval potentate did not read or write (and probably could not) because he had neither the need nor the wish, having others (i.e. the clergy) to do these things for him; social prejudice rendered reading and writing *infra dig* for the noble class" (9). By the 16th century the crude, illiterate warrior was becoming a gentleman, interested in literature and art. Nevertheless in 1848 a Hungarian poet could quote a Hungarian nobleman as proclaiming with glee: "I do not read, I do not write, for I am a Hungarian nobleman!" One result of the growing sophistication and wealth of the nobility was that the distinction between lord and peasant became more pronounced, making it almost impossible for one not born into a knightly family to enter the nobility in Europe. In Japan, the only other truly feudal society, feudalism lasted until the 19th century.

The priestly class was of supreme importance in India - Brahmins ranked higher than warriors - in Egypt, in Mesopotamia and in West Europe. For the clergy could read and write! They carried out five essential functions. First, they performed the rituals essential for the welfare of society - whether in the great Egyptian temples described above, the temples of Mesopotamia and Hindu and Buddhist societies (including Japan), and the cathedrals and churches of Christendom. Second, they were the scribes who copied the scriptures and also wrote the documents essential for government. Vast collections of clay tablets have been found in Egypt and Mesopotamia on which officials of the two empires communicated with each other on all sorts of matters. If an individual wanted to write a letter, he found a priest-scribe who would do it for him. The situation was the same in medieval Europe King John did not sign the *Magna Carta* because he could not write! India's second greatest and most intellectual emperor, Akbar, who ruled northern India from 1556 - 1605 A.D., was also illiterate. Third, they were administrators, acting often as civil servants for the ruler. Fourth, they were teachers, carrying out the only kind of education which generally existed - studying the scriptures and getting the next generation of male priests to memorise them (see Chapter 8). And finally they were lawyers; in societies where, except in Europe, there was no distinction between civil and religious law, it was their function

54

to extrapolate law from the scriptures. In Western Europe after the Reformation all these functions except the first passed into lay hands.

At this point we must glance at the unique development of China. From 221 B.C., when the Emperor Qin abolished feudalism, China was ruled by a bureaucracy of scholar-gentry, who came to be called "Mandarins" by the Portuguese who came to China in the 16th century (from the Latin *mandare,* to command). They were salaried, non-titled, appointed, and in theory non-hereditary. Often they were also land-owners, for it was laid down by imperial decree that a man should divide his land equally between his sons, thus preventing the development of the huge estates of the nobility in societies where primogeniture prevailed - and younger sons became priests or unruly under-employed knights. The mandarins were unique in that they were recruited by the emperor by taking examinations in the Confucian scriptures. The underlying idea was the Platonic ideal that the country should be ruled by the wise and the good. Writing in the mid-19th century, a British consular officer summed up the causes for the long duration and political stability of the Chinese Empire as consisting of three doctrines and an institution. "The doctrines are: (I) That the nation must be governed by moral agency in preference to physical force; (II) That the services of the wisest and ablest men in the nation are indispensable to its good government; and (III), That the people have the right to depose a sovereign who . . . gives cause to oppressive and tyrannical rule. The institution is: The system of public service competitive examinations" (10). In the year 1056 two brothers went to the capital, then Kaifeng (in Honan province), journeying two months by land, to take the examinations. Here is an account of their experience. "Ouyand Shiu was nominated by the Emperor to be chief examiner, together with a number of distinguished scholars as judges. The approach to this most critical moment in a scholar's life was always filled with keen excitement, tense hope, and a nervous fear of failure. It was the moment to which all his years of grinding labour and burning the midnight oil were supposed to lead. The candidates had to get up in the middle of the night and come to the palace at dawn, bringing their cold meals with them. During the examination, they were shut up in cubicles under the supervision of palace guards . . .[They] were examined first on questions of history or principles of government.

There was a second examination in the classics [i.e. the writing of Confucius, Lao Tzu and other ancient sages], and finally, after the successful ones had been graded, there was one - under the direct supervision of the emperor - on lyrics, descriptive poetry (*fu*), and again, essays on politics. Emperor Jentsung . . . took a personal interest in these tests. He sent out the subjects for the papers by his own personal servants, and sometimes . . . changed them at the last moment" (11).

The Peasants

"Where are the peasants?" asked Nikita Khrushchev in astonishment, when he visited the USA in 1959 as the guest of President Eisenhower. The son of a peasant himself, he was the first ruler of the USSR to be invited as a guest to the first great country of non-peasants, and he was very flattered.

In the traditional societies, with the exception of Greece and Rome, normally 90 per cent or more of the population were peasants, whose lives, in the famous words of the 16th century English philosopher Thomas Hobbes, were "nasty, brutish and short". In some non-feudal civilisations, for example those of Egypt and China, labour conscription prevailed. In Egypt the peasants were conscripted to carry out the irrigation works, planting and harvesting planned by the government officials who worked under the Pharaoh's Viziers. The great pyramids, temples and tombs were probably built in the season when the Nile was in flood. From the time of the Middle Kingdom onwards (c.2000 B.C.) the tombs of the well-off often contained statuettes of peasants, with their tools, to ensure that the tomb owner would not have to do peasant work himself in the after-life. Inscriptions "demonstrate with no possibility of doubt how disagreeable the Egyptian considered it was to have his name on the call-up list for the agricultural corvée". This system lasted in a modified form until the late 19th century A.D., when it was abolished under the British administration (12). The peasants lived in two-room houses made of bricks of mud and straw - similar to those I saw myself in Egypt in 1950.

In China, 2,000 years ago, imperial government officials organised land registers and household censuses on the basis of which state taxes, a land tax and a poll tax, were levied, paid in crops, textiles, services or cash. In addition, all males aged 23 - 56 had to work for the government for one month a year, building roads, irrigation and flood control works, state tombs for emperors and mandarins, and the Great Wall, completed in 214 B.C. - the only man-made object visible from the Moon!

The living conditions of peasants were much the same all over the world. Here is a description by a distinguished American scholar: "The Chinese people are still mostly peasants tilling the soil, living mainly in villages, in houses of brown, sun-dried brick, bamboo or whitewashed wattle . . . with earth floors, oil lamps, if any, and paper, not glass, in the windows. Half to three quarters of their meagre income is used for food . . . The houses have usually about four small room sections for every three persons. Sometimes family members of both sexes and two or three generations must all sleep on the same brick bed. There is little or no meat in the diet, and iron is scarce for tools". . . Until recently, life expectancy was 26 years (13).

Peasants were illiterate and superstitious. Here is a description by a famous Italian writer of religion in a village in southern Italy in the 1930s. "In the peasants' world there is no room for reason, religion and history. There is no room for religion because to them everything participates in divinity, everything is actually, not merely symbolically, divine: Christ and the goat; the heavens above and the beasts of the fields below; everything is locked up in natural magic. Even the ceremonies of the Church become pagan rites, celebrating the existence of inanimate things, which the peasants endow with a soul, and the innumerable earthy divinities of the village" (14). We might be in any village in the ancient world!

Peasants were serfs, sharecroppers, tenants, or, at best, owned their little plots of land. The serf was not actually a slave, in that he was bound to the land and not to its owner as a human chattel (see Chapter 6). But he could not leave his holding or his village, marry, change his occupation or dispose of his property without his lord's permission. In Western Europe serfdom was reduced in the 14th century by the plague of the Black Death, which created a great demand for labour. It had died out in England by Tudor times, though it lingered on in France until the Revolution of 1789. In Germany it was abolished after the Revolutions of 1848. In Russia the system achieved its most ferocious manifestation. A law of 1649 enforced serfdom on the peasantry. They were forced not only to cultivate their lords' lands, but to build vast palaces and even whole cities, such as St Petersburg, built by Peter the Great (1672-1729) for the Czar and his nobles. Catherine the Great, the patron of Voltaire and other West European luminaries of the Enlightenment, in a Code of 1767 increased the nobles' right to punish their serfs - which often meant exile to Siberia, if not execution - but also "turned over nearly a million free peasants to private proprietors . . . She gave General Rumyantsov 5,000 serfs after his victory over the Turks, to correspond with the number of enemy slain, and to her favourites (i.e. lovers), anywhere from 7 to 10,000 each" (15).

Peasant revolts constantly occurred. In England, in 1381, Wat Tyler led a revolt to London demanding from King Richard II that serfdom should be abolished, together with the hated poll tax. He was murdered. Peasant revolts normally failed; but they fuelled revolutions, which succeeded. The French Revolution of 1789, the Russian Revolution of 1917, and the Chinese Revolution of 1911, which finally swept away traditional kingship and nobility, were led by the educated and often well-travelled intellectuals.

The Merchants

The fourth class in the standard social structure was that of the merchants. In the Confucian description of the four-class structure, the order of prestige is: scholars (mandarins); farmers; artisans; and merchants. The warriors are not included and the merchants come last! Merchants, who moved around, made money - often charging interest - forbidden in Christian and Islamic law, and thus gained status through wealth. They flourished in Greece and Rome (see below), and again came into their own in the time of the Western European Renaissance. One reason was that trade was an acceptable alternative profession to the army or the church for the younger sons of the noble landowners, in systems based on primogeniture. The existence of a large, wealthy, adventurous class of merchants and bankers was a major reason for the start of the Industrial Revolution in England in the late 18th century.

The Hindu Caste System

Finally, we must mention the major ancient social aberration, the Hindu caste system. The four basic castes, the Brahmins (priests), warriors, traders and peasants, laid down in the ancient Vedic scriptures, gradually developed into about 3,000 exclusive sub-castes, based on profession, endogamy (prohibition of inter-marriage), distinctive custom or creed, and religious taboos. A person could not do a task unrelated to his caste, for example, a gardener could not obey his British employer's request to put his pet horse's droppings on the flower beds. Certain tasks, such as sweeping up excreta or dealing with corpses or womens' menstruation and childbirth fluids, were regarded as ritually impure, and contact with those who performed them, the "Outcastes", or "Untouchables", would pollute members of the higher castes, the "twice-born". A Brahmin could only eat food cooked by a Brahmin. Mahatma Gandhi made it one of his main aims to break down this ancient taboo. He called the Untouchables "Harijans" - "children of God" - and invited as many as possible to live with him in his Community or Ashram. Eventually the leader of the Harijans, Dr Ambedkar, who started life as a child beggar and married a Brahmin girl, became independent India's first Minister of Law and drafted her first constitution of 1947. He also persuaded Harijans to become Buddhists, since the Buddha had rejected the caste system.

The modern idea of equality before the law was unthought of in traditional societies - except to some extent in those described below - India's ancient legal code, the *Code of Manu*, based on the Vedic scriptures, upheld the caste system. It laid down fines of 1,000 cows for killing a warrior, 100 for killing a merchant, 10 for killing a peasant, or a woman of any class. The killing of a peasant by a Brahmin was said to be equivalent merely to the killing of a cat, a mongoose, a blue jay, a frog, an owl or crow.

Government and Law in Greece and Rome

The Development of the Polis. In Homeric days, around 1200 B.C., Greece was ruled by hereditary warrior-kings. Since there were no "scriptures", there was no organised caste of priests or scholar-jurists;

Homer had no word for "law". From about 1000 B.C., when the invading Dorians from the North took the place of the Mycenaeans, until the conquests of Alexander the Great in the fourth century B.C., the basic political unit was the *polis* or "city state"; some 200 were scattered around the coasts of the Eastern Mediterranean and the Black Sea. These states developed secular government based on written constitutions, a unique form of government which, after the collapse of the Roman Empire, did not crop up again until Oliver Cromwell produced a written constitution in 17th century England. Aristotle analysed the constitutions of 158 Greek states; only that of Athens has survived.

In the *polis* the Greeks made the transition from tribal rule to secular constitutional government. The *polis* became a laboratory in which new forms of government were being constantly tried out: aristocracy* - rule by the best, the nobility; oligarchy* - rule by the few; plutocracy* - rule by the rich; monarchy* - rule by one *(monos);* and democracy* - rule by the people *(demos).* All these constitutional systems were regarded as rule under the law. A ruler who placed himself above the law was called a tyrant* (*stands for Greek word).

Where is man to find wisdom, harmony and justice - the moral source of law - without the guidance of the scriptures? The answer suggested by the Greek philosophers was: in his own mind or "soul". (See Chapter 3). Thus was born the concept of "Natural Law", which was to play a potent role, 2,500 years later, in ushering in the modern age.

The "democracy" which flourished in the *polis* of Athens for some 150 years left a lasting imprint on the European mind, and provides, in certain respects, a model for the world in the 21st century. Its basic feature was that it was direct and participatory: the idea that the "government of the people" should be expressed indirectly, through elected representatives, would have been horrifying to the 100,000 or so Athenian citizens. But so also would have been the idea that the participants should include women, slaves or non-Athenians - "resident aliens" from other Greek cities, of whom there were many in Athens, or "barbarians" from other countries.

The sovereign body of the Athenian polis was the *Ecclesia*, or General Assembly, which met 40 times a year. Its members, who were paid to attend the open-air meetings, put forward any topic and spoke on it as they pleased, and then there was a vote. The judiciary was vested in panels drawn from the Assembly. The administration was carried out by a Council of Five Hundred, chosen every year by ballot from the members of the Assembly. It met in groups of 50, one for each tenth of the year, to supervise execution of the Assembly's business. The administration of particular matters, such as finance, education, religion, docks, was vested in boards of citizens chosen by lot - about 1,900 men would be involved at any given time. Only the ten generals who commanded the army and the fleet were chosen by election. And all citizens did stints of military service. Every Athenian citizen was thus called upon to be an active legislator and judge, and at some time in his life, an administrator. How far removed in consciousness was he, therefore, from the peasants and even the nobles of other ancient societies, who perforce thought what they were told to think and did what they were told to do!

Originally, as in other traditional societies, land was owned communally by the kith and kin. But as the modern idea of personal freedom developed, so did the modern idea of private property. Solon, elected magistrate for the year 594 B.C., established the farmers of Athens as private peasant proprietors, and added the right of freedom of bequest. Status thus became linked to wealth rather than birth. Cleisthenes, magistrate for the year 525 B.C., destroyed the old clan-based tribes, and so cleared the ground for the *polis* to emerge as the group which claimed the citizens' loyalty. This was a "modern" situation; and in modern times the "right" to private property is complemented by the duty of the individual to pay direct taxes to the state. The Athenian citizen led an essentially public life; his "private life" in his small insanitary brick house was largely confined to his sleeping hours. But as a free man, he was expected to finance this public life by free giving. So instead of filling in forms and signing cheques, he would volunteer to pay for a ship, a statue, the production of a public play, or to make a contribution to the building of a temple, a theatre*, a Gymnasium*, or some other item which would link him personally to the *polis*. The Greeks' attitude to property was thus in a sense post-modern, since it assumed that free people would freely contribute to the welfare and beauty of the state. For a basic function of the *polis* was to instil a sense of beauty into all its inhabitants. "Let our artists", wrote Plato, "be those who are gifted to discern the true nature of the beautiful and the graceful. Then will our youth dwell in the land of health, amid fair sights and sounds, and receive the good in everything; and beauty, the effluence of fair works, shall flow into the eye and ear, like a health-giving breeze from a purer region, and insensibly draw the soul from earliest years into likeness and sympathy with the beauty of reason".

The Dissemination of the Achievements of the Polis. Like all human societies, Athenian democracy was riddled with intrigues, quarrels and vice - well described by its own historians*. It was based on the toil of women and slaves, who were denied the rights of citizens, and it assumed that Greeks were superior to all other races. Yet there was apparently something about the unique nature of the *polis* which made the extraordinary achievements of the Greeks possible. It was in principle a community of freemen, and the main principle of their unity was not the traditional ties of kith and kin, nor the common adherence to a religious revelation, as in Judaism and in Islam (see below), but the ethical ideals involved in the search for "excellence". This made it "modern" in the sense discussed in this book.

If the Athenian *polis* was in many ways more than 2,500 years ahead of its time, it is not surprising that it did not last very long. The Peloponnesian War (431 - 404 B.C.) led to the conquest of Greece by King Philip of Macedonia; and Greece did not become a free, self-governing nation again until the 19th century. Yet the downfall of the *polis* ensured the triumph of the Greek spirit. The achievements of the exclusive little *polis* were universalised by the Macedonian and Roman barbarians who conquered it.

Roman Government and Law. Rome, profoundly influenced by Greece, produced her own model of a modern state in the ancient world. The little Latin-speaking state on the banks of the Tiber river was probably founded about 1000 B.C. It was ruled by Homeric-type high priests of Etruscan lineage until 510 B.C., when a Republic was set up (Latin word), and kings were abolished until the 19th century. During a 200-year contest between the aristocracy - "patricians" - and the common folk - "plebeians" - a secular constitution was worked out, providing for elected executive officials, "consuls", who, when their annual term of office was ended, entered the 300-man legislature, the famous Senate, for life. All owners of private property were electors; the institution of private land ownership was well established. For 500 years real power was delegated by the people to the Senate, which directed Rome's expansion, first throughout Italy (conquered by 272 B.C.), and then throughout the Mediterranean world. The extent and speed of the Roman conquests, stretching from Spain to Syria, from the Danube and the Rhine and the Scottish border to North Africa from Morocco to Egypt, and in Western Asia from Turkey to Armenia, Mesopotamia, and Syria, eventually made a military dictatorship the only practical form of government. And so, in 27 B.C., the Republic gave way to the Empire, and Augustus, the first Emperor, established its constitution, which lasted until 476 A.D. Legally the Emperor derived his authority from the people. Real power, however, became vested in the hands of the army, which made and unmade Emperors - though the letters SPQR - "For the Roman Senate and People" - remained on the banners of the legions until the end of the Empire. The institution of compulsory Emperor-worship was not, therefore, an integral feature of the nature of the state, as it was elsewhere - e.g. in China, Japan and Pharonic Egypt - but rather a practical device, like modern dictator-worship, to hold the huge and disparate Empire together.

The long-term influence of Greek philosophy, art and science, which flourished for 1,000 years under the aegis of the Roman Empire, is discussed in other Chapters. We must now turn to the influence of Roman law. Perhaps the greatest Roman heritage to humankind was to embody the ideals of Greek philosophy in the practical principles and precepts of law. "There is not a problem of jurisprudence which it does not touch; there is scarcely a corner of political science on which its light has not fallen", wrote Lord Bryce, a leading British jurist in the early 20th century. Rome, like Athens, had developed a written code - the "Twelve Tablets" (451 B.C.), which was regarded as emanating from man's reason, and not from divine revelation, and which was administered by secular magistrates. During the expansion of the Empire this *jus civile,* civil law, which applied only to Roman citizens, was supplemented by the *jus gentium,* the law of peoples, developed for non-citizens by lay administrators. By the third century A.D. the *jus gentium* had superseded the *jus civile*. It was gradually supplemented by the legislation passed by the Senate and the decrees of the Emperors; and finally this whole corpus of secular, cosmopolitan law was infused with the Greek concept of the universal law of Nature, the cosmos or ordered universe. A class of legal experts arose, the *jurisprudentes,* who for 200 years worked to relate the practical provisions of the law of nations to the philosophical principles of the Law of Nature. "The aim of the law was thus to move closer to the objective standards enshrined in the Law of Nature which were based on . . . the reason, not of one man, or of one nation, but of man as part of Nature", writes a British scholar. "The result was that in all their (the jurisprudentes') labours of making law, of amending and interpreting existing laws, they had a norm or criterion to guide them, the ideal of natural justice, of an objective good, more sublime and comprehensive than any of man's devising, which lawyer and philosopher would strive to discover and embody progressively in the laws of the Roman Empire". "Justice is the constant and perpetual will to give each man his right", states the famous Code of the Emperor Justinian (483 - 565 A.D.). It is "the art of the good and the fair". "We worship justice". "In a new sense", adds the scholar, "the lawyers were priests concerned with absolute and eternal values, valid for all men at all times and in all places, which they strove to express in the form of 'equity' for the use of mankind" (16).

This Classical concept of the Law of Nature differed in two ways from the concept of absolute, divine justice embodied in the legal systems of other traditional societies, which derived from scriptures or ancient religious tradition. First, the knowledge of the divine law was to be found in the "reason" of the ordinary person, not in the authoritative pronouncements of scriptures, kings, priests or theologians. It was thus a fundamentally democratic concept, complementary to the great innovative idea of popular sovereignty. Second, whereas the traditional religious law emphasised the duties of the individual, this secular law emphasised his rights. A new legal emphasis was therefore given to the concept of individuality - which, as we have seen, was basic to the Greek experience. The Romans expressed this emphasis in a practical way by providing for the legal right to private land ownership. It is suggested in Part II that the right to own property is not an absolute moral right. But its assertion in those ancient days was an affirmation of the individual's independence of the group which was to prove vital, centuries later, to the awakening of the modern mind.

Islamic Society, Government and Law

Apart from the cultures of Greece and Rome, there was one other traditional society which, in theory at least, departed fundamentally from the standard structure of a divinely appointed ruler heading a divinely ordained stratified class structure. This was the social structure created by Islam, a religion which today has about 700 million adherents.

In Chapter 3 we described how the Prophet Muhammad (570 - 632 A.D.), the Arabian camel-driver, "received" the *Koran* in a series of visions, and on its basis founded the religion of Islam.

Islam arose out of the basic Arabian social unit, the family united by blood ties. Unlike all the other regions of South West Asia, by Muhammad's time Arabia had never been conquered by another and more advanced civilisation. Muhammad's message was simple: reject idols and worship only Allah, "the One and All-Powerful, Creator and Sustainer, Master of the Universe, the Merciful and Compassionate, but also the Just Judge who will reward and punish all His creations on the Last Day". The confession of faith testifies that: "There is no God but God and Muhammad is His Prophet". Under Islam, therefore, the tribal leaders and their gods were replaced as the source of religious and political authority with God, and the precepts and canon of the *Koran* (see Chapter 3) replaced unwritten tribal custom as law. How was this sudden, tremendous change to be put into practice? Muhammad's solution was brilliant. The concept of the family was retained, but the blood tie of the Arab tribe was replaced by the community of the faithful, the *Ummah,* or Brotherhood. As such it was pitted against all other groups not worshipping the same God. "Brethren in the Faith, partners in sharing of booty, allies against the common foe", said Abu Bakr, the father of Muhammad's youngest wife, of the *Ummah.* The concept of a Brotherhood of equal men (women remained appendages of men) united by the spiritual ties of worship

65

of the One Creator, is therefore the political and social basis of Islam. It has no clergy nor priesthood, no religious nor political hierarchy. This is in essence a concept which is relevant to the 21st century. But in the 7th century there were problems in its application. First, how should the leader of the *Ummah,* a person who must combine religious and political leadership, be chosen? Muhammad apparently left no instructions on this matter. So the leading "Companions of the Prophet" elected Ali, Muhammad's son-in-law and cousin, as Caliph, or "Successor to the Prophet", sometimes called Imam when expressing his spiritual authority. Soon there was dissension among the "brothers". One sect, the Shi'a, asserted that the Prophet had appointed Ali. The main group, the Sunnis, believed in the canonical scriptures (see Chapter 3) rather than a human authority. Sectarian conflict ensued. Meanwhile, filled with proselytising energy, invoking the Koranic doctrine of the *Jihad* or Holy War, the Islamic Arabs burst out of their barren peninsula, and within a century of Muhammad's death had conquered Syria, Iraq, Persia, regions of south-east Asia, large parts of India, Egypt, and in the west, Morocco and Spain. All these regimes adopted the Sunni doctrine of the origin of the *Ummah* except for Persia, which became (and remains) almost completely committed to the Shi'a version, together with half the population of Iraq. In an age when the succession was held to signify the inheritance of a stream of spiritual power, feelings ran - and still run - very deep on this matter.

In 660 A.D. the Muslim Arabs shifted their political capital from Medina in Arabia to Damascus, where the Ummayyad dynasty of Caliphs ruled; in 750 A.D. the Abbasid Caliphs founded a new dynasty centred in Baghdad. The great outpouring of cosmopolitan intellectual energy and learning which spread forth from Baghdad in the 9th and 10th centuries is discussed in Chapter 10. (In particular, Islam was profoundly affected by its encounter with Greek thought, while Western Europe languished in the Dark Ages). Here we are concerned with how this vast empire was governed. Essentially a fairly small group of unsophisticated Arabs, just emerging from tribalism, found themselves ruling over a large number of ancient and diverse cultures with many different languages, scripts, scriptures and customs. The fracture of the *Ummah* into a number of military dictatorships was inevitable. The office of Caliph, chosen under the Abbasids by a process of consultation, nomination and election, was claimed by a number of lesser rulers or Sultans until it fell into Turkish hands; it became moribund and was finally abolished as a religious office by Kemal Ataturk, the founder of modern Turkey, in 1924. The rulers of the various Islamic countries took the title of Sultan; and although in theory succession was hereditary, in practice it was often carried out by assassination. An American scholar writes of the *Ummah:* "The effort of modern Muslims to depict the early community as the archetype of egalitarian participatory nationalism is by no means entirely an unhistorical ideological fabrication. In a way the failure of the early community, the relapse into pre-Islamic principles of social organisation, is an added proof of the modernity of the early experiment. It was too modern to succeed" (17). In a world essentially full of mighty lords and miserable peasants, the very concept of the *Ummah* was revolutionary. Although the Sultans were autocrats, they were not necessarily tyrants. They were committed to rule in accordance with the teachings of the *Koran*. And Muslim intellectuals, after turning away from Greek philosophy, threw their energies into the development of Islamic law. In contrast to the Christian situation, there was no distinction between canon or ecclesiastical law and civil law which, being made by man and not by God, could change with the times. Great law schools arose in Medina in Arabia, Kufa in Iraq and other centres, and they developed different interpretations of the *Shari'a*, the body of Islamic law based on the *Koran* and the *Hadith*, the sayings of the Prophet handed down by tradition. The scholars who formulated the law were called Ulema - "religious men", and the judges who administered it Quadi. By the 10th century Islamic law had become finalised, institutionalised and canonised (see Chapter 3). To use the Arabic expression, the doors of *ijtihad* (personal interpretation) were closed." Jurists were not henceforth to write law books but commentaries". This was the situation until the modern age.

Muslim society was divided into four major social classes. The elites were the Arab Muslims. Next came the non-Arab converts to Islam. Third were the "People of the Book", Jews and Christians who possessed a revealed monotheistic scripture. As we have seen in Chapter 3, they were tolerated provided that they paid taxes. Finally, there were the slaves, drawn from captives in battle. Neither Muslims, Jews nor

Christians could be enslaved in early Islam. (It will be noted that Muslim treatment of Jews and Christians compares very favourably with Christian treatment of Jews and Muslims in the long centuries before the modern age).

After the brilliant Muslim culture of the 9th and 10th centuries had declined, and narrowed down into the study of law, a new Islamic impulse arose in the 11th and 12th centuries. By this time the ancient empires of southern Asia, from India and China to Russia and Eastern Europe, had been overrun by wild nomadic Mongols from the steppes of central Asia. (Japan was only saved from their invasion by a mighty typhoon). The Mongols, and their Turkish brethren, became converted to Islam and, having no script, adopted the Arabic alphabet. Under the rule of these barbarians a new version of Islamic spiritual energy welled up among some of their subjects, ranging from the highly educated to simple craftsmen. This was Muslim mysticism, called Sufism, because the Sufis wore woollen cloaks *(suf:* "wool"). Like the mystics of all religions, they sought personal experience of the divine Love which pervades the universe, and we have seen in Chapter 3 that some Sufis were persecuted for heresy. Anyone who, like me, has been privileged to see the magnificent tombs and colleges built at Samarkand in Uzbekistan by the murderous marauder Timur (1336 - 1405) cannot but be profoundly uplifted by the celestial geometry and unearthly colours of these wonders of the world, and know that in the hearts of the architects, artists and hosts of anonymous craftsmen who created them for one of the world's most brutal conquerors was the celestial love which Sufism cultivated. The time may come, in the 21st century, when Islam will help to create the world *Ummah* - of women as well as of men - irradiated by the celestial love which the Sufis seek to reveal.

The Mother of Parliaments

In the Middle Ages all over Western Europe assemblies were formed, representing three of the four main classes: nobles, clergy and untitled gentry or "bourgeoisie". These were called "Estates", and when the three Estates met together the gathering was called the States General. The fourth class, the peasants, was not of course included. The Estates

68

were summoned by the ruler when he needed them, which was usually to ask for money to finance Crusades and other enterprises. Throughout most of Europe these assemblies had little power or influence. Normally the First and Second Estates, the clergy and the nobility, united to out-vote the commoners and support the King. In France the total number of meetings of the States General between 1300 and 1789 exceeded only by two the total number of Parliaments (as they were called in England) summoned in the reign of Edward III (1327 - 1377). When in the momentous year of 1789 Louis XVI finally summoned the States General, the Third Estate was led by wealthy intellectuals inspired by the ideas of Voltaire and Rousseau about the Rights of Man, who launched the Revolution which changed the world. This will be discussed in Part II.

Things developed differently in England. First, in 1215 the barons, supported by the clergy and the commoners, forced King John to initial the Magna Carta, the "Great Charter". This famous document, the first English statute, had been regarded all over the world as the forerunner of democracy. The barons, and the people in general, were furious with the King, his father, Henry II, and his elder brother, Richard I, for their profligate expenditure on wars with France and on the Crusades. Moreover, there were quarrels with the Pope over Church appointments in England, and the Pope had placed the country under an "Interdict", which meant that no-one could take the sacraments; and the next year he excommunicated King John. Many people therefore feared that because of the King's behaviour they would go to Hell! The Charter with which the barons confronted the King in the field of Runnymede in the county of Surrey on 15 June 1215 made a number of specific demands, of which the most famous is that no freeman should be arrested, imprisoned or punished except by the judgement of his peers or the law of the land. Since most of the inhabitants of England were serfs, this in no way amounted to a demand for democracy or the Human Rights of the French Revolution. "The barons were not concerned to make new law, but to prevent the violation by the Crown of existing rights. They had no theory of liberty as such. The liberties which they were concerned to defend were feudal, ecclesiastical or municipal privileges. Against royal caprice they offered the bulwark of legal custom", writes the historian H. A. L. Fisher. But

69

he adds that: "Magna Carta is rightly regarded as the corner-stone of English liberties" (18).

In the next reign, that of Henry III (1216 - 72) the quarrel between king and barons erupted into civil war, and the King's forces were routed in 1264 by the nobles led by Simon de Montfort. He held the old king and his young heir, the future Edward I, captive, while he summoned England's first Parliament to Westminster in 1265. It was the beginning of a new epoch in two ways. First, the aim of the clergy and the barons was to place the erratic and profligate kings under their permanent control; and secondly, in order to strengthen this control, the commoners included, for the first time, not only two knights from every shire (county), but two burgesses from every chartered town. In the 14th century these groups formed themselves into two "Houses"; the "lords spiritual and temporal" became the "House of Lords", and the squires and the burgesses became the "House of Commons", while the lesser clergy dropped out. The reduction of the Estates from three to two made it possible to avoid the situation which prevailed in continental Europe, where the nobles and the clergy regularly united forces against the commoners, the rising middle class. The process of legislation developed. Laws no longer originated with the king, as in all other traditional societies except for Greece and Rome, but became "Acts of Parliament", which the king accepted and signed.

The next momentous development occurred during the reigns of the Tudors (1485 - 1603). Henry VIII, whose father, an obscure Welsh baron, came to the throne after another civil war between baronial groups (the Wars of the Roses), decided to take an unprecedented step: to cut England off from allegiance to the Pope because the latter would not give him permission to divorce his first wife, Catherine of Aragon, and to make himself Head of the "Church of England". He also decided to plunder and disband the monasteries which dotted the country. To make these changes acceptable to a devout and simple-minded populace, and to ensure the support of their leaders at the ground level, while playing down his natural challengers, the great barons, he consulted and cultivated the House of Commons and embodied these changes in Acts of Parliament. His great daughter, Queen Elizabeth I (1558 - 1603), followed in his footsteps, holding the country together in the face of the dire threat of Spanish invasion and cultivating art

70

and exploration to the full in close collaboration with Parliament. At the end of her long life she said to her last Parliament: "Though you have had and may have many mightier and wiser princes sitting on the throne, yet you never had nor shall have any that loved you better".

But the battle was not over. In the early 17th century the Stuart kings, James I and Charles I, tried to rule without Parliament, mainly to crush the threat of Puritanism, which was seeping in from Scotland, with its democratic system of Church government. "A Scottish presbytery agreeth as well with a monarchy as God with the Devil", declared James I. (1603 - 25). The Civil War between Charles I and Parliament - or a large faction of Parliament - led to the execution of the King, the establishment of the Puritan "Commonwealth" by Oliver Cromwell, who tried to introduce a written constitution, and the restoration of the old status quo with the recall of Charles II from exile in France in 1660. But there was one great change. Parliament, in inviting the King back, insisted that he should have no sources of revenue which were not voted for by themselves. So the wily King set himself to control Parliament from within, by building up his own Party, the "Tories", who were opposed by the "Whigs", both led by great lords. Charles was succeeded on his death in 1685 by his brother, James II. The leakage of a secret plot between James and Louis XIV to turn England Roman Catholic and abolish Parliament with the aid of French troops led to immediate action by the Tory and Whig leaders. They sent a deputation to Holland to invite Mary Stuart, James's elder daughter and heir, and wife of William of Orange, the ruler of Holland, to replace James. The couple accepted the invitation, provided that they could rule jointly, and James fled to France, dropping the Great Seal of the monarch into the sea as he went. Parliament passed the Bill of Rights which in effect established Parliamentary control over the monarch - it had nothing to do with modern Human Rights. This was the so-called "Glorious" or "Bloodless" Revolution.

The King remained head of the executive branch of government as well as head of the State - the position of the American President under the U.S. Constitution, except that the monarchy was (and is) hereditary. The next step was to secure the separation of these two functions. At the beginning of the 18th century this was hardly a conscious policy. George I, who succeeded Queen Anne in 1714 after all her 17 children had died before her, was a German who could not speak English and was happy to leave the conduct of affairs to his chief ministers, who were prudently drawn from the majority Party in Parliament and who took to meeting in a small room called a "cabinet". Insensibly their leader became the "Prime Minister", *primus inter pares*. It took nearly a century for this system to become established as constitutional practice, under the pressure of two events: the madness of George III which made him unfit to govern during the great crisis of the American revolt, and the mortal threat to Britain in the French Revolutionary and Napoleonic Wars. Fortunately a strong Prime Minister emerged, William Pitt the younger, who was capable of dealing with this threat, and by 1815, when Napoleon was defeated in the Battle of Waterloo, the transfer of real executive power from the King to the leader of the majority party in the House of Commons had become definite. Britain (for Scotland had been joined to England in 1707 and Ireland by 1801) had in practice - but not in theory - changed from a monarchy into an aristocracy. To make it into a democracy, two further developments were needed. The first was to shift real power from Parliament to the people by establishing the principle of "one person one vote" for the House of Commons. This was carried out in stages between 1832, when the property qualification for voting was first established, then gradually removed, and 1918, when women were finally given the vote. The second was to deprive the House of Lords, consisting of hereditary peers appointed by the Monarch, of the power to veto Bills passed by the House of Commons. This was done in the Parliament Acts of 1911 and 1949, which confined the powers of the House of Lords to discussion and delay, and introduced the creation of "life peers". Thus the British Constitution evolved gradually, in piecemeal developments, from the day when King John signed the Magna Carta in 1215, until the second Parliament Act of 1949. The monarch is Head of State but not head of the Government, and the hereditary peers are a medieval anachronism.

The fundamental significance of the long historical development of the British constitution is that when the modern age dawned very suddenly at the end of the 18th century, a working model for a potentially democratic constitution based on "the will of the people" rather than the "divine right of kings" was already coming clearly into existence. The French and American intellectuals studied it carefully, but, unwritten and hand-to-mouth as it was, they misunderstood it. So the Americans produced a different model of a democratic constitution, based on the separation rather than the integration of legislative and executive powers. In the modern world there are two working models for democracy, the American and the British constitutions. As we shall see, countries which cannot yet cope with democracy have adopted ephemeral dictatorships. Since the annexation of Tibet by China in 1959 there is only one country in the world which deliberately retains a completely traditional system of government: Saudi Arabia, whose constitution is still the *Koran*. And there is only one other democratic country which, like Britain, has no written constitution: Israel.

The Meiji Revolution in Japan

The extraordinary phenomenon of the modernisation of Japan deserves special mention. Like China, Japan, which had excluded or executed Western missionaries and traders since the Renaissance, came face to face with Western modernity in the 19th century. But her reaction was utterly different. The Chinese deposed the Emperor, the "Son of Heaven", and tried in a confused way to assimilate modernity, producing chaos in the country. The Japanese took a deliberate decision to copy and outdo the challenge of Western science and secular liberalism, and for this purpose, to revive the ancient authority of the divine Emperor, the "son of the Sun-Goddess". This is known as the "Meiji Restoration", initiated in 1868, and it was based on the destruction of the ruling feudal caste, the warriors or Samurai. The Emperor had already decreed that "knowledge shall be sought around the world to strengthen the foundations of Imperial rule". Emissaries were sent to Europe and America to study their science and technology, and their governmental, legal, military and education systems. The findings of these systems were then coolly put into practice. Long centuries of learning from China had given the Japanese no inhibition against adopting foreign models. Universal military service was introduced. The army was organised on the German model, the navy on the British. Equality before the law was granted to all, even the *Eta*, the Untouchables. A constitution was promulgated, based on that of Bismarck in Germany. It provided for a Parliament called, like that of Germany, the Diet, elected by a narrow male suffrage with a high property qualification, and involving a Cabinet responsible to the Emperor, not the Diet. The legal system was copied from France, the business structure from America. A modern currency and banking system were established, and universal education was introduced, organised and controlled by the Government. But one basic modern development was rejected. There was to be no religious toleration. Shinto - ancient spirit-worship - was proclaimed the state religion, and the Buddhists were persecuted (19). From this basis Japan launched on a career of conquest which ended with the catastrophes of Hiroshima and Nagasaki. But since 1945 she has again become a rich and powerful country, rivalling those in the West, while China, from whom she derived all her traditional culture and education, remains poor and underdeveloped. (In 1990 Japan's *per caput* GNP was $25,000, higher than that of the USA, while that of China was $370). Why is this so? One answer is given by Professor Edwin Reischauer: "The age-old assumption that theirs was the only land of true civilisation made it extremely difficult for China to adapt herself to new ideas" (20). And in the long view of history the answer cannot simply lie in the idiosyncrasies of 50 years of Marxist Communism – the commissars replacing the mandarins and Marxist dogma replacing Confucian scripture. Perhaps there is an inherent quality in the Chinese culture, the sense of harmony embodied in the concept of *tao*, which makes it impossible for the Chinese to behave in as amoral and aggressive a manner as have the Japanese in the last century. As dogmatic Marxism crumbles in China under the influence, among other factors, of mass education based on science, *tao* may shine forth to bring China's ancient spiritual wisdom to the modern world.

Conclusion

For 5,000 years government in the ancient civilisations, except those of Greece and Rome, was based on authority held to be flowing from a divine source - in Islamic and Judaic societies, from a Book, elsewhere direct from God or the gods, transmitted through rulers. And on the same principle the structure of society was hierarchical – priests, nobles, teachers had a divine right to wield authority over the "lower" orders, the craftsmen, peasants, serfs, slaves and women. In Part II we shall describe how in the modern world, the concept of hierarchical power is fundamentally rejected. Authority is in principle based on "the will of the people", and the existence or non-existence of God or the gods is irrelevant to government. What if God and the gods do exist after all? Divine hierarchy can only be reconciled with human democracy if *all* persons become philosopher kings, that is, set their feet on the path to the realisation of their creative potential, the power of the soul. Then the Greek vision of the world as a *cosmos*, a "City of Men and Gods", may dawn in the post-modern world. We will discuss the future of modern democracy in Part II.

Chapter 5

WOMEN

MEN dominated traditional societies, and men had five main uses for woman.

First and foremost, the function of women was to produce children. The family and the clan must be carried on; this was imperative for the ancestors and the gods as well as for the humans. Specifically, a woman must produce sons, for only the male could act as the link with the ancestral spirits; a girl would, on marriage, move into another family. A wife who did not produce sons could normally be cast aside. Men believed that, at conception, they alone produced the seed of the future child, planting it in the passive seed-bed of the woman's womb. It was not until modern anatomical dissection was developed that it was revealed that women play an equal part in creating the foetus! A woman's second function was to look after the home, to cook and clean, to spin and weave - or to supervise the servants or slaves who did the hard work. Her third function was to provide sexual pleasure, and for this purpose a whole class of unmarried women was normally encouraged to serve as concubines, entertainers and prostitutes. Fourthly, in many societies women also worked outside the home in the fields, cultivating while the men hunted or performed other tasks - a great many men spent much of their time fighting (see Chapter 7). Finally, in many societies, there was a sense in which men regarded "woman" as a goddess. The celestial feminine was the inherent complement to the god-head, the Moon to the Sun, Yin to Yang (in Chinese philosophy). In most of the great traditional religions, such as those in India, Egypt, Mesopotamia, China, Japan, Greece, Rome, Africa and America, goddesses were as prominent and as powerful as gods. And goddess-reverence spilled over into human life in such phenomena as medieval chivalry - see below. In some societies there was a significant role for women to play as priestesses, soothsayers and oracles. The world's most famous oracle, that at Delphi in Greece, always made its utterances through the voice of a woman. But one crucial attitude was missing: the idea that men should treat women as *persons* - as friends, companions, cronies, colleagues, kindred spirits - and thus as *equals!*

In some societies sex discrimination started at birth. Infanticide of girls was a common form of family planning in China and in ancient Greece. Married, normally, at puberty, the average healthy woman bore ten to twenty children by the age of 35; by then she looked an old hag, and her life expectation was over. If before then some form of triage had to be practised because there was not food and shelter enough for all, boys had priority in selection to live. The harsh choice was not confined to the illiterate masses. In post-Pharonic Egypt a husband wrote to his wife as follows: "Hilarion to Alis, very many greetings . . . know that we are still in Alexandria . . . I entreat you, take care of the little one, and as soon as we receive our pay I will send it up to you. If by good fortune you bear a child, if it is a male, let it be; if it is a female, throw it out" (1). The alternative method of pruning the crop was to sell girl children into prostitution or slavery.

From her earliest years a respectable girl would be brought up to regard marriage and motherhood as the central purpose of her life - a life which would be lived in the all-embracing *ambience* of the family - before marriage, her own family, after marriage, her husband's family. If her husband died before her, she would be married off to another member of his family, or, in traditional Hindu India, expected to commit suicide by throwing herself on his funerary pyre in order that she might continue to serve him in the next life. In Buddhist countries, and in the medieval Christendom, a husbandless woman could become a nun. The idea of a woman remaining deliberately single and "doing her own thing" was unthought of anywhere.

The girl's husband would be chosen by her parents. In some societies, such as those of China, Japan and India, a professional matchmaker might be employed. Much care was involved. First, there was the question of tribal relationship, or family suitability, for essentially the marriage was concerned not with linking two individuals but two families and even two tribes. Would the marriage be to the advantage of each family in terms of social status? Would it be appropriate in terms of caste, religion, consanguinity? Although modern India is a secular state, and laws passed in the 1950s gave women legal rights of a modern nature, including the right to choose their own partners (see Part II), the following incident shows how deep-rooted are the emotions about caste, which date back about 4,000 years. In February 1991, in the village of Mehrana in the State of Uttar Pradesh, Roshni, age 15, the daughter of an upper caste landowner, eloped with Brijayendra, a lower caste boy, with the help of his lower caste friend, Ram Kishan. The village elders decided to make their punishment a terrible deterrent for violating the principles of the caste system, which is being destroyed by intermarriage. Their own fathers were ordered to hang them publicly. The weeping fathers botched the job. The two lovers were dragged alive, along with the corpse of Ram Kishan, to the burning funeral pyre, and when they tried to extricate themselves, the mob pushed them into the flames with sticks (2).

Religious barriers against marriage between cults were, and often still are, equally deep, for the thorny question arises: in which of the parents' religion shall the children be raised? The grandfather of a friend of mine was a countryman with strong Calvinistic Protestant convictions; he did not - probably could not - prevent his son's marriage to a Roman Catholic girl; but he never spoke to her for the rest of his life. Jews to this day are troubled about intermarriage with non-Jews, not only on religious grounds but also on ethnic grounds.

Secondly, there was the crucial matter of the exchange of money or goods: the dowry brought by the wife to her husband in some societies, such as those of India, Ancient Greece and medieval Europe, or the "bride-price" paid by the husband for the wife, often in the form of cattle, in societies such as those of Africa. In medieval Europe daughters of both nobles and peasants were often sold by their parents to the highest bidder. In the 16th century England "John Rigmorden, aged three, was carried in the arms of a clergyman who coaxed him to repeat the words of matrimony to a bride of five. Before the end he struggled to get down, saying he would learn no more that day, but the parson said, 'You must speak a little more and then go play you' " (3).

Thirdly, in many ancient societies, such as those of Egypt, Mesopotamia, Mexico, India, Greece and Rome, it was felt important to ensure, through horoscopes and oracles, that the couple was spiritually compatible and that the omens for their marriage were benign.

Traditional attitudes to the expectations from women in arranged marriages are clearly expressed in the following advertisement from Oteocho, Japan, which appeared in the *New York Times:* "Wanted: 8,000 brides for 8,000 grooms. Young women must be willing to work hard in the house and fields. Daily cooking. Also husband's bath preparation. Desire for many children imperative. Must be respectful of and obedient to in-laws. Taste for long winters away from town preferable. One-way fare provided. Apply Hokkaido Farmland Bride Liaison Bureau . . . " (4).

These factors meant that a legal contract, crowned by a religious ceremony, was central to marriage. It was essentially a religious and social matter, part of the cosmic order, brooded over by the ancestors, the gods, or God, concerned with the present and future interests of the family. Any behaviour by the woman, before or after marriage, which threatened these interests was normally strictly punished, for the paternity of the child was crucial. Female adultery was thus a monstrous crime, while men could normally have several wives, or many concubines, or enjoy the favours of prostitutes, with impunity. To give just one example, a Chinese diplomat, visiting Cambodia in 1296 A.D., found that the monarch of that small country had five wives and between 3 and 5,000 concubines. In democratic Ancient Greece, the law required the husband of an adulterous wife to repudiate her - and return her dowry - on pain of loss of his civil rights. But she could claim no legal rights if he committed adultery. Perhaps the starkest attitude to female adultery prevails in the Muslim world. The *Koran* lays down that a woman who commits adultery shall be executed by stoning. And today all Muslim states except Turkey still operate under Koranic law in family matters. A British nurse of my acquaintance worked in a British-staffed military hospital established by the King of Saudi Arabia in Riyadh, the capital, in the late 1970s. She told me that executions - and other punishments, such as chopping off the right hand of thieves - were carried out on Fridays - the holy day of Muslims - in front of the Government Court House; and that adulteresses had large slabs of stone dropped from trucks on top of them. Koranic law thus institutionalises a very deep-rooted male emotional reaction.

Once married, the sexes normally lived separate lives. In ancient Athens, the women lived in one part of the house, the *gynaikeion* - small and mean though these houses mostly were - and the men in another part, the *andron*. The wives of Athenian citizens had no more political or legal rights than their slaves, and since slaves did the shopping and other errands, the wives had little opportunity to go out of doors. "Adolescent girls were lucky if they were allowed as far as the inner courtyard, since they had to stay where they could not be seen . . . even by the male members of their own family" (5) . They were educated at home by their mothers or other women; the philosopher Xenophon's hero Ischomachus refers to his 15 year old wife as "trained from childhood to see and hear as little as possible, and ask an absolute minimum of questions" (6). Meanwhile the men were strolling round the magnificent public buildings, bathed in the glorious Grecian sunshine, discussing politics, philosophy, science, art, drama, athletics, "love" - laughing, joking, arguing in what was perhaps the most creative social atmosphere which the world has ever known. And in the evenings, when the philosophers settled down at their dinner parties to the discussions which laid the basis for European philosophical thinking for the next 2,500 years, they were served by slaves and entertained by dancing and flute-playing courtesans. The female members of the family never ate with the men. Nor were they allowed to attend the political Assemblies, nor that marvellous Greek institution, the public games. They were allowed to attend the theatres, but only to sit in the very topmost tiers. Small wonder that when Socrates asked Critobulus: "Is there anyone of your acquaintance with whom you have less conversation with than your wife?", Critobulus replied: "hardly anyone, I think" (7 The numerous religious processions and rituals were the only public events in which Greek women fully participated.

In some societies, such as those of Ancient Egypt, Rome and medieval Europe, upper class women did mix socially with men. In his fascinating book, *Life Under the Pharaohs,* Leonard Cottrell reconstructs from historical evidence a dinner party given by Vizier Rekhmire in the time of the 18th Dynasty (1580-1321 B.C.) (8). He describes the guests and their wives chatting, flirting, drinking and eating, entertained by singers and dancers of both sexes. The girl entertainers are naked except for beads and loin cloths; the women guests wear the standard garment which upper class Egyptian women wore for 3,000 years: a long, sleeveless robe of virtually transparent white linen. It all seems very modern. In Egypt, uniquely, kingship and landed property were inherited from the wife, not the husband; this gave women a built-in legal status in society. Yet "the few professions open to them were the priesthood, midwifery, dancing and mourning."

But for Egyptian peasant women - as for almost all peasant women everywhere - "life . . . was a hard round of menial toil, regularly but briefly interrupted by childbirth leading to premature ageing and early death. If her son rose to high office - and this was possible in Egypt - she and her husband might be given a tomb instead of a nameless grave. But for the great majority 'it is as if they had never been' " (9).

Perhaps the most poignant symbol of the separation of the sexes in the Muslim world was and is the exclusion of women from the mosques. What for religious people is the most fundamental act of life, worship, has to be performed separately.

In Hindu India the sexes were similarly separated. The Hindus took over from the Muslims, who invaded India in the 12th century A.D., the custom of *purdah,* under which a woman was not allowed to meet any man outside her family, and had to be veiled from top to bottom if she went out. An American missionary who lived for five years in the village of Karimpur near Agra in the 1920s described the situation of women there: "in their own courtyards the women go about their work scolding, laughing, chaffing, grumbling without reserve. But the instant a man from the family enters they become self-conscious, covering their faces, bowing their heads, and in every way emphasising their sex and their role as subordinates . . . But the lot of a lower caste woman was perhaps better that of one of the higher castes. A young Brahmin woman in the village lives in a house whose walls are joined on all three sides by the house walls of other castes. She has never seen the other Brahmin women of the village, because she would have to cross a lane to get to them. Her knowledge of the lanes and houses and families of the village comes to her through her small sons and serving women. Beyond the village she knows only the road to her home village, seen through the holes in a carefully covered

81

bullockcart. Railway trains pass a few miles away, but she has never seen one. She cannot read and does not possess a book or picture" (10).

These are just a few examples of the general situation of women in traditional societies. Their marriages were arranged without their consent. They lived under the domination and control of their fathers and husbands - control which was symbolised in China by the habit of binding their feet so that they could not stray away far, and in parts of central and eastern Africa by the custom of female circumcision, to ensure their fidelity by making sex painful. If they belonged to the great peasant masses - 90 per cent or more of most traditional populations - their lives were filled with hard physical toil punctuated by continuous childbearing. If they were attached to the upper classes their lives might be filled with long hours of humiliating idleness in the harems of kings and prices, guarded by that equally humiliated class of men, eunuchs. In either case they had little daily contact with men as companions. Affection and respect must have crept into man-women relationships; but the flow of such feelings was too slight to transform ancient society. An American journalist who visited rural North China in 1947-8, just before the Communist Revolution, wrote as follows: "The lowly position of Chinese women not only had a terrible effect on the women themselves, but also succeeded in degrading and debauching all human relations within society . . . No social revolution - either good or bad - ever took place without the existence of a great mass of disinherited people who could furnish a new group with a base of support. In the women of China the Communists possessed . . . one of the greatest masses of disinherited human beings the world had ever seen" (11).

Ordinary men, therefore, took it for granted that their females were their property, to be used, cherished or punished as they felt fit. Theologians, philosophers and lawyers rationalised the situation. And for some of them there was a further motive: the desire, not to indulge in sex but to avoid it! Woman was not only inferior to man physically and intellectually; she was also a temptress luring him away from Heaven down to Hell! Here are some astonishing statements: "The deliberative faculty", wrote Aristotle, "is not present at all in the slave"; "in the female it is inoperative, in the child underdeveloped". In the family "as regards male and female this relationship of superior and inferior is permanent" (12). *The Code of Manu,* the ancient legal code of Hinduism (200 B.C.) lays down that: "though he be uncouth and prone to pleasure, though he have no good points at all, the virtuous wife should ever worship her lord as a god". "I feel that nothing more turns the masculine mind from the heights than female blandishments and that contact of bodies without which life may not be had", wrote St Augustine, who abandoned the woman who had been his devoted mistress for 20 years to follow Christ. St Jerome, the famous translator of the Bible into Latin, wrote to a Spanish Christian who had vowed to live apart from his wife: "you have with you one who was once your partner in the flesh but is now your partner in the spirit; once your wife but now your sister; once a woman but now a man; once an inferior but now an equal". A modern Indian scholar writes that: "Buddhist thought gives honour to woman to this extent, that it never doubts the possibility of her putting off woman's nature, and even in this life becoming, as it were, a man" (13).

But some masculine mystics saw the situation in reverse: the essential function of woman is not to lure man to Hell but to lead him to Heaven. "Woman is the everlasting field in which the Self is born", proclaims the great Hindu epic, the *Mahaharata* (400 - 200 B.C.) This theme is marvellously developed by three of the greatest European writers, Dante, Goethe and Ibsen. In the *The Divine Comedy,* Dante is led to Paradise by the spirit of Beatrice. Goethe's Faust is redeemed in Heaven by the spirit of the girl whom he ruined on earth, and the poem ends with the famous line: *Das ewig Weibliche zieht uns hinan -* "the eternal feminine leads us onwards". Ibsen's Peer Gynt spends a life of ego-centred experience and experiment before he returns in old age to Solveig, the love of his youth, now old, blind and apparently childless. "Peer Gynt: 'tell me, then - where was my real self, complete and true, the Peer who bore the stamp of God upon his brow?' Solveig: 'In my faith, in my hope, and in my love'. Peer Gynt: 'Mother and wife! You stainless woman! Oh hide me, hide me in your love!' (Clings to her and buries his face in her lap. There is a long silence. The sun rises.)"

This vision is all-important, but it is one-sided. What about the situation of the woman's soul?

As the British historian G. M. Trevelyan has pointed out, the way forward towards the modern conception of love between man and woman as a bond between two equal souls, developing their potential togther, was embodied in mediaeval chivalry. "It has been shrewdly said", he writes, "that any idealisation of sexual love in a society where marriage is purely utilitarian must begin by being an idealisation of adultery'. But it need not so end. The great gift of the medieval poets to the Western world was their new conception of love of man and woman as a spiritual thing - the best of all spiritual things, raising men and women above their normal selves in all gentleness and virtue."

"Here", writes Trevelyan, "was a new and constant source of inspiration to the life of mankind, based on the facts of nature. It was an idea unknown to the Ancients, and to the early Church. Could this thrice precious concept of the medieval poets be allied, by a further revolution, to the state of Marriage? . . . Could the bond of young love be prolonged till age and death? This change has actually taken place in England in the gradual evolution of the idea and practice of marriage" (14). The noble vision, based on the concept of the *gentleman*, will be discussed in Part II.

It is hard to imagine a more profound statement of human love than that in Shakespeare's cryptic poem *The Phoenix and the Turtle:*

> *"So they loved, as love in twain*
> *Had the essence but in one;*
> *Two distincts, division none:*
> *Number there in love was slain.*
>
> *Hearts remote, yet not asunder;*
> *Distance, and no space was seen*
> *'Twixt the turtle and his queen:*
> *But in them it were a wonder . . .*
> *. . . Either was the other's mine . . ."*

Chapter 6

SLAVERY

SLAVERY was - and is - the vilest institution ever devised by humankind. It involves treating persons as chattels - things - to be possessed, used, abused and destroyed indiscriminately by their owners. A slave was, in Aristotle's phrase, "a living tool" (1), or if a female concubine, a mere toy. Legally and often socially a slave had no kin. His owner controlled his work and often his right to physical reproduction. In all known slave societies masters had the legal right to punish their slaves physically, to whip and brand, and often to kill them (2).

Slavery must be clearly distinguished from serfdom, which prevailed throughout medieval West Europe, and throughout Europe east of the Rhine until the 19th century. The serf was an agriculturist, whereas the slave could be made to do any work, from household shopping and copying of manuscripts in Greece and Rome to murderous labour in mines or rowing in galley ships. The serf was a peasant, bound to the land, and bought and sold with it, while the slave was bound to his master. The serf owned his means of production, such as his tools, while the slave owned nothing, not even his clothes. The serf was normally subject to the law, which gave him some rights, while the slave had none. There were exceptions: for example, in Sumerian law, as set out in the code of Hammurabi (c.1700 B.C.), and in the Roman Empire, slaves could acquire property and education, and buy their freedom.

Slavery was and is rare in hunter-gatherer societies, that is, pre-civilisation societies as "civilisation" has been defined in Chapter 1. It seems that for slavery to flourish, social differentiation is essential. But slavery existed in Africa - see below.

Slavery was endemic in traditional civilisations. It was the vital basis of society in those of Greece and Rome; in the Islamic Empire which stretched from Morocco and Spain to Indonesia; in the European colonies in the Caribbean and parts of South America after their discovery in the 15th and 16th centuries; in the Southern States of the USA until the Civil War of 1861-5.

In Attica the slave population probably equalled the estimated population of about 100,000 free citizens in the fifth century B.C. Allowing for "resident aliens", about one in three of the Athenian population was probably a slave. Their status was proclaimed by their shaven heads, and if they tried to run away, they were branded. Most were employed as domestic servants. "All citizens aspired to own at least one slave; one might compare it with the modern European's attitude to owning a car" (3). In both Greece and Rome it was felt that being a servant, taking orders from another, was degrading for a free man. A rich man, such as Plato, might have about 40 slaves in his household (4). Another main Greek use of slaves was in their silver mines at Laurion, where their survival life-time was about three years. In the Roman Republic and Empire slaves were also used for domestic service. A Roman Senator in the first century A.D. might have 400 slaves in his town household. Slaves were also used for crafts, such as copying books - many written by Greeks. The philosopher Seneca (died 65 A.D.) estimated that in Rome there were three slaves for every five free men. Their second main use was in agriculture. Many free men were called up for an active life-time of military service in Rome's huge armies - Rome had, in the second and third centuries B.C., the highest proportion of male conscripts known to history - and it was therefore left to gangs of slaves to cultivate the huge multi-purpose farms owned by the multi-millionaires. And as in Greece, slaves manned the galleys - again an occupation where life was short. It is estimated that in the Roman Empire in the first century A.D. and later, the richest five per cent of Italy's population owned a million house slaves, and that another two million were employed elsewhere, out of a total Italian population of about 7.5 million. In the whole Empire about 30 per cent of the population were enslaved. Finally, after the fall of the Empire, they were converted into serfs.

The second main civilisation of antiquity whose economy was based on slavery was that of Islam. The great Arab conquests of Western Asia, North Africa and Spain which began immediately after the Prophet Muhammad's death in 632 A.D. required large armies. The

Arabian population was small, so the Arab leaders and later the Turks, Mongols and other Asian races converted to Islam recruited slaves for their armies from the great "population reservoirs" of Eastern Europe, Russia, Iran and sub-Saharan Africa. They were used mainly for fighting, for domestic service and to stock the harems of the ruling class with girls and their wardens, castrated males. The word "slave" derives from "Slav". Its military basis made the Islamic slave's situation mobile; many rose up to positions of influence and power. Finally, in the Far East, for about 1,000 years before the 18th century, the economy of Korea depended on slave labour; about a third to half the population were enslaved.

In other civilisations slavery existed but was not basic to the economy. In ancient Egypt slaves became numerous after the Egyptian conquests in Asia Minor and Nubia (the modern Sudan) in the time of the New Kingdom (1555-712 B.C.) The pyramids were built by peasants who were paid by the state in food and drink, the standard method of payment in a culture which did not invent money, and who were free for architectural work during the months of the Nile flood. Slaves could not enter temple courtyards because they were regarded as ritually impure. In a culture obsessed with the need for a ritual burial as a passport to well-being in the next life, the corpses of slaves were simply thrown into the Nile for the crocodiles to eat. Slavery continued to exist in Egypt during the thousand years of post-Pharonic - pre - Muslim rule (c.300 B.C. - c.600 A.D.) mainly as a domestic institution. A letter of condolence states: "I too have had a loss, a young house-born slave worth two talents" (5). In China domestic slavery existed from the dawn of Chinese history in the second millennium B.C. until the 20th century. China did not need slaves for military purposes, agriculture or public works such as the building of roads, irrigation works and the Great Wall, because it developed an efficient system of government conscription of its huge peasant population (see Chapter 4). The children of impoverished and indebted peasants were sometimes sold into domestic slavery, a practice which did not end until 1949. In Japan and elsewhere in the Far East slavery was on a similar scale. The slaves who kept the Buddhist pagoda temples clean in Burma were themselves treated as ritually unclean. In Hindu India there was a small class of slaves, outside the caste system (see Chapter 4), and derived mainly from people captured in battle. Slavery existed in ancient Mexico. Some were war prisoners captured for ritual sacrifice. Although the economy of medieval Europe was based on serfdom, slavery was endemic. In England 10 per cent of the population was entered as slaves in the Doomsday Book of 1086. However, by the end of the Middle Ages slavery no longer existed in England, and the famous Cartwright decision of the reign of Elizabeth I (1569) held that "England was too pure an air for slaves to breathe in". Not so elsewhere in Europe. To meet the labour shortage caused by the Black Death of 1348, slaves were kidnapped by Tartar raiders or Italian traders from North Africa and West Asia and sold in Italy for domestic work. "By the end of the 14th century there was hardly a well-to-do household in Tuscany without at least one slave. Brides brought them as part of their dowry, doctors accepted them from their patients in lieu of fees - and it was not unusual to find them even in the service of a priest". The Church condoned the trade provided that the slaves were "infidels" (6). Finally, slavery existed in Black Africa throughout recorded history; it was practised everywhere even before the rise of Islam and the Islamic thirst for African slaves. In addition to the slaves owned in the regions of East and West Africa which became converted to Islam, it has been calculated that about 18 million African were delivered to the Islamic trans-Saharan and Indian Ocean slave traders between 650 and 1905 A.D. European trade in West Coast African slaves started in the second half of the 15th century; by 1867, 7 to 10 million Africans had been shipped to the New World. The Africans at home wanted women and children slaves; the New World plantation owners wanted males - whom the Africans would have otherwise slaughtered when they seized their females. The Africans were also anxious to buy guns from the Europeans in return for their slaves (7).

There was one traditional state which forswore slavery - Macedonia, the homeland of Alexander the Great (356 - 323 B.C.). Its people were all free. Alexander's father, Philip II, conquered Greece and abolished slavery in Athens.

Such in barest outline was the situation of slavery around the world when Columbus discovered the New World in 1492. As a result, a new dimension of slavery emerged between the 16th and the 19th centuries.

First, let us note the harsh Spanish rule on the South American mainland. The Spaniards soon found that they had discovered vast resources of precious metals, both as ore and as artifacts. In Peru, where there was no wheeled transport, Indian slaves, chained together with iron collars, were forced to transport ore, goods and artillery for hundreds of miles on foot in the high Andes. In Mexico the Aztec Indians were forced to work as slaves in the gold and silver mines.

In the Caribbean the Spaniards, and the British, French and Dutch who followed in their wake, started to grow tobacco, and, after tobacco growing had shifted to Virginia in the 17th century, sugar. They found the native Indians untameable, and so they slaughtered them and imported African slaves. By 1730 slaves constituted 30 per cent of the population of Cuba and 90 per cent of the population of Jamaica. In Portuguese-conquered Brazil the same process occurred. The coffee plant was imported from Arabia and Ethiopia, and by 1800 half the population were African slaves.

Meanwhile slavery was instituted by the white immigrants throughout colonial America; but it died out in the North simply because it did not pay, and by the time of the Revolution of 1775 against British rule most Americans, North and South alike, considered that eventually it would go out of existence everywhere. The situation was transformed by the invention of the cotton gin in USA in 1793, which launched the Southern States into the production of short-staple cotton suitable for production of cotton goods for the world market; while simultaneously Britain was launching the Industrial Revolution and establishing factories for making such goods. A three-way trade developed. Slave ships brought slaves from Africa to America, and raw cotton, tobacco and sugar from America to Europe. In 1800 the USA exported $5 million worth of cotton, in 1810 $10 million worth, in 1860 $191 million worth - 57 per cent of all American exports, produced by nearly four million slaves, whose value as "slave property" was estimated at, at least, $2 billion. It took the four-year Civil War, and the loss of 600,000 American lives (over twice American losses in World War II), to prevent the Southern States seceding from the North in order to retain "the peculiar institution" (8).

If we look back now over the whole scene, we may note that slaves were acquired in four main ways. The first was by capture in war. The second was slave trading, which went on all over the Western world until the 19th century, making sea travel a precarious undertaking for millennia. The third was by slave procreation, which accounted for most of the slaves of the Roman Empire and of the New World, and the fourth was by purchase in the slave markets. In ancient Mesopotamia the average price of a slave in the Sumerian market was 20 shekels of silver, less that the price of a donkey. Around the year 100 B.C., one of the major slave markets of the ancient world was held in the sacred island of Delos, which according to the Greek geographer Strabo handled 10,000 slaves a day.

And here is how slaves were sold in the Caribbean, according to an announcement in the official gazette of the French colony Martinique dated 22 June 1840: "in the name of the King, Law and Justice, Be it known . . . that on Sunday 26th instant, in the market place of the town of Saint-Esprit, at the termination of the mass, the following will be sold at public action: The slave Suzanne, negress, aged about forty, with her six children of 13, 11, 8, 7, 6 and 3 years. Proceeding from a distress. Payable in cash" (9).

The institution of slavery added enormously to the precariousness of life for ordinary people. Here is a *cri de coeur* from someone in Roman Egypt in the late third or early fourth century A.D., who set out on a papyrus questions to put to an oracle: "72: Shall I get my pay? . . . 74. Shall I be sold up? . . . 85. Am I to be sold as a slave? 86. Shall I go into exile? 87. Shall I go on an embassy? 88. Am I to become a town councillor? 90. Shall I be separated from my wife? 91. Am I under a spell?" (10).

What did the world's great religions say about slavery? We have seen that in antiquity institutions were grounded on a specific religion. And all these religions in fact sanctioned slavery. "The Judeo-Christian-Islamic tradition has been the most tolerant of slavery. Judaic and Islamic canonical texts refer frequently to slavery and treat it as a natural condition that might befall anyone. But they view it as a condition that should be gotten over quickly. Islamic practice was based on the assumption that the outsider rapidly became an insider and consequently had to be manumitted (freed) after six years. New Testament Christianity, on the other hand, had no prescriptions that slaves be manumitted. Canon law sanctioned slavery. This is attributable at least partially to Christianity's primary focus on spiritual values and salvation after death rather than on temporal conditions and the present life. Under such a regime it mattered little whether someone was a slave or a free person while living on earth".

Since law stemmed from religion, every slave-owning society had laws regulating slavery. "Islamic law", derived from the *Koran*, "regulated in detail every part of the institution of slavery, from the *jihad* (holy war) and the distribution of booty and treatment of slaves and their emancipation. The last Islamic slave law was promulgated in 1936 by King Ibn Sa'ud of Saudi Arabia. It required owners to register slaves with the government and licensed slave traders . . . Slavery was a relatively prominent institution in the Chinese T'ang Code of the 7th century A.D. Subsequently it was mentioned in every Chinese law down to the 20th century".

The great Greek philosophers made no protest against slavery. Plato merely advised, in his last book, *The Laws*, against the enslavement of Greek citizens, and exhorted masters to treat their slaves decently. Aristotle wrote, in his *Politics*, that "the human race contains certain individuals as inferior to the rest as the body is to the mind or brute beasts to men; (they) will respond best to brute force. Such persons are destined by nature itself for enslavement, since there is nothing which suits them better than to obey". And "warfare is a legitimate method of acquiring slaves, since it allows for one's need to hunt, not wild beasts only, but also men, who are born to obey yet refuse to submit to a yoke." (11).

But in the later Roman Empire twinges of conscience set in. The Code of Justinian (483 - 565) changed the definition of a slave from a thing to a person and prescribed the death penalty for an owner who killed his slave by torture, poison or fire. By the year 400 A.D. the Roman Empire had become Christianised, and there was moral unease among many Christians about the institution. "Gregory of Nyssa boldly attacked the institution of slavery, Augustine thought the domination of man over his neighbour an inherent wrong, but saw no way of ending it and concluded that, since the ordering of society prevented the misery of anarchic disruption, slavery was both a consequence of the Fall of man and at the same time a wrong that Providence prevented from being wholly harmful" (12).

When we come to the U.S.A., the one slave society which was

91

established in the secular climate of modern times, and which claimed in its Constitution to be based on the morality of Human Rights, we find an atmosphere of embarrassment about slave law. There was no federal slave law; the 10th Amendment to the Constitution of 1791 left the issue of slavery to the States. The following summarised extract from a History of the U.S.A. shows how the Southern States slipped inexorably into a dehumanising slave regime. (Far worse, however, were the 20th century slave regimes of Stalin's Gulags and Hitler's slave camps). "In 1660 the Maryland Assembly declared that 'all Negroes and other slaves shall serve Durante Vita, and in 1670 Virginia declared that 'all servants not being Christians' brought in by sea were to be slaves for life. The other Southern colonies followed in insisting that conversion to Christianity was not a prelude to inevitable manumission. As it became obvious that Negroes, as chattels to be bought and sold, were the source of their profits, so did the callousness of the system increase. Although talk of Human Rights was in the air, it was generally assumed by Southerners that such concern could not, need not, and indeed must not, be applied to Negroes. There followed, at this late stage in the 18th century, the argument that Negroes were, after all, rather less than human, and that their subservient status had been predefined by Holy Writ" (13).

In Part II we shall see how in the modern age the concept of Human Rights, embodying the idea that all individuals are intrinsically persons, is outlawing and gradually ending chattel slavery.

Chapter 7

FIGHTING AND WAR

IN 1986 twenty distinguished scientists from 12 countries - physiologists, biologists, professors of animal behaviour - drew up the "Seville Statement on Violence". They were concerned that "the theory of evolution has been used to justify not only war, but also genocide, colonialism, and suppression of the weak". They affirmed that it is "scientifically incorrect to say that war or any other violent behaviour is genetically programmed into our human nature . . . that there is nothing in our neurophysiology that compels us to react violently; . . . that in all well-studied species, status within the group is achieved by the ability to co-operate and to fulfil social functions relevant to the structure of that group". "Warfare is a peculiarly human phenomenon and does not occur in other animals"; and "the same species which invented war is capable of inventing peace". Why, therefore, is the history of ancient civilisations a long chronicle of fighting, war and generally violent behaviour, accompanied by continuous acts of vandalism and cruelty?

Wars were fought by tribes, states, empires, religious sects - by any body of people which had developed a group consciousness, and could thus regard other groups as "enemies". Perhaps the most basic motive was the urge to gain or protect land. There was also the need to capture slaves, important, in particular, for the Greeks and Romans; to acquire sacrificial victims, important for the Mayas and Aztecs; and to seize booty, important for everyone. There were wars of religion, fought, in particular, by Christians and Muslims. The *Koran* exhorts the Faithful to fight the *Jihad,* or Holy War, and asserts that the sinner will go to Paradise if he dies in battle against the infidel. The Christians fought the Crusades to capture the Holy City of Jerusalem from the infidel Muslims, and Christian sects fought each other to stamp out heresy. The only major ancient civilisations which lived for centuries in a state of relative peace seem to have been those of Ancient Egypt before the Hyksos invasion (3200 - 1700 B.C.), and Crete (2000 - 1400 B.C.). In

93

both cases the kingdom was self-sufficient in foodstuffs and basic necessities, and there was little or no external threat.

War was surrounded by an aura of glory. Kings, who normally led their troops in battle themselves, boasted to posterity of their military exploits in engravings on temples and tombs, showing the enemy trodden under foot and hoof, or by building huge triumphal arches. The *Arc de Triomphe* in Paris, commissioned by Napoleon to commemorate his victories, and completed in 1836 after his death, shows how continuous the glorification of war has been. The Roman motto: *Dulce et decorum est pro patria mori* - "sweet and fitting is it to die for one's country" - echoes in our psyches today. Traditional rulers normally believed that they had divine support. One of the most momentous events in history, the conversion of the Roman Empire to Christianity by the Emperor Constantine (280 - 337 A.D.), occurred because, as a result of a vision, Constantine believed that the Christian God would be more effective than the pagan gods in bringing him success in war and government. In fact, his vision proved sound; he was fighting throughout most of his reign, and he never lost a battle.

For thousands of years weapons remained essentially unchanged: bows and arrows, swords, daggers, spears, javelins, axes and catapults. An arrow killed Harold, the Saxon King of England, in the famous Battle of Hastings, fought on 14 October 1066; this ensured the Norman Conquest and thus determined the fate of England. Shields and helmets were standard equipment, and some form of armour or protective clothing's was usually worn. Almost every city was walled for protection, and battering rams were used for sieges. The Assyrians had battering rams 20 stories high. The Chinese invented gunpowder in the third or fourth century A.D., used it in weapons such as grenades in the tenth century, and in early forms of cannon in the 14th century. In Europe it came into use in the 14th century. The hitherto impregnable walls of Constantinople were breached by the Turks in 1453 in 40 days of bombardment with a siege train of 70 cannon. An Assyrian of 700 B.C. would have found little to astonish him in the attack and defence of walled strongholds in Europe 2,000 years later. By the time of the French Revolution in 1789 rifles with bayonets, pistols and cannon were supplementing or replacing the traditional weapons. Armour was abandoned by the 18th century, and men fought

94

in elegant, brightly coloured town clothes, with tall or tricornered hats covered with braid.

From about the sixth century B.C., when cavalry began to play a key role in warfare, until World War 1, when tanks were invented, the basic components of land warfare remained unchanged: soldiers on foot (infantry), and soldiers on horseback (cavalry), or riding some other animal - elephant or camel - or driving horse-drawn chariots, particularly favoured by the Mesopotamians and the Egyptians. The art of battle, which usually lasted a day, lay in the skilful deployment of cavalry and infantry. The Battle of Adrianople of A.D. 377, when the Roman Emperor Valens was defeated by the barbarian Visigoths, "was of vast significance for the future of warfare, for it represented the first victory of heavy cavalry over infantry" (1). And then there were the nomad warmongers the Mongols, circling around on their fast little horses, armed with bows and arrows, swept from the Yangtse to the Vistula in the 13th century without a major defeat. Their greatest ruler, Genghis Khan (ruled 1206 - 1227) - whose cult is being revived in Mongolia today - conquered the largest empire in history with a force of 150 - 200,000 horsemen, moving with a speed not repeated until the tank warfare of World War II. (For comparison, a census of 220 B.C. assessed the armies of Rome and her allies at 700,000 foot soldiers and 70,000 cavalry).

A comparison of the Battle of Cannae, fought near Rome on 2 August 216 B.C. between the invading Carthaginian General Hannibal and the Romans, with the Battle of Waterloo, fought in Belgium on 18 June 1815 between Napoleon and two armies of British, Dutch and Germans, will illustrate how little essential change in the nature of warfare had occurred in 2,000 years, despite the invention of gunpowder. At Cannae Hannibal's 40,000 infantry and 10,000 cavalry confronted 80,000 Roman infantry and 7,000 cavalry. Hannibal's superior tactics and use of cavalry to envelop the enemy secured him a resounding victory; the Romans, according to the Roman historian Pliny, lost 60 - 70,000 men (2). At the Battle of Waterloo, fought from 11.30 a.m. till 8.00 p.m., Wellington commanded an Anglo-Dutch force of infantry and cavalry, and was later in the day joined by the Prussian Marshal Blücher with a force of infantry and cavalry. The only essential difference between the two battles was that at Waterloo the soldiers fought with pistols and rifles as well as swords, and were supported by horse-drawn cannons, firing indiscriminately. French casualties are estimated at 40,000, Allied at 25,000. When night came, 40,000 men and 10,000 horses lay dead or dying on the two square mile battlefield. Napoleon had fled. Wellington, appearing dejected, rode back to his quarters in Waterloo, ate his supper in silence and then went to sleep on the floor - an officer lay dying in his bed. No doctors, no nurses, no clergy, no ambulances went to the darkened battlefield, only looters robbing - and then killing off - the wounded (3).

The manpower of traditional armies fell into three categories: conscripts, standing armies and mercenaries. Conscripts were the general rule. In some societies - China, Egypt, Mesopotamia, Greece, Rome, Aztec Mexico - the peasant or citizen was called up for state service, such as building canals or roads or performing military service, for a certain period of each year. In China conscripts built the Great Wall to keep the barbarians out in the third century B.C. The Athenian citizen did two years' military service from the age of 18 to 20.

European feudalism was based on the principle that the king owned the land; the barons held land from him in return for military support, and the knights similarly held land from the barons. But feudal levies were often inadequate, so conscripts were hired from unemployed knights (see below); other vassals paid the king to be let off going to war. The knights and squires in their turn called up their peasants - who were mostly serfs (see Chapter 4).

The Egyptians found it necessary to form a standing, professional army when they became involved in wars with their neighbours. Sparta alone among the Greek city states had a standing army. In Rome, the Consul Marius (157 - 86 B.C.) transformed the old citizen-militia into a highly organised professional force of well-trained career soldiers, the most efficient army in the ancient world, rewarded by allotments of land - equipped to build Rome's huge empire and to hold back the barbarian hordes. The Emperor Constantine, in the third century A.D., transformed the core of this army from infantry to cavalry, thus enabling it to hold back the barbarians for another century, and making it the model for medieval armies. Charles VII of France created medieval Europe's first standing army in order to fight the English invaders in the Hundred Years' War (1338 - 1453 A.D.).

In Britain, the inadequacy of the old feudal levy was shown up in 1639, when Charles I called up the "knights of the shires", now solid landed gentry, or "squires", to fight the Scots in order to impose Anglican bishops on that stubborn Puritan people. The squires failed to turn up, the Scots invaded the north of England and demanded a large sum of money from the King before they would go away. In order to get the squires to pay up, the King was obliged to summon them to meet him in Parliament - for the House of Commons was composed of squires and merchants. This led on to the outbreak of the Civil War between King and Parliament (1641 - 49). When Charles II came to the throne in 1660, he established England's first standing army.

The third category of soldiers were the mercenaries, hired troops who were employed by kings throughout history, from the Pharaohs of Egypt and Alexander the Great to West European rulers up to the end of the 18th century. Slaves were debarred from military service for fear that they would turn their weapons on their masters. Instead, they were employed in navies as "galley slaves", manning the oars, and often worked or beaten to death. After the Battle of Lepanto, fought off the coast of Greece on 7 October, 1571 A.D. between a Turkish and a West European fleet, 12,000 Christian slaves were freed from 250 Turkish ships.

To complete the picture, we must mention the barbarian hordes which, for hundreds of years, swept down from Northern Europe and Asia into the more civilised regions to the south. Barbarians from Western Europe - Goths and Vandals - overthrew the mighty Roman Empire in the West; the last puppet Emperor abdicated in 476 A.D. For another 1,000 years barbarian tribes from Eastern Europe ravaged the Greek-speaking Roman Empire in the East (Byzantium), which finally fell to the Turks in 1453 A.D. The Great Wall of China did not succeed in keeping the Mongols out of China in the 13th century A.D.; nor did the Himalayas keep the Turks and Mongols out of India in the 12th and 13th centuries. In the Middle Ages Norsemen from Scandinavia roamed the seas around Europe, from Britain and Ireland to the Dnieper, pillaging and sacking, though some settled down in East Anglia, Normandy and Sicily. In the Western hemisphere the high seas were not cleared of pirates until the 19th century, and in the Eastern hemisphere they infested the China seas until today.

Battles may have normally lasted for a few hours; but invasions and wars often lasted for years or decades. Alexander the Great, aiming at conquering the world with his army of Macedonians and Greeks, spent eleven years (334 - 323 B.C.) invading an area which stretched from the pyramids of Egypt to the Indus valley. The Thirty Years War of 1618 - 1648 was fought in Germany between German and Swedish Protestants and German and Austrian Roman Catholics; these are but two episodes of centuries of war between the emerging European nation states. In between battles - and this often meant for whole seasons in which the climate was not suitable for fighting - the armies settled down to "live off the land". It was physically impossible for them to come with their long-term supplies - as, for example, the Americans went to Saudi Arabia in 1990 - 91 to fight in the Gulf War. In the 14th century, when cannon appeared in Western Europe, "a big gun", its ammunition and other equipment might need 6 wagons, 100 horses and 70 men just to travel across country at 10 miles (16 kilometres) a day - on dirt or mud tracks! (4).

Moreover, the soldiers were out for pillage; it was the way that the unemployed, illiterate knight or underpaid mercenary kept himself. "There must be no mistake about the undiminished gusto with which soldiers, Swedish, French and Imperial (i.e. Austrians and Germans) carried on their trade to the end", writes the British historian H.A.L. Fisher of the Thirty Years' War. After the great cultural flowering of the Renaissance, this war, writes Fisher, "plunged a large area of central Europe into an abysm of barbarism and misery . . . It is impossible to exaggerate the miseries which the helpless peasants of the German Empire were compelled to endure . . . There was marauding, there was starvation, there was even cannibalism. Whole villages died out . . . moral restraints broke down and ceded to wild bursts of profligacy. At the beginning of the 16th century Germany stood in the forefront of European civilisation. By the end of the Thirty Years' War the country was barren of literature and art, burdened by an almost unmanageable language, and in social manners and customs sunk to a Muscovite barbarity" (5). As for the Hundred Years' War, "it has been calculated that it diminished the French population by a least a third, while it kept that of England (the invader) stationary" (6). What did this long absence of their men on campaigns do to the millions of women and children left behind? What did it do to the psyches of the soldiers, deprived of normal family life and normal methods of livelihood?

But there was worse. Throughout the ages it was standard practice for the conqueror, not merely to loot and pillage - including the seizure of slaves - but also to render the enemy helpless by wholesale massacre and devastation - a terrible kind of deterrence or vengeance. We can but mention two or three episodes to illustrate a general practice. We have already referred to the illiterate Mongol empire builder Genghis Khan (1157 - 1227 A.D.). The ruler of Turkestan sent an envoy to Peking to find out what was happening after Genghis Khan had invaded China in 1221. "Signs of terrible devastation were everywhere visible, the bones of the slaughtered formed whole mountains and the soil was greasy with human fat. At the gate of Peking lay a vast heap of bones" (7). His behaviour in Persia was equally ferocious. In the province of Khorasan nearly a million people were massacred, and according to a Persian historian, at Nishapur, "it was commanded that the town should be laid waste in such a manner that the site could be plowed upon and that in the exaction of vengeance not even cats and dogs should be left alive" (8). Genghis Khan was an illiterate barbarian. Those highly literate and cultured people, the Athenians, at the height of their civilisation, were capable of similar behaviour. In 416 B.C. the people of the island of Melos refused an Athenian request to ally with them in the Peloponnesian War (431 - 404 B.C.) which they were fighting with Sparta; but the Melians insisted on remaining neutral. The Athenians thereupon slaughtered the whole male population and enslaved the women and children. The island never recovered its prosperity. In 146 B.C. the Romans decided to put an end to "the Carthaginian problem" by razing the city of Carthage (modern Tunis) to the ground. A Roman army under the command of Cornelius Scipio Aemilianus attacked the city and set it on fire. Living and dead were thrown together into pits, or crushed by horses under foot. For ten days the Roman troops plundered the city. The Carthaginian leader, Hasdrubal, came out of the temple of Eshmoun, the local god, with his wife and two children, to ask for mercy. But 900 Roman deserters, faced with crucifixion as a punishment, set fire to the temple; and Hasdrubal's wife, calling her husband a coward and a traitor, threw herself and her children into the flames. The fifty thousand half-starved civilians who surrendered were sold into slavery (9). Equally ferocious was the Romans' "final solution" to "the Jewish problem". In the first century A.D. the Jews refused to settle down under Roman rule, mainly because the Romans would not respect and finally tried to suppress their religious practices, and imposed on them such abominations as sacrifices to the Emperor. So in 70 A.D. the Romans razed the Temple in Jerusalem to the ground, and in 135 A.D., after further Jewish revolts, the city of Jerusalem was destroyed. "The names Judea and Jerusalem were blotted from the Roman language. The country was renamed Palestina, and Aelia Capitolina, which no Jew might enter, rose as a Roman city on the ruins of Jerusalem" (10).

How did the kings and generals who ordered these massacres and devastations feel about them? Genghis Khan felt glee. He is recorded as having declared that "a man's highest joy in life is to break his enemies, to drive them before him, to take from them all the things that have been theirs, to hear the weeping of those who cherished them, to take their horses between his knees, to press in his arms the most desirable of their women" (11). King William the Conqueror (1027 - 1085 A.D.), who ruled both England and Normandy with a harsh hand, had a different reaction on his death bed. He died as a result of a fall from his horse after totally destroying the city of Nantes near Paris. The man " 'who was too relentless to care though all might hate him', as an English chronicler wrote, burst into floods of tears as he prayed for divine mercy, worried about the future and invoking the Virgin Mary. He expressed penitence for the vast bloodshed which had been the price of his greatness" (12).

We have seen that fighting and war were generally regarded as intrinsically glorious activities. They developed the qualities of character which were most admired: courage, discipline, resourcefulness, loyalty, and above all, a sense of honour. The warrior was a hero, a role model. His aim was, of course, to kill; and his likely fate was an early death in battle - what true warrior wanted to live on into old age, his ultimate state as a feeble old man undermining his hero image? In Homer's *Iliad,* the basic textbook of male education for hundreds of years in Greece, Rome and Byzantium, the father-god Zeus says of one of his two main heroes, Hector: "I guarantee power to Hector to kill until he comes to beached vessels, until the sun goes down and blessed darkness comes over". And Hector prays for his baby son: "Zeus, and you other immortals, grant that this boy may be as I am, pre-eminent among the Trojans . . . And let him kill his enemy and bring home the bloodied spoils, and delight the heart of his mother" - who would, of course, by then be a widow (13). Homer is thought by scholars to have lived between 750 and 650 B.C., and to have been recording events which occurred in the Mycenaean Age - about 1400 to 1100 B.C. Over two thousand years later we find the same attitude attached to the archetypal hero of medieval England, King Arthur - for whose actual existence scholars have little hard evidence. According to legend, King Arthur led the Britons against the invading Saxons in the Battle of Badon Hill, fought around 500 A.D., and, says the chronicler Nennius, writing 300 years later, "The twelfth battle (fought by Arthur) was on mount Badon where nine hundred and sixty men fell in one day from one charge by Arthur, and no one overthrew them except himself alone. And in all the battles he stood forth as victor". (14). Aeschylus, the Greek tragedian, one of the greatest dramatists the world has produced, composed his own epitaph, and all it referred to was the fact that he had fought in the Battle of Marathon in 490 B.C. "This memorial in barley bearing Gela covers the Athenian Aeschylus, son of Euphorion. The grove of Marathon could tell of his glorious valour, and the flowing-haired Mede knows it well" (15).

Underneath the glamour of heroism, the urge to demonstrate what the Romans called "manliness", the macho qualities outlined above, we can discern three psychological attitudes in the cult of war. The first is an immense egoism. History is full of examples of kings and nobles fighting for motives of personal power and glory. The second is the psychology of what may be called groupism: when the social group is a closed structure it tends to regard other groups as "the enemy"; it may be easier to fight than to fraternise - particularly when the other group speaks a different language and worships a different god; and as regards property, it is easier to seize than to share. The war culture fans the herd instinct. A group of soldiers on parade, marching in their uniforms like robots, symbolises the suppression of individuality and personality which militarism entails. The third is the fundamental indifference not only of the warrior class, including the highest nobility, but also of the priests, sages and even those most high-minded of men, the Greek philosophers, to the sufferings which war brought to the weak and lowly, the women and children, the peasants and slaves. A writer says of the "Heroic Epoch", 3000 - 500 B.C., "A total lack of respect for human life and indifference to suffering runs through all the literature and records of the epoch. We see expressed in stone hero kings boasting of unthinkable atrocities. We read in sacred books that 'God' commands us to destroy man, woman, child and beast, every living thing in a conquered city. We . . . are looking at an age that we cannot possibly understand. We cannot grasp that 3,000 years ago only horses counted, ordinary people were animals and even less than animals" (16). The culture of fifth century Athens, which came at the end of the heroic epoch, is generally regarded as representing one of the periods of the highest achievements of the human race in politics, philosophy, art and literature. But the attitude to war of the Greeks of this time was a hang-over from the heroic age. "The heroic outlook of the Greeks confirmed them in their taste for war, and was itself confirmed by it. It was in this that the famous heroes of the past had proved their superiority, and their descendants wished to rival them. Greek states went to war with each other almost as part of political routine, and it is significant that neither Plato nor Aristotle thought it unusual or undesirable or suggested any means to avoid it", writes an Oxford scholar (17).

One practical pacifist proposal did, however, emerge in Ancient Greece. In his play *Lysistrata* the comedian Aristophanes describes the women of Greece successfully stopping their men from fighting by refusing them sex until they desist. Even more extraordinary, the women transform the attitude of the men in the two armies from hostility to friendship! This was a portent for the modern age.

In the 2,500 years since the Heroic Age war has continued to be treated as glamorous, in order to hypnotise both soldiers and civilians. Uniforms, medals, flags, parades, war music, religious blessings have been the order of the day. The author of the book already quoted on the Battle of Waterloo describes the psychological importance of "regimental colours" (flags). "The colours in all armies were presented to the regiments by their Sovereign in solemn ceremony, and so became precious tokens of patriotism and regimental pride. They were also blessed by priests, and when they were honourably shot to pieces the tattered remains were hung up in cathedrals. So they were given a holy significance. To lose its standard to the enemy was a disgrace which could haunt a regiment for a whole generation; to defend it, men cast away their lives; to capture an enemy's standard was every good soldier's ultimate ambition, the height of his concept of glory" (18).

We have seen in Chapter 3 that the "higher religions" injected an attitude and outlook into the world which negated the glorification of war. The calm, dispassionate benevolence inculcated by the Hindu *rishis* or seers; the cosmic harmony affirmed by the Chinese sages Confucius and Lao Tzu; the harmlessness and compassion preached by the Buddha; the injection "Thou shalt not kill" laid down in the Ten Commandments revealed by God to Moses; the great statements of Jesus Christ: "Turn the other cheek"; "forgive seventy times seven"; the Muslim assertion that Allah (God) is "All-Compassionate", constitute a mighty affirmation that attitudes of love and forgiveness should replace attitudes of hatred and vengeance, if the human race is truly to express its humanity. However much these pronouncements are flouted and these commandments violated, they echo in the psyche of the world; their inner power cannot be obliterated.

The humane attitudes of higher religion have had a more profound effect on the structure of society in the Orient than in the cultures of Christianity and Islam. The dominant caste in Hindu India, in Confucian China, and in the Buddhist countries of South East Asia and Tibet, has been that of the priests and sages: the Brahmins of India, the mandarins of China and the monks of Buddhism. "In India, as in China", wrote Jawaharlal Nehru in his famous book, *The Discovery of India,* "learning and erudition have always stood high in public esteem, for learning was supposed to imply both superior knowledge and virtue. Before the learned man the ruler and the warrior have always bowed . . . The task of determining values and the preservation of ethical standards was allotted to a class of thinkers who were freed from material cares . . . and obligations, so that they could consider life's problems in a spirit of detachment. This class of thinkers and philosophers was thus supposed to be at the top of the social structure, honoured and respected by all. The men of action, the rulers and warriors, came after them and, however powerful they might be, did not command the same respect. The possession of wealth was still less entitled to honour and respect. The warrior class, though not on the top, held a high position, and not as in China, where it was looked upon with contempt" (19). A British scholar writes of the 3,000 years of Chinese imperial rule: "According to Confucian ethic, emperors had no need to call on force; the strength of their example and precepts which they both preached and practised would be sufficient to ensure the willing submission of all peoples of the earth to their beneficent dispensation. It followed that the overwhelming stress in Chinese institutions was on those organs which were devoted to cultural pursuits *(wen)* rather than to the practice of military arts *(wu)*. Dynasties might well depend on the courage and tactical qualities of those who led troops in battle, whether to establish a regime, to put down rebels or to engage the armies of enemy confederacies; but while local protagonists, fighting like Robin Hood to protect the weak from oppression, would earn praise for their exploits, successful generals would not merit the reputation of heroes, in a manner comparable with Alexander, Hector and Lysander" (20). An American scholar givers the same verdict. " . . . Few empires in history have had a more impressive military record than the Chinese. In periods of strong government . . . powerful military expeditions have gone beyond China's borders . . . Meanwhile every dynasty has been founded by the sword. Decades at a time have seen an endless succession of rebel hordes, imperial armies, and alien invaders marching across the face of the land". Nevertheless, he continues, "The Chinese military tradition is of a different type from the European or the Japanese. Once an imperial government has been instituted, civilian government has been esteemed over military. It took a soldier to found a dynasty but he and his descendants invariably found it easier to rule as sages, through civilian officials" (21).

Another American scholar writes that: "As an eyewitness of the Communist triumph in China in 1949, this writer had ample opportunity to observe the high esteem enjoyed by the soldiers of the Red armies, and to compare it with the fear, dislike or contempt only too commonly accorded the Chinese soldier in the past. On the basis of what he has seen, it is hard for him to believe that the present attitude represents nothing new in Chinese history" (22).

Feudal Japan was dominated by the caste of professional warriors, the Samurai, from the 12th to the 19th centuries. Medieval Europe was similarly dominated by knights and nobles, who were usually illiterate. "The high-born of our country distain letters", said a scholar in the reign of Henry II of England (1133-89). North of the Alps "there was clearly no Norman provision for the education of boys and girls of the noble class in the feudal age" (23). The Church provided the scribes who did the book work for kings and nobles and produced what literature there was; the Middle Ages resounded with the noise of quarrels between clergy and nobility. The value system of the Japanese Samurai had its roots in pagan Shinto, which was not concerned with ethics, rather than in Japan's other main religion, Buddhism (see Chapter 3). The value system of medieval European knights was drawn from prehistoric, pagan traditions. In both societies group loyalty and obedience to the tribal chief, and Spartan courage and discipline, were paramount. As we shall see in Part II, the Imperial Japanese and Nazi Germany regimes of the 1930s deliberately revived these ancient warrior energies. The medieval Church did not itself oppose war as intrinsically immoral. Lord Soper, a leading Methodist minister, has pointed out that St. Paul, who initially organised the scattered groups of Christians into embryonic churches, "was more concerned with the eternal Christ than the human Christ", and failed to inject into his groups the revolutionary pacifist teachings of Jesus. He thus "paved the way for a concordat between the Empire and the Church in which the evidence of war could be justified in the presentation of a 'Holy Roman Empire'. A martial Christendom came into being and stayed there through the Crusades. It is still the official Christianity in the nation state and capitalist systems" (24). The Church justified its support of warriors by the doctrine of "the Just War", formulated by St. Augustine and developed by St. Thomas Aquinas. This doctrine has been summed up by a Sorbonne professor of law as follows: "The duty of the prince was to guarantee the reign of justice, the chief means to be used to this end being law, which should respect the rights of God and the Church, and war. War was an act of vindictive justice which only the prince could perform. It must not be entered into with a view to conquest but only for the restoration of peace, the punishment of evil-doers, and the recovery of stolen property. An attack made on another without justification, in a mere spirit of revenge or gain, was held to be unjust. In this way the Church limited the *casus belli*" (25). This ancient doctrine was evoked by Prime Minister John Major of Britain and President Bush of the USA in 1991 to justify the war which they declared against Iraq. Islam proclaimed the Koranic doctrine of the *Jihad* or Holy War to justify military conquests and conversion across the globe, in a region stretching from Spain to Indonesia. Thus in many societies religion, instead of working to transmute militarist psychological attitudes, was evoked to justify - though in the case of Christianity also to control - them.

There is, however, another way of looking at the whole situation. A marvellous interpretation of the medieval knight's spiritual commitment to serve God and man - and woman - has been given by Sir George Trevelyan, former Director of the Wrekin Trust in England, in an essay on heraldry. "Picture", he writes, "the young aspirant for knighthood in vigil all night before the altar, his sword and armour, his helm and shield set before him, in prayer to Christ the King in preparation for the day when his earthly king should, in the accolade, touch him on the shoulder with the Sword of Michael (i.e. a sacred sword) and say 'Rise, Sir Roger'. Then he is to go forth into the world to carry light and justice into the confusion and cruelty of daily life. There he is to do doughty deeds and rescue fair ladies from the clutches of dragons or wicked men." Chivalry and heraldry are, Sir George suggests, "closely allied with the medieval vision of the Arthurian legends", which, like all legends, is an allegory about the human soul and its passage through the darkness of life on the earth plane. Medieval heraldry is a form of sacred art in which this allegory is portrayed. "The full coat of arms" is called THE ACHIEVEMENT. It pictures that which the soul is called on to "achieve" during its journey through the dark forest of life . . . The SHIELD represents the body or personality with which we live out our lives. The HELM is the potentiality of higher thinking. The MANTLING, weaving all around in colour, is the symbol for the aura from which the trends of the soul can be read, The CREST is the symbol for the quintessence of the higher self, the SUPPORTERS are guides or guardians from the supersensible spiritual realms, and the MOTTO in a few concentrated words gives a mantrum for aspiration" (26).

Such may have been the vision embodied in medieval chivalry and hinted at in the Arthurian legend. But what was the reality of the knight's psychology? Here is a brief analysis. "The Arthurian heroes are not bovine men, too stupid to feel fear and too stolid to be a prey to self-doubt . . . They tend to be highly-strung, emotional and sensitive. They know what fear is and have to steel themselves against it. They can be knocked off their psychological balance, as well as their horses. When the redoubtable Saracen knight Palomides sees that Tristram will outdo him in a tournament, he bursts into tears, Lancelot and Tristram, parted from the women they love, are so distraught they go mad . . . A man who lives by stretching his nerve is likely to be a mass of nerves. A man who only feels fully himself in action feels inadequate out of it. This is as true in the Arthurian romance as in real life" (27).

Here we reach the paradox at the heart of the cult of heroism. Is the knight's spiritual commitment made during his vigil in the chapel to serve Christ the King compatible with his return to his place at the Round Table in King Arthur's castle with severed heads hanging from his saddle? Can one both love one's enemy and slaughter him - and his wife, children and old parents? Today some modern Christians - and non-Christians - are committed pacifists: they will not fight in war in any circumstances. This attitude was pioneered by the Quakers, a sect founded in 17th century England; to escape persecution many Quakers emigrated to America, where they have had a profound influence. Some modern Muslim scholars are interpreting the doctrine of the *Jihad* as the war between good and evil impulses in the human soul. Modern psychology is powerfully reinforcing the symbolic attitude to fighting expressed in Sir George Trevelyan's interpretation of medieval heraldry. Outside the Headquarters of the United Nations is a statue, donated by the Soviet Union in 1949, of a man beating a sword into a ploughshare. This man surely symbolises the hero of the future reminding us that, as the Seville Statement on Violence says, "the same species which invented war is capable of inventing peace".

Chapter 8

EDUCATION

THE word "education" is loosely used today to denote two complementary concepts: to "draw out" - *e ducare* in Latin - and to "push in", which may be called "learning" or "training". Traditional education has been essentially concerned with training in the broadest sense. In the modern age, education has begun to shift towards "drawing out". The meaning behind this change is proclaimed in Article 26 of the United Nations' Universal Declaration of Human Rights of 1948 (see chapter 13). "Everyone has a right to education . . . *Education shall be directed to the full development of the human personality . . .* " This concept was almost entirely unthought of in traditional societies, the partial exception being those of ancient Greece and Rome.

Traditional education, in general, had three main aspects. First, the moulding of character, the inculcation of the values laid down by Heaven which held the particular society together - whether family, clan, tribe, state or empire: values such as honour, loyalty, courage, piety and obedience - the *mors maiorum* of the Romans, the "Five Relationships" laid down by Confucius in which harmony should prevail: between (i) ruler and minister; (ii) father and son; (iii) husband and wife; (iv) elder and younger brothers; and (v) friend and friend. This kind of conditioning produced intense cohesion and psychological security within the groups concerned, but it did not develop relationships between persons as such, between individuals who were simply "being themselves". Therefore "love" between "persons" as we conceive it today was not a feature of the traditional ethos.

The second aspect of traditional education consisted in training that class of men (very rarely women) destined to be priests, scribes, lawyers and teachers. This normally involved learning to read and write, memorising the revealed scriptures, especially in the periods when they were transmitted orally; training in the performance of ritual; learning the skills of mathematical calculation for the purposes of astronomy, architecture, engineering - e.g. road and canal building - and commerce, and the study of medicine. (see Chapter 10).

The third aspect was the training in practical skills needed by the vast majority of the population who performed the manual and menial jobs. Skills in architecture, engineering and sculpture were transmitted outside formal schooling. Such training did not involve literacy. In 1945 the literacy rate of the "developing" continents of Africa, Asia and Latin America was about 5 per cent. Probably in 1800 the literacy rate for the whole world was about 5 per cent for men, and one per cent for women.

Let us now glance at the development in traditional societies of the second aspect of traditional education, the formal education in literacy and numerically given to a special class or caste.

Education in Ancient Egypt, Mesopotamia and Mexico

In Egypt and Mesopotamia the boys chosen to be scribes were attached to temple schools at an early age. There they learned to write the appropriate phrases for dealing with one or more aspects of the state's affairs, or to write out the culture's epic stories and sacred texts. In societies which had pictorial scripts this was a most exacting task, requiring long years of memory training. "King Ashurbanipal (of Assyria, 668-626 B.C.) who boasted his complete knowledge of cuneiform writing, completed the establishment of a large library in his palace at Nineveh (now in the British Museum) which aimed at embracing all branches of learning" (1). The public scribe and the public story-teller were essential figures in Mesopotamian society. In Egypt the scribes were also a privileged class, free from the forced labour to which all other non-noble classes, including the priests, were subject. They paid no taxes because they produced no goods (in Egypt, where money did not exist, taxes were paid in produce). They were an elite corps of civil servants, with a long, hard 12-year education in the difficult art of writing hieroglyphics. This elite administered the country well for centuries; and as a result "there is plenty of evidence to show that there was a substantial level of literacy throughout Egypt" (2). In both Eygpt and Mesopotamia rigid methods and harsh discipline were used to achieve uniformity and cultural transmission; variations from traditional patterns of thought were strictly prohibited. The hieroglyphics were "the word of God". They were written in stone as

109

well as on papyrus in order to radiate their inner power in perpetuity. Similarly, in the Aztec culture in Mexico, boys destined to be priests or administrators, chosen not on the basis of family or class but of character and ability, were trained at special temple schools called *calmecacs*. The rest of the youngsters had a less exacting education at schools called *tgelpochcalli*. "The priests taught the young men all the songs that are called holy, which were written in their books by means of their characters, as well as the astrology of the Indians, the interpretation of dreams and the reckoning of the years". Girls destined to be priestesses underwent a similar training. Boys not destined to be priests were trained for war. Aztec children received some education related to their future life's tasks. This compares favourably with medieval Europe and with the Graeco-Roman civilisation (3). The Incas in Peru also ensured that all children had oral education (since they had no script) from the age of five.

Education in China

"For two millennia learning was the basis of civilised life in China. Even the modern word for culture, *wen-hua*, means 'to be transformed through writing'. Learning began with the reading of the classics. The 'Way of Confucius' was the most sacred spiritual possession of the Chinese people, enduring as such throughout Chinese history, until the 20th century, as the basis of Chinese culture" (4). This "Way" was the simple affirmation that a man is naturally good, that he is innately in tune with *Tao,* the cosmic harmony which pervades the universe, and that if people apply *Tao* in their family life, in village life, and in the life of the Empire, harmony and happiness will result. We have already discussed in Chapters 3 and 4 the unique system of government in China: imperial autocracy based on administration of scholar-gentry - "mandarins" - trained by years of study and memorisation of the Confucian texts and recruited by written examination in them. The process and spread of learning was enormously facilitated by the invention of paper about 200 B.C., of block printing in the 8th century A.D., and moveable type in the 11th century (see Chapter 10). We have noted in Chapter 2 the vast output of printed books in China up to the close of the 18th century. Since Confucianism is an ethical system propounded by a philosophy rather that a supposedly divine, authoritative revelation, and since the scholars were expected to be government administrators and also encouraged to be poets, education was of a wider nature than in the other ancient civilisations - leaving aside the Greeks and Romans (see below). Schools abounded at every level. Students from Korea and Japan came to study in China and took back the lunar calendar and the texts of the Buddhist sects, as well as the examination system and the Confucian theories of government and social life. Chinese culture also penetrated Indochina. The examinees gained degrees, comparable to those of Western Europe. During the Ming dynasty (1368-1644) 2,000 scholars, working for five years, produced an encyclopaedia of 11,000 volumes costing so much to print that only two extra copies were made.

This rich and unified cultural and educational system was spread over the biggest empire in the world in a common language and script. (According to an ancient census the population of the Empire was about 60 million in 2 A.D. A modern scholar estimates it at 430 million in 1850) (5). The Mongol conquerors (1206-1368) had the classics translated into the Mongol language. This led to the popularisation of vernacular Chinese, preparing the ground for a vernacular literature. The Manchu rulers (1644-1912) were afraid of innovation. By the modern age, therefore, the 2000-year old system of education and government, intrinsically backward looking as it was, had become stagnant and rigid. Modern science and technology were ignored. The almost unique social mobility of the past, whereby peasants could rise through the school system to the highest positions, died away. "By the 17th or 18th centuries the opportunities for men of humble origin to rise to the front ranks of the state had been diminished very severely" (6). It has been estimated that essentially, during the imperial era, 80 per cent of the population were illiterate. In these circumstances China was almost totally unprepared for the assault of modernity from the West in the 19th century.

Education in Japan

In Japan, the ancient indigenous clans formed an Empire under a supposedly divine Emperor in 645 A.D., and developed a class of nobles who ruled under his nominal authority until 1868. The descendants of the longest reigning dynasty in the world then effectively took control until 1945, when he finally renounced his divine status as well as his political authority. Shinto, "the Way of the Gods'" was the ancient indigenous religion which affirmed the Emperor's descent from the Sun Goddess, and inculcated belief in familiar spirits, ghosts and ancestors - *kami* - amoral beings who could ensure weal or woe but were not concerned with spiritual development. Japanese culture developed as the Japanese imported the Chinese script in the 5th and 6th centuries - although the Japanese language is as different from the Chinese as it is from English. Chinese art and Chinese ideas about education flowed in, and so did the teachings of Confucius and Buddha. The ruling nobles lapped up the foreign religions, which supplied the ethical and philosophical element lacking in Shintoism, and a rich and poetic literature developed. And for the simple-minded, the Buddha was a superior *kami* who had more power than the local spirits to ensure material prosperity. Confucian style education was developed for the nobility, who were also the administrators, in a College House in the capital, Kyoto (formerly called Heian), and in provincial colleges. In the ensuing feudal period, 1192-1867 A.D., power passed from the poetry-writing nobility to the warrior class, the *samurai,* and education shifted to a combination of military training with reading and writing - necessary if the military were to govern. Buddhist temples became centres of culture and learning, equivalent to universities. And as the military enforced peace on the nobles during the period 1603-1867, a middle class arose, leading to the provision of schools for commoners. The curriculum of all the schools established for both the warriors and the commoners continued to be based on Chinese Confucianism. By 1870, according to two scholars, the literacy rate for men was 40-45 per cent, and for women 10-15 per cent. Levels were comparable with those of Europe at that time and far ahead of any other part of Asia (7). Such was the educational background to the Meiji Revolution of 1867, the sudden decision to modernise Japan described in Chapter 4.

Education in India

We described in Chapter 4 how by about 500 B.C. the four traditional

112

classes, priests, warriors, traders and cultivators, had become hardened into rigid castes, each with its own customs, privileges and taboos, prescribed in the Vedic scriptures. Religion saturated educational ideals and the study of the Vedic literature was indispensable to the higher castes. The boys of the first three castes were in ancient days given compulsory, free secondary education in the ashram or spiritual retreat of their mentor from the age of 8 to 16. The curriculum consisted of phonetics, grammar, astronomy, prosody and etymology. They had to observe celibacy, sleep on hard beds, eat simple food and wear simple clothes. Memorisation of the scriptures was basic. Girls were educated at home. Gradually this secondary education became confined to the Brahmin or priestly caste, until it was challenged by Buddha (c. 563-483 B.C.) and Mahavira (599-527 B.C.), the founder of the Jain religion. Both these great sages rejected the authority of the Vedas, condemned the caste system, and challenged the exclusive claims of the Brahmins to the priesthood. They taught in the common languages and offered education to all, regardless of sex, caste and creed. But as time went on, the Buddhists, organised, unlike the Hindus, into monasteries and nunneries, also became more exclusive. Education was given to monks and not to laymen. Meanwhile the Mauryan and Guptan dynasties of India (321 B.C. - 500 A.D.) began to develop secular education, from the village to the university. Law, medicine, military science, botany and astronomy were studied, and students were allowed to choose their subjects freely, and not according to caste. In the second century A.D. Indian education spilled right across South East Asia, from Sumatra to New Guinea. For 1500 years there was a fusion of cultures. Hinduism continued to wield its influence in these lands until the Muslim invasions of India, which started in the 13th century.

The Education of the Jews

The history of the Jews is a unique phenomenon. Their peculiar contribution is not only the production of one of the great scriptures of the world, the Old Testament, but also the way in which they have related to education. We described in Chapter 3 how the Old Testament and its commentary, the *Talmud,* were written down in Hebrew and proclaimed as canon by the Rabbis in the 4th century A.D. The two great works together constitute a corpus of theological pronouncements, ethical principles and social rules claiming to govern every aspect and provide for every contingency in life. Other religions which have made similar claims were written and interpreted by a specialised corps of priests and scribes. The Jews were unique in that every male Jew was expected to study and discuss the scriptures and the Law derived from them. The synagogue, the "House of the Book'" was introduced during the Babylonian exile of 597-538 B.C. It consists in principle of a gathering in a private room of ten or more male Jews for study and prayer. After the scriptures were written down, therefore, all male Jews were expected to become literate, and to memorise them. After the destruction of the Temple and of the city of Jerusalem by the Romans in 70 and 135 A.D., this special literate democracy, based on an unchanging curriculum, kept the Jews united all over the world, from China to Spain. At the age of 13 every boy, in the ceremony of Bar Mitzvah, became personally responsible for fulfilling the Law. When the modern age dawned in the 19th century there were, it is estimated, some 3 million Jews in the world (there had been about 6 million in the Roman Empire; today there are 12 and a half million). They then began to emerge from their secluded groups and ghettos and to produce many of the seminal thinkers, artists and men and women of action of our time. Freud, Marx and Einstein are but figures on the tip of the iceberg. Is this phenomenon to be at least partly explained by 2,500 years of exacting, democratic mental and moral education?

Education in Greece and Rome

The two factors which made Greece and Rome different from all other traditional civilisations, viz, the absence of revealed scriptures combined with the possession of a rich written literature, and the institution of secular democracy, inevitably affected their education systems. A boy living in fifth century Athens was expected, in the first place, to learn to read, to write - with a stylus on a waxed wooden tablet - and probably to know enough arithmetic to add, subtract, multiply and divide. (The Greeks used letters for numbers and had not invented the concept of zero, so mathematics was an onerous subject). Secondly, he was expected to study music and to learn to play a musical instrument. The Greeks were passionately attached to music and dancing, which they regarded as the earthly reflection of the harmony and music of the spheres. Their main instruments were the lyre and the flute. (In the year 480 B.C., after the Greek victory over the Persians in the battle of Salamis, the future dramatist Sophocles, aged about 15, stripped naked and gleaming with oil, lyre in hand, led the boys' chorus which chanted the victory paean) (8). The teachers were hired by the parents, sometimes for a pittance, and slaves were often attached to the boys of wealthier families to accompany them to school and supervise the performance of their studies. Homer's epics would be learnt by heart, and recited orally, for they embodied the qualities which were universally admired in traditional societies, such as courage and honour. Memorisation of Homer's works was still a basic educational requirement in the Christian Byzantine Empire 1,000 years later. Meanwhile girls stayed at home, indoors. At the age of 12 or so came the climax of the boy's education: gymnastics. In every Greek city there are two buildings which sum up their civilisation; the theatre and the stadium. Gymnastics *(gymnos,* "bare") were everywhere, supervised by paid instructors. The boys stripped naked, then rubbed their bodies with olive oil and sand, which combined with sweat to make a fine coating. Fitness exercises were supplemented with running, wrestling, jumping and discus and javelin throwing. The main purpose of this aspect of Greek education was not simply psychological - *mens sana in corpore sano* - but the practical one of preparing good soldiers. It was taken to extreme lengths in Sparta, where the education system for boys made them spend their childhood in a military system which resembled a cross between the Hitler Youth and the Boy Scouts; girls, almost as naked as boys, participated in the system, to prepare them to be healthy mothers of future soldiers. Roman girls, unlike Greek girls, were sent to primary school from the age of 7 to 14, when they were withdrawn into the home to prepare for marriage.

If the Athenians were unique in making all male youths - that is, these who were Athenian citizens, barbarians and slaves were excluded - practise gymnastics and music, they were even more unique in fostering universal higher education for males. In many parts of the

115

Greaco-Roman world there existed centres of higher learning for an elite of scholars and intellectuals. Philosophers and scientists were already taking advantage of the free intellectual climate of thought to put forward a variety of unconventional and stimulating ideas. These were disseminated and discussed by a class of proto-professors, travelling lecturers, permanently "on circuit", called Sophists. "Their demonstrations of learning and verbal fluency brought them pupils who attached themselves to the maestro and followed him from town to town: they were, first and foremost, educators. Under the general heading of 'philosophy' they taught all the subject then available that had not been covered by the elementary school curriculum: geometry, physics, astronomy, medicine, arts and crafts, philosophy in the narrower sense of the word, and rhetoric" . . . "It is in large measure due to the Sophists that subjects such as grammar, logic, ethics, politics, physics and metaphysics first emerged as separate entities" (9). Their teaching, like that of Socrates, involved argument and discussion. In other countries an ordinary citizen had only a small arena - if any - in which to air his views. In democratic Athens a man with a cause to make in the ruling assemblies "faced an audience of several thousand, the majority complete strangers, who were by no means bound to listen to, let alone accept, what he said." An understanding of public speaking, "rhetoric", "persuasion" - "the ability to make someone acquiesce peacefully" was essential. According to tradition, the first handbooks of rhetorical technique were produced in the democratic city state of Syracuse in the 460s B.C. and quickly reached Athens. The modern policy of "conflict resolution" by discussion in a free society was born. A classical scholar of modern Oxford University sums up the situation: "Literacy in Greece was never a craft skill, possessed only by experts; from the start writing was used for a great range of activities, from composing poetry to cursing enemies, from displaying laws to voting, from inscribing tombstones or dedications to writing shopping lists . . . Our evidence suggests that there existed all levels of skill in writing, spelling and grammar . . . There is no sign that women were expected or encouraged to read, though many of them could. To be cautious, we may say that in Athens well over half the male population could read and write, and that levels of literacy in the Greek cities in the classical and Hellenistic periods were higher than in any period of Western

116

culture before this century" (10).

In the broadest sense, the Panhellenic Festivals and Olympic Games which took place every four years were an aspect of Greek education. No similar institution existed in any other traditional society. They established a model which is being revived today, albeit in the context of modern culture.

According to tradition, the Games were organised at Olympia in the Peloponnese in honour of the God Zeus in very early times. They were revived in 776 B.C. when the Delphic Oracle prescribed them as a means of avoiding civil wars and plague. Thereafter they were held every four years until 393 A.D. - a period of 1168 years. The athletes, who came from all over Greece, participated as individuals, representing themselves, not their clans. The Sacred Truce, concluded by the rulers of all the Greek city states, laid down that the district of Olympia (Elis) should be inviolable; no army or armed men could enter the sacred area, dominated by the Temple of Zeus containing Pheidias's marvellous statue of the god. Throughout Greece conflicts should cease for the month of the Games, and for one month before and one month after, while the athletes and spectators journeyed to and from the sacred arena. The Olympic Council, which organised the Games, fined those who violated the truce, including the city of Sparta. Among those who regularly turned up were philosophers such as Plato and Aristotle, poets, artists, historians and statesmen. "It is reported that after the Persian wars, in 476 B.C., Themistocles was also present at the most brilliant Olympics which had ever taken place. As he entered the Stadium . . . the Greeks stopped watching the games in order to cheer. That day in the Stadium the gratitude of all Greeks was concentrated on honouring the heroic victor of Salamis" (11). Only one woman, the priestess of the goddess Demeter, was allowed to attend the Games. Any woman who slunk in was thrown over the edge of a local mountain to her death. Slaves were forbidden to take part, although slaves and barbarians could be spectators. The Games were divided into athletic and equestrian contests. The athletics included foot-racing, wrestling, the long jump, discus-throwing and boxing. The equestrian included chariot racing. The athletes were naked. The prize for the victors in all the races was a crown of wild olive leaves. Girls took part in foot races in honour of the goddess Hera, held at a different time from the

117

Olympiad. But only virgins from the district of Elis were permitted to take part, and they only ran half the length of the Stadium (160 metres), wearing a short tunic.

The ideal which the Games affirmed for over a thousand years is summed up in a report made by the ancient Greek historian Herodotus. After the Battle of Thermopylae the Persian King, Xerxes, was talking to some Greek deserters, led by Mardonius, about the Olympic Games. The King asked what the prizes for the winners were. "They replied: 'A crown of wild olive'. Then a staff officer, Tritandaechmes, son of Artabanus, spoke to Mardonius . . . 'Alas, Mardonius, against whom have you brought us to fight? With men who compete not for money but for virtue' " (12).

Finally, in 394 A.D., the Christian Emperor Theodosius the Great abolished the Games. Pheidias's wonderful statue of the fatherly Zeus was taken to Constantinople, and in 426 A.D. Christian fanatics destroyed the deserted sanctuary after Theodosius II had decreed that the temple should be burnt.

But the model for the cultivation of the combined excellence of body and mind, inculcating brotherhood, peace and virtue, was not forgotten. At the end of the 19th century, at the instigation of a French aristocrat, the Games were revived as the International Olympiad, open to athletes of all nationalities and both sexes, and since 1896 they have been held every four years (except during the two World Wars) in different countries and cities. But the prize of victory is no longer a crown of wild olive leaves, but a gold, silver or bronze medal.

The Greeks had another famous educational institution, the theatre. In other cultures, for example, those of the Japanese and medieval Europe, there were dramatic public performances of a religious and poetic nature, but they were not drama in the Greek sense and the sense of Shakespearean England: the acting out of stories - admittedly based on ancient legends and dedicated to the god Dionysius - written by known contemporary dramatists about the interplay of human emotions at their deepest and also their most comic levels. The plays, like the games, were competitive. There were two festivals in Athens, in the theatre at the foot of the great rock on which the Parthenon stands. One was for comedies, when five playwrights competed for the prize with the production of five single plays, and the other was

118

for tragedies, when three playwrights entered four plays each. The playwright was his own producer, and trained the three actors, who were all male, as well as the chorus. The Festival lasted five days, one for the comedies and three for three collections of tragedies. The audience watched a total of 17 plays! The prizes, presented by ten elected judges, consisted of plain ivy wreaths. Such was the setting of the greatest comedies and tragedies (both Greek words) before Shakespeare: the plays of Aeschylus, Sophocles, Euripides, Aristophanes and a few lesser authors. The Athenian theatre held 14,000 people. The great theatre of Epidaurus in the Peloponnese held 12,000. Women were apparently admitted but made to sit at the back. One could call the whole phenomenon of the Greek theatre a form of adult education (13).

Such was the general setting in which the most famous development of higher education before the modern age emerged. Against the background of the Sophists and of a group of the world's first scientific thinkers in Ionia (see Chapter 10), three of the greatest philosophers in the world emerged in fifth century Athens: Socrates, Plato and Aristotle (see Chapter 3). Plato founded a school for higher study, which he called the Academy, after an early hero, Academios. It can be considered the world's first university. It flourished, drawing to itself, later, intellectuals from all over the Roman Empire, until it was closed, together with all other "pagan" institutions, by the Christian Emperor Justinian in 529 A.D. (The word "pagan" is defined in Collins' Dictionary as "a member of a group professing a polytheistic religion or any other religion than Christianity, Judaism or Islam"). These institutions of higher education proliferated: Aristotle's Lyceum, the "Garden" of the philosopher Epicurus, the "Porch" or Stoa which gave its name to the sect of philosophers called Stoics (the Roman Emperor Marcus Aurelius was a Stoic); and above all the *Mouseion* (Museum, Temple of the Muses) established at Alexandria in the 4th century B.C.. In the 3rd century B.C. Greek scholars met at the Museum to produce the "best text" of all surviving Greek literature. A huge activity in collecting and editing educational material took place. Alexander the Great spread Greek learning and education throughout the area which he conquered, from Egypt to India, in his short life (356 - 323 B.C.), and "universities" and large libraries were also established during the Hellenistic period in Rhodes (1st century B.C.), Smyrna, Antioch, Beirut, and later Constantinople. The study of mathematics and science was also highly developed (see Chapter 10). Huge libraries were assembled at Alexandria (half a million scrolls), Pergamum (200,000 scrolls, said to have been given by Antony to Cleopatra for the Alexandrian library) and elsewhere. Rich men established their own libraries - and some Romans, in particular, were very rich! Books were being copied everywhere. The best authors' works became school text books. One corner of the Agora or central market place of Athens was reserved for book shops. All this intellectual activity was cosmopolitan. Jews, Persians, Egyptians, Romans and others, even Welshmen, travelled to these centres of learning to equip themselves for their life's work. Cicero (106 - 43 B.C.), Rome's greatest orator and one of her greatest writers, spent three years in Athens and Rhodes studying oratory and philosophy. Greek therefore became the cosmopolitan language of education during the Hellenistic and throughout the imperial Roman periods. Most well-educated Romans were bilingual in Greek and Latin. As the Roman poet Horace put it: "Captive Greece captured her rude conqueror and introduced the arts to rustic Latium".

This brings us to Roman education. Republican Rome was a nation of small farmers and soldiers and its education was suitable for a rural, traditional people, instilling an unquestioned respect for the customs of the ancestors, as in other traditional civilisations. Early Roman education was therefore practical; and in contrast to that of Greece it was familial. The Romans, unlike the Greeks, believed in the virtues and the happiness of family life. Cicero waxed eloquent on returning from exile and finding his house torn down by his enemies. "Is there anything" he asked "more hallowed . . . than the home of each individual citizen. Therein he has his altars, his hearth, his household gods, . . . his rites and ceremonies. For all of us this is a sanctuary so holy that to tear a man away therefrom is an outrage to the law of heaven". Marcus Portius Cato (234 - 149 B.C.), a senior politician, said that "a wife and a son are the holiest of holy things" (14). Roman boys and girls were therefore educated at home until they were 16 - although in later times a rich man might hire a Greek tutor for his son. At 16, the boy became a man, adopting adult dress, the white woollen toga; and

120

at 18 he was called up for military service. Later, when Rome had annexed Greece, Macedonia, Pergamum and the whole Hellenic Orient, upper class Romans patterned their studies on those of the Greek schools, except that instead of Homer their own great writers - Virgil, Horace, Cicero, Terence, Tacitus, Caesar, Ovid, Quintillian and others - were adopted as texts. In higher education priority was given to oratory rather than philosophy and law, which had no equivalent in Greek education, was added. The Emperor Marcus Aurelius (121 - 180 A.D.) endowed four chairs of philosophy in Athens, one each for the four great sects - Platonism, Aristotelianism, Epicureanism and Stoicism. This illustrates the freedom from dogma in the Graeco-Roman world. The Roman Empire was covered with a network of schools: private primary schools, grammar, i.e. reading and writing secondary schools, supported by private foundations or municipal funds; and the institutions of higher education which we have outlined.

There is, however, a dark aspect of Roman culture which should be mentioned to complete the picture. The Romans supplemented the Greek stadiums and theatres all over their Empire with amphitheatres (*amphi*, Greek for "around"), huge circular or oval buildings in which the spectators sat all around watching the events in the arena below. The Emperor himself attended the performances in the Colosseum in Rome, built in 80 A.D., which seated 50,000 spectators. And what did this Roman form of "adult education" involve? Gladiators (Latin *gladus,* a sword), trained fighters, recruited from slaves, criminals and prisoners of war, fought each other to death for the entertainment of the spectators. Or else they fought defenceless victims: Christians, or wild animals imported from afar at great expense: tigers, crocodiles, giraffes, lynxes, rhinoceroses, ostriches, hippopotami, lions - 600 in a single show - and elephants, some bred in Italy. (After Roman times no hippopotami were seen in Europe until 1850). All classes, participated in the shows, whose purpose was not only to entertain, but to terrorise those who failed to please their masters. "No Roman temple was ever as impressive as the amphitheatre. Public slaughter was already, for the Romans, a fundamental institution, a social, if not a religious, ritual" (15). It was a far cry from the games and plays which ended with crowns of olive and ivy leaves.

Education in The Byzantine Empire

The Graeco-Roman system of education was inherited by the Byzantine Empire, which lasted virtually unchanged for 1,000 years, until Constantinople fell to the Muslim Turks in 1453 A.D. There were many villages as well as town schools in which boys aged 6 to 10 learned reading and writing - in Greek. From 10 - 16 they studied the "classics", Homer and a selection of classical Greek texts, memorised partly because of lack of written copies. Higher education, as in Greece, consisted of rhetoric and philosophy. For a time Neoplatonic philosophy, the philosophy of Plato developed by the Roman philosopher Plotinus (205 - 270 A.D.), was integrated into Christian doctrine by some of the early Christian Fathers; but, as we have seen, in 529 A.D. the Emperor Justinian closed the Academy of Athens, and the Arab conquest of Egypt in 640 ended the teaching of Christian Neoplatonism in Alexandria. (The only known woman philosopher, the Neoplatonist Hypatia, who taught at the Museum, had been torn to pieces by a fanatical Christian mob). Aristotle's logic therefore became the main content of Byzantine higher education. "In such a society, where so few calls were made on reason - that tool of a materialistic world - the brain atrophies; in Byzantium the whole intellectual life was stagnant. Literature was . . . living on what it had inherited from Greece and Rome. The most popular writings were chronicles from past times in which, in a jumble of 'futility, idle talk and convent gossip', the author usually limited himself to copying a predecessor. For a religious writer, the highest achievement was reproduction of the thoughts of the (early Christian) Fathers with appropriate ecstasy . . . The schools produced not the full man, but the erudite. The pupil had to commit to memory a host of facts and dates, to learn Homer by heart and to stifle any personal opinion", writes a French scholar (15). Byzantium's greatest cultural achievement was that it preserved the literature, science, philosophy and law of classical Greece and Rome, to be taken up by the Arabs, and later to burst into medieval and Renaissance West Europe.

Islamic Education

Muslim education must be considered against the background of Islam's concept of *Ummah,* the brotherhood of all believers, (see Chapter 3). Wherever possible, therefore, basic education in the teachings and practices laid down in the *Koran* was provided for all Muslim men (not women). Writing schools, *maktab,* which date back to the pre-Islamic period in the Arab world, were common all over the Muslim world. Elementary schools, *masjids,* were attached to mosques. There were reported to be 3,000 mosques in Baghdad in the early 10th century, and 12,000 in Alexandria in the 14th century, most with schools attached. The main purpose of the elementary schools was to learn to memorise, recite and if possible read the *Koran* in Arabic. (It was supposed to lose spiritual potency in translation). This form of primary education has gone on into this century in some Muslim countries. "In many places children under ten are required to learn by heart its 6,200 odd verses. They accomplish this prodigious feat at the expense of their reasoning faculty, for often their minds are so stretched by the effort of memory that they are of little good for serious thought. Where there are schools of a modern type it is common to require a selection of passages rather than the whole book to be memorised" (17).

Secondary education took place in *madrasas,* "institutions for theological instruction, with an official status, salaried teachers, and in many institutions also provision for the maintenance of students as well. During the 10th to 12th centuries hundreds of these *madrasas* were set up throughout the eastern Islamic lands and in Egypt, and brought the control of higher education more and more into the hands of the theologians. In these institutions the upper classes and all the educated elements received a grounding in the traditional disciplines and fundamental doctrines and principles of Islam, which served to counteract the attitudes and heresies of the Sufi groups" (see below). Thus "there was created in every country an influential body of men, who had the task of leading the half-converted masses gradually into the orthodox fold". But this had negative results. "Originality and vitality were gradually crushed out of existence; the field of study was restricted . . . to a narrowing circle of traditional subjects acquired by rote and endlessly produced in lifeless commentaries. The theology of Islam as taught in the *madrasas* remained in the grip of the dead hand, so going far to give colour to the charge of petrified medievalism which has been laid against the *Ulama* almost down to our own day".

The *Ulama,* "the learned", "the doctors", correspond to Christian clergy or Jewish "scribes". They represented the "consensus of the community", and their decisions came to be regarded as irrevocable (18).

But as the Muslim conquerors spread across the Middle East, they encountered the vast body of Greek literature described above. The impact was both shattering and transforming (see Chapter 3). The very idea of philosophy had been unknown to the desert Arabs. Universities sprang up in Spain, North Africa (such as the famous University of Al Azhar in Cairo), and the Middle East, notably in Baghdad and Iran. The universities performed three great services to humanity. First, they brought Islamic scholars into contact with Indian, Jewish, Persian, Greek and Graeco-Christian thought from Byzantium. Second, they collected the Greek manuscripts - many acquired from Byzantium - and translated them, first from Greek into Arabic, and later, from Greek into Latin and Hebrew, thus making them readable for scholars in medieval West Europe where knowledge of Greek had died out. They also flooded out from their universities translations of Islamic literature from Arabic and Persian into Greek and Latin (see Chapter 10). Third, they seized on and developed Greek scientific knowledge - the intellectual way was clear because the *Koran* makes no pronouncements on science and mathematics. Book shops, copyists and book dealers sprang up in centres such as Damascus, Cordoba and Baghdad. But "before the days of printing the life of a scholar must always have abounded in irritation and disappointment. Until, and even after, the foundation of the Muslim universities in East and West, many a student set out . . . on a journey of a thousand miles or more in quest of a teacher. Vast journeys from Spain to Mecca or from Morocco to Baghdad were undertaken by young men who left their home practically penniless to sit at the feet of a chosen master" (19).

We have already referred in Chapter 3 to the Sufi movement, the mystical expression of Islam. We have shown that orthodox Islam was - and is - a religion of authoritative teachings to be accepted, rituals to be performed, and social rules to be practised, all without question. Mysticism, the search for personal communion with the Divine, for the experience of celestial Love, was not emphasised - in fact, was often treated as a heresy - see the fate of Al Hallaj of Iraq in 922 A.D.

recounted in Chapter 3. Nevertheless mystics, like weeds, are irrepressible. Sufism sprang up originally in Iraq in the 7th century, and spread gradually throughout the Muslim world. It was expressed in a rich poetry of love and adoration; in the personal attachment of disciples to *shaiks* or spiritual "Masters", somewhat comparable to the Yogi-disciple relationship in Hinduism (the *shaik*, like the Hindu Master, only accepted as disciples those with whom he felt that he had a spiritual affinity); and in the veneration of saints - often departed *shaiks*. Sufism therefore became attractive at the popular level as the emotional complement to the mental austerity of orthodoxy, and it spread among the masses throughout the Islamic world. It also became attractive to theologians of the noblest calibre, who studied Greek, Neoplatonic and Christian writings, and who, like St Thomas Aquinas, in the end penetrated to an insight that was unattainable by the intellect alone. One such theologian was al-Ghazali of Baghdad (A.D. 1058 - 1111), "a man who stands on a level with Augustine and Luther in religious insight and intellectual vigour . . . He revolted against the casuistry of the theologians and set out to seek the ultimate Reality through all the Muslim religious systems and philosophies of his time . . . At length, after a long struggle, bodily, mental and intellectual, he fell back in sheer philosophic agnosticism on personal experience of God and found it in the Sufi path" (20). The repression of the Sufis proved futile, and in time it was more or less accepted by the orthodox as a fact of life. Great Masters established themselves in the 10th and 11th centuries in such centres as Bokhara, Samarkand and Tashkent. But in the 12th century the Mongols, led by the illiterate Genghis Khan (1160 - 1227) swept down from the steppes of East Asia and laid low all the civilisations which they encountered, from China to central Europe. (It has been said of the Mongols that what they did not understand they despised, and what they despised they destroyed). Meanwhile a reaction against the Sufis had set in amongst the Ulamas. By now they had created in every Islamic country an influential body of educated men, "who had the task of leading the half-converted masses gradually into the orthodox fold". But in the process "originality and vitality were gradually crushed out of existence; the field of study was restricted, except among a favoured few, to a narrowing circle of traditional subjects acquired by rote and endlessly reproduced in lifeless commentaries. The theology of Islam as taught in the *madrasas* remained in the grip of the dead hand . . ." (21). By 1300 the valuable body of Muslim scientific, philosophic, and social learning had been transmitted to European school-men through Latin translations; and European scholars stood again on the basis of Hellenistic thought, enriched and modified by Muslim and Byzantine efforts. The creative period of orthodox Islam was then over. But Sufism lived on, and it could prove to be the elixir which transfigures orthodox Islam and enables it to blend with the spiritual forces which are transforming the other great religions (see Part II).

Education in Western Europe

The modern age, the age of science and Human Rights, which we shall discuss in Part II, was launched in Western Europe. The great revolution in scientific thought occurred in Western Europe in the 17th century (see Chapter 10). It was followed in the 18th century by what is often called "the Age of Reason", or "the Age of Enlightenment" - they are not, strictly speaking, the same thing, for "Enlightenment" implies more than "Reason"; it implies vision.

After the confusion of the barbarian invasions which brought about the collapse of the Western Roman Empire in A.D. 467 and the "Dark Ages" which followed, Western Europe settled down into the feudal structure of kings, nobles, clergy, burgesses and peasants, crowned and controlled by a public religion. But, uniquely, this religion was organised into a separate structure from the state, the Roman Catholic Church (see Chapter 4). Education throughout this period was controlled and organised by the Church. "In England, from the first . . . education was the creature of religion; the school was an adjunct of the Church, and the schoolmaster was an ecclesiastical officer . . . From 598 to 1670 A.D., all educational institutions were exclusively under ecclesiastical control. The law of education was a branch of the Canon Law. The Church courts had exclusive jurisdiction over schools and universities and colleges, and until 1540 all schoolmasters and scholars were clerks, or clerics or clergy" (22). The same applied everywhere north of the Alps. Both local synods and Pope Eugenius II (826) decreed that the local priest should conduct an elementary school in every

126

parish. One problem was the poor quality of text and reference books. A much greater problem was that education was conducted in Latin, which most medieval people, including kings and nobles, could not speak; and was concerned with Latin texts, which most medieval people, including kings, could not read. "From 597 to 1100 it is exceptional for an (English) king to be able to write at all, or to read Latin; in the 12th and 13th centuries kings learnt to read Latin but do not (even if they can) write it; in the 14th and 15th centuries they are taught in youth both to read and write Latin, but in fact are far more occupied with French and English" (23). It was a far cry from the cultured Emperors and mandarins who ruled China until the 20th century! As in other cultures, education consisted essentially in memorising the scriptures. Even schoolmasters could excommunicate heretical students! Free thought was suppressed more savagely by another unique institution, the Inquisition (see Chapter 3).

The clergy were thus the class which read, wrote and copied. Schools which trained them, "Grammar Schools", in Latin, in Bible studies, and in music to sing in Church, were attached to every cathedral. The curriculum also involved memorising manuals of excerpts from the classics, as well as the main liturgies of the Church. In the later Middle Ages town councils set up business schools which taught arithmetic for use in commerce. But the vast majority of the population remained peasants, toiling in the fields, with no schooling - and the gentry saw to it that they should remain untaught. In 1391 the House of Commons (see Chapter 4) petitioned the King of England that no bondsman should be suffered to send his sons to school "in order to advance them by clergy". Professor Coulton estimates that at the time of the Dissolution of the Monasteries in Henry VIII's reign (1509 - 47), there were about 26,000 boys in Grammar and elementary schools out of a population of about 5 million in England and Wales (24). In France there were about 1000 cathedral schools, developing the study of classical literature and philosophy as well as theology - in Latin. The advantage of Latin was that it was an international language.

In the 12th century universities were established, essentially guilds or corporations spontaneously created by groups of people interested in the pursuit of higher learning - though lawyers asserted that a papal or imperial licence was necessary. The most famous, in Paris, Bologna,

Cordoba, Oxford and Cambridge, developed "by custom". They made their own statutes, appointed their own professors (called Doctors or Masters) and received private endowments. By 1500 there were 20 in Italy, 18 in France, 16 in Germany, 14 in Iberia, 3 in Scotland and 2 in England. (By 1800 there were still only 2 in England). The training "consisted in hearing lectures which took the form of commentaries on set texts; the examination was always oral" (25). The subjects studied consisted of the *trivium* - rhetoric, logic, metaphysics - including moral philosophy and natural philosophy (physics); and the *quadrivium* - arithmetic, astronomy, geometry and music (the Greek model is clear!) Law, both civil and canon, was also included in the greatest universities. And it must be emphasised that civil law was secular law, a Graeco-Roman construct; canon law was for the government of the Church only. Justinian's Code and the laws of Rome had reached West Europe in the 11th century. The arrival of the works of Averroes and Avicenna in medicine, and, in the 13th century, those of Aristotle, caused a revolution of thought in the universities. Medieval thought became a complete system, wholly different from the fragmentary Platonism of previous centuries. Aristotle was "the Philosopher", with an authority almost that of the Bible. The teaching of these classical subjects as well as Christian theology in the new universities loosened the ties with orthodoxy, and by the 14th century a flow of great literature in the vernacular languages produced, for example, the writings of Dante in Tuscan Italian and Chaucer in English.

During the period between the Reformation and the French Revolution new attitudes towards education began to spread in Western and Central Europe. The state gained control of the Church in Roman Catholic as well as in Protestant countries. It wanted to promote national power and wealth, which meant encouraging the education of the middle class. The scientific revolution of the 17th century (see Chapter 10) led to the introduction of scientific rationalism and the thinking out of problems in schools - promoted by such leading philosophers as Descartes, Leibniz and Spinoza. And in Protestant countries an immense leap forward in the spread of education was propelled by the new decision that Christians should read the Bible themselves, now that it was being translated into the vernacular languages. By the 19th century Protestant Northern Europe was far more literate than Catholic Southern Europe at the popular level. In the mid-20th century many of the peasants of Italy and Spain were still mentally in the Middle Ages. In Sicily and Sardinia, in the 1950s, there were shepherd boys who said: "I've heard tell of the Pope, but what sort of thing is it?", and who believed that Russia was a little island (26).

In this atmosphere the idea of education as "drawing out" rather than "pushing in" suddenly emerged. Two seminal thinkers stand out. The Czech cleric Comenius (1592 - 1670), who as a victim of the wars of the period wandered from country to country, spreading his ideas of education based on the child's capacity to experience and proclaiming the concept of *panosophy*. In his last book, *Pampaedia* or *Universal Education,* whose MS was only discovered in 1935, he argued that "the whole human race may become educated, men of all ages, all conditions, both sexes and all nations". His aim was *pansophia* - universal wisdom - which meant that "all men should be educated to full rationality, morality and happiness". The second seminal thinker in promoting "child-centred education" was Rousseau (1712 - 78), whose novel *Emile* described a boy educated until the age of 15 by play and by exposure to nature and ordinary life; the only book he was allowed to read until then was *Robinson Crusoe.* As we shall see in Part II, he was the pioneer of the modern transformation of traditional educational philosophy.

Thus, between the Renaissance and the end of the 18th century the fixed opinions of medieval Europe began to break down. Fixed opinions of millennia had already partially broken down once before, in ancient Greece and Rome. The infusion into the European education system of classical philosophy, law, science and political models of democracy acted as an enzyme to break them down completely in Europe in the 19th and 20th centuries. In other civilisations, as we have seen, traditional cultures became more and ossified and atrophied. In Western Europe the urge dawned, in the 18th century, to establish a world community of free-thinking self-actualising persons.

Chapter 9

COMMUNICATIONS

THE first passenger train in the world ran in England from Stockton to Darlington, a distance of 9.6 miles (15.4 km), in 1825. Soon the railways, which by the middle of the 19th century were spreading across England and America, were flanked by telegraph posts and wires. And with them came the invention by an altruistic Englishman, Rowland Hill, of the penny post. "Rowland Hill's plan (opposed by Government and Establishment, but supported by popular demand) for a postal delivery prepaid by a cheap adhesive stamp, enabled the poor, for the first time in the history of man, to communicate with the loved ones from whom they were separated" (1).

Before these great 19th century inventions, the steam engine and the telegraph, land travel, everywhere, was based on human or animal muscle power. Between 4 and 3,000 B.C. wheeled carts and chariots appeared, and animals were used for haulage, and later, for riding: horses, oxen, mules, camels, yaks, elephants and in the high Andes, llamas. In Africa south of Egypt the wheel was not thought of, and animals were not used for transport until the era of Arab penetration (see Chapter 12). Nor did the horse appear in America until brought by the Spaniards in the 16th century. According to Collier's Encyclopaedia, an ordinary man can carry only about 40 kg (90 lbs) for any distance, walking at a speed of 2.7 km (1.7 miles) an hour; so progress on foot was slow. The average road was a dirt track. Greece, a small land bustling with travelling politicians, artists, philosophers, scientist, athletes and businessmen, native and foreign, had only one paved road fit for chariots and processions: that from Athens to Eleusis, the site of the sacred Mysteries, a distance of 22 km. Travelling was further complicated by lack of maps. When Alexander and his army crossed the Hindu Kush in 326 B.C., neither he nor his companions "quite knew where they were going. Without maps or compasses, they marched onwards, as though driven by a fanatical ambition to conquer the world. The Greeks thought when they first saw the river Indus that they had reached the Nile" (2).

Some great Empires did develop systems of solidly-built roads, which facilitated the transport of troops and goods and made the development of postal services possible. Between 312 B.C. when the 132-mile Via Appia from Rome to Capua was constructed, and the fall of the Empire in 467 A.D., the Roman's had built some 53,000 miles of excellent roads in West Europe, North Africa and the Near East. Their mastery of the arch enabled them to construct bridges, causeways and viaducts. The half-mile long Roman bridge over the Tagus river at Alcantara in Spain, with 60 arches, bears an inscription from the architect: *Pontem perfect mansuram in saecula* - "I have built a bridge that shall endure through the ages" (3). (By contrast, the Egyptians built no bridges across the Nile, and the only bridge across the Euphrates, at Babylon, consisted of stone piers covered by wooden platforms). Along this road system sped the Imperial Mail Service, instituted by the Emperor Augustus, at an average speed of 75 km a day - the ordinary traveller could expect to make 45 km a day.

In China, the first Emperor (221-207 B.C.) built a network of roads, radiating from the capital city (then Hsienyang) based on five major trunk roads about 15 metres wide, lined with trees, policed and provided with post-stations at which were stables, couriers and inns. In the Han period (206 B.C. - 200 A.D.) a fast postal system was developed which lasted until the 20th century. In 1842 the official schedule of mail from Peking to Canton was 32 days, by horse (4).

In South America the Incas, during their brief period of imperial rule (1438 - 1532 A.D.) before their overthrow by 168 Spanish soldiers (of which 62 were mounted), built a superb system of roads linking their capital, Cuzco, with Quito in the north and Santiago in the south. One major road went along the coast, and the other through the immense mountains, involving tunnels cut through rock and suspension bridges flung over canyons. Trained runners carried messages at a speed of 240 km a day (5).

The Persian Empire, under the Achaemenid dynasty (7th to 4th century B.C.) constructed a road system, including an all-weather road from Susa, in central Iran, to Sardis, in Western Turkey.

In these few road-building empires modes of travel for the elite were sometimes sophisticated. Wealthy Romans travelled in a *carruca-dormitoria* with soft beds - "the huge, luxurious Rolls Royce of antiquity". Cicero (106-43 B.C.) bumped into Vedius "in the depths of Asia, with two chariots, a carriage, a litter, numerous slaves and a monkey on a little cart and a number of wild asses" (6). Nearly 2,000 years later, the travel style of the rich had not greatly changed. In 1816 Lord Byron, the English poet, ordered a replica of Napoleon's coach, the *dormeuse,* which had been captured at Waterloo by the Prussians. "He paid £500 for it - and never settled the debt. The panels were made bullet-proof. The interior was adapted to various purposes of office, bedroom, wardrobe and store. Beneath the coachman's seat was a small box containing a folding bedstead, mattress and linen. Byron could compose his poems on a collapsible writing desk. There were also holsters for pistols, a chronometer and a commode. Between 1816 and 1832, when he disembarked at Genoa for Greece, Byron rode on this coach from town to town in Italy. It was followed by a cortege of smaller coaches containing servants, books and a menagerie of animals" (7).

Sailing ships, and ships propelled by oars, often manned by slaves, plied the rivers and the seas from about 6000 B.C. But until the compass and the sextant came into use about the time of the European Renaissance (16th century A.D.) navigation was hazardous. Ships tended to hug the coasts and to avoid sailing in winter. In the 18th century A.D. it took several weeks for the British monarch to send a message to a Governor of one of his colonies on the east coast of North America and receive a reply, and several months to communicate similarly with his Viceroy in India.

Let us cast an eye over the traditional scene. Millions of men and women were cultivating the soil or tending their flocks, often involving long walks or climbs. Hundreds of thousands were walking on long journeys - pilgrimages, trade missions, military exercises, personal visits; many others were riding on horseback or in carts, carriages, or litters carried by men (especially in China) or on sledges; while merchandise was loaded on to pack animals - "beasts of burden" - plodding for thousands of miles in long convoys. The great majority of people did not venture far from home. Their range of personal experience was limited to their village and perhaps their local market town, or for millions of women, particularly in Asia, to the family compound. For everyone, everywhere, without mechanical transport, maps, books, photographs (invented 1889), telegraphs (invented 1837) or telephones (invented 1876) knowledge of the wider world in which they lived was based on hearsay.

How did this affect their attitudes of mind? The following account of a conversation between an American woman woodcarver and a small store keeper in Liberia, which took place during World War II, illustrates the situation. "Baysah turned to me again. 'The world is how big?' . . . How should I tell him the size of the world? Liberians measure distance to a given point by how many sundowns they have to walk to reach it. 'I used to think', he said, 'that the world was as big as the distance from where I was to the farthest place where a man I know has his house. I know a Mandigo trader. He carries goat hair blankets from way back of Sierra Leone to the Ivory coast. He brings back a head-load of carved ivory bangles. He has got a house and a set of wives and many children at both ends of the trail. He stops here at night and we sit late. He tells me about both places and all that is in between. So I thought the world started where his wives weave goat-hair blankets and ended in the courtyard where the ivory carvers sit to file the bangles.

"All right! That world was big enough! Then you brought me papers which I could read if I took a long time to it and put my finger under every word. That way, the white people's country got into the world for me . . . and I can't get it out, even in my sleep' . . . 'When you first learned to read, I asked him, didn't that spread your world beyond Sierra Leone and the Ivory Coast?' 'It did not', he said. 'The missionary who taught me to read taught me from the Bible. That was just like reading about our own people. They had tribes and chiefs and rain-makers and many wives and goats and they hated government tax collectors! They kept people with leprosy outside the villages and they liked bright coats and they had drums and if the chief did not hold them hard, they broke the laws. They acted just like Lomas (his tribe). Those are plenty fine stories in the Bible' " (8).

This conversation surely indicates that while the communications systems - or lack of them - were a major factor in moulding the consciousness of traditional men and women, they were also an expression of that consciousness. Just as individual birds do not leave the flock and fly off to explore for themselves, so the individual person remained ensconced in his group consciousness, profoundly threatened by the intrusion of something different from outside. Looked at negatively, traditional communications fostered ignorance and fear of the world beyond the pad of the feet of horses and of men, or the shores visited by sailing ships. Looked at positively, they fostered peaceful and stable life-styles in which the soul could actively turn to Nature and to Heaven. In A.D. 1059-60 two young Chinese scholars travelled 1,100 miles, by boat on the Yangtse River and by cart on the roads, to take the examinations for the Imperial Civil Service. The journey took them five months, and on the way they composed 100 poems (9).

Chapter 10

SCIENCE AND TECHNOLOGY

Introduction

THE word "science" derives from the Latin *scientia* - knowledge. But what kind of knowledge is sought, and how is it obtained? Modern science is the systematic study of the physical universe by observation and experiment and the formulation of laws to describe the results. Isaac Newton's deduction in the 17th century of the law of gravity, from his observation of the behaviour of an apple falling off a tree beside him in his garden, is a familiar example of the scientific way of thinking. It follows that modern science is intellectually open-ended. If further facts were to emerge which did not fit into the law already deduced, the law would have to be changed or abandoned. Newtonian mechanics were modified in the early 20th century in the light of discoveries such as those made in the Michelson - Morley experiment of 1887 on light, which paved the way for Einstein's Special Theory of Relativity. The creative imagination may act as the engine of reason, showing the scientist's mind in a flash of "insight" where to look for clues to the organisation of his facts into scientific laws. These laws are normally expressed in mathematical terms. Mathematics is the language of science. And, finally, "pure science", the result of observation, thought and calculation, is converted into "applied science", producing our modern technological civilisation.

Professor Joseph Needham of Cambridge University, the great expert on traditional Chinese science, sums up "the modern science which developed only in Western Europe at the time of Galileo [the 17th century A.D.] as the application of mathematical hypotheses to Nature, the full understanding and use of the experimental method, the distinction between primary and secondary qualities, the geometrisation of space, and the acceptance of the mechanical model of reality" (1).

The Ancients did not look at science in this way. Science was "natural philosophy", the process of fitting the facts of nature into the

135

revelations of religion. The Encyclopaedia Britannica puts it well: "If the history of science is to make any sense whatsoever, it is necessary to deal with the past on its own terms, and the fact is that for most of the history of science natural philosophers appealed to causes which would be summarily rejected by modern scientists. Spiritual and divine forces were accepted as both real and necessary until the end of the 18th century, and, in areas such as biology, deep into the 19th century as well" (2).

Needham poses two key question which will be discussed in this Chapter. "Why did modern science, the mathematization of hypotheses about Nature, with all its implications for advanced technology, take its meteoric rise in the West at the time of Galileo?" And "why was it that between the second century B.C. and the 16th century A.D. East Asian culture was much more efficient than the European West in applying human knowledge of Nature to useful purposes?" (3).

Science Before the Greeks

The belief, held in traditional civilisations - with the major but partial exception of Greece - that natural phenomena are the expression of spiritual forces, has been outlined in Chapter 3. Let us therefore glance first at the scientific achievements of the great traditions which preceded the Greeks, those of Mesopotamia, China and Egypt - not forgetting that indecipherable scientific knowledge is also demonstrated in the temples of Mexico, Peru and Ancient Britain. These achievements fall into four main categories: astronomy; mathematics; medicine; and technological inventions.

Astronomy was the dominant physical science throughout antiquity. The combination of religion and astronomy was integral to the early study of science for 4,000 years. Astronomy was studied essentially in order to tune into the gods and the cosmic harmony of the universe. Teachings about the structure of the universe were developed by priests and seers and became accepted for millennia as revealed truth. For example, the Chinese, the Hindus, the Mesopotamians and the Egyptians believed that the earth was flat. The Sumerians of Mesopotamia were convinced that it was "a circular disc bounded at its circumference by a rim of mountains on which the sky rested like a dish cover. There were two outlets in the cover, one for the rising and one for the setting sun". At the centre of the disc lay Babylon (4). The Chinese thought that the disc was square, and at its centre was China! The Egyptians, the Incas and the Mayas also each believed that their civilisation lay at the centre of the universe, and was the place where its creation was initiated by God. The Hindus, Buddhist and Jains of India located the centre of the earth at "Mount Meru", north of India, directly under the Pole Star, and Hindu temples soar to the sky in graduated stages, like Chinese pagodas and Babylonian ziggurats, to symbolise the ascent of Mount Meru (5). It followed that the sun, moon and planets, whose motions were carefully studied from the tops of pagodas, ziggurats, pyramids and temples, were regarded as circling the earth. And beyond the solar system were the "fixed stars", whose psychic influence was also important. The Egyptians, the Chinese and the Mesopotamians all made charts and catalogues of these stars - that of China, which no longer survives, included over 1,100 stars - and their only instrument was, of course, the naked eye. From these data they predicted such phenomena as eclipses and discerned sun spots, and, most important, calculated calendars, all of which were based on the lunar month except that of Egypt, which forms the basis of our modern calendar. And everywhere, from China to Peru, cities were laid out and temples constructed in alignment with the supposed celestial pattern. In China, since the earth was square, city plans were square, with special areas assigned to each social class. The town plan symbolised the physical universe and each man's place in it. The Egyptian temple was not just a building but a miniature image of the world, a model representing symbolically the regions of the universe where the gods moved. The Mexican Oscar Paz writes: "The pyramid is time transformed into geometry and space. The pyramid of Tenayuca has 52 serpent heads, the 52 years of the Aztec century. The pyramid of Kukalkan at Chichen Itza has 9 double terraces; the 18 months of the years, while its staircase has 364 steps plus one on the top platform, the 365 days of the solar calendar. In Teotihuacun, each one of the two staircases of the Pyramid of the Sun has 182 steps - 364 plus one for the platform at the apex, and the temple of Quetzalcoatl has 364 serpent fangs . . . Marriage of space and time.

Movement expressed by the geometry of stone" (6). Of the ancient Andeans and their modern descendants an American scholar writes: "The solstices of the Milky Way mark the wet and dry seasons, providing a way of predicting river floods. The movements of the sun and moon help in the planning of planting and harvest. A vast reservoir of astronomical knowledge was integral to Andean agriculture and to religious belief" (7). In general, calendars and time keeping were vital for the performance of most of the ordinary activities of life, from agriculture to ritual. In China, Mesopotamia and Egypt there was a special branch of astronomers in the imperial civil service, which was also the imperial priesthood (see Chapter 4). In Egypt this branch was charged with "establishing the hour and specifying, day and night, the moment in which each act of the cult should start" (8).

Astronomy was accompanied, in these civilisations, by astrology, the study and calculation of the relationships between the supposed psychic qualities of the stars and the psychic human and natural forces on earth. It was a popular as well as official activity in China, India and Mesopotamia. "From Gupta times (c. 300 A.D.) to these days [astrology] has been implicitly believed in by nearly all Indians" (9). A comparison of horoscopes was essential in arranging marriages. Later, astrology seeped from Mesopotamia into the Graeco-Roman-Egyptian world - and thence into medieval Europe (see below).

Mathematics was essential for three main purposes: first, for astronomy and its derivatives, the calendar and navigational charts and maps; second, for the architecture of all the huge temples, palaces and tombs which all these civilisations were building; and third, for public works - land surveys, roads, irrigation canals, aqueducts, amphitheatres, and so on. The priests of Egypt and Mesopotamia and the scholars and sages of India and China were mathematicians. From the 11th century A.D., mathematics and astronomy were included in the Chinese State Civil Service examination. Around the beginning of our era, the Indians invented the ten numerical symbols, plus the zero, which we use today, replacing the cumbersome Roman system based on letters. In his book "The Discovery of India", Jawaharlal Nehru, independent India's first prime minister, quotes Professor Halstead: "The importance of the creation of the zero mark can never be exaggerated. This giving to airy nothing, not merely a local habitat and a name, a picture, a symbol, but helpful power, is the characteristic of the Hindu race from whence it sprang. It is like coining the Nirvana into dynamos. No single mathematical creation has been more potent for the general on-go of intelligence and power" (10). The Indians also invented algebra. Indian mathematics developed in Gupta times (320-550 A.D.) to a stage more advanced than any known in antiquity. They were ahead of the Greeks in arithmetic and algebra, but not in geometry. They invented the decimal, the place-value system and the zero mark. The Romans, Greeks and Hebrews struggled with separate symbols for tens and hundreds. These inventions were brought to the Muslim world by Indian scholars in the great period of Arab civilisation in the Middle Ages (see below). "Very little original work in mathematics was done in India after the 12th century A.D. until the modern age" (11).

The Chinese rivalled the Indians. According to Professor Needham, "Decimal place value and a blank space for the zero had begun in the land of the Yellow River earlier than anywhere else, and decimal metrology had gone along with it. By the first century Chinese artisans were checking their work with sliding callipers decimally graduated. Chinese mathematical thought was always profoundly algebraic, not geometrical, and in the Sung and Yuan periods (12th to 14th centuries A.D.] the Chinese school led the world in the solution of equations" (12). According to another scholar, "the world's first comprehensive treaties on arithmetic" was the "Text book of Calculations in nine Sections", completed at the beginning of the Christian era (13). "The Chinese were the first, as early as the 14th century B.C., to be able to express any desired number, however large, with no more than nine signs" (14). Euclidean geometry only really took root in China with the arrival of the Jesuits in the 16th century A.D. (15).

"The pyramid builders of Egypt understood geometry, but they never attempted to prove theorems or to pose abstract questions . . . True multiplication and division, the imaginative short-cuts to calculation, were unknown" (16). But they knew as much mathematics as they wanted to know, for "Sir Flinders Petrie's measurements of the Great Pyramid indicate a maximum error at the corners of only 12 seconds of arc, an accuracy of 1 in 27,000, or the order normally associated with watchmakers rather than structural engineers" (17). To the

Egyptians, "as art was devoted to the particular demands of immortality, so science was there to solve down-to-earth problems. It was left to Euclid and his fellow Greeks to show that mathematics is capable of beautiful constructions and abstract propositions" (18). The Babylonians were also able to calculate the exact volume of a pyramid and a truncated cone, and made giant strides in the development of algebra. Like the Egyptians, they were not concerned with abstractions, such as the proofs of elegant geometric theorems.

Medicine. The general attitude in traditional societies was that illness was due to the presence of evil spirits or dark magical forces, resulting, perhaps, from the imposition of spells by some enemy. It had, therefore, to be cured by counter-magical measures, by invoking, perhaps with the aid of a magician, the power of the gods and benign spirits. No demonstration of this attitude could be more vivid that the New Testament's account of Jesus Christ's acts of healing and the casting out of devils from the psyches of obsessed persons. Innumerable accounts exists of similar acts performed by saints and healers, and even their clothes and dead bones, and by apparitions of spirits, in all ancient cultures.

There was also, particularly in India and China, some objective study of anatomy and physiology. In the Tang dynasty of China (618-907 A.D.) Chinese anatomy "was ahead of anything in Europe," but anatomical illustrations made then, "continued to be reproduced, mainly in books on forensic medicine for the use of magistrates, in the Ching dynasty (1644-1912), long after European anatomy had passed out of sight" (19). By the Sung period (960-1127) Chinese physicians had discovered the secret of vaccination. Similarly in India in the period 1000-600 B.C., surgery was carried out and possibly dissections made. 121 different surgical instruments are described in ancient medical treatises. There were doctors for horses and elephants as well as for humans. But although Indian doctors made fruitful contact with Arab medicine and science in the Middle Ages (see below), "a mystical intuitive tendency which settled down over every branch of Hindu thought during the medieval period discouraged the development of any objective scientific attitude . . . The arts and crafts were left more and more to the lower castes, and anatomy and surgery fell into disuse. Empirical medicine decayed as diseases came to be regarded as the inevitable result of *karma"* (20). Chinese and Hindu medicine thus combined with philosophy to make a unique contribution, not so much to medicine as to health. Professor Needham says of the Chinese view of causation: "Conceptions are not subsumed under one another but placed side by side in a pattern, and things influence each other not as acts of mechanical causation, but by a kind of 'inductance' . . . The key word in Chinese thought is Order, and above all Pattern. Things behave in particular ways not necessarily because of prior actions or impulsions of other things, but because their positions in the ever-moving cyclical universe was such that they were endowed with intrinsic natures which made that behaviour inevitable for them . . . They were thus parts in existential dependence upon the whole world organism" (21). Hindu philosophy, although perhaps more transcendental in expression, is fundamentally similar. Both cultures affirmed that body and soul are intrinsically at one with the harmonious Order of the universe, and that it is for the individual, by his or her own effort, to attune his mind, heart and will to this order. Then - and only then - will he become calm, benevolent, wise - healthy! In order to achieve this self-transformation, the Hindu sages, some 3,000 years ago, devised the most subtle and psychologically perceptive techniques of meditation known to the world - and later the Buddhists added their own version. Collectively the Hindu system is known as *Yoga* - "to yoke". One form is Hatha Yoga, exercises for controlling and relaxing the body, which today are being practised all over the Western world! (see Chapter 18). Here is a description of the effect of the practice of Hatha Yoga on an Indian prince who was interviewed by a British journalist in London in the 1930s (i.e. before the independence of India). "I had discovered beforehand that the rajah was over 70, and knowing that Indians age early, I was prepared for even more of the sagging muscles and profound wrinkles which mark the majority of 'old people' everywhere. Imagine my astonishment, therefore, to meet (in the Savoy Hotel) a man with the agile, supple movements of youth, eyes shining like a boy's, strong, brilliantly white teeth, firm muscles, radiant smile, and a mind that worked like summer lightning. He looked a young middle age. He told me that he had known no illness, not even a cold for 28 years . . .

The secret lay in a series of exercises called 'Surya Namaskars', or 'Sun Prayers'. They were simplicity itself, he explained, taking only five or six minutes to complete a round of 25 cycles and requiring no sort of equipment whatsoever. Breathing was fundamental, three controlled breaths being taken for each cycle of ten positions. Anyone of any age could try them. All that was necessary was a flat floor space about two by seven feet" (22). This is just one of hundreds of yoga exercises which rhythmically relax and strengthen every organ in the body. Before the modern age thousands of Hindu sages and Buddhist monks practised various forms of yoga, both physical exercises and meditation, in ashrams (Hindu religious communities), Buddhist monasteries, and solitary forest glades and mountain caves. And ordinary people practised it in their daily lives.

The Chinese through the ages developed a complementary system of exercises called T'ai Chi Chuan, derived partly from the philosophy of Confucius and partly from that of Lao Tzu (see Chapter 3). T'ai Chi answered the need for self-defence without aggression, since the monks were frequently attacked and robbed in their mountain monasteries. For many centuries T'ai Chi was taught on a village basis. But at the end of the 19th century the last Imperial Physician, Grand Master Cheng Man-Ch'ing, developed it into a national system for "strengthening race and nation". And today hundreds of millions of Chinese do their T'ai Chi exercises on the pavement before going to work in the morning. The new national system consists of 37 upright movements performed in slow, continuous motion. They are designed to enhance co-ordination and circulation, to balance all body functions, and to promote a sense of calm, clarity and effortless action. A round of T'ai Chi takes 7 to 10 minutes and can be practised by young and old alike. It needs a smooth floor space and flat cotton-soled shoes (23).

Another traditional Chinese therapy, now practised all over the world, is the system of acupuncture. This involves assessing the state of the lines of psychic energy which flow through the body and adjusting the flow by inserting needles in the meridians. Acupuncture has been incorporated into the modern Chinese health system, together with Western medicine, and has been found particularly helpful for inducing anaesthesia.

In the art of keeping healthy, as distinct from curing illness, China and India have much to offer the West in the modern age! (see Part II).

Technical Inventions. Throughout the 5,000 years when the traditional civilisations flourished, there were very few technical inventions. Attempts by myself and two friends to tabulate them have produced in each case only two to three pages! Since it is difficult for a non-scientist to be exact on this matter, I will confine myself to certain general points and certain specific examples.

First, there were two kinds of inventions which were fundamental in preparing the ground for civilisation and all its achievements. The first was the transition from a hunter-gatherer life-style to a settled agricultural life-style, which came about first in the Middle East some 10,000 years ago. Plants and animals were domesticated. The second was the discovery of how to mine and smelt minerals: first bronze, by mixing copper with tin, later iron, gold and silver. Following these developments marvellous artifacts were produced all over the world. An attempt is made in Chapter 11 to give a brief impression of these artifacts, expressed not only in enormous temples and churches, statues and carvings, but in millions of small objects such as jewellery, goblets and garments. The artifacts of the Ancients involved craftsmanship of the highest skill.

Why, then, did technology fail to develop? Here is a rough list of most of the outstanding technical inventions between 3000 B.C. and 1800 A.D.: the wheel (but not in Africa or America); the hand-pushed or animal-drawn plough (but not in Africa or America); the wheel barrow (in China c.300 A.D.); the windmill; the watermill; carts, chariots and carriages; weapons such as bows and arrows, swords, spears and daggers; helmets and armour; the stirrup (China, c.300 A.D.), crucial for cavalry; gunpowder (c. 9th century A.D. in China and 13th century A.D. in Europe); the magnetic compass (China); the astrolobe for determining the direction of the stars (Greece); the calendar (invented everywhere except in Africa); coins (China, 2000 B.C. and Lydia in Asia Minor, 7th century B.C.); paper money (China 8th century A.D. and Sweden 1648); paper (China 2nd century A.D.); printing (China 9th century A.D., Europe 15th century A.D.); spectacles (Italy, 1232 A.D.); watch (Germany 1509 A.D.); microscope (Holland,

1590 A.D.); telescope (Holland 1609 A.D.).

A comparison of this rough list of the technical inventions produced by the whole human race between 3000 B.C. and 1800 A.D. with the technology of the past 200 years must produce amazement - particularly since, as already mentioned, the wonderful artefacts of the pre-modern era show that technological capacity was not lacking. The fundamental reason must be that the ancients did not want technological progress. Their religions taught them that the existing order was divinely ordained; and they were more concerned with their celestial than their earthly welfare. Even the Greeks, who initiated rational scientific thinking, were not prepared to apply it to the transformation of ordinary life. They were content that slaves should do the work which machines do today. The same principle applied throughout the ancient world - whether the workers were slaves, serfs, peasants or women.

Finally, it is notable that a high proportion of these inventions originated in ancient China, and none in Japan. Today Japan is the richest country in the world, and China among the poorest. We shall discuss this paradoxical situation in Part II.

Greek Science

It is generally agreed today that modern scientific thinking was born in ancient Greece between 600 and 400 B.C. Its main exponents were a small number of philosophers who lived in the Greek cities of Ionia (Western Turkey today), Thrace in Northern Greece, and Sicily. But they soon became associated with the intellectuals of Athens. Some are said to have travelled to Egypt, Mesopotamia, Persia and even India to make contact with the priests and sages in those realms. Their revolutionary attitude was the assertion that material phenomena have material causes. Aristotle (384-322 B.C.) later drew the logical distinction between "efficient causes", such as "the egg boils because the water is hot", and "final causes", such as "the egg boils because I want to eat it".

Traditional philosophers looked to a spiritual explanation of both kinds of cause: these Greek philosophers looked to a physical explanation for both. The first, Thales of Miletus, sought the final cause in water; Anaximenes of Miletus in mist; Heraclitus of Ephesus

144

in fire; Anaximander of Miletus in mist, earth and fire; Democritus of Abdera in Thrace in atoms. "It was a great advance in human thinking when Thales reduced the manifold appearances of things to one First Principle" - a natural principle. "What Thales did was to leave Marduk out", writes a historian of Greek science (24). (Marduk was the Creator-God of the Babylonians). The tremendous implications of this thinking were three-fold. First, each philosopher was thinking for himself, and all were arguing with each other. Secondly, the thinking was creative, open-ended, dynamic; no blue-prints were laid down. And thirdly, the impulse to verify ideas by experiment was born. Anaximander, the pupil of Thales, made a map of the known world. Aristarchos of Samos (c. 260 B.C.) anticipated Copernicus in propounding the theory that the sun was at the centre of the solar system. Eratosthenes of Alexandria calculated the circumference of the earth and reached a figure within 16 per cent of the "correct" one of modern geographers. Anaximander and Aristotle deduced from observation that the earth is a sphere and not a flat disc. Empedocles of Agrigentum in Sicily devised an experiment to show the corporeality of the viewless air. This experiment "was crucial for the whole future of Greek theory on the nature of matter and the degree of validity of sense-evidence . . . Empedocles has shown how we can overcome the limitations of our sensuous apprehension and discover, by a process of inference based on observation, truths we cannot directly perceive. He had . . . conquered, in the name of science, a world that lay beyond the normal range of man's perceptions. He had revealed the existence of an imperceptible physical universe by examining its effects on the physical world. The importance of this as a step towards the atomic theory was decisive" (25). This kind of thinking led not only to open-ended discussion, but, for the first time in history, secular discussion. Agnostics, atheists, cynics, sophists, Epicureans, Stoics went around airing their views. The attitude to the gods, expressed by Xenophanes in the 6th century, was that of a modern psychologist: "if horses or oxen had hands and could draw or make statues, horses would represent the forms of the gods like horses, oxen like oxen". Politically, economic and social conditions were propitious. The system of government was democratic and essentially secular - laws were made by the citizens and not derived from scripture. In Ionia in particular the ruling class was a mercantile aristocracy anxious to promote wealth. Books were being written and circulated. But the Greeks did not believe that the free man should concern himself with manual labour. "The practical applied sciences, the productive techniques, continued to be handed down exclusively by oral tradition among the members of the deprived classes in society" - who remained illiterate. And there were plenty of slaves and women to do the manual work (see Chapters 5 and 6).

The materialistic outlook of these philosophers produced its philosophical counterpart or reaction. Pythagoras, Socrates, Plato and Aristotle (the latter with reservations), could not accept a world-view which to them was flawed in two ways. First, it ignored the ancient vision of the essential spirituality of the cosmos and the immortality of the soul. Secondly, it failed to explain such non-material qualities and values as beauty, goodness, justice and love - that is, it failed to answer the great questions of ethics. So they turned to the exposition of a simple metaphysical system based on the hypothesis of the Divine Creator, God, as immanent and transcendent, and the soul as immortal. And, as we have seen in Chapter 3, Plato added the doctrine of divine forms - archetypes, models, "ideas in the Mind of God" - as the underlying basis for all material phenomena. So these philosophers looked at mathematics, astronomy and music as the sciences through which the divine is revealed. "The function of geometry is to draw us away from the sensible and perishable to the intelligible and eternal. For the contemplation of the eternal is the end of philosophy, as the contemplation of the mysteries is the end of religion", wrote Plutarch, another philosopher. A number of modern philosophers and historians of science, including Bertrand Russell, Charles Singer, Benjamin Farrington and Carl Sagan, have criticised these philosophers, and in particular Plato, for holding up the progress of natural science and technology for 2,000 years by clamping these metaphysical concepts on to the world of Nature. "We see the advent into the Greek world of a great intellectual movement as a result of which the department of philosophy that dealt with nature receded before Ethics. Of that intellectual revolution - perhaps the greatest the world has seen - Athens was the site and Socrates (470-399) the protagonist . . . His great successor [Plato] . . . gives us in the *Timaeus* a picture of the depth to which natural science can be degraded in the effort to give a specific teleological meaning to all parts of the visible Universe. The picture which the book draws, dark and repulsive to the mind trained in modern scientific method, enthralled the imagination of a large part of mankind for well-nigh two thousand years", writes Charles Singer, a professor of the history of medicine (26). He thus raises in stark form an essential problem with which this book is concerned: the relationship of science to religion, ethics and philosophy.

We have seen in Chapter 6 that Plato and Aristotle supported the institution of slavery, which inhibited the incentive to develop applied science. Moreover, while all modern-minded people can accept as objective truth the basic discoveries of modern science, there is still, after 2,000 years, no general agreement about the objective nature of beauty, justice and love, and about the question of the immortality of the soul. Aristotle, who was Plato's disciple for 20 years in his early manhood, eventually came to disagree with his teacher's idealism. He turned his mind away from transcendental mysteries and mathematics and dedicated himself to studying the world around him: its physics, including astronomy; its politics - which had also concerned Plato - and above all its biology. He studied and classified some 500 species of birds, fish, mammals and insects. Yet Aristotle interpreted biology in terms of teleology, the evolution of organisms towards their inherent goals, and conceived the planets as perfect orbs making perfect circles around the earth. Although "saving the phenomena" - accounting for observed facts - was a professed Hellenic ideal, and no dogmatic scriptural authority stood in the way, if the facts conflicted with the deeply felt attitude about the innate harmony of the universe, they tended to be brushed aside. Ultimately Greek science was swallowed up in Greek philosophy. When it came to the crunch, the Greek was an introvert after all, believing that he could discover the macrocosm of the universe within the microcosm of his own mind. This may be the deeper explanation of why the Greek scientists did not, as a whole, carry out much experimentation and produced very little technology.

Meanwhile another group of Greek thinkers turned their minds to medicine. The school of medicine founded in the 6th century B.C. on the island of Cos, and developed by Hippocrates of Cos about 400 B.C., produced about 60 or more treatises on medical practice which were

147

preserved in the Library at Alexandria (see below). They show how their physicians - that is, naturalists; *physis* is the Greek for "nature" - deliberately rejected the dogmatic cosmological approach of the Pythagoreans - and the Egyptians, Mesopotamians, and other ancient cultures - linking illness with the stars, evil spirits and so on, and "practised a system of medicine based not on theory but on observation accumulated systematically as time went on. The teaching of Hippocrates and his school is the substantial basis of instruction in the wards of a modern hospital. We are concerned with the earliest evolutionary (i.e. open-ended) medicine" (27). Hippocrates was renowned not only for his methods but for his attitude. He embodied, apparently, the benevolence and wisdom of an ideal physician; this is expressed in the Hippocratic Oath taken by some doctors today.

After Alexander the Great, having over-run Greece, conquered Egypt in 332 B.C., the centre of Greek learning shifted to his capital city, Alexandria. On Alexander's death in 323 B.C. the Macedonian general Ptolemy proclaimed himself King of Egypt, and his successors ruled the country until it became a Roman province in 30 B.C. The first two Ptolemies established the "Museum", officially "the Temple of the Muses", in practice a teaching and research institute modelled on the Lyceum. Its library contained over half a million scrolls (a volume of Homer might constitute 50 scrolls) and it was staffed by 100 professors paid by the King. This great and unique institution became a cosmopolitan centre of learning, where Jews, Persians, Romans and others mingled with Greek scholars and citizens. Among its most eminent scholars were the astronomer Ptolemy, the geometer Euclid and the physician Galen. Ptolemy wrote a 13-volume work expanding and organising the geocentric theory of the planetary system developed over the centuries by the Greek astronomers. It became known by the title later given to it by the Arabs as the *Almagest*. Galen, who in his youth was surgeon to the gladiators in the Ionian city of Pergamum, wrote a 22-volume work covering every known department of medicine. He is said to have carried out dissections, but mainly on apes, not humans. (Human dissection was forbidden in the Hellenic world as elsewhere, for religious reasons). Finally, Euclid wrote a 13-volume book, *The Elements,* in which he collected and systematised Greek geometry so completely that it was the standard geometry text book in western schools for many centuries. The Alexandrian Library was destroyed by the Muslim Arab Caliph Omar when he conquered Egypt in 642 A.D. But these great textbooks, together with much of the works of Plato, Aristotle and other Greek writers, were already widely disseminated throughout the Roman Empire and the Empires to the east.

The Middle Ages - Islamic and Christian

In the centuries preceding the Arab invasion of Egypt in the 7th century A.D., Greek science in Alexandria had faded. The Arabs who flooded out of the Arabian deserts into the Near East and South West Europe had no culture except that of Islam. They spilled over into Western Asia, Christian Syria and Byzantium and Zoroastrian Persia, where, as we have seen in Chapters 4 and 8, they encountered Greek and Asian scholars who had brought their books and were studying science and medicine. Since the *Koran* is silent on these subjects, the Arabs made no attempt to interfere with them. From about 750 until about 900 A.D., during the rule of the Abbasid dynasty, science and medicine flourished throughout the region. The major activity was the translation of the Greek text books of Aristotle, Galen, Ptolemy and Euclid into Syriac (the language of the Near East and Mesopotamia), Arabic, Persian and even Sanskrit, and the translation of the works of Asian scholars into Greek and Arabic. A library and translation school was founded in Baghdad. Paper was introduced from China into the Islamic world in the 8th century, and in 794 the first paper manufacturer was established in Baghdad. "At the end of the period of translation, the physicians and scientists of the Islamic world stood on a firm foundation of Greek science, increased by a large share of Indian thought and experience. Their work had been learned but not very original. From this time they began to rely on their resources and to develop from within" (28). Between about 900 and 1100 A.D. a number of great physicians appeared in the region, of whom the most famous was Abu Ali al-Husayn ibn Sina, known in the West as Avicenna. (980-1037). Born in Bokhara, "his influence on European medicine has been overwhelming. He concentrated the legacy of Greek medical knowledge with the addition of the Arabs' contribution in his gigantic

Canon of Medicine (al Qanun fi't Tibb), which is the culmination and masterpiece of Arabic systemization . . ." The book was translated into Latin by Gerard of Cremona in the 12th century, and circulated in Europe in innumerable manuscripts, and later, in print, and continued to be read until the second half of the 17th century. "Probably no medical work ever written has been so much studied", and it was in current use in the Orient in the 20th century (29). During this golden age of Islamic science hospitals were founded throughout the Islamic world in which doctors were trained as well as patients cured. Other sciences were taught in mosques, which had libraries of philosophical and scientific was well as theological works. On the annual pilgrimage to Mecca scholars from different regions met and exchanged views. But from about 1100 A.D., after the death of the leading religious teacher al Ghazali (d.1111), orthodoxy began to clamp down on Muslim scientific speculation. Al Ghazali, in a book called *Destruction of the Philosophers,* pointed out that since all necessary truth is in the *Koran,* there is no need of speculation independent of revelation. Yaqub al Mansur, Caliph (ruler) of Spain, "published an edict to the effect that God had decreed hell-fire for all those who thought that truth could be found by the unaided reason. All the books that could be found on logic and metaphysics were given to the flames" (30). More generally, the Muslims treasured and disseminated their great legacy of Greek science, but failed to make any major additions of theory or thought. It must be remembered that they were hampered by the strict prohibition by Islamic law of human or animal dissection. Finally, in 1256 the sophisticated and luxurious empire of the Abbasid dynasty in Baghdad was overthrown by the crude Mongols from the east, who put the last Caliph to death "along with 800,000 inhabitants of Baghdad" (31).

Meanwhile, what was happening in medieval Western Europe? We described in Chapter 3 how the Roman Catholic Church sought to impose its interpretation of knowledge and ethics on rulers and their subjects, and how those who challenged the authority of the Church were branded as heretics, and were often burnt to death. (The 73-year old mother of the great Renaissance astronomer Johannes Kepler (1571-1630) was only saved from being burnt as a witch, after torture, by the persistent efforts of her son). The Bible, like the *Koran,* lacked

150

scientific and medical information. So when, in the 13th century, the great Greek textbooks were made available through Muslim and Jewish-organised translations from Arabic into Latin, the Church simply added them to the canon. The writings of Galen, Ptolemy, Euclid and Aristotle(the latter partially integrated into Christian theology by St. Thomas Aquinas (1225-74) became authoritative. When Galileo (1564-1642) began to flaunt his Dutch-made telescope some of the orthodox theologians refused to look through it, saying: "If we see what is written in Aristotle, there is no point in looking through the telescope. If we see what is not written there, it can't be true". This remark sums up a significant paradox: the culture whose treatment of unorthodoxy and heresy was perhaps the most vicious in pre-modern history (see Chapter 3) was the culture where modern science was born. Medieval Europe was far more barren in scientific activity and development than any of the other civilisations discussed in this chapter; medieval medicine was no more than a corrupted version of Galenism. The Cambridge medieval historian, G. G. Coulton, writes: "Medical science stood still - or even, to some extent, went backwards, from 200 A.D. to nearly 1500". And the same applies to science generally. "Even when we do find traces of patient original observation, this is scarcely ever turned to proper account by bold philosophic synthesis. Roger Bacon (1214-92) and Cardinal Nicholas of Cusa (1401-64) are perhaps the only two who can be specified, within a whole thousand years of Western Europe, who combined both the essentials, original observation and bold synthesis" (32). And Roger Bacon, an English scholar who foresaw magnifying lenses, gunpowder, mechanical cars, boats and flying machines, spent 15 years in prison for heresy!

There is, however, another aspect of the medieval scientific situation whose significance will be discussed in Part II. The medieval synthesis, integrated science, philosophy and theology into a whole. The vision of the greatest medieval poets, Dante and Chaucer, confirmed medieval astronomy's picture (inspired by Aristotle and Ptolemy) of a divinely organised, personified universe. At its centre God had placed man "that he may both serve and be served", as Peter Lombard, the 12th century Paris University theologian, explained. Immediately round the Earth was the "sublunary sphere", the realm of change, growth and decay, of evil, Hell and Purgatory. Beyond the Moon was the locus of Heaven, where the Sun and the five known planets rotated in their perfect orbs, incorruptible and eternal, populated by angels. Beyond this zone was the sphere of the "fixed stars", and beyond that the "last heaven", where the throne of God was situated. Dante and Chaucer affirmed that love is the force which pervades the universe. Yet on 16 February 1600 the Neoplatonist philosopher Giordano Bruno was burnt alive in the Square of Flowers in Rome, after seven years' imprisonment, for teaching about the infinity of the universe and the plurality of inhabited worlds. Where was love then?.

A very important development occurred, however, in medieval Europe in the 14th to 15th centuries, which amounted to an industrial-economic revolution. A bourgeois class of independent craftsmen, entrepreneurs, traders and bankers arose in the small political regions and cities which were flourishing in decentralised states such as Italy and Germany. They formed an economic-intellectual network throughout Europe, developing intellectual concepts such as banking, accounting, and long-term rational planning, all "in the Name of God and profit", as the 14th century Tuscan Merchant of Prato put it. This was accompanied by well-planned industrial development: new industries, promoted on a large scale by banker merchants, for the first time planned provision for the future through the planting of forests; a whole industry of differentiated tool-makers; the development of intricate mining technologies; and, finally, the pearl of all: book printing, which was the *conditio qua non* of modern technological development - not as the chance discovery of one person but a planned economic process.

The European Scientific Revolution

The revolution in scientific thinking which developed in Western Europe in the 17th century has had consequences greater than those of any other intellectual event in human history. It was launched when the Polish cleric Nicolas Koppernigk - known by his Latinised name Copernicus - published in 1543 a book *On the Revolution of the Heavenly Spheres* in which he showed that the observations of the mathematicians were best interpreted by the hypothesis that the earth and the planets encircle the sun. At one stroke he undermined the Ptolemaic astronomical system and the vision of the cosmos set out by Aristotle and injected by the Church and the greatest medieval poet into the medieval W*eltanschauung*. He deliberately held up the publication of his book until he was dying - or he might have suffered Bruno's fate. He was followed by the Danish astronomer Tycho Brahe, who carried out more accurate measurements of the planetary positions than had ever been made before, which provided the factual material for Kepler's discoveries. Meanwhile Galileo had acquired his telescope, and opened up the spectacle of the countless stars in the Milky Way. This struck at the very roots of the Aristotelian system of the crystalline spheres. And in Germany the astronomer Johannes Kepler showed that the planets moved round the sun in ellipses. William Gilbert in England had already shown in 1600 that the Earth is a great magnet. Finally, Isaac Newton (1642-1721), after inventing the mathematical tool of the calculus, integrated all these discoveries of his predecessors into a complete system of the laws of physical motion, based on gravity, publishing his book *The Mathematical Principles of Natural Philosophy* in 1687. For this intellectual achievement he has been regarded as perhaps the greatest scientist of all time.

Nature and Nature's laws lay hid in night.

God said: 'Let Newton be!' and all was light,

wrote the 18th century poet Alexander Pope. It was only 87 years since Bruno was burnt!

The world of nature now became divorced from the world of spirit. This divorce was expressed in the "dualistic system" of the French philosopher René Descartes (1596-1650), which postulated that the spiritual universe is governed by divine laws, and the physical universe by "natural" laws, the two connected by man, whose soul is held to reside in the divine world and whose body in the natural world. Cartesian philosophy, as Descartes' system is called, formulated the fundamental distinction between quantitative knowledge about things which can be measured, derived from rational thought, and qualitative knowledge about values, derived from imaginative experience. This distinction, which we have discussed in Chapter 3, pervades all modern thinking. When Napoleon asked the French astronomer Laplace why, in his huge work on celestial mechanics, he had made no mention of

God, the reply was: "I have no need for that hypothesis".

The mighty revolution in knowledge of physics was accompanied by an equally mighty revolution in biology and medicine. Newton, who was a devout Christian, was content to accept Archbishop Ussher's calculation, made from the Bible, that the world was created by God at 8.0 P.M. on Saturday, 22 October, 4004 B.C. Until the 19th century scientists assumed, as men had assumed through the ages, that each species of plant and animal was created by God in its distinct and final form, with man at the apex. The static view of the natural world was complementary to the static view of society which prevailed generally in traditional societies (see Chapter 4). Darwin's great book, *The Origin of Species,* was published in 1859. He delayed its publication for about 30 years, since if it had appeared when he first wrote it, in the 1830s, he might have been prosecuted and imprisoned under a medieval Blasphemy Law, still in force. His theory, supported by massive evidence collected during his voyage to South America in 1831-6, asserts that the world of living things is not static, but in a state of continuous change or "evolution". This theory has provided the keynote for the modern age, the first age in history which can be called "dynamic". Does this change imply progress towards inherent goals - Aristotle's teleology - and towards ideal models - Plato's archetypes? We shall see in Part II that this is a crucial question confronting the 21st century.

Darwin's researches coincided with the origin of the modern sciences of geology and anthropology. Charles Lyell's seminal book, *Principles of Geology,* was published in 1830. The geologists began, for the first time, to assess the earth's ages and phases of physical evolution through a study of the rocks and fossils of animals and plants, and anthropologists to study the early origins of man (see Chapter 1).

If there is a single founder of modern medicine it is Andreas Vesalius (1514-65) known as the "Father of Anatomy" and the first to question the authority of Galen. Even in his time dissection of the human body was bitterly opposed by the Church; Leonardo da Vinci (1452-1516) carried out dissections, but this only became known many years later. William Harvey (1578-1659) studied at Padua (where he was a contemporary of Galileo) and shortly afterwards taught his discovery of the circulation of the blood. Harvey's work was incomplete because he could only infer the existence of the capillaries which join the arteries to the veins; these were first seen four years after Harvey's death by Marcello Malpighi (1628-94) with the newly-discovered microscope. At about the same time plant cells were seen and named by Robert Hooke (1635-1703, a contemporary of Newton, who persuaded the latter to publish his theory of gravitation, and spermatozoa and bacteria were observed by Antonie van Leeuwenhoek (1632-1723). But further progress in medicine needed modern chemistry, in particular the work of Antoine Lavoisier (1743-94, a victim of the guillotine) who first explained combustion and, with Laplace, showed that respiration is a form of combustion. Based on this work, Louis Pasteur (1822-95) was able to demonstrate that micro-organisms were indeed a form of life, were not spontaneously generated, and were the cause of infections. Joseph Lister (1827-1912) used Pasteur's discoveries in antiseptic surgery almost immediately.

About a century later came the complementary technological revolution, "the industrial revolution". Darwin wrote his book in the late 1830s by candlelight, but he was using gas light by the time he published it in 1859. The invention of the steam engine (end 18th century); the railway engine (1825); the telegraph (1837); the telephone (1876); the harnessing of electricity (1826); the motor car (mid 1880s) and in general the machinery of the "dark satanic mills" which began to flood the world with mechanical equipment and mass-produced consumer goods, ushered in a new kind of civilisation. It can be no coincidence that the industrial revolution was contemporaneous with the emergence of the doctrine of the Rights of Man. The great humanist thinkers of "the Enlightenment" - Voltaire, Rousseau, Thomas Paine, William Blake, Jeremy Bentham, John Stuart Mill, Shelley, Coleridge, Walt Whitman, Jefferson, Goethe, Schiller and others - were asserting something which the Greeks had ignored, which had never before (except by a few fringe sects) been proclaimed as the basis for society: the *Right of every person to the conditions for self-development*. In order to implement these rights, an entirely new kind of material environment has become necessary for all human beings. The crucial link between Human Rights and modern technology will be discussed in Part II.

Conclusion

At the end of the 18th century, at the time of the French and American Revolutions, it could not have been foreseen that Western Europe and its offspring, North America, were on the threshold of a scientific explosion which would open up a completely new kind of society - the modern society. Scholars conclude that up to 1500 A.D., China was ahead of the world in inventions, and the Muslim world had developed a rich scientific culture, though of an imitative rather than a creative nature. West Europe had been intellectually and scientifically stagnant for a thousand years - and East Europe even more so under the rule of the Romanovs in Russia and the Turks in the Balkans. In the 19th and 20th centuries the explosion of Western science and technology not only took these ancient civilisations by surprise; it gave them a traumatic psychological shock - enhanced by the aggression of "colonialism" (see Part II). This is why today many of the leaders and thinkers in the East and the South identify "modernity" with "The West". One of the aims of this book is to show that modernity is a global phenomenon which happened to occur first in the West. As Professor Joseph Needham has put it: "Modern universal science, yes; Western science, no!". Why, then, did it happen that modern science was launched in the West? We may suggest four reasons.

The first was the mental domination of revealed religion, set out in authoritarian and dogmatic scriptures or in unchangeable sacred customs. It is significant that the only civilisation which replaced backward-looking religion with open-ended philosophy, that of Greece, produced the first signs of authentic science.

The second was the almost universal rigid class - caste structure, laid down and sanctified by the prevailing religion, which controlled work, education and all aspects of economic as well as social life, and thus proscribed self-expression and inventiveness. And this was underpinned by the dead hand of the institution of slavery.

The third was the fact that the Western European civilisation was the only one in which Church and State were separated. This division between Church and State opened the door for the self-expression of the individual, in intellectual activity - enormously expanded by the invention of printing, and in trading and exploring and generally

156

amassing private wealth. It was the Europeans, not the Chinese or Japanese, who discovered North and South America and Australia - before the days of steam ships.

The fourth reason is that the enzyme of Greek thought and experience was at work in the European sub-conscious - and later, conscious - mind. In the Muslim world the rigidity of Koranic law, institutions and theology kept Greek thought at bay except in the field of a rich but imitative scientific output. In Europe, Greek philosophy, democracy and secularity became embedded in Roman Law, which was later adopted by all West European countries (including Scotland) except England; and it profoundly influenced Christian theology, art and literature. After the Renaissance "the classics", became the core of a gentleman's education. The enzyme of modernity promoted the urge to experiment and explore, while other cultures remained ensconced in their traditions, looking backwards to the past for inspiration. "New bottles for new wine" said Jesus Christ. And the new wine involved the opening up, in an unprecedented way, of the great question of the relationship of matter to spirit.

Chapter 11

ART

WE have discussed how all traditional societies were rooted in the public worship of God or "the gods", in the evocation of celestial forces. We have seen how this ethos inspired the building of huge temples, churches, mosques, palaces and tombs. We have noted that while priests and rulers lived in relative splendour, the living conditions of ordinary people were simple and crude, for the amenities produced by modern science did not exist - anywhere. We must now look at the glorious by-product of the culture of huge temples and simple huts: Art. We might describe traditional art as the vesture in which all man-made objects were clothed. "The art of the ancients", a friend said to me, "is their great bequest to us moderns". (To this must be added literature, scriptures, epics and philosophical texts - see Chapter 3).

What, then, is art? What is the nature of this 5,000 year-old bequest from all over the world? Webster's Dictionary seems to find it difficult to define. "Art", it says, "is the application of skill and taste to production according to aesthetic principles; specifically, such application to the production of beauty by imitation or design, as in painting and sculpture." "Aesthetic" is defined by the Dictionary as "pertaining to the beautiful, as distinguished from the moral, and especially the useful". And "beauty" is defined as "that quality or aggregation of qualities in a thing which gives pleasure to the senses or pleasurably exalts the mind or spirit; physical, moral or spiritual loveliness". We seem to be going round in circles, significantly - as we shall see later, ending on a new word - "love". Before we try to unravel the knots of Webster's definitions, let us look at the basic characteristics of traditional art, that is European art until the Renaissance, and all other art until the 20th century.

First, each civilisation, each culture, had its own distinctive artistic style. A modern person knows at a glance that a pyramid is Egyptian, a Doric temple Greek, a pagoda Chinese or Japanese, a mosque Islamic, a Gothic cathedral a building of medieval Western Europe, a temple festooned with friezes of eight-armed deities Hindu, and so on. And this distinctiveness and this identity is reflected at the level of the individual, as in the Greek tunic, the Roman toga, the Japanese kimono, the Egyptian wig and white linen kilt, the Hindu sari, the Muslim burqua, the American-Indian feathered head-dress. The sub-cultures within each culture had their own artistic expression, in costume, design, song and dance and other modes.

Although this art was expressed at the personal level, it was not personal, in the sense in which we have defined "personality". There was no scope for an individual to break out of the tradition and simply produce artefacts, or dress as he or she felt inclined, in a personal style. (As we shall see below, the classical art of Greece and Rome was a partial exception). Traditional art was collective art. The names of some of the greatest architects and artists are known to us, particularly those who designed some of the Greek temples and Gothic cathedrals. But the great majority who chiselled the statues and painted the murals and made the mosaics and the stained glass windows will be forever anonymous. Yet there must have been immense emotional fulfilment in working in teams to embody celestial visions in physical forms.

There seems to have been some scope for personal expression, or naturalism, at the edges, as it were. The humans who were depicted in standardised forms in sculptures and paintings were the great ones, who were often deified, or who wanted to leave a record of their human might and glory for posterity. In ancient Egypt, according to one art historian, realism was permitted in depicting "inferiors" - "poverty, disease, old age are all from time to time depicted" - and also the dead and dying in battle scenes. "This departure from the standardised calm and dignity of the principals" was not inconsistent with the cult, for "the condition of inferiors was of small importance in the world of Egyptian draughtsmen" (1). The same might be said of the art of medieval Europe: peasants performing their common tasks abound as background for the principals - saints, angels, kings, queens, nobles, bishops and archbishops.

Second, these collective art styles prevailed unchanged for centuries, even millennia. Temples, churches and mosques were constantly being destroyed by earthquakes, wars, fires or other calamities; they would be rebuilt on the same model - but often bigger and better - as happened, for example, when fires burnt down parts of Chartres and Canterbury

159

cathedrals in 12th century Europe. The Egyptians evolved a style for the depiction of two-dimensional human figures on the walls of temples and tombs which remained unchanged for 3,000 years. "The head is drawn in profile, but with the eye in its frontal aspect, the shoulders are seen from the front, the breast in profile, and the waist and hips in a three quarters view, while both feet usually show the inside and the hands are often identical" (1). In India, "in architecture and sculpture, by the 6th or 7th century A.D., prescriptions for the measure and lay-out of designs had been codified and come into use; by the 10th century they were fully evolved and certainly written down. These were schemes of overall proportion, both for different types of building with their detail, and for bodies of various human and superhuman beings in the figurative arts, which would authenticate each work as the reflection of the transcendent reality it was supposed to express" (2). To please the god, to earth the divine, it was essential to adhere exactly to the divinely prescribed standards and forms. Experiment and change would have invited calamity.

Third, it followed, therefore, that there was no clear distinction between art and craft. The ancient Egyptian language had no word for "artist"; painters and sculptors were "craftsmen". Clothes, ornaments, carpets, pots, furniture - the objects in the home were as much an expression of the cosmic order as the objects in the temple. The function of ornament in Indian art has been well put: "Every individual in India strove to present an elegant social persona. The figures in art represent ideal versions of divine persons (Sanskrit *deva,* from the verbal root *div,* to shine) and their ornaments. For the role of ornaments is 'displaying wealth'. . . the body's inner feeling of wealth, fullness and fertility, raising its status towards the divine. One of the features of Indian personal ornament - as well as of architectural mouldings and profiles - is repetition and multiplicity. Units multiplied into a long series exalt the mind with the suggestion of wealth . . . Ornament is an active expression of praise and adoration. A temple, a deity, a wife deprived of ornament is unthinkable" (2). (Just after I had written this I turned on my television, and found myself watching an instalment of the B.B.C's dramatised version of the *Mahabharata,* acted by Indians, speaking Hindi. A king was discussing the bequest of his kingdom with his advisers and his son. All were covered with

160

jewels - necklaces, bracelets, jewelled belts, and fantastic jewelled crowns. What a contrast to any modern group of politicians in their dreary, unadorned grey suits of standardised cut, white shirts, and hatless shorn heads!). In Islamic societies "everything, whether made for common or for ceremonial use, is lavishly enlivened with ornament, so justly planned and expressed that the patterns seem to be living creatures rather than artificial embellishments" (3). Medieval European cathedrals were similarly adorned with designs and forms of humans, animals and plants, in stone and on cloth and glass. In Chartres Cathedral over 10,000 figures in glass and stone survived break-up by the French revolutionaries. Dead bodies in their tombs were often likewise adorned. The body of the Chinese Emperor Liu Sheng (reigned 154 - 112 B.C.), was found in his tomb in a suit made from 2,499 pieces of jade - regarded as a magical stone which counteracted bodily corruption. Through ornamentation traditional art sought to link common things with the celestial realms.

Fourth, there was a fundamental unity between the arts, bound together as aspects of the great ritual of the cosmos. Architecture, sculpture, painting, music, dance and costume were all expressions of the harmony of creative activity. Here is an account of the Dancing Dervishes of Islam, witnessed by a German visitor, Herr Vett, to a mosque in Turkey in the 1920s:

"After half an hour the singsong (of the *Koran*) gave place to a reed pipe whose faint music caressed the ears and soothed the audience into what was almost a light trance. It was like the whispering of a virgin forest . . . all the life and movement of nature was gathered together in the almost infinite variations of that music . . . The dervishes rose. They were wearing long white shirt-like garments with many folds that rose and fell in rhythmically moving lines as they danced. On their heads were brown turbans, three times as tall as an upturned flowerpot.

Each dervish revolved on his own axis, and at the same time circled about the hall with his hands and arms held off at an angle from his body. The palm of the right hand was turned upwards, and the palm of the left hand was turned downwards. One after another, the dervishes whirled past us. The wooing enticement of the music held them enthralled. My thoughts were led to planets moving to the music of the spheres, revolving on their axes and at the same time circling about their sun . . . This sublime ceremony is probably a representation of an ancient insight, that God created the mind of man in his own image as a microcosm of the macrocosm. The dancers whirled for an hour, each making approximately 365 turns".

Much Indian sculpture, in particular, is concerned with dancing figures, often with multiple arms, standing, sitting or lying in all sorts of complex and graceful attitudes, very different from the stiff and stylised figures of the Egyptians. As a scholar writes of the sculpture of a celestial musician playing a flute, cut on an 11th century A.D. temple at Bhuraneshvara, Orissa:

"It illustrates music as the heavenly art intimately related to the dance. All the arts are believed to originate in, and connect humanity with, the heavenly regions. The modes of music are essentially divine, and to play them well depends upon transcendent inspiration" (4).

Greek culture was also suffused with music. The Olympic Games were performed to music; the philosophers held their discussions against a background of music. Unfortunately, no scores of Greek music have survived.

In the great medieval cathedrals of Western Europe the soaring columns, vaults, flying buttresses and spires; the exquisite stained glass windows turning the light into jewelled rays; the myriads of carvings of saints, angels, humans, animals and plants; the glorious music of voice and instrument (the organ was developed in the 14th century), the majestic Latin liturgy, and the magnificent vestments of priests and nobles - all this in combination must have made all participants in the services feel that they belonged to a community which embraced heaven and earth.

Fifth, most traditional art linked the human world with the worlds of animals and of nature in a fundamental way. The distinction between animals and humans so clearly drawn in the modern society was blurred in the ancient world. Both men and animals had god-like qualities. Statues and murals of beings with human heads and animal bodies - of which the most famous of all is the great Egyptian Sphinx - and with animal heads and human bodies, abound in the pantheons of the Egyptians, the Mesopotamians, the Central American cultures.

To cite one example of an artefact depicting this intermingling of man and beast: a relief of the Hellenistic period, found in the Egyptian town of Oxyrhnchus, of the god Aion, representing eternal time. This figure has a lion's head with a number of solar rays, a man's body and human-size legs which seem to be covered with animal fur. Each hand holds a key; in one is also a torch; and between the thumbs a bolt of lightning. At his back are four wings. What strange powers were thought to be locked up in this small figure - found at a place where in the Roman period there were some eleven temples shared by Greek, Roman, Egyptian and Syrian gods and goddesses! (5).

Chinese art also had its fair share of animals, from flying horses of wonderful rhythm and energy, to grimacing dragons guarding tombs and temples. But it had something else, not found in any other traditional culture except that of its cultural off-shoot, Japan: painting depicting man-in-nature, which reached its apogee in the Sung dynasty (960 - 1279 A.D.). The influence of Taoism, with its affirmation of the inner harmony which unites all living things, enhanced by the benign serenity cultivated by Buddhism (see Chapter 3) was fundamental. A modern scholar writes:

"Throughout Chinese poetry and painting we find this awareness of the beauty and mystery of Nature - always, however, a Nature in which man holds an integral but not an assertive place. Never, on the one hand, are the mountains, rivers, and forests of the great Chinese landscape painters mere decorative backdrops for man and his activities, as so often in pre-romantic Western art ... Always they are peopled by human figures, tiny yet distinct: a fisherman in his boat, a woodcutter, a cowherd, a recluse sitting in contemplation on a rock. So too in the paintings of animals, birds, insects and plants, in which the Chinese excel: always these creatures must be shown alive and in their natural surroundings" (6).

Su Tungpo, (1036 - 1101 A.D.) a famous civil servant-philosopher-poet-artist (a "mandarin" - see Chapter 4) wrote as follows about the painting of a friend, Wen Tung:

"There are plenty of craftsmen who can copy the minute details of objects, but the inner law of things can be comprehended only by the highest human spirits. Wen Tung's paintings of bamboo, rocks and dried up trees may be said to have truly seized the inner spirit of the objects. He understands how these things grow and decay, how they twist and turn and are sometimes blocked and compressed, and how they prosper and thrive in freedom. The roots, stalks, joints, and leaves go through infinite variations, following different rhythms independent of one another. And yet they are all true to nature and completely satisfying to the human spirit".

"Chinese painting", comments Su Tungpo's biographer, "is an unconscious expression of the philosophy of the oneness of man with nature and the essential unity of the great mystic procession of life in which the human being occupies but a small and transitory part". It may be described, he says, as a "pantheistic revelry" (7).

Japanese painting, developed by Zen Buddhist monks in close contact with China, followed the model and the spirit of Chinese painting. And they added three other naturalistic art forms, also adopted from China, which have become world famous as Japanese forms of self-expression: landscape gardening; indoor flower arrangements; and the tea ceremony (8).

Sixth, the concept of cosmic relationship extended not only to all things on and in the earth, but also to all things in the heavens. The sun, moon and planets, and the 5000 or more stars discerned with the naked eye, were regarded as celestial bodies, the habitat of gods and angels, who produced "the music of the spheres" and ordered the affairs of earth. A central function of traditional art, therefore, was to reflect and embody the cosmic harmonies. Here is how a journalist describes the "Forbidden City", the great palace of the ancient Chinese Emperors in Beijing: "The geomancers who ordained the laying out of Peking (Beijing) designed the Forbidden City . . . Its palaces were arrayed along a north-south axis, bringing earth and sky into equilibrium and the elements into harmony. From this sacred mid-point, the emperor could preside over a universe whose immortality he was supposed to share. His domain contained 9,999 rooms, falling just short of the 10,000 which would be at his disposal in heaven. Looking down from the man-made hill behind the Forbidden City (erected to shield the emperor from the invasive spirits of the north), the maze of dragon-guarded peaks resembles the cross-section of an ingenious, multi-cameral brain. Each roof caps a different idea, or houses a separate function. The emperor did his schoolwork in the Hall of Mental

Cultivation; he marched to war through the Gate of Martial Valour; he spent his retirement in the Hall of Permanent Longevity; his excrement was evacuated through the Gate of Certain Peace. The Forbidden City was an ideogram, a model both of the world and of the mind" (9).

Another example may be given from the opposite side of the world. Medieval English cathedrals contain three architectural features in their upper level: a triforium or gallery forming an upper story of the aisle, "often having three openings to each bay...above the triforium rises the clerestory . . . the story that gives light above the roofs of the aisles, carrying the main roof or high vaulting of the church and containing the windows lighting the upper reaches of the building". (Magnificent hangings would be draped over the edge of the openings in the triforium). The three fold division is a symbol of the Trinity; and the whole building a symbol of the universe. The foundations, columns and bays represented the physical world; the stage above that, the triforium, represented the soul of the World and the clerestory represented the Divine Mind illuminated by the light of the sky" (10).

A further example may be given from Cuzco, the capital city of the Incas of Peru. The Quechuas today still think of the celestial river (the Milky Way) as connected to the flow of rivers on earth. In Cuzco, the city divisions crossed one another close to the junction of the two streams which flowed through it. At this central point the Temple of the Sun was situated. The empire, the Milky Way and the sacred rivers were all drawn together in a union of earth, sky and mankind (11).

As a final example, Hindu and Buddhist temples were built as three dimensional mandalas, geometric figures which were believed to reflect the structure of the universe. The idea that architecture and city planning should link humanity to the stars was universal.

We have noted that the traditional cultures produced collective rather than personal art. Before the modern age dawned in the 19th century there were three bodies of art which were exceptions to this principle, producing art which may be called personal or even superpersonal, and these may throw light on the questions raised at the beginning of this chapter.

The first lasted only 16 years; it occurred during the reign of the heretic Egyptian Pharaoh Akhenaten (1378 -62 B.C.) This Pharaoh

165

banned the worship of Egypt's myriad gods and decreed that only the *Aten*, the Spiritual Sun, should be worshipped. He proclaimed as its symbol a sun beaming out rays; at the end of each ray depicted on the murals is a kindly hand. He built a huge temple to the *Aten* at Karnak, and placed it in colossal statues of himself which showed that his body was highly deformed - no other ancient ruler would thus reveal his physical defects! (Modern scholars conclude that he suffered from a disease of the endocrine glands). Murals also show him in a natural, affectionate relationship with his lovely wife Nefertiti, in contrast to the usual stilted depiction of spouses. His reign ended in military disaster. "Among later generations Akhenaten, alone of all the Pharaohs, was remembered with opprobrium as ' the Great Criminal' and 'the Conquered One of Amarna' " (12). Yet to the modern mind, Akhenaten's image, alone of those of all the pharaohs, shines out as that of a *person* who would be comfortable in the United Nations of the 21st century!

The second period is that of the thousand year flowering of Greek and Roman art between the 5th century B.C. and the 5th century A.D. Why does Greek sculpture affect us so profoundly? The Greeks moved from the stylised human form depicted by the Mesopotamians and the Egyptians to the real human form - bones, muscles, flowing movements as they are in nature - and then idealised it. The greatest statues, such as the Venus of Milos and the Hermes of Praxiteles, reach beyond the personal to the superpersonal. Heaven is earthed, the ideal and the natural are blended, in a "natural" person. The Greeks looked for perfection in the human figure which was also the form of the gods. The highest form of art was thus usually the human nude, chiefly male. The Games held at Olympia for 1,168 years (776 B.C. until 393 A.D.) were dedicated to the Father God Zeus, and the winner's much coveted prize was a crown of wild olive leaves. In the great temple in the centre of the grounds was a 40 foot statue of the god, carved by the sculptor Pheidias. The expression on the god's face was so serene and kindly that the Greek philosopher Dio Crysostom exclaimed that "the sight drew the beholder away from himself to the contemplation of the divine. If a man heavy of heart . . . should stand before it, he would remember no longer the bitter hardships of life. Your work, O Pheidias, is grief's cure". The Olympic Games were a unique phenomenon in the ancient world. And the finest Greek art was not anonymous, but the work of known individual artists, citizens of a democracy. (The same applies to the great plays, the tragedies and the comedies). Roman art descends from the superpersonal to the personal. In depicting the gods, the Romans copied the Greeks. In depicting humans, they produced, in statues, the first great body of humanistic portraits in the ancient world. (Many of the sculptors of these portraits were Greeks).

There were two civilisations whose reaction to the stylised portrayal of divine personalities which tradition demanded was in stark contrast to that of the Greeks. The Jews and the Muslims regarded the artistic portrayal of human or animal forms as impious. For orthodox Jews the Second Commandment put a total ban on artistic representation of living things: "You shall not make yourself a graven image, or any likeness of anything that is in heaven above, or in the earth beneath, or under the earth". When the Prophet Muhammad returned to Mecca after his flight to Medina he rode on camelback round the *Kaaba,* the small square building, allegedly built by Abraham, which is the only Islamic sanctuary comparable in sacredness to a temple, and smashed up the 360 images which surrounded it. Depiction of the human and the natural world spelt magic, "idols" which embodied satanic forces. And even if the image were benign, it was (and is) held that contemplation of images of living forms traps the mind in the world of phenomena, of "psychological idols", and prevents it from entering "the unfathomable peace symbolised by the desert landscape in which the *Koran* was written". Islamic art is therefore essentially concerned with abstract forms and shapes "whose unbroken rhythm and endless interweaving enhances the quality of contemplative emptiness" (13). It is often described as "sacred geometry", and the Arabic script in which the *Koran* is written is an expression of sacred art. (As in Ancient Egypt, in Islam naturalistic art expressed in portrayal of human and animal figures is allowed "round the edges" in domestic and palace art, but never in mosques). This attitude reflects the emphasis which Judaism and Islam place on the transcendence of God. But it removes the living object, the person, from the subject, the artist or the viewer. One cannot love a pattern or a script in the way that one can love a human or an animal.

Medieval European art is profoundly concerned with evoking celestial persons through picture and statue. An ancient Egyptian would have nodded assent to the following statement about Byzantine icons; a Muslim would regard it as heresy:

"From the very first the Orthodox theologians did not interpret icons as works of man at all. Rather, they regarded them as manifestations of heavenly archetypes. Icons . . . were a kind of window . . . through which the inhabitants of the celestial world looked down into ours and on which the true features of the heavenly archetypes were printed two-dimensionally. The countenances of Christ, the Blessed Virgin or a saint on the icons were therefore a true epiphany (appearance) . . . Any alteration of a celestial archetype would be heretical in the same sense as wilful alteration of ecclesiastical dogma . . . Thus the iconography of the Eastern Church keeps alive a kind of primitive script used to record archetypal religious experience. It is an art which goes back to the earliest age of the Church, when the power of visionary insight was as yet unbroken" (14).

Iconography implies love, in the union between the human worshipper and the celestial being who has "appeared". In Western medieval Europe this same approach finds its highest expression in Dante's Divine Comedy. "Shelley has well said", writes an editor of the poem, "that the *Paradiso* is the story of 'how all things are transfigured except Love' . . . [Dante] conceives of the whole universe as one cosmic dance of love, beginning in the Seraphim, that highest Angelic order which knows most and therefore loves most, and continued through all nature" (15). And it is through Beatrice, who is no abstract figure but a human person in the spirit world, that this love has been revealed to him (see Chapter 5).

And now we come to an extraordinary intermediate period between the art of traditional societies and modern art, the art of Western Europe from the dawn of the Renaissance in the 14th century until the latter half of the 19th century. The political, economic and social context of this unique outpouring of creativity is significant. Until the outbreak of the French Revolution in 1789 the old order still prevailed, the order of kings and nobles and peasants and established churches, the order of "God bless the squire and his relations and keep us in our proper stations". But within this order the symptoms of the modern age were stirring. The emergence of scientific thinking in the 17th century began to shatter all traditional ideas about the nature of matter; ideas about personal liberty and human brotherhood were proclaimed by the thinkers of the 18th century "Enlightenment"; and a rising middle class was producing new wealth, so that money was around for the patronage of the arts. Let us outline the essential features of Renaissance and post-Renaissance art.

First, it was individualistic; the great artists emerged who are household names today; the anonymity and collectivism of traditional art was ending. Secondly, these great artists felt free to develop their own styles; no-one with any knowledge of art could mistake a picture of Rubens for one by Leonardo da Vinci, or a symphony by Mozart for one by Beethoven. Third, it was naturalistic. After 1,000 years of concealment since the days of Greece and Rome, the naked body was again depicted in statues and pictures. Landscapes were painted with a realism not hitherto expressed except in China and Japan. Portraits showing people as they are, outwardly and inwardly, were produced with exuberance. "Paint the face in such a way that it will be easy to understand what is going on in the mind", said Leonardo da Vinci. Fourth, it was innovative; the artists felt free to draw on completely different models from those of the medieval tradition. A striking example is the fate of St. Paul's Cathedral in London. When cathedrals were burnt down in the Middle Ages, as happened to those in Chartres and Canterbury, they were replaced by bigger and better versions of the old building. When St. Paul's Cathedral was burnt down in 1666, it was replaced by something entirely different, Christopher Wren's great classical structure with its golden dome. Fifth, a new attitude to the feminine was emerging. We have noted in Chapter 5 how some of the greatest writers - Dante, Goethe, Ibsen - extolled "woman" as representing man's higher self. A different attitude was expressed by certain other great artists, notably Shakespeare and Mozart, an attitude already hinted at in the poetry of medieval chivalry. Shakespeare's mysterious poem, *The Phoenix and the Turtle* - "the most profound statement about love in literature" (16), and Mozart's opera *The Magic Flute,* describe the union of man and woman as the union of equal persons, an ideal which, as we shall see in Part II, the modern age is seeking, for the first time in history, to put into practice in ordinary life. Sixth, a new note of compassion for suffering humanity was appearing in this art. Compare the anguish and horror evoked by Goya's picture, called "3 May 1808", of a firing squad of soldiers executing a small group of "inconvenient citizens" with the glee with which ancient Mesopotamians, Egyptians, Greeks, Romans and others portrayed conquerors trampling their victims under foot. Seventh, the corollary to this compassion was the proclamation of ideals of personal freedom and universal brotherhood. Beethoven's opera *Fidelio* contains "the greatest of all hymns of liberty, as the victims of injustice struggle up from their dungeons towards the light" (17). Beethoven's Choral Symphony ends with the singing of Schiller's *Ode to Joy* with its affirmation that "all men will become brothers" - now the anthem of the European Community! The ideal of a universal religion embodied in Masonic teachings prompted Mozart, Goethe, Schiller, Herder, King Frederick the Great of Prussia (a patron of the arts), Voltaire, George Washington and Benjamin Franklin, among others, to become Freemasons.

Finally, this period produced two new art forms, the opera, with its child, the ballet, and the novel, both secular art forms peculiarly suited to the exploration of the lives, characters and relationships of individual persons. The art historian Kenneth Clark thinks that the appeal of opera is that it is irrational. " 'What is too silly to be said may be sung' - well, yes; but what is too subtle to be said, or too revealing or too mysterious - these things can be sung and only be sung" (18). The novel is of fundamental significance. Its production requires no more material assets than a pen and paper: no workshops, bulky materials, complex equipment. It can be read anywhere and at any time; its enjoyment requires no art galleries, concert performances or fixed sites. As an artefact it can flit anywhere like an insect; as an art form it is equally fluid, tied to no traditional conventions of structure, style or content. The European novel burst upon the scene in the 18th century, and began to come into its own in the 19th century in Russia as well as in Western Europe. It is a supremely suitable means for exploring, not only the thoughts and feelings of individual persons, but also the thoughts and feelings of the groups who were the passive spectators of art in traditional societies: the toilers and workers at the bottom of the social pyramid; the women who stood in the shadows behind the men. Moreover, in traditional societies the artists were almost all men; women now began to write novels!

In the great Western European art of this period, therefore, the individual person began to move into the centre of the stage. The words which the 17th century poet John Milton puts into the mouth of his hero, Satan, in his great poem *Paradise Lost,* sum up the emerging attitude:

The mind is its own place, and in itself
Can make a Hell of Heaven, a Heaven of Hell!

But it must be remembered that this great art was produced for the upper classes and the rapidly growing body of middle class intelligentsia who were patrons of the arts. The mass of the people were still illiterate peasants or, in the 19th century, factory workers, to whom the works of Michelangelo, Mozart, Shakespeare and all the others were unknown. When the modern age dawned, and the toilers and workers began to become literate and materially comfortable, and to have access to the wider world through the mass media instead of the local town crier, many of them would ignore traditional art and demand "pop" culture - an entirely new and secular phenomenon.

In conclusion, let us return to Webster's Dictionary's attempt to define "art". This brief and inadequate attempt to outline the vast corpus of traditional art raises two fundamental questions. First, is the beauty which we "see" in traditional art a subjective or an objective value? Is the experience of this beauty simply a reaction of our own psyches, or is it, as the ancients believed, a reflection of a divine quality in the universe, which we call, not "a god", but God? Second, do the gods, saints, angels, demons and other non-material beings with whom much of this traditional art was concerned really exist, or are they fantasies of the ancient mind? Could everyone, all over the world, have been totally deluded for 5,000 years of civilised creativity, not to speak of the millenia of pre-history?

In Part II of this book I shall suggest that the post-modern age which is likely to dawn in the 21st century will involve an integration of the insights of ancient art with the discoveries of modern science and the modern humanism of human rights. Sacred art is the gateway to the New Age!

Chapter 12

AFRICA

"**B**Y the mid 1870s no explorer had penetrated far along the dangerous latitude of zero towards the interior. No one knew which was Africa's greatest river or where it led. Europeans pictured most of the continent as 'vacant'; legally *res nullius,* a no-man's land . . . Beyond the trading posts on the coastal fringe and the strategically important colonies in Angola, Mozambique and South Africa, Europe saw no reason to intervene. Suddenly, in half a generation, the 'Scramble for Africa' (a term coined in 1884) gave Europe virtually the whole continent. Thirty new colonies and protectorates, 10 million miles of new territory and 110 million dazed new subjects were acquired by some method or another by five rival nations: Germany, Italy, Portugal, France and Britain, with Spain taking some scraps" (1).

In Chapter 1 we adopted for the purpose of this book a definition of traditional civilisation quoted by Colin Renfrew: a "civilisation" should include at least two of the following three factors: towns of over 5,000 inhabitants, a written language and monumental ceremonial centres. Apart from the countries north of the Sahara, from modern Tunisia to Egypt, and the Sudan and Ethiopia, Black Africa does not fit very comfortably into this definition. Two thousand years ago the population of the region south of the first parallel may have contained 3-4 million black-skinned people. By 1945 no censuses had been taken by the white colonial powers; but Professor Basil Davidson estimates that in 1900 it may have been 150 million people (2). According to estimates by the United Nations, in 1992 the population of Africa south of the Sahara was 560 millions.

Africa's Pre-modern Contact with Other Civilisations

Before the scramble for Africa other civilisations had made contact

172

with or even colonised some of its edges. About 800 B.C. Phoenician traders from the Near East established the state of Carthage in what is now Tunisia. The Romans later razed its capital city to the ground (see Chapter 7), and later the Roman Empire included the whole of Africa north of the Sahara from Tunisia to Egypt. By the end of the 7th century A.D. this region had been conquered by the Arabs and converted to Islam. Gradually Arab traders and missionaries began to penetrate into black Africa across the Sahara by camel and by sea from Arabia and Asia, bringing with them not only the teachings, rules and rituals of Islam, but also the Arabic script. In Egypt, which the Romans had Christianised (see Chapter 3), the Christians did not lose effective power until the later 13th century, and Ethiopia retained the Coptic form of Christianity which it had received from Egypt till this day. The Sudan, Christian since the 4th century A.D., became permanently Arabised in language and culture in the 15th century, except for its southern region - hence the civil war which has been raging in the Sudan between the southern Christians and the northern Muslims since its independence from Britain in 1955. The result of these Arab incursions in the medieval period is summed up by Professor John Mbiti: "Africa is predominantly Muslim in the areas approximately north of the tenth parallel. These stretch eastwards from Senegal up to Ethiopia, the whole of Somalia and the east coast as far as Mozambique, with comparatively small clusters of Muslims in the fringing regions, Uganda and Tanzania. Over 40 per cent of the population of Senegal, Mauritania, Gambia, Niger, Chad, Northern Nigeria and the Sudan is Muslim, the percentage rising above 90 in the Muslim States of Africa [i.e. North Africa]. The total number of Muslims in Africa is estimated at 70-100 million, compared with 50-70 million Christians" (3). (The Christians, of course, are the results of the "Scramble for Africa in the modern age). To complete the picture of the pre-modern penetration of Africa, we must note that small groups of Europeans settled on the African coast. This was made possible by the maritime revolution of the 15th century, when new designs of ship construction produced a type of sailing ship, the caravel, which could withstand the adverse winds and currents which surrounded the southern half of the continent. "Within a few decades European ships could reach any part of the ocean." This revolution coincided with the

173

invention of gunpowder in China, leading to the production "of the first effective artillery. By the 16th century cannon were being used . . . across the whole belt of countries stretching from Morocco to Japan. The coasts of Africa therefore emerged from isolation confronted by intruders who were both mobile and well armed. As the use of firearms spread rapidly through the Muslim world, a similar confrontation emerged along the fringes of the desert, from the Senegal River to the Red Sea. Africans thus faced better armed neighbours on all sides" (4). As a result of these developments, the Portuguese established trading posts on the "Gold Coast" to export gold and slaves from present day Senegal, Benin in southern Nigeria and Congo. In 1471 they seized and colonised the uninhabited island of Sao Tomé, establishing sugar, coffee and cocoa plantations worked by slave labour. Angola on the south west coast became a Portuguese colony in 1491, and Mozambique on the east coast in 1505. Portugal proceeded to exploit the resources of these colonies for gold, ivory and slaves. Finally, after the Cape of Good Hope had been rounded by the Portuguese Bartholomew Diaz in 1488, the Dutch founded Cape Town as a port of call to India in 1652, and this Dutch town and its hinterland, settled by Dutch farmers who called themselves Boers and spoke a form of Dutch called Afrikaans, was occupied by the British in the Napoleonic wars, and finally purchased by them in 1814. Until the British victory over the Dutch in the Boer War of 1899-1902, South Africa, the southern tip of the vast continent, was colonised by a mixture of Boers and British.

Africa's Religious Culture

Such was black Africa's relationship with the rest of the world before 1870. Now let us look at the ancient, indigenous culture which the Europeans discovered when they colonised the continent at the end of the 19th century.

There are five distinct racial groups in black Africa, organised into almost 3,000 clans, or extended families based on kinship. These ethnic groups speak at least 1,000 distinct languages. Some are widely used, for example, Swahili in East Africa, which was declared the official language of Tanzania in 1967 and of Kenya in 1973. There are about 50 major languages, but others are spoken by only the inhabitants of one small village or region. The distribution of language patterns has not changed much in the last 2,000 years.

The vast majority of African ethnic and linguistic groups never developed indigenous scripts. The Via of Sierra Leone, the Mum of Cameroon and the Tuareg and some other southern Sahara clans are a tiny group of exceptions. The Berbers of North Africa used Greek scripts before the region north of the Sahara was conquered by the Arabs. In Ethiopia the Amharic language, today the country's official language, spoken by some 6 million of its population of 23 million, developed an alphabet of 33 characters. A script was produced for the Somali language in 1976. Where the Arabs traded and raided and converted the natives to Islam (see above), the Arabic script was used for Swahili and other languages. When the European explorers finally penetrated into the interior in the late 19th century, they regarded it as their mission, in the words of David Livingstone, the Scottish missionary who discovered the source of the Nile, to bring "Commerce, Christianity and Civilisation" to Africa.

Not only did traditional Africa have no scripts; it had no number systems. Mathematics was unknown. There were no numerical calendars, no system of dates. Many an elderly African born in this century has no idea of the date of his birth. There was no concept of linear time as conceived in traditional civilisations. The African attitude to time is well described by one of their leading modern theologians: "The question of time is of little or no academic concern to African peoples in their traditional life. For them, time is simply a composition of events which have occurred, those which are taking place now and those which are immediately to occur. The linear concept of time in Western thought, with an indefinite past, present and infinite future, is practically foreign to African thinking . . . people set their minds not on future things, but chiefly on what has taken place. This time orientation, governed by the two main dimensions of the present and the past, dominates African understanding of the individual, the community and the universe . . . Time has to be experienced in order to make sense or become real . . . Since what is in the future has not been experienced, it does not make sense . . . unless of course, it falls within the rhythm of natural phenomena . . . Man is not a slave of time; instead, he 'makes' as much time as he wants. When Westerners come to Africa and see people sitting down somewhere without, evidently, doing anything, they often remark: These Africans waste their time by just sitting down idle!' Another common cry is: 'Oh, Africans are always late'. . . [But] those who are seen sitting down are actually not wasting time, but either waiting for time or in the process of [producing] time . . . [This] basic concept of time underlines the life and attitudes of the African in the villages," and profoundly influences their economic and religious life (5).

Now let us look at traditional Africa's economic sub-structure. This has been described by Basil Davidson. "If you tramp through the African bush you will soon wonder how anyone could ever impose human settlement on this land . . . All this wild profusion stands there vast and looming . . . Give this giant the merest chance, you feel, and the whole surrounding scenery will again invade these narrow fields and possess the land once more . . . as though humanity had never been. Every African culture bears profound witness to this dominating 'spirit of the land'. Yet the appearance of lush natural wealth is often misleading. Much of Africa is paved with a lateritic soil of low fertility and shallow depth. Much of it is covered by fruitless bush and poorly timbered trees. Much of it is pestered by tsetse fly inimical to beast or man. Only the development of an inherent immunity - but this never complete - has enabled Africans to withstand widespread malaria. Other pesticides demand their toll, jiggers and locusts, pestilential water snails, fever-bearing clouds of flying creature" - and now AIDS. "Initially, moreover, Africa had few good food and plants. Early farming was of dry rice and local yams in western Africa, and of millet and sorghum elsewhere, but of little else until the coming of Indonesian and Asian yams in the 4th or the 5th centuries, and of American cassava, maize, sweet potatoes, pawpaw and pineapples in the 16th century (6). Cattle, sheep, goats and chickens were domesticated from the first millennium B.C., and later horses and camels. By the first century A.D. the Iron Age revolution had penetrated into Africa; hunter-gathering was giving way to shifting agriculture, and the Africans were using iron hoes instead of stone tools. But they never invented the plough or the wheel, nor the sailing ship; nor did they make the roads and irrigation canals which were basic to the development of Mesopotamia, Egypt, China and other cultures.

African Religion

Every aspect of African life was inspired by and infused with religion. In Chapter 3 we discussed the distinction between imaginative and rational knowledge. African religion was pre-eminently imaginative; the rational dimension remained undeveloped - as is indicated by the absence of scripts. Thus African religion was essentially what may be called popular religion. It did not have the intellectual elements of the dogmatic religions, based on canonical scriptures, which produced written legal systems (though African societies were governed in every detail by ancient and supposedly divinely inspired customs, as we shall see). Nor did it, therefore, have temples, churches, priests or religious teachers such as rabbis and imams. Though different local groups often had different gods, as in the Near East and the classical world, the fundamental pattern of African religious belief is clear-cut. First, there is universal belief in a Supreme God or Creator, Who may be He-She-It - a mixture of all three. An African theologian, Dr. Gabriel M. Setiloane, gives an interesting list of the Names of the Creator used in different parts of the continent, with their English translations. These include: "Ancestor of days: One who has been from the beginning" (Cameroon); "The Supreme, Omnipotent Being, Determiner" (Ghana); "The Unknown" (Guinea); "Great Spirit"; "The Owner of Life" (Nigeria, Sierra Leone); "The One Who Penetrates and Permeates all Existence; The Source of Being" (Southern Africa); The Great and Supreme One (Zimbabwe); The Breath of all Life" (Zambia) (7).

Secondly, the belief in life after death and a constant communion between the living and the dead - "the living dead", especially the family ancestors, is basic. (Compare the religion of ancient China and Japan). Dr. Setiloane writes of "our" (i.e. the Africans') "very strong objection to the translation of "the living dead" as "ancestral spirits". "Whenever an African speaks about this contact with the 'living dead' *(babimo)* it is about a person-to-person contact, not a vision or apparition," a deity or spirit. "There is an interaction of being which transcends the mechanical, chemical and physiological interactions" in human communications. "Because this is the level at which real communication takes place, it is at this level that it continues even after the death of one of the parties. This I see as a much deeper or higher level of living than Western estimates of the human person teach or admit". *[I prefer the word "communion" to "communication" in this context - author]*. The living dead share in the essence of Divinity, "in Rudolf Otto's phrase, in the quality of *mysterium tremendum et fascinans* . . . Numinusness. But . . . this quality can be experienced also when one comes into contact with people alive in the flesh . . . with some more than others, for example a chief, a *ngaka*" (8). Animals also participate in this communion, this *force vitale* which pervades the universe.

Thirdly, in addition to the spirits of the ancestors, the Africans believe - as was almost universally believed in other traditional civilisations (see Chapter 3) - in the existence of spirits of all moral levels - gods, saints, angels, witches, devils and so on, which can draw on the morally neutral psychic energy which pervades the universe to heal or to harm, to make the crops grow or wither, the rain fall or drought prevail, enemies fall sick and die, friends recover from illness. Here is one modern example, from an Englishman working in 1990 in a hospital in Bolobo, Zaire. "The wailing started somewhere in the hospital, to herald yet another death . . . Within a few minutes the first *nkokos* (normally elderly female relations) appear, some wailing . . . Then comes a group of younger male relatives, grim faced and silent, carrying the body of a teenage girl. They are followed by the rest of the family carrying few possessions - a couple of pots, a bundle of clothes, their sleeping mats . . . There was nothing physically wrong with the dead girl. She died simply because someone had put *ndoki* [witchcraft] on her. Because her belief in the curse was so strong, she had lost the will to live . . . Witchcraft and tribalism pervade the whole of society here . . . Witch doctors are a common sight, even in the hospital. Tribal medicine is the cause of death in a high percentage of the children brought into the hospital" (9).

This brings us to the fourth aspect of African religion: the existence of customs and ritual relating to every stage and every aspect of life, from the cradle to the grave. One of the most crucial of these customs is that of circumcision, applied to both sexes, which marks the entry into manhood and womanhood and opens the path to marriage and parenthood. This ritual, which takes place at puberty, is very painful

178

for both sexes, and often physically dangerous, since it is performed by old men and women unversed in modern surgery and with unsterilised knives. But it is far worse for girls than for boys, since it makes the experience of the sexual act painful for them all their lives. (The World Health Organisation estimated in 1993 that there are at present 90 million females in the world who have been subjected to genital mutilation, which is practised in more than 25 African countries). Mbiti asserts that "through the initiation ceremony of both girls and boys the corporate life of the nation is revived . . . its vitality renewed . . . The ceremony is a deeply sacred one, for in it lies the survival of the nation" (10). No modern-minded person can give moral support to this operation on girls; but Amnesty International has recently pointed out that Western assertions that the fundamental purpose of the girls' operation is to make the sex act painful in order to ensure fidelity are an inadequate explanation.

Edwin Smith, a Canadian missionary who "spent the happiest years of my life" in Central Africa, writing in the 1940s, says that: "The Gospel has a prodigious task before it in Africa. It finds nothing in heathen systems into which to engraft itself. To subvert and supplant is its mission". Yet after this devastating statement he proceeds to bless African religion in glowing terms: "You feel religion is everywhere, not as an organised cult separable from the rest of their life, but as part and parcel of it, all-pervasive, motivating, controlling, guiding, strengthening . . . Religion is there as an attitude of the spirit - a reverence and a trust; as a cult; as an adoration and a worship; as a social bond, an organising, architectonic force, as a concern with the supernatural; as in some sense a theology, a philosophy . . . If there is one universal article of the African's creed, it is the conviction that death is not the end of all things . . . but a stage in the human spirit's experience" (11). This moving statement makes the inner philosophy of African religion relevant to the modern world. This is reinforced by a similar statement by Geoffrey Parrinder, Reader in Comparative Religion at London University. He writes that "African philosophy of being is not too far distant from that philosophy of life, power and consciousness which appears in the writings of Teilhard de Chardin [see Chapter 16] . . . and in modern physics. The older [i.e. 19th century] notion of 'dead matter' has been replaced by a science which sees mind or life from the lowest level of creation to the highest". Modern "scientists also share the vision of Wordsworth who felt a 'sentiment of being spread o'er all that moves and all that seemeth still'. This may be a kind of pantheism, though, as Chardin insists, for Christian belief it must be a personal pantheism, and the same may be said for African belief " (12).

The main impact of Islam on traditional African religion was legalistic. The traders, with their caravans of camels, were not scholars; probably most of them, like the Prophet himself, were illiterate. Many of those from the Maghreb (North Africa) must have been imbued with the Sufi cult of reverence for holy men and worship of saints, which would be congenial to African religious feeling. The result, according to Dr. Trimingham, was not a culture clash but a "parallelism". Islamic rituals, and Islamic personal law - e.g. the prohibiting of men from having more than four wives - were adopted, but community life continued as before. "In Afro-Islamic culture, when Islamic law collided with strong family-centred systems, it was quite simply ignored . . . Everywhere the traditional world remains real and its emotional hold is vivid" (13).

And when the great centre of the continent was opened up to modernity at the end of the 19th century, Africans did not want to learn to speak or write Arabic - which would be of little use to them in the modern world! As a result, the literature of Islam, other than its legislation, remained practically unknown to the clerical leaders of non-Arabic speaking Africa (14).

The Impact of Islam on African Society

The general effect of the impact of Islam on traditional African society may be summed up as follows: (i) to undermine traditional customary law and "communalistic morality" by introducing the concepts of rigid law and legal morality - e.g. in matters of marriage and divorce, in the law of death as the punishment for apostasy, and the concept of the *jihad* or holy war against the infidel; (ii) this created a fundamental sense of dualism - also later fostered by Christianity - which was incompatible with African pantheism: God versus the Devil - Heaven versus Hell; the believers versus the infidel; (iii) to drive a wedge between the sexes. In the Muslim world only men are generally admitted to the mosques and women cannot perform the basic prayers and rituals which are the spiritual "work" of a Muslim until after the menopause, when they are no longer regarded as real women. As a result, when African men became Muslims, their women remained pagan, and kept up the ancient cults; (iv) to undermine the religious basis of the community, including the concept of kingship as divine. Relationships became contractual and personal (v) to introduce clothing - with all its implications for distinctions of class, sex and age; (vi) to forbid representational art - and African art is essentially representational, symbolising - or embodying - the psychic and spiritual forces in gods, humans and animals; (vii) to undermine traditional magic and animism; (viii) to promote the concept of the *Ummah,* the brotherhood of believers, a wider brotherhood than that of the kinship group (see Chapter 3); to promote the basic literary of Islamic boys and (ix) to introduce the concept of linear time (15).

It is obvious that although in many regions and for many periods African religion and Islam co-existed comfortably, the ingredients for a basic and inevitable clash were there, particularly after Christianity arrived to challenge both "paganism" and Islam. "It is only since the modernistic type of religion invaded Africa that religion has become a cause of division and conflict between peoples and individuals. Religion has changed in Africa from being the regulatory principle of life to becoming a theology or law that man can use to forward secular urges." Christianity and Islam "have treated African society as a largely passive 'object' of their missionary activity and have had little concern for the religious African as 'subject' (16). The result has been, in the 20th century, religious conflicts of peculiar ferocity between African Christians and African Muslims in certain regions, e.g. Nigeria and the Sudan.

African Government and Society

Let us now turn to traditional African systems of government and life styles, which are embraced in the word "community". The philosophy underlying the African concept of "community" is well summed up by John Mbiti. "In human relationships there is emphasis on the concept of hierarchy based on age and partly on status . . . a ladder ranging from God to the youngest child. God is the creator and hence parent of mankind . . . Beneath him are the divinities and spirits, some of whom are founders of different societies. Next come the ancestors . . . Among human beings the hierarchy includes kings, rulers, rainmakers, priests, diviners, medicine men, elders in each household, parents, older brothers and sisters and finally the youngest members of the community. Authority is recognised as increasing from the youngest child to the highest being. As for the individual, the highest authority is the community of which he is the corporate member. The authority also has degrees, so that some of it is in the hands of the household-family, some is invested in the elders of a given area, part is in the hands of the clan, and part is in the whole nation, which may or may not be invested in central rulers (17).

The Africans lived mostly in villages of small huts, some grouped together in kingdoms, many self-governing and self-sufficient in fulfilling their modest needs. In about 80 per cent of these communities there was an institution called *limbry* (now illegal everywhere); "it was a form of institutionalised marginality in which individuals such as prisoners and criminals were restricted in their participation in society, but were not on the whole mistreated, dehumanised or exploited" (18). Government was carried out by Councils of Elders, general assemblies, or meetings of the whole village or tribe - men only - talking and talking until they reached agreement by consensus. Marriages were arranged by family elders. Normally girls were married at puberty, as soon as they had been circumcised, but boys at a considerably older age, because they had to wait until they could afford to buy their bride - with cattle. (This is the opposite of the Indian system, where brides must have dowries). Polygamy is practised in 98 per cent of African societies, for the fundamental purpose of marriage is to produce children, for the sake of both of the ancestors and of future generations. Since large numbers of the children die in infancy, and since men must not have sexual relations with their wives either during pregnancy or during the two years of breast feeding, many women cheerfully accept the existence of co-wives - who in pagan tribes may be very numerous if the husband is rich in cattle. Each wife normally has her own hut, where she lives with her children and where her husband visits her. Most African women are busy all day working in the communally owned fields, fetching wood and water - often from miles away - and cooking. There are normally rigid customs about what kind of work should be done by men, and what by women. The children play around, or help; and there are always plenty of elders to look after them.

Africa did not bequeath to the world a great collection of temples, palaces and tombs. Africa does not have much stone, so buildings in alternative materials and under tropical conditions have generally decayed - and the archaeologists have not been so intensively at work in Africa as in other continents. Nevertheless, there were impressive developments, particularly where Arab influence penetrated on the west and east coasts. On the west coast, for example, Timbuktu, the capital of the 14th century empire of Mali, was a magnificent place. "In his atlas of Africa, produced in 1375, Abraham Cresques, the Majorcan cartographer, shows the Emperor of Mali seated in majesty on his throne, holding an orb and sceptre, while the traders of all North Africa made their way towards his country's markets. The maritime nations of Southern Europe recognised Mali, at the time, as one of the great empires of the modern world. In the 14th century Mali gold fuelled the trade of half the civilised world, and provided the metal for Europe's first gold currencies since Roman times. Timbuktu . . . was described a century and a half later by Leo Africanus, as a city of learning and letters. He noted the big market for manuscript books, and reported that more profit was made from the sale of books than from any other merchandise. The Malian cities of Timbuktu and Jenne became, under Emperor Mansu Musa in the 14th century, places of scholarship and learning, and the reputation of their schools of Theology and Law was well-known in the furthest parts of Moslem Asia" (19).

On the eastern side of the continent there were also large empires, and one famous complex of ancient stone ruins remains today in Zimbabwe. "By as early as the 4th century A.D., the people of this area were skilled metal workers, smelting iron and extracting gold from extensive mines", which was exported to the Indian Ocean world" (20).

Conclusion

In the fundamental ethos of its profoundly spiritual religion - when shorn of magic and superstition - and the fundamental structure of its communitarian societies, Africa, generally regarded as "primitive" and "backward", offers models for the world society of the future. In contrast to the societies where the great traditional civilisations prevailed, the Africans have little or no "cultural baggage" of dogmatic scriptural religions and rigid class and caste systems to shed. On the contrary, the underlying assumptions of their religion add to the rationalism of modern science the spiritual dimension which it needs. And the spiritual communitarianism of African society shows the way towards lifting Western capitalism out of the rut of competition and greed, and of Marxist Communism - where it still prevails, in China and Cuba in particular - out of dictatorial "command" planning and non-democratic public ownership. But a third factor is needed in Africa: individuation, enabling *the person* to emerge and develop and express his or her unique potential. Edwin Smith observes that "I have never succeeded in finding in any African language an equivalent for 'person'". (see Part II on Human Rights) (21). Here Islam and Christianity provide a goad. Inevitably the impact of modernity on Africa has been profoundly traumatic. But it is possible that the basic spirituality and communitarianism of the "dark continent" will cause it to play a leading role, in the 21st century, in the process of world transformation.

PART II

THE
MODERN
CIVILISATION

Chapter 13

THE PHILOSOPHY OF HUMAN RIGHTS

B Y the 18th century the ideas let loose from the East into the European body politic by the pre-Renaissance (the arrival of the texts of the works of Greek philosophers and scientists and of Justinian's legal code), the Renaissance, the Reformation and the scientific revolution of the 17th century had, like potent enzymes, prepared the ground for the emergence of the modern age. It sprang from the last great movement, the 18th century "Age of Reason and of Enlightenment", which brought the seminal modern idea that "people matter" into clear expression, and also sounded the clarion call to action - to reform and regenerate human society everywhere.

The idea that "people matter" is based upon a supremely optimistic assumption about human nature. It is that all people, of whatever sex, race, colour or social status, are, *as persons,* endowed with creative powers, and that it is the purpose of society to provide the conditions for the development of these powers - which may range from scientific or artistic genius to the blessing which the craftsman bestows on the humble object which he fashions. This idea inspired the American Declaration of Independence, drafted by Thomas Jefferson in 1776, who inserted in it, uniquely, the "Right to Happiness"; the Declaration of the Rights of Man proclaimed by the French Revolutionaries in 1789; and the American Constitution's Bill of Rights of 1791. And 150 years later, in 1948, it was affirmed for all humanity in the United Nations' Universal Declaration of Human Rights, the first universally agreed moral code in history (see Appendix I). Since then the Rights have been embodied in two United Nations' Covenants of Human Rights, approved unanimously by the U.N. General Assembly in 1966 and in force as international law since 1976, after ratification by 35 states - at the time of writing the USA has only ratified one of them, that concerned with political and Civil Rights: There have also been other treaties such as the European Convention on Human Rights and the European Social Charter, drawn up by a body called the Council of Europe (not the European Community), consisting in 1994 of 31 democratic European states. This Council has a unique institution, a Court of Human Rights to which individuals can appeal over the heads of their governments. Meanwhile all the states which sign and ratify these Conventions thereby commit themselves to putting them into practice in their countries. A Declaration of Human Rights has now been written into most modern constitutions.

Categories of Human Rights

The Human Rights set out in these documents fall into four categories: (i) *The personal or civil rights* comprise freedom of worship, speech, writing and assembly; freedom to travel inside and outside one's own country; equality before the law; the right to a fair trial and not to be tortured, or held in slavery, or subjected to "cruel, inhuman or degrading treatment or punishment"; the presumption of innocence unless proved guilty; the right to asylum from persecution in other countries; and the right to marry freely and found a family. (ii) *The basic political right* is "the right to take part in the government of one's country, directly or through freely chosen representatives", and implies the right to form political parties, known today as "pluralism". The firm statement that "the will of the people shall be the basis of all government" finally destroys the moral validity of ancient systems of rule by gods, priests or divinely ordained kings. (iii) *The economic rights* consist essentially in the right to "own private property, alone as well as in association with others"; the right to form trade unions, to strike and freely choose one's employment; the right to work, to free choice of employment, to just and favourable conditions of work; to equal pay for equal work without discrimination, to "just and favourable renumeration", remuneration to protection against unemployment; the right to rest and leisure, including reasonable limitation of working hours and periodic holidays with pay. Finally, (iv) *the social rights* include the right to social security, to education, and to "food, clothing, housing and care in sickness and old age". These social rights are, according to the Universal Declaration, "the economic, social and cultural rights indispensable for a person's dignity and the free development of his personality". The affirmation in Article 26 of the Universal Declaration on the right to education is particularly

189

significant: "Education shall be directed to the full development of the human personality". Gone is the attitude of traditional societies that from king to slave, from warrior to housewife, an individual should be trained to perform his or her allotted function in his divinely assigned station. The liberation of human creativity implied in these two short statements is as momentous as the liberation of physical energy involved in the splitting of the atom.

If all the Human Rights were to be implemented, the framework of an ideal society would be established, grounded on the principles of Liberty, Equality and Fraternity, in which love, or affection, would unite people and in so doing stimulate their individual creativity. This surely is the blueprint for the modern consciousness which is dawning today.

In the past 200 years most societies have taken some measures to implement Human Rights, measures which have been made possible by that other pillar of modernity, applied science. The societies which initiated these measures in the 19th century have laid the basis of the modern model. And since the rights are universal, the process has also involved the creation of global institutions. This will discussed in Chapter 18.

Why are the Human Rights "Right"?

We have seen that in all traditional cultures except those of Greece and Rome, the authority of the public moral code was derived from the prevailing public religion. In Western Europe traditional Christianity was the life-blood of the old order which imposed the chains of authority on peoples' thoughts and actions. So the 18th century proponents of the Rights of Man were impelled to reject orthodox Christianity - *écraser l'infâme* - "crush the vile thing" - was Voltaire's famous indictment of the Roman Catholic Church. To clear the way for "the idea whose time had come" these European thinkers had to demolish three of the foundation stones of the orthodox religion. The first was the concept of a static spiritual cosmos, a hierarchically structured organism, to which human society should conform - a concept which had already been partially undermined when the formulation of the scientific laws of Nature in the 17th century dehumanised the physical universe, turning it into a mechanism. The second was the doctrine, first propounded by St. Augustine, that man is born in "original sin", with its corollary that only through the intervention of Christ the Redeemer can he attain salvation in this life or the next. The third was the inculcation of dependence upon religious authority - that of scriptures, and of the Church and its priests (see Chapter 3). The philosophers asserted that the "naturally good", the adult man, needs no such props. "Enlightenment" wrote the philosopher Kant, "is the emancipation of man from a state . . . of incapacity to use his intelligence without external guidance". "Man is born free, but everywhere he is in chains", are the famous opening words of Rousseau's seminal book, *The Social Contract.*. The free man, said Kant, will naturally direct his *will* towards the exercise of his moral duty. He is no longer to be regarded as a helpless child, reaching out to hold the hand of God the Father. "Fixed opinions are like standing water, they breed reptiles of the mind", wrote the poet William Blake. Today the words "heresy", "excommunication" and "hell" no longer echo through the psychological air - although a secular version of these dread concepts has pervaded those modern societies which have been, or still are, grounded on "the Gospel according to St. Marx."

This leaves to every individual the responsibility for deciding for himself on his moral duty, his philosophical attitude, and his religious beliefs and spiritual faith - if any. The world-wide affirmation of this attitude is new in history - although it was anticipated in ancient Greece and Rome.

The rejection of these concepts and attitudes led the philosophers to break new ground in three main ways. First, if man be "naturally good", and, as Rousseau said, it is bad institutions which make him bad, than all that he has to do is to liberate himself from the bondage imposed by tyrannical kings and authoritarian priests, and he will be able, *by his own powers,* to create the ideal society. Secondly, this affirmation implied that the adult man should live in a dynamic, not a static, society, in which he himself would bring about progress towards the goals specifically outlined two centuries later in the Universal Declaration of Human Rights. In the 19th century, the Darwinian theory of evolution reinforced this affirmation by demonstrating that in the natural world evolution from simpler to more complex forms was spontaneously taking place. "Sin" could now be explained as "backwardness"; through natural evolution it would be outgrown, and a society based on Human Rights would spontaneously evolve. Darwinism thus reinforced the rejection of the idea that only through divine intervention could man be "saved". Moreover, by freeing man from dependence on the apparently arbitrary acts of God, it opened up the amazing prospect that man can and should steer the evolution of the planet himself - an attitude also entirely new in history, and pregnant with the potential for global transformation or destruction. Thirdly, if the unique person is to express his potential, he must be liberated from all the social customs and institutions which had traditionally inhibited his self expression. This involved the revolutionary transformation of society: the development of new attitudes to marriage, education, work, leisure, the treatment of crime, and so on. Marriage should be regarded as a union of loving persons, not a legal contract based on social considerations:

> *Children of a future age,*
> *Reading this indignant page,*
> *Know that in a former time*
> *Love, sweet love, was thought a crime.*

cried William Blake. Love between a man and a woman, as persons, the sweetest relationship on earth, has been placed at the core of modern society. Education, said Rousseau in his book *Emile*, should be "child-centred", related to the child's needs and capacities. His imaginary hero, Emile, was allowed to read no books except *Robinson Crusoe* until he was 15, so that he was spared the experience of "inert minds pumping inert material into other inert minds", discussed in Chapter 8. Careers should be opened to talent; the implementation of this principle, proclaimed in the French Revolution, has enabled innumerable men and women, who in olden days would have been forced to "keep in their proper stations", to make outstanding contributions to the world. And people should be able to chose their leisure activities - often expressed in joining churches, clubs and groups according to their natural interests - without regard for social status, race, sex or other external consideration. The vast proliferation of clubs, societies, "Non-Governmental Organisations" and voluntary groups of every kind is a modern phenomenon, in which persons relate,

192

not on the basis of social status but of human interests. Anyone can join a group of bird- watchers, chess players, actors, anti-war activists - and they make *friends* of either sex. This is new in history. The aim of punishment, said the Italian jurist Beccaria, should not be retributive or even merely deterrent, but reformatory - a revolutionary idea when barbaric executions by such methods as "breaking on the wheel" (in 18th century France) or flogging to death (in Russia), were a form of public entertainment. And to symbolise that the New Age stood for the shedding of the role-playing of the past, William Blake and his wife would sit outside their English cottage stark naked.

The 18th century philosophers placed the source of Human Rights in "the People". (The preambles of the American Constitution (1776) and of the United Nations' Universal Declaration of Human Rights (1948) open with the phrase: "We, the People"). How do "the People" know that the Human Rights are "right"? Most of the 18th century philosophers were Deists. They believed that God had implanted in the hearts of people the ideals for which they were struggling. Jefferson's Declaration of Independence speaks of "the Laws of Nature and of Nature's God", and Alexander Hamilton wrote that the Laws of Nature "are not to be rummaged for among old parchments or musty records. They are written, as with a sunbeam, by the hand of Divinity itself, and can never be erased any mortal power". Voltaire, the high priest of the Age of Reason, said that "the only book which should be read is the great book of Nature. The sole religion is to worship God and to be an honourable man". But suppose that people cease to believe in God - for religious freedom is a basic human right? Can moral rights derive from people who are "merely" superior animals?

Let us approach the problem from another angle. If all men were naturally good, free men would spontaneously associate fraternally in communities, and the need for government, in the sense of law enforced by compulsion, would disappear. "Religion is politics and politics is brotherhood", wrote William Blake. "Government, like dress, is the badge of lost innocence . . . The palaces of kings are built on the ruins of the bowers of Paradise", commented Tom Paine. But the majority of the 18th century thinkers were more realistic. At the end of the 17th century the English philosopher John Locke, whose writings profoundly influenced the Founding Fathers of America, had given the most powerful formulation of the age to the "contract theory", the complement to the scientific theories of natural law. This theory asserts that in principle human society is based on a contract made between free and equal individuals to set up a sovereign ruling *power*. The establishment of this power is, in the view of Locke and his famous predecessor Thomas Hobbes, the alternative to anarchy; it is motivated by the desire for self-preservation. The contract theory is thus based on a purely pragmatic view of human nature. To Rousseau, on the other hand, the "social contract" was the means of establishing liberty as a moral value. The urge for democracy stems from man's moral sense. This is perhaps the most fundamentally revolutionary idea in the whole corpus of revolutionary philosophy of the modern age, for it implies the democratisation of the Platonic vision that government should be in the hands of the wise and good. Churchill summed the situation up in a famous sentence: "Democracy would be the worst form of government if every other system were not worse". In other words, democracy is the only system of government which attempts to combine order and law with freedom and fraternity.

The Problem of Evil

This bring us to the problem of evil, for if free men behave unfraternally, chaos and crime will result. We noted in Chapter 4 the tremendous fear of "disorder" as a cosmic phenomenon in the philosophies of traditional societies. Rousseau realised in a confused way that his "General Will", the will for the common good, is not necessarily the same thing as the will of the majority: and so he asserted that it might be possible for one man only to know the General Will. In that case, he wisely advised, the will of the majority should prevail. His disciples did not heed him, and some of them, declaring that "for the sake of the Rights of Man we must violate the Rights of Man", proceeded to guillotine their opponents, and to establish in the Jacobin regime in France the first modern totalitarian state. The poet Shelley had a premonition of what was to come. His beautiful poem *Hellas* opens by triumphantly hailing the collapse of the old order and the coming of the golden age:

The world's great age begins anew
  The golden years return
The earth doth like a snake renew
  Her winter weeds outworn:
Heaven smiles, and faiths and empires gleam
  Like wrecks of a dissolved dream.
But it ends on a note of anguish:
  Oh, cease! Must hate and death return?
Cease! Must men kill and die?
  Cease! Drain not its dregs the urn
Of bitter prophecy.
  The world is weary of the past,
Oh, might it die or rest at last!

Perhaps it was inevitable that the seers who saw the vision of the perfect state on earth could not grapple with the problem of the redemption of evil. For how can the two extremes be endured together - the vision of a Golden Age and the vision of the immemorial wickedness and suffering of humanity - unless the seer has reached the stature of a saint?

This brings us back to Plato and to Christianity. As soon as the doctrine of natural goodness is recognised to be but a half-truth, the Platonic distinction between the soul and the mind, between man's "higher" self, the divine soul, and his "lower" self, the ego, and the Christian doctrine that only through love, which stems from God, can the lower self be "redeemed", become relevant. In this metaphysical context the status of modern "democracy" becomes clear. If it is to be regarded as a system of government which is "right" because it stems from God, as Rousseau and the Founding Fathers of America believed it to be, then all men and women must develop the powers of their souls; all must become philosopher-kings. Only thus can Rousseau's problem be solved, the problem, as he put it, of how "to find a form of association . . . by which each man, uniting himself to all, nevertheless renders obedience to no-one but himself and remains as free as before"; the problem of creating *communities*. Man is born both good and bad, a "mixed up kid". He must develop his natural goodness and overcome his natural badness if he is to enter into the Human Rights which are his heritage.

Modern Political Theory

Modern political theory, in trying to grapple with the problem of reconciling Liberty, Equality and Fraternity, has developed in three main directions. The first, that of Western liberal democracy, assumes that free individuals are normally motivated by self-interest and must therefore set up a sovereign power, which will control them in their own interests, and which they in turn will control by majority voting. In this thinking, the main problem becomes: how much freedom shall the individual have, and how much power shall be given to the sovereign? Here we may note the famous definition of sovereignty formulated by the British jurist Austin: "If a determinate human superior, not in the habit of obedience to a like superior, receive habitual obedience from the bulk of a given society, that determinate superior is sovereign in that society, and that society (including the superior) is a society political and independent". With the emergence of this amoral concept of sovereignty as secular "power", law has become essentially "positive law", divorced from its ancient roots in the Natural Law which was held to stem from God (see Chapter 4), so that "command and obedience appear as the essential attributes of law". "The abandonment of Natural Law marks the rise of modern jurisprudence". In the past two hundred years, sovereignty has generally been considered to reside in the "nation state"; but it can in fact be exercised at any level in what Austin calls "society". The principles of federalism and "subsidiarity" - that each task should be performed at its appropriate governmental level - provide for the exercise of sovereignty at various levels - global, regional, national, local. As we shall see in Chapter 18, the surrender or sharing of sovereignty to institutions operating at all these levels is developing rapidly at the end of the 20th century - though the first modern federal state, the USA, was established in 1787.

The second trend may be termed the Hegelian heresy. It lies at the root of the Fascist ideology developed by Mussolini, Hitler and lesser dictators who took their cue from these satanic characters. This philosophy originated in Germany in the early 19th century, and was developed by Hegel, Treitschke and other highly respected German philosophers. They gave the Platonic philosophy a profoundly sinister twist. Instead of saying that the actual state is only an imperfect reflection of the perfect state which exists in heaven, the German philosophers asserted that the actual state - for Hegel the Prussian State and for Treitschke the newly united Second German *Reich - is* the ideal state - "the march of God on earth", as Hegel put it. "The absolute ethical totality is nothing but *ein Volk* - a people or a nation", he wrote. The individual is only truly free in so far as he submerges his mind, heart and body in the life of the actual state, which demands his *total* allegiance - hence the term "totalitarian state". The Hegelian heresy, as applied to the German state, had an important influence in instigating the two World Wars, and is now, therefore, totally discredited. Paradoxically, however, by immersing the absolute in the actual and reducing Natural Law from a transcendental standard to the product of an historical process, Hegel provided the basic concept for Marx's famous "materialistic' philosophy of history.

The third trend is embodied in Leninism. Marx asserted, from his nook in the British Museum in London, that once the Communist revolution had occurred, the sovereign state would "wither away", and the way of life which we have called "community" would inevitably prevail. Lenin, the man of action involved in carrying out the first Communist revolution, saw that this could not happen in the immediate future in Russia. So he formulated the doctrine of the "dictatorship of the proletariat" as the form of government required to guide a society through the transition stage until the circumstances were ripe for the establishment of "Communism". And since the Communist Party was regarded as "the vanguard of the proletariat" this amounted to the dictatorship of the Communist Party. In fact, in the half century since the Russian Revolution, the dictatorship of the Communist Party became entrenched in all Communist countries, and those who defied it were treated as heretics. But the contradiction of applying traditional dogmatic political attitudes to a well-educated, science-oriented and increasingly sophisticated and affluent modern population has caused Marxism-Leninism to be discredited in Europe. And as the great masses of Chinese peasants get educated and China develops a modern technological economy, the same ideological breakdown seems to be occurring in that great country.

Now let us look at the application of the concepts of Liberty, Equality and Fraternity to the four kinds of Human Rights.

Civil Rights

The civil personal rights may be regarded as negative in the sense that they aim at removing restrictions on the individual's freedom of action. Without freedom - to strive, to create, to explore, to destroy, to err - he or she cannot grow; he cannot love. A distinction must therefore be drawn between the moral principles of negative freedom, and the use to which this freedom is put. No power in the world can force the "free" man to perform acts of fraternal love, or make him equal in achievement to the genius who lives next door, or fill his heart with a song of joy. Every society which has tried to establish civil rights has therefore been obliged to hedge than around with restrictions in order to prevent the selfish interests of one person from disturbing the freedom of another: restrictions which range from laws about stopping one's car at red traffic lights to laws forbidding slander, libel, theft, torture, murder, racial and religious discrimination, and so on. And rules must be enforced by sanctions. In a "democracy" (see below) "the people" make these laws and set up the mechanism for their enforcement: this becomes the "positive" legal system, secular in nature, replacing the customary law of traditional societies which stemmed from religious revelation. As long as the free man is conceived to be free to behave badly, so long will legal systems and enforcement procedures, with all the grim panoply of police, law courts and prisons, be necessary. But can we return to the system of the olden days, when man was expected to behave as a moral being but was not free in the sphere of his personal life? No!

The Right to Private Property

The right to own private property and to do what one likes with it falls, in a sense, into the same category as that of the civil rights. Most of the early protagonists of the Human Rights regarded the possession of some private property as essential to the self-expression of the free individual, and as constituting, therefore, the necessary complement to the civil and political rights. John Locke wrote that "the great and chief end of men's uniting into commonwealths and putting themselves under government is the preservation of property". The French Revolutionaries' Declaration of the Rights of Man included the right to own property, and this right is affirmed in the United Nations' Universal Declaration of Human Rights. Although Jefferson substituted the word "happiness" for the word "property" in the American Declaration of Independence, his vision of the new society which he was trying to found in the United States was one of sturdy, self-supporting small-holders, a concept adopted by the Conservative Party of Britain after World War II under the slogan of a "property-owning democracy". The *philosphes* of France, the Founding Fathers of America and the liberal statesmen of 19th century England all had deep reservations about granting the vote to those who had no property; Voltaire called them "cattle": Montesquieu described them as "so mean as to have no will of their own", and in the French Revolution they turned into that terrifying phenomenon, the mob. Under France's first constitution of 1791 the vote was restricted to male taxpayers; in the United States and in Britain this inhibition was not overcome until 1918.

As in the case of the civil rights, the "right" to possess private property must be distinguished from the use to which the property is put. The selfish person will acquire property in order to enhance his ego through the power which it brings him, rather than as a means of promoting his creative self-expression. The Marxist maxim: "From each according to his ability, to each according to his need" appears to hold the key to this problem. All people have "basic needs", a concept defined in 1976 by the World Employment Conference of the International Labour Organisation; and in addition, all people have individual needs in relation to their individual creative powers - needs which may well be unequal. Some will need new books, some gardens, some means of rapid travel, some scope for political or economic service and so on. One of the greatest men of this century, Mahatma Gandhi (see Chapter 17), who devoted his life to the promotion of Human Rights, possessed at the time of his death a cheap pair of spectacles, a cheap watch, two eating bowls, two pairs of wooden sandals, a copy of the *Bhagavad Gita,* and little else. "Forget wants; concentrate on needs", he said in his old age to a young man who asked him for a thought to guide his life. The fact that the exercise of the "right" to accumulate private property frequently leads to the economic, political and social exploitation of other people and to the abuse of the environment has prompted liberal societies to hedge it around with legal restrictions, and Communist societies deleted it from the list of fundamental Human Rights affirmed in their constitutions. Although this right is included in the United Nations' Universal Declaration of 1948, it was omitted, at Communist insistence, from the United Nations Covenants of 1966 (see above).

We would therefore assert that the right to own private property cannot philosophically be classified with civil, political and social rights as a moral principle.

Political Rights

The implementation of the political rights requires *positive* action to establish and operate secular constitutional systems through which "the people" will govern themselves, replacing the "divine right" of kings, priests and scriptures by the authority of man-made law. Modern democratic constitutions are normally drawn up by "the people" represented in elected constituent assemblies. Since they are the product of a culture which believes in dynamic change and progress, they provide for their own amendment - the United States' Constitution had had 26 amendments between 1789 and 1979. An existing constitution which is considered unsatisfactory can legitimately be replaced by another - by 1988 France had had 16 constitutions since its first one in 1791; and a constitutional government can at any time enact, amend or repeal specific statutes dealing with any aspect of the nation's life. There is thus ample provision for making orderly changes in order to implement new ideas or to adjust to pragmatic needs. The ancient fear of upsetting the ancestral spirits or of violating revealed codes has been removed. In all modern political democracies the "will of the people" is expressed indirectly; the people elect the legislative and executive bodies which carry out the government. (This may be compared with the system of direct government by the people in Athens, the country which invented democracy - see Chapter 4). They do this through organising political parties. A country which calls itself a "one party state" is not generally considered democratic today. There are two standard modern democratic constitutions which in general have served as models for the modern implementation of political rights: the British and the American. (The Communist countries call or called themselves "democratic"; but in practice they were, or are, secular theocracies ruled by secular priesthoods - the Communist Parties - promoting Marxist secular theology).

The evolution of the British form of democracy from its origins in 1215 A.D. was described in Chapter 4. In order to make the modern situation clear let us briefly outline its present structure. The British people elect the main legislative body, the House of Commons, for a specific term of years (at present five years), and the leader of the party with the majority of seats in this House automatically becomes the Prime Minister, the head of the executive branch, and chooses his ministers - known as "the Cabinet" from other members of his own party in the House of Commons or the House of Lords - a medieval anachronism, see Chapter 4. If he loses his majority within the five year period, he and his Government must resign, and an election be held. If he personally loses the confidence of the House of Commons he must resign, as Neville Chamberlain did in May 1940, when Hitler was threatening to invade Britain, to be replaced by Winston Churchill. Thus the executive is, in principle, controlled by the legislature elected by the people. If, as in many countries, there is a multiplication of parties, due partly to the system of proportional representation under which parties are allotted seats according to the number of votes they receive, rather than, as in Britain, according to winning a majority in a constituency, coalitions may be necessary "to form a Government", a process which may take weeks or months. The confusion and inefficiency caused by this situation between the two world wars has, since 1945, produced in West European countries more or less effective systems based on modified forms of proportional representation, which imply government by consensus rather than confrontation. In Britain the judges are appointed by the government, but they and the juries who give the verdicts can adjudicate against the executive. Parliament, however, is sovereign except at election time, when sovereignty reverts to the people. There is no appeal against its laws - except now to two European bodies, the European Community and the Council of Europe

- see Chapter 18. The hereditary monarch remains Head of the State, representing the country as a whole, but with no political power. The leading Opposition Party is an essential part of the system; it is called "Her Majesty's Opposition." This is a far cry from the situation in countries where political opponents are treated as enemies. Unlike all other modern constitutions except that of Israel, the British constitution, having evolved so gradually and imperceptibly, has never been written down. This is likely to be changed soon. A written constitution, which provides procedures for its own amendment, is a necessary framework for a modern state in its task of implementing Human Rights.

The British Constitution is thus based on the harmonisation of powers, on legislature, executive and judiciary working together. This was misunderstood by the French thinkers of the 18th century, who, visiting England, noted that the Parliament controlled the King, and concluded that the freedom which they found there, in contrast to the repressive rule of the French autocracy, was the result of the se*paration* of powers. This concept was adopted by the authors of the American Constitution. This great document provides that the President, who is head of state and head of the executive rolled into one, should be directly elected every four years. The legislature, Congress, is divided into two Chambers, the House of Representatives, whose members are elected for two years only in constituencies organised on a population basis (as in the British system), and the Senate, which has two members for each of the 50 states of which the USA is composed, a third of whom are elected every other year, for six years. Both President and Congress can initiate legislation, which must be passed by both Houses. The President can veto a bill initiated by Congress; but Congress can over-ride his veto by a two-thirds majority. The judiciary is headed by the Supreme Court of nine judges, appointed for life by the President, which interprets the Constitution and whose decisions are final, short of a constitutional amendment. Thus in the American system of separation of powers sovereignty resides essentially in the Constitution itself. Meanwhile, the possibility of conflicts and blockages between executive, legislature and judiciary remains a difficulty.

Most democratic constitutions in the world are more or less based on these two models. In general the countries of Western Europe, Asia - in particular India - and Africa have adopted the British model, while those of Latin America have adopted the American model.

The USA, unlike Britain, is a federal state - the first modern federal state. But federalism does not affect the model chosen for the form of democracy: India, Canada, Australia and Germany are examples of federations which are based on the British model.

Social Rights

The social rights fall into a different category from the other three kinds of right. Their implementation implies some assessment of the "basic needs" of all human beings in terms of their material standards of living (see Chapter 18). Then *positive action* is taken by the societies concerned. Schools, hospitals and other institutions must be built, and teachers, doctors and other workers trained. When established through democratic institutions, the social rights imply fraternity - that people care sufficiently about each other voluntarily to surrender some personal freedom and private property - for instance by paying high taxes - to ensure the material well-being of their fellows. In the modern world the state is normally responsible for implementing the social rights, replacing or supplementing the care traditionally provided by family, church, guild, caste or other private groups; and such a state is called a *welfare state,* because for the first time this care, regarded as a *right* enjoyed by *persons* as such, is in principle systematically given; through the welfare state the individual's basic needs are met.

How is the provision of all these social rights paid for? One of the great inventions of the modern world is the concept of income tax. The major form of taxation through the ages has been indirect taxation on goods, whether locally produced or imported, and often placed on necessities, such as salt in pre-refrigeration days, which means that the poor are hurt far more than the rich. In England William Pitt introduced an income tax to finance the wars with revolutionary and Napoleonic France, but it was so unpopular that all records of it were destroyed when it was abolished. Sir Robert Peel reintroduced the tax in 1842 and it has been levied ever since (1). At its lowest, in 1874-6, it was 0.83 per cent of income; at its highest, in 1941-46 (i.e. during the Second World War) the standard rate was 50 per cent. In the USA income tax was levied during the Civil War, but an attempt to make it a permanent federal tax was ruled unconstitutional. The 16th Amendment to the Constitution of 1913 authorised the Federal Government to levy the tax (2). We shall see in Chapters 14 and 18 that the concept of a new kind of benefit, which would give a basic income to all citizens without conditions, is emerging in Europe, and that a world taxation system is in the offing.

While the civil, political and economic rights are thus concerned with providing the individual with liberty, which he can put to moral or immoral use, the social rights assume that he is a moral being, that he desires to behave as a member of a community.

Conclusion

The idea of building a world society upon the foundations of a moral code which would give practical expression to the ideals of Liberty, Equality and Fraternity for all persons, providing the conditions for the fulfilment of their human potential, is new in history. We are moving into an age when it is realistic, indeed imperative, to envisage planetary policies for the implementation of Human Rights. But we shall not see our goals clearly unless we face the key philosophical question: is the source of this modern moral code man or God? If "man is the measure of all things", as some ancient Greek philosophers put it, he will be tempted to use his rights for selfish and wicked purposes. Following the principle that "by their fruits shall ye know them", we suggest that the criterion for assessing the morality of the use to which Human Rights are put lies in the extent to which they are applied to promoting the development of "community". We have already suggested that this criterion applies by their very nature to the social rights.

The future of the world depends upon the transmutation of the negative, irrational forces which the process of implementing Human Rights is unleashing, fomented by the explosion of science. It depends upon "tuning in" to the Source of the Rights and thus liberating the creative energies locked up in all human souls. These fundamental questions will be discussed in the rest of the book.

Chapter 14

THE IMPLEMENTATION OF HUMAN RIGHTS

The Sovereign State

A T present (1994) the main organs responsible for implementing Human Rights are the 185 sovereign states. Some of these responsibilities are being delegated by the states to supranational bodies, such as the United Nations and its Specialised Agencies, and the European Union (see Chapter 18), and some to local bodies - provinces, districts, villages. Such delegation is in accordance with the principle of "subsidiarity" - every task should be performed at its appropriate level - which is the official policy of the European Union and the Roman Catholic Church. It involves a certain sharing or surrender of sovereignty - both words are being used. Some of these states are tiny, under 2,000 square miles; some are huge, over 5,000,000 square miles. Some have a few thousand citizens, some tens or hundreds of millions. China, with 1.4 billion citizens, contains a fifth of the human race. Some are very poor; some are rich beyond the wildest dreams of traditional societies. But whatever its nature, the sovereign "state" is essentially providing government, with all the functions which modern government involves - defence, police, financial and economic policies, welfare services and so on. It gains an emotive character, a group personality, when it is identified with the concept of a "nation" - a modern secular group which is tending to absorb the emotions traditionally attached to family, tribe and religious group.

Secularity

Since the Human Rights constitute a secular ethical code, the state must be secular. Everywhere modern states are inexorably pushing religion out of public life. The Founding Fathers of the United States, who deliberately created the first state in the world founded *ab initio* on the basis of Human Rights, felt it necessary to make constitutional provision to limit the sphere of religion to private life. The only state in the world today which has a constitution based on a traditional scripture (the *Koran*) is Saudi Arabia. In Britain, the "Church of England", the national Church, created by King Henry VIII (1509-47) in order to defy the Pope and divorce his Spanish wife, and whose clergy are to this day therefore appointed by the lay Prime Minister who represents the royal power, is a historical anachronism.

Let no one think, therefore, that the old groups, even the most sacred, the family and the religious community, are changing today because our modern society is decadent. They are changing in order that the groups which truly express Human Rights may emerge. Although blood relationships and traditional religious affiliations have their place, modern groups are based essentially on empathy, on fraternity, on "the chemistry is right", on shared interests - on *personhood*. Let us now briefly consider how the modern state is carrying out this great transformation. We shall discuss the role of international and supranational bodies in Chapter 18.

The Economic and Social Rights up to 1939

For reasons that will be apparent, we will start our discussion with the group of Rights, the Social Rights, the need for which historically emerged last on the scene.

The affirmation of the right to an adequate standard of living (Article 25 of the United Nations' Universal Declaration of Human Rights) is surely one of the most important statements in the modern world. It was taken a step further when the World Employment Conference of the International Labour Organisation, held in 1976, formulated the policy of "Basic Needs First". "National strategies and development plans and policies should include specifically as a *priority objective* the promotion of full employment and the satisfaction of the basic needs of each country's population". It is likely to be further developed by the United Nations' Social Summit to be held in Copenhagen in 1995. The idea of establishing criteria of economic equity is new in history.

How will these rights and these criteria be fulfilled? For the past century this question has thrown the modern world into a ferment.

The Industrial Revolution was launched in 19th century West Europe and America by the accumulation of capital by private enterprise. The traditional idea that the basic "commons" are a trust from Heaven has been replaced by the modern concept of the right to own private property as "real estate", to be bought, sold or even grabbed at will. This attitude inspired the "laissez-faire" philosophy developed by Adam Smith in the late 18th century. Economists and politicians believed that the government regulation of the economy was not necessary, because the "laws" of supply and demand would automatically allocate goods and resources effectively. One man's wealth would produce another man's wealth, by creating demand. This philosophy was later reinforced by "Social Darwinism", the concept of the survival of the fittest in the economic struggle. "Classical economic thought . . . held that economic activity was subject to its own inbuilt constraints, and these, by implication, also neutralised political power. If the economy worked automatically and well, there was no case for intrusion by the state . . . The general commitment to classical thought was deep in the United States; in no other country was it so fully adopted as a guiding principle", writes Professor J. K. Galbraith of Harvard University (1).

During the second half of the 19th century the social and economic horrors of the Industrial Revolution became apparent.

They included:

(a) The wretched housing, working and living conditions of the masses who had left the countryside to work in "the dark Satanic mills" and live in the new urban slums.

(b) The cyclical booms and slumps, or "depressions", as they are called today, to which the capitalist system was prone, producing unemployment and other forms of social distress.

(c) The widening gulf between the owners and managers, on the one hand, and the "workers" on the other. The grant of the right to strike produced an ugly confrontational atmosphere.

(d) The cut-throat, war-like nature of economic competition - "I win the contract, you lose it - ha ha!".

(e) The built-in tendency to pander to consumer greed rather

207

than to minister to "basic needs". This involves advertising, lobbying and other forms of consumer manipulation, ranging from boosting gums which keep peoples' dentures in place while they kiss in the dark ("Polydent" and "Fixident"), to the huge trade in lethal weapons - the "military-industrial complex".

(e)   The distortion of fair competition through take-overs, mergers and stock exchange speculation.

These phenomena produced several kinds of policy reaction:

(i)   Recognition of the need for *social programmes* to meet the social needs of the people for decent housing, health care, pensions, unemployment benefit, minimum wages, reasonable working hours and so on. Those countries which have ratified the United Nations' Covenant of Economic, Social and Cultural Rights (which, in August 1994, does not include the USA!), the Council of Europe's Social Charter, and the Social Chapter attached to the European Union's Treaty of Maastricht of 1993 (which does not include Britain!), are committed in principle to putting them into law - although there exists as yet no system for enforcing international social law (see Chapter 18). The state provision of comprehensive social services, which take care of every normal contingency, is called the *umbrella welfare state*. The concept was first formulated in war-time Britain in the Beveridge Report of 1942, and has become the standard policy for West Europe since then.

(ii)   The idea of *direct taxation* of personal wealth through income tax, property tax and death duties, to supplement the indirect taxation of goods and services, which affects rich and poor alike.

(iii)   The idea, associated with the British economist Maynard Keynes, that national governments should "manage" the capitalist economy, through taxation, trade and monetary policies. This was a direct attack on the classical economic system described above.

(iv)   The idea that the *relationship of national currencies* to each other should be stabilised at fixed rates by the stabilisation of all to the "gold standard".

(v) The concept of *socialism,* developed by Karl Marx and a host of other thinkers, who felt passionately that the capitalist system is morally wrong. Socialism substitutes public for private ownership of major *economic* assets - "the means of production, distribution and exchange", as it was defined in the British Labour Party's Constitution of 1918. This, it was thought, would end "the exploitation of man by man" expressed in the gulf between the shareholders who own the capital of a private business and the workers who produce the wealth which the shares represent.

(vi) National economic and social *planning,* based on agreed priorities and setting production targets.

(vii) Laws, administered by government agencies, to *control or forbid monopolies and cartels.*

By 1939 the first three policies had been partially accepted in Europe, the USSR and USA. Direct taxes were generally imposed. Throughout West Europe and in the USA the need for social services was met by piecemeal government schemes for pensions, unemployment and health insurance, to which workers and employers contributed; working class housing, and government hand-outs - the "dole" aid to the unemployed who fell below the ignominious "means test". The system was patchy, leaving many contingencies and people uncovered; the insurance schemes applied only to wage and salary earners; others paid fees for private and better services. Only in the USSR were comprehensive social services - the "umbrella welfare state" - introduced by Stalin as the citizen's *right* - and the Soviet welfare state was not fully implemented until the 1960s. Keynesian policies for economic management by the state did not prevail in Europe until after the War, in spite of the breakdown of the system based on classical economics in the Great Depression of 1929-33. But in the USA they powerfully influenced the thinking behind President Roosevelt's New Deal of 1933-39, whose lasting bequest to the country was the Social Security Act of 1935, which provided and still provides contributory state pensions for all. Anti-trust legislation was enacted in the USA from 1890 onwards - somewhat illogically, since the system was supposed to work for itself without state intervention! In the USSR, after the 1917 Revolution, comprehensive socialism was established, the state owned all economic assets, from mines and fields to shoe shops and hairdressers, and in 1928 Stalin introduced comprehensive, authoritarian or "command" state economic planning - a conceptual break-through in economic affairs.

Economic and *social* policies have to be administered through *political* systems. We must next, therefore, consider the implementation of the political rights.

The Political Rights

We noted in Chapter 13 that political rights are universally expressed through secular *constitutional government.* There seem to be, in 1994, only six states which are structured on traditional feudal lines: Saudi Arabia and five other small Persian Gulf States - Kuwait, Qatar, the United Arab Emirates, Oman and Bahrain. Tibet was a feudal theocracy until the Chinese invasion of 1959. And since 1979 Iran has been a constitutional theocracy, ruled by the clergy.

There is one provision which in the Western world is generally regarded as basic to "democracy": "pluralism"; the right to form political parties. The existence of a legal and lively "Opposition", poised to take over from the ruling Party if the electors vote it in, is an essential feature of the two constitutions which are the democratic models for most of the world, the British and American Constitutions (see Chapter 13).

But the modern world is riddled with one-party states. They are of three kinds. First, crude dictators who rule by force and guile need a Party through which to dominate the people, and some sort of constitutional framework to give their rule legitimacy - this may necessitate vestigial opposition parties as well.

Secondly, in Africa especially, benign rulers of considerable moral stature in international experience, such as Presidents Nyerere of Tanzania (now retired), Kaunda of Zambia (also retired) and Mugabe of Zimbabwe, have tried to create one-party systems as a modern expression of the traditional concept of the tribe as a family in which all members talk and talk until they reach an agreement - by consensus.

In societies which have been tribal rather than feudal, the main function of the single party is to unite the tribes, transcending ancient rivalries. It is a mass party through which the leader seeks to inspire a new level of consciousness, blending modern science and humanism with traditional communitarianism. "Consciousness-raising" is a rapidly spreading concept. The third kind of one-party state is the Communist state, where the Communist Party was or is an elite, with the mission to lead the masses into the ideal Communist society. In 1994 it still exists in China, Cuba and North Korea.

Communist Philosophy in the USSR up to 1989

Marxism is not simply an economic policy which advocates socialism. It is also a philosophy of history, an apocalyptic vision, which asserts dogmatically that socialism is the inevitable climax of the historical process. In Marxist theory, beyond socialism comes communism; when socialism has been fully established, and man has therefore ceased to exploit man, the state, as a legal and coercive system, will "wither away". "Under socialism", wrote Lenin, "all will take part in the government in turn and will soon become accustomed to no one governing at all". The transition from legalism to community, discussed in Chapter 18, will have been made. Such a vision appealed to the idealistic Russian character which, in 1917, knew little or nothing of the "classical economy" of the Western world. In the Russian language the word *mir* means "village", "peace" and "world".

The Soviet Constitution of 1977 - the third revision of the USSR's original Constitution of 1918 - opens with a ringing annunciation, which in the light of subsequent events reads with sad irony:

"The great October Revolution [of 1917], made by the workers and peasants of Russia under the leadership of the Communist Party by Lenin, overthrew capitalist and landowner rule, established the *dictatorship of the proletariat,* and created the Soviet state, *a new type of state,* the basic instrument . . . for building socialism and communism. Humanity thereby began the epoch-making turn from capitalism to socialism". The Communist Party is "the vanguard of all the people", created to play "the leading role" in building the ideal socialist society. It is no more possible for a Communist state to admit party pluralism, that is, to admit the functioning of parties which stand for capitalism or any non-communist type of society, than it was for the medieval Church to admit the existence of heretical sects. But by implementing the Social Rights, and in particular the right to education, while denying democracy in political and economic matters, the USSR prepared the way for the downfall of its Communist system in 1989. The demand of millions of educated people for political and economic freedom became irrepressible.

West European Social Democracy up to 1980

In the inter-war years, throughout capitalist democratic Europe, the Communist parties, directed by Moscow, were separate from, and often in conflict with, Social Democratic Parties, of which the British Labour Party and the German Social Democratic Party are the most famous. These Social Democratic parties believed that the *political* system of a modern state should be that of pluralistic democracy. In *economic* matters they stood for a "mixed economy", involving the public ownership of the "commanding heights" of the economy, the great public utilities and some major industries, and the retention of a "private sector" for consumer goods and services. In *social* matters they advocated the creation of an umbrella welfare state. Since they put the political system - pluralist democracy - before the economic system - socialism - they did not, like the Communists, believe in eliminating the pro-capitalist parties which were in power everywhere except in Scandinavia. Although some of these Social Democratic parties were profoundly influenced by Marxism - the German Social Democrats did not formally abandon it until 1959 - their attitude was essentially pragmatic, concerned with what is sensible in a free and mixed-up world, rather than with actualising an ideal by force.

After World War II, Keynesian policies of managing the economy by a measure of state intervention enabled West European Social Democracy to come into its own. The pragmatic model of the mixed economy and the umbrella welfare state, grounded solidly on pluralistic democracy, was adopted throughout the region. It met the needs of the time. The War had jolted millions out of the rut of fixed opinions and narrow interests and awakened a deeper sense of morality.

212

"Freedom From Want" was one of the "Four Freedoms" proclaimed as their War Aim by Roosevelt and Churchill in the Atlantic Charter of 1941. There was a widespread consensus that the creation of the umbrella welfare state was a moral imperative. And public ownership of the commanding heights of the economy was felt to be not only morally right, but practical, for post-war reconstruction necessitated a measure of planning for which the capitalist system, geared to the vagaries of consumer demand, is less well adapted. (Comprehensive planning had, of course, been essential during the War). Finally, the terrible experiences of Nazi dictatorship had made the Europeans regard political democracy as their most precious possession. When, in the British election of July 1945, Churchill's Conservative Party was roundly defeated by the Labour Party, with its social democratic programme, the great war leader is said to have stumped out of his den in tears, growling: "This is what we fought the war for".

Pragmatic, consensus politics prevailed in West Europe till the early 1980s. The Conservative parties were willing to accept the mixed economy, the welfare state, and a measure of "indicative" or guideline planning and Keynesian economic management. And the Communist as well as the Socialist parties, powerful in some countries, notably Italy, were willing to work within the pluralist political framework. Thus a system was created which probably goes further than any other in the world towards implementing all three kinds of Human Right. And it was based on *consensus,* the urge to co-operate rather than to compete. The following account of its basic achievements was written by a senior United Nations' economist:

"The immediate need to repair the terrible devastation brought about in Western Europe by the War was given great impetus by the USA, which in the Marshall Aid plan allocated 13 million dollars as a gift to 18 countries on the sole condition that they co-operated together in plans for spending it. The aid was also offered to the Communist bloc, but Stalin did not allow them to accept it . . . Stimulated by this initial help, Western Europe experienced under the aegis of its system of Social Democracy nearly a half century of unprecedented prosperity . . . The granting of wage increases and the development of social services were made possible by two factors: first, the vast increase in the sheer production of goods brought about by technology; and second, the redistribution of wealth which took place in every country. The aristocracy were either eliminated by war and revolution, as in East Europe, or persuaded, as in West Europe, to surrender much of their incomes and property through such devices as income tax and death duties - 19th century inventions. Throughout Europe many of the great mansions and castles whose owners had lorded it over serfs and peasants became museums, amusement parks, schools or trade union rest homes. West and East Europe have experienced a fundamental social revolution since 1945. By 1970, for the first time in the history of the continent, the majority of their inhabitants were adequately fed and clothed. Millions were living in new houses or flats of a standard and aesthetic design unthought of before the war. Public utilities - piped water, modern sewage, gas, electricity and telephone services - had vastly expanded . . . In Britain, a million houses were built between 1948 and 1952, 90 per cent financed by public funds. In the USSR, where 25 million people had been made homeless in the war, the government pioneered the technology of mass produced housing units of pre-cast, pre-stressed, reinforced concrete elements that can be pre-assembled in the factory and erected on any site in minimum time and with minimum labour . . . This housing breakthrough constituted a kind of 'architectural Sputnik' . . . Cars are a significant indication of living standards. In 1922, there were only 854,000 passenger cars in the whole of Europe. By 1970, on an average every other household in West Europe had a car. Better living conditions combined with the developments of medical science and the introduction of free health systems financed by governments, to transform the health of Europeans. Between 1900 and 1970 the death rate was halved, and life expectancy at birth prolonged by 20 years. Many hitherto fatal diseases were brought under control. In both West and East Europe, though on different scales, the Social Rights had been essentially implemented since the War" (2). But now a new spectre has cast a dark shadow over the scene: unemployment. Meanwhile in the USA classical economic theory still dictated social policies. The welfare state was not created; the poor were given handouts as state charity - apart from the social security system already mentioned, and the provision of "Medicare" - state medical care for the aged, enacted by the Johnson Administration (1961-68).

The Need for an Economic Revolution in the Developed Countries.

Since the mid 1980s the capitalist economic system of the Western World has begun to break down, although orthodox economics proclaims that the prevailing "recession" is nothing more than a natural, self regulating ailment, as a cold is to a healthy person.

By 1994 unemployment had reached 30 million in western Europe. Social welfare systems were stretched to the limit and in Britain were beginning to collapse. Conservative Governments, particularly in Britain and the USA under Mrs Thatcher and President Reagan respectively, were widening the gulf between the rich and poor by reducing income tax, and, in Britain and the European Union countries, imposing a tax, known as VAT, on consumer goods. Small businesses were being ruined by giant firms, and speculation in uncontrolled currencies was making and unmaking fortunes. (The International Monetary Fund (IMF), set up in 1946, had failed to replace the defunct gold standard as a world currency stabiliser). In 1994, in the USA and West Europe, nearly 15 per cent of the population were living below the poverty line (3). "The economy must grow"; "We must be competitive in world markets", was the constant cry of politicians, projected through the media. This was the system which the naive East European and ex-Soviet citizens, starved of consumer goods, were rushing to introduce as a replacement to Communism, which had developed their industrial infrastructures and comprehensive social welfare systems, but failed to improve agricultural production or provide adequate consumer goods for the needs of a modernised people (4).

Those who believe, however, that the current economic depression in the industrialised world is merely a minor illness of the ethically sound and practically efficient capitalist system are closing their eyes to the flashing storm signals of the dangers ahead. The world is facing an entirely new phase in the process of dynamic "development". The combination of population explosion, depletion of natural resources, the misuse of resources and technology for arms, the threat of environmental breakdown, and the widening gulf between the three quarters of the human race who live in the developing countries and the quarter - soon to be a tenth - who live in the industrialised countries (which include those of East Europe) calls for an entirely new economic philosophy to inspire entirely new economic policies. The industrialised countries will have to replace the shibboleth of "growth" by the concept, first launched on to the international scene in 1972 by the Club of Rome (a prestigious international Think-Tank) in a seminal book, *Limits to Growth* (5). They will have to recognise the significance of the slogan coined by E. F. Schumacher in Britain: "Small is Beautiful," (6); of Mahatma Gandhi's statement: "Forget wants, concentrate on needs" (see Chapter 16), and of the International Labour Organisation's policy of "Basic Needs First". They will have to give speedy and effective help to the developing countries to enable them to leap forward into the modern world, building an industrial infrastructure based on modern and perhaps post-modern technology suited to their particular needs, including adequate social services. And they will also have to help the East European countries to develop post-modern economies. The emerging global problem and the new ethical attitudes needed for their solution will necessitate the abandonment of the classical economic philosophy which has dominated non-Communist European and American policies since the time of Adam Smith. The dawning economic revolution in the industrialised countries calls for such policies as shorter working hours (already in practice in major firms in France and Germany), education for creative leisure as well as training for technological skills; the payment by the state to all of a "social wage" - just as old people get "social security" - to remove the nightmare of the unemployment dole; heavy taxation of the rich; and environmental control measures which will probably involve major changes in standards and styles of living, and consultation and co-operation between labour and management in industry (this is at the heart of the "Social Chapter" of the European Union's Maastricht Treaty of 1992 which Britain refused to sign). Fundamentally, competition will have to be transformed into co-operation, and, when basic needs have been met, human progress will have to be directed into non-materialistic creative channels; the ingredients of this economic revolution are being worked out by the New Economics Foundation in London. Meanwhile, during his short rule in the USSR from 1985 to 1991 Mikhail Gorbachev tried to start such an economic revolution, based on two concepts: *Glasnost* - "openness", the right of every person to express him or herself freely, the end of the medieval tyranny of Marxist dogma; and *Perestroika,* or restructuring. "The essence of *perestroika",* Gorbachev has written, "lies in the fact that it *unites socialism with democracy* . . . Today our main job is to lift the individual spiritually, respecting his inner world and giving him moral strength" (7). As we shall see in Chapter 16, a global ethic is emerging which supports the economic revolution.

Human Rights in the Developing Countries

The developing countries, which have emerged into statehood in the second half of the 20th century, have before them these three models, the American, the West European and the Soviet, for implementing economic, social, political and civil rights. Only China and a handful of small states adopted the Soviet model, most as a result of the particular circumstances of war-time occupation (North Korea and Ethiopia), or decolonisation (Vietnam, Angola and Mozambique), or as a reaction against dictatorships supported by the USA (Cuba and Nicaragua). The Latin American states have generally adopted the American model, which is easily distorted into dictatorship by entrenching the presidency, turning the legislature into a rubber-stamping body and outlawing opposition parties as "subversive". India, the most populous country in the world after China, has adopted West European parliamentary democracy and the mixed economy; but in contrast to Communist China, she has not yet managed to create even a rudimentary welfare state, except in the provision of education (see below).

In general, outside pressures - political interference by the great powers, and economic involvement with the West-based multinational corporations - combine with backwardness and poverty to make it difficult for these societies to develop appropriate institutions for implementing human rights. Their problems will be discussed in Chapters 17 and 18.

The Right to Education

Article 26 of the United Nations' Universal Declaration of Human Rights not only asserts that "Everyone has the right to education", but expounds a revolutionary education philosophy: "Education shall be directed to the full development of the human personality . . . "

In order to appreciate the explosive nature of this statement, we must glance again at the theory and practice of education in traditional societies - recalling always the exceptional character of those of Greece and Rome.

Education consisted of *training* for the adult role laid down by the kinship or caste group. Intellectual training, involving learning to read and write, was therefore reserved for the priests, scholars and jurists - almost all male - and involved essentially studying and interpreting the scriptures. By the dawn of the modern era most of the classical languages in which these texts were written were "dead" languages, and scholars were generally unable to relate the traditional pedantic learning either to modern spiritual needs or to modern ideas of liberalism and science. The abolition by the Chinese Imperial Government in 1905 of the ancient system of examining civil service candidates in the 2,500 year-old Confucian scriptures was a symbolic gesture as well as a practical reform.

The peasants who formed the vast majority of the population everywhere except in North America were illiterate; and it was felt best to keep them that way. In 1803 the Bishop of London said that "It is safest for both Government and the religion of the country to let the lower classes remain in that state of ignorance in which nature originally placed them". But with the advent in the 19th century of democracy and of the Industrial Revolution, the idea of *universal education* was born. As the franchise was extended to the working man, politicians realised that "we must educate our masters"; and industrialists realised that illiterate workers would not be efficient "hands" in the technocratic age. And so, in the 19th century, decades before the Social Rights came to be generally accepted, in Western Europe and North America the state assumed the responsibility for providing universal education. By the mid 20th century this region

218

was 90 to 100 per cent literate, and so, now, is East Europe and the former Soviet Union. Simultaneously higher education was gradually made available to all who could profit from it, regardless of social status, and in Europe since 1945, at the cost of the state for those who could not afford to pay.

In the 20th century the idea that education "should be directed to the full development of the human personality" has begun to penetrate the massive state education systems of the Western world. The British Education Act of 1944, abandoning the legal injunction of the first national Education Act of 1879 that all children should be instructed in the "three Rs" (reading, writing and 'rithmetic), laid down that all children should receive an education related to "their age, aptitude and ability" - the "three As". But despite growing recognition that education should be "child-centred", one of the greatest weaknesses of the modern system is that "subjects" are often taught in an excessively rational mode. Literature, art and history tend to be analysed as if they were objects in the laboratory, rather than experienced in such a way that they create a resonance in the soul. The education of the creative imagination, through which alone *values* are understood, is essential to the development of the person.

Japan was the first non-white nation to realise the relationship between Western education and industrial development. By 1905 she had made herself an industrial power capable of defeating a European nation - Russia - and to do this she had created a secular state education system which had produced a literacy rate of 90 per cent - but by methods which treated the children as creatures to be moulded into future servants of the state rather than as persons to be developed to be themselves. Japanese education has remained far ahead of the rest of the non-white world, much of it under colonial rule until after World War II. In 1945 there was, throughout most of Asia, the Middle East and Latin America, only a sprinkling of colleges and schools in which the elite received a Western-type education - from Westerners, and in Western languages. Indian children recited Shakespeare, African children studied the fertilisation of the chestnut tree, which does not grow on their continent. Eighty to eighty-five per cent of African, Arabs, Chinese and Indians, and forty-five per cent of the Latin Americans, were still illiterate.

The problems of language and script compound the problems of education. There are some 3-5,000 languages in the world today (see Chapter 2). In order to gain a "modern" education, a person may have to master two languages in addition to his mother tongue; the national language used in secondary education, administration and the law courts - for example, Spanish in most of South America, Swahili in Tanzania, Hindi in India, Bahasa Indonesian in Indonesia; and finally a European language. And each of these languages may have a different script. Kemal Ataturk, the Turkish reformer of the 1920s and 1930s, outraged orthodox Islamic feelings by ordering that the Turkish language should henceforth be written in the Roman instead of the Arabic alphabet, the sacred alphabet of the *Koran*. The Chinese Communists have considered the Romanisation of their ideograms, but have so far only simplified them - even this has cut them off from their literary heritage and from the writings of overseas Chinese, and enclosed them in a "closed-circuit Communist culture". This points to another vast problem, that of translating the huge flood of Western literature, much of it concerned with science, technology, psychology, economics, politics, sociology and other matters which are now of vital import to educated people everywhere. (An Egyptian scholar told me in 1992 that very little of the vast body of modern literature has yet been translated into Arabic; educated Egyptians read modern subjects in English or French). English is now the language of the world elite, the language used at international conferences, particularly scientific conferences, and of most scientific and technological literature. But it is spoken by only ten per cent of the world's population. The question of developing a world language will be discussed in Chapter 18.

Since 1945 the developing countries have given a very high priority to the quantitative expansion of education: gross enrolments of school children more than doubled between 1955 and 1975 - although this expansion has only just kept ahead of population growth. As regards content, the idea of making education "functional", relevant to the practical needs of development, is spreading. Adult education is expanding: in 1970 42 per cent of the adults in the developing countries were literate; by 1992 the figure had risen to 69 per cent, and 80 per cent of children aged 15 to 19 were at school (8). The major success stories are those of China, Cuba and Nicaragua. In China, by the early seventies almost all children were in school, and most adults had become literate on the basis of the simplified characters. In Cuba and Nicaragua adult literacy was achieved in one year's crash campaign, carried out in 1961 and 1980 respectively. The World Conference on Education for All, held in Thailand in 1990, set the goal to provide primary education for the 100 million children in the world with no access to schooling, and basic education for all illiterate adults by the year 2000. The first of these goals is estimated to cost $40-50 billion over the decade of the 1990s - from a world which is spending in 1994, an estimated $767 billion on arms (9).

The development of mass media since 1945 offers a new means of mass education. The range of a traditional peasant's consciousness of the world was normally restricted to his village or market town. Today the village radio, the old second hand TV in the coffee shop, the Western advertisements, the travelling movies (India has the second largest movie industry in the world) are taking the peasant's mind to the four corners of the earth, and showing him ways of life beyond the wildest ken of his ancestors. Future technological development may greatly accelerate the spread of education. India has pioneered in launching a communications satellite which beams down educational programmes on a nation-wide basis. Such developments may do much to promote international co-operation, for in areas like East and West Africa, the Middle East and Central America, satellite programmes will only make sense on a regional basis.

And so, for the first time in history, the whole population of the world is becoming educated. This tremendous process is producing an inevitable turmoil. Modern education has three significant characteristics. The first is the emphasis on science. Every modern state must encourage scientific education, for without scientific knowledge it cannot establish decent standards of living. The study of science inculcates certain qualities - objectivity, initiative, curiosity and universality - which are incompatible with dogmatism, authoritarianism and repression of free enquiry. Hitler and Mussolini knew that their grip on the psyches of their subjects depended on playing down serious education in rational thought and on whipping up the base emotions. "We are barbarians . . . We shall rejuvenate the world!" screamed Hitler's Propaganda Minister. "We need to give

221

our youth the sense of virility, of power and conquest," cried Mussolini. The Fascist dictators had to go to war to keep up this emotional momentum. The Communist regimes of Eastern Europe, however, have transformed the masses of credulous, illiterate peasants into a large, well-educated science-oriented bourgeoisie - thereby pointing a dagger at the dogmatism built into their system.

The second is the use of education to raise the "consciousness" of the masses in the developing countries, for social transformation cannot be satisfactorily imposed from above. This has been well understood by Mao, Castro, Che Guevara, the radical clergy in Latin America, Gandhi, President Julius Nyerere of Tanzania and other far-sighted leaders of the new countries.

The third is the development of government by the "brainy". In traditional societies, power and privilege were inherited. In modern societies, where caste has given way to class, "Social Darwinism" has tended to award power to those who are ambitious, aggressive and wealthy. But in Western Europe a century of mass public education, including the construction of a ladder whereby able children of any background can ascend at the state's expense to the highest levels, together with stringent laws about the financing of elections, have produced the new phenomenon: "meritocracy". Thus the world may be beginning to put into practice, on a democratic basic, Plato's concept of government by the wise, although, since the brainy are not necessarily the good, a leap into another dimension of consciousness will have to take place before this concept is really established.

Civil Rights

In all countries of the Western world civil rights are now well protected by secular constitutional and legal systems. The only one whose implementation is weak is the right to reformatory punishment - in general prisoners are still treated as individuals to be locked up, rather than as persons to be understood and helped for the sake of the contribution which they can make to society although this attitude is developing.

Communist countries drew up legal codes which, on paper, safeguarded the main personal freedoms and provided for fair trials.

But Communist ideology produced four main differences from the Western democracies. First, *economic actions* which in the Western world would not be considered criminal, such as slacking at work, were crimes against the state.

Second, the primary aim of the courts was to reform rather than to deter - this is in accordance with Article 10 of the United Nations' Covenant of the Civil and Political Rights - and the Courts therefore take or took into account the defendant's whole personality, background and moral attitude. The Communist legal system has forced into the open one of Marxism's most glaring weaknesses. According to Marxist theology, when capitalism has been eliminated, crime should die away. The fact that in the more advanced Communist societies - in the USSR and East Europe before 1989 and in China - crime is on the increase demonstrates the failure of Communism to produce the "new man". Yet the attempt to consider the criminal or litigant "in the round" in the context of his relationship with and duties to the community, is, we suggest, in line with the trends of the future.

Third, in Communist countries all non-political groups, from trade unions to dancing classes, have hitherto been organised by the state within the context of Marxist ideology. The only autonomous groups hitherto permitted have been the churches, and they were strictly controlled by the state (see Chapter 16). Now, Mikhail Gorbachev's new policy of *glasnost* - "openness" - is opening the door to the emergence of private groups inside the state. The importance of this development cannot be over-estimated.

Fourth, Communist dictatorships, like all dictatorships, have maintained themselves in power through the apparatus of the "police state". Crimes against the state, ranging from petty economic crimes to criticisms of government policy or attacks on government institutions, are or were dealt with by special courts and arbitrary procedures outside "the due process of law".

The indigenous cultures of non Muslim Asia and Africa have had little *theological* difficulty in adjusting to modern legal ideas. A devout Hindu, for instance, can give his allegiance to a legal system which abolishes traditional Hindu personal law and still base his life on the ethical and metaphysical teachings of the *Upanishads* and the *Bhagavad Gita,* while fully accepting what an Indian writer has described as: "the imposing and truly magnificent legal structure of British law, under which [the] people of India have lived during the last 100 years", in particular, the British principle of equality before the law. Buddhism finds in modern civil rights an affirmation of its ancient principle of personal equality and responsibility and universal brotherhood. Taoist and African concepts of universal cosmic harmony can be regard as complementary to the concepts of Western individualism. Very different, however, is the situation of the devout Muslim. He cannot, theologically speaking, accept some of the teachings of the *Koran* and reject others. The Prophet's Revelation is regarded as final and complete for all time and all contingencies. Alien legal codes which violate Koranic law are therefore profoundly sacrilegious. The same attitude is held by the Orthodox Jewish Rabbis who at present dominate the religious establishment of Israel.

All over the developing world, traditional law is being "modernised" and Western legal systems are being introduced. Japan, for instance, has based its modern legal code, completed in 1899, on those of France and Germany, and almost all ex-colonial countries have adopted the legal code of their former rulers. In the spheres of criminal and commercial law these Western systems are largely concerned with the kind of modern problem which traditional law never had to face: problems of mass production, trade, ownership of capital equipment, strikes, immigration and emigration, etc. In the sphere of personal law, which the colonial rulers had generally left alone, a traumatic clash between the traditional and modern arises. Here modern individualism confronts the ancient sense of group identity at its most sensitive point.

In non-Muslim Asia and Africa, personal law is being modernised in accordance with the principles of Human Rights. India, for instance, has affirmed that it is a secular state. Dowries, polygamy, child marriage and caste discrimination are legally forbidden, and provision has been made for modern-style civil marriage, divorce, equal rights of inheritance for women, and so on. But the 90 million Muslims in Indian (15 per cent of the population) are allowed to practise Muslim personal law - though a polygamous Muslim cannot hold a government or civil service post.

All Muslim countries, except Saudi Arabia, have in the twentieth century adopted Western secular codes of criminal and commercial law. But in the sphere of personal law, only Turkey has completely abolished the *Shari'a*, adopting the Swiss code in 1926. Mustapha Kemal, Ataturk the great reformer who ruled Turkey from 1923-38, prohibited polygamy, instituted civil marriage and divorce, and legalised equal rights for women in education, entry into the professions and ownership of property. The wearing of the veil by women was prohibited. All these new codes were to be administered by secular judges - thrusting the *Ulama* out of the legal life. These are blows directed at the very heart of the Koranic social ethic. At the other end of the scale Saudi Arabia has continued to base its whole policy on the Koranic law, and Iran is doing likewise since the Revolution of 1979. Adulterers and adulteresses are publicly executed; thieves have their hands chopped off in the market place; women remain secluded and veiled; and the oil-rich princes who rule the land have large harems. Since 1979 Pakistan has reintroduced Koranic personal law and thrust women back into the home and the black shroud. Other Islamic states have produced statute law, administered in secular courts, which apply a blend of traditional and modern principles in the sphere of personal law. In Syria and Tunisia, for example, laws passed in the fifties effectively prohibit polygamy by laying down stringent rules about a man's ability to support more than one wife, and by giving legal content to the Koranic injunction that all wives should be treated with complete impartiality. The Koranic prohibition of usury has been reinterpreted in such a way as to permit capitalism to flourish.

African customary law is a flexible system. Its role is to decide what is "right", and in the African context this is whatever will assure the cohesion of the group. There is no question of ensuring respect for private rights, or of attributing to each his "just due". Customary justice is thus essentially conciliation. But the Western colonial rulers introduced the concept of personal rights, which, apart from any sense of their "rightness", were the necessary basis for economic and social development. When the African countries gained their independence in the early 1960s, they retained the criminal and commercial codes of their European rulers. They are trying to complement these codes by reforming and consolidating their customary law, which varies from tribe to tribe. If its great assets - its fluidity, adaptability and conciliatory nature - and the values on which it is based - the sense of community, respect for the aged, absence of class antagonisms, and the habit of talking and talking until all are in agreement - can be combined with the basic modern ingredient of personal freedom, African law may provide a model for the future.

Conclusion

The thrust towards the implementation of all three kinds of Human Rights is surely irreversible. This thrust is liberating human energy and creativity on as mighty a scale as the splitting of the atom has liberated physical energy. "People, human beings with all their creative diversity, are the making of history", writes Gorbachev. And since Human Rights are intrinsically the same everywhere, it is a thrust towards a universal society of persons, united by that which is the essence of personhood, love. Inevitably the sudden breakdown of the rigid attitudes of past ages and the hubris and greed generated by modern science and technology are producing chaotic and negative reactions. Inevitably the different modes, stages and concepts of implementing Human Rights are producing confusion. Millions see the groups of the past collapsing and have no vision of the groups of the future; they take refuge in various forms of rage, escapism, fantasy and fundamentalism. Millions exploit the psychological vacuum to give rein to their base instincts. But modern psychology claims that the maturation of a person cannot take place until the dark forces repressed in the "unconscious" psyche have been dredged up into the consciousness and confronted (see Chapter 15). The peculiar anguish of the 20th century may represent the collective confrontation of the emotional murk of the ages. What Wordsworth wrote of the French Revolution seems even more relevant to the 20th century scene:

But a terrific reservoir of guilt
And ignorance filled up from age to age,
That could no longer hold its loathsome charge,
But burst and spread its deluge through the land.

But out of this turmoil and confusion a wonderful pattern is emerging. At the spiritual level, the models which we have considered are complementary! The Western system, having liberated the individual, must now develop community - as it is doing, to some extent in Western Europe. The Communist system, having established the framework of community, must liberate the individual. And the developing countries, recently appearing on the modern scene, may in the next century combine the best of East and West, learning from their experience. There is one vital factor which may enable them to achieve this: that they are still close in their psyches to the great currents of spiritual energy which infused their ancient religious traditions. They may, for good reason, cease to be religious, but they remain at heart profoundly spiritual; and this energy, even though partially destroyed by the materialism and cynicism of the West, will surely mould their political, economic and social institutions in the 21st century.

We will explore the spiritual impulse to promote Human Rights in Chapter 16.

Chapter 15

THE ERUPTION OF THE IMAGINATION:
PSYCHOLOGY, FEMINISM AND ART.

W E suggested in Chapter 10 that science as it developed in Western Europe in the 17th, 18th and 19th centuries tended to exalt rational knowing at the expense of visionary imagination, and that this ended up in "reducing" both nature and man to mechanisms.

The modern climate of thought has come to be dominated by scientific rationalism, affecting every sphere of activity, political, economic, social and theological, except art (see below), and pushing scientific discovery and technical development to the point of giving man the power to destroy or transform the whole world of nature. But if the universe *is* a cosmos, a harmoniously ordered living organism, it abhors imbalance. If there is too much emphasis on *Yang, Yin* will reassert itself. And so in the modern world the repressed imaginative faculties are exploding into the scientific atmosphere like volcanoes of psychic energy. The purpose of this chapter is to discuss three major forms which this eruption is taking, in order that we may consider whether a new level of consciousness is emerging in which reason and imagination will be harmoniously blended.

Psychology:
The Exploration of the Irrational and the Superrational

In the 19th century "psychology" emerged as a scientific study of the mind, dominated, like all other modern scientific studies, by mechanistic thinking, "reducing" it to what the writer Arthur Koestler called "ratomorphism" - dealing with persons in the terms of the chemistry of rats' brains. While this academic discipline has produced impressive results in terms of knowledge about how the physical brain works and ability to treat mental diseases which have a chemical basis (such as schizophrenia and manic-depression), it is in fact just one more component of the scientific world picture. In the 20th century, however, another kind of psychology has emerged, depth psychology, the probing into the "irrational" contents of the "unconscious" sphere of the psyche. This was initiated, as the world knows, by Sigmund Freud (1856 - 1939).

In the last half century depth psychology has begun subtly to transform the modern climate of thought. Its fundamental achievement has been to assert the existence of what Freud called the "unconscious" sphere of the psyche, from which erupt non-rational forces. This assertion is of profound significance in two ways. First, it restores validity to the realm of the imagination - for the "unconscious" expresses itself often in imaginings, dreams and visions. And secondly, it impels modern man to confront the neurotic and demonic forces within his own nature - the concept of the "repressions" in the "unconscious" can be used as a secular term for "sin". By combining the rational consciousness with the irrational unconsciousness the concept of natural goodness - the basis, we have suggested, for the whole structure of modern liberal and humanistic thought - is confronted by the phenomenom of natural badness. Humans must deal with their neuroses and their demonic urges if they are to build a society based on liberty, equality and fraternity. External circumstances certainly have a profound effect on man; but he cannot transform them, nor they him, unless he simultaneously transforms himself. To "know oneself", as the Greek Oracle of Delphi taught; to "withdraw one's projections"; to dissipate one's fantasies; to transmute anger or fear into compassion and calm: what a heroic task! Freud has generalised what the mystics have always known: that the true battle must be fought in the psyche. This involves the painful realisation that in hating one's enemy, one is really hating oneself; that in projecting adoration on to an idol figure, one is evading the challenge of independence. The recognition of the "unconscious" part of the psyche and of the irrational forces fermenting in it is thus the prerequisite of adulthood. Freud's theories are helping 20th century man to understand why the mighty attempts to implement Human Rights, described in the next chapter, have been accompanied by the eruption of neurotic and demonic forces on an unprecedented scale.

Freud was a philosophical materialist, asserting that all psychological phenomena have their origins in the physical instincts or the sense impressions. He therefore regarded the idea of "God" as a projection or a fantasy created by the childish need for security and certainty embodied in a father-figure; psychological maturity involved dispelling this fantasy. But this metaphysical materialism produces, surely, an unbalanced formulation of the nature of the psyche. For if the mystics' "intimations of immortality" and the artists' flashes of inspiration do not originate in repressed instinctual drives, where do they come from? If we cannot agree that Beethoven wrote the Ninth Symphony to "compensate" for the lack of a happy sex life, and that Jesus' statement that "I and My Father are one" represents the fantasy of an insecure adolescent, then we must postulate that the "unconscious" or "subconscious" is complemented by a "super-conscious" level of the psyche, the "soul" of perennial mystical metaphysics, whose emotional content is derived from "heaven".

This leads to a third point. It has been noted, for example by such psychologists as Roberto Assagioli, that depth psychology gives an inadequate place to the role of the *will*. Freudian psychologists seem to assume that if the complexes and repressions created by heredity or circumstances are brought into the conscious mind, the patient will be spontaneously liberated from the forces which inhibit his creativity. But will these forces just go away when confronted by the ego or conscious mind? Does not psychological liberation depend upon *transmuting* these forces? If so, the patient will have to direct his *will* to replace "lower" by "higher" emotions, to draw the contents of the "super-conscious" or soul into the conscious mind. This brings us back to the Platonic concept of archetypes, derived from heaven, as the source of super-rational self-expression, and of heaven itself as the source of that power from which the will derives its strength. From this point of view depth psychology provides a modern version of the psychological techniques developed by the Hindus, Buddhists, Sufis and other traditional mystical schools to prepare the ground for mystical experience (1). The Freudian theory of the "unconscious" either points the way towards such experience, or else demands to be turned, somehow, into a "real" science, based on verified data - the direction so far taken by the majority of Freud's followers.

Freud's famous disciple, Carl Gustav Jung (1875 - 1962), broke away from him on this issue. Jung found that the dreams of his patients often threw up symbols connected with the great traditional religions, such as the cross, the sun and the child. He made a life-long study of comparative religion, and particularly of religious symbology. Applying the fruits of these studies to his practical experiences as a psychologist, he postulated a number of "archetypes", not divine forms like Plato's archetypes, but basic patterns of human behaviour, such as "the great mother"; the "wise old man"; the "animus" and the "anima" representing the masculine and feminine principles; the "shadow" - a different term for "sin". These archetypes, he said, were not related specifically to the physical urges - Freud tended to relate most subconscious motivation to sex - but stemmed from the "Collective Unconscious", a kind of reservoir of the unconscious experience of the human race from which the individual unconscious mind draws vitality and knowledge.

In contrast to Freud, Jung believed that man is a spiritual being inhabiting a spiritual universe. But like Freud, his determination to adhere to the "scientific" mode of enquiry prevented him from firmly grounding his teachings in the affirmation that the spiritual universe is *objectively* real. While he used the Platonic term "archetype", he did not give it the full Platonic meaning - that of perfect forms and patterns of behaviour in the *objective* transcendental world of eternal perfection. Like Freud, he regarded psychological experience in essentially *subjective* terms; he internalised the archetypes. What the mystic would interpret as a vision of objective reality would be explained by a Freudian psychologist as a manifestation of unconscious material, and by a Jungian as some residue or emanation of the archetypal material in the "Collective Unconscious". This subjectivisation of unconscious experience means that values remain as relative to the Jungian as to the Freudian. There are no clear-cut transcendental terms of reference; and both Freudians and Jungians therefore seem to evade the central questions of redemption and transformation. Christianity asserts that redemption is achieved through love; and love demands an "other". To give a simple example: I dream that I meet my late father, whose ideas, when he was alive, were the original inspiration of this book. In my dream I see a piece of paper in his handwriting. Does this mean that I have objectively contacted the personality of my father, or that I am afflicted with a childish longing for a father-figure? The first explanation provides for one *person* loving and helping another; the second tells me to grow up, but leaves me lonely, brooding on the immature state of my psyche. The first provides for the transformation of the lower nature by help "from above"; the second talks only of coming to terms with it. In the final analysis, therefore, the forces which motivate the will must be drawn into the psyche from a source outside as well as inside it.

Feminism

The attitude to women in traditional societies was described in Chapter 5. The following account from Morocco in 1976 shows that despite the Declarations and Covenants of Human Rights, despite the rapid spread of modern ideas throughout the world, it is still deeply entrenched.

"A respectable Moroccan townswoman, outside the educated classes (and only 8 per cent of Moroccan girls go even to primary school) never leaves her home except for a weekly purifying bath at the Hamman, and a male-escorted visit perhaps monthly to relatives, in each case heavily chaperoned, and swathed from head to foot in jallaba and veil. It is immoral for her to figure in any way in the public sphere, defined according to the severity or sanctity of fathers, husbands and brothers as work, public entertainment, education, contact with men of any sort beyond the closest degree of relationship, and, remarkably commonly even contacts with women neighbours. She will rarely talk to or see her husband - because men who spend too much time with families or women are ridiculous in traditional townships. They spend their time with their male friends at their business places (semi-clubs) and cafés, where women are forbidden" (2).

How do these Moroccan men sitting out in the pavement café react as they see young male and female Western tourists pass by, dressed alike in brightly coloured short pants and sleeveless shirts, their strong bare legs gleaming in the sun, their backs laden with large packs, chatting and laughing in a companionable way? When I was in India staying in the foothills of the Himalayas in 1973 I fell into conversation on the hillside with a merchant from the town of Amritsar who was on holiday with his family. A lady in a green *sari* appeared out of the morning mist. "Here is my wife", he said, "and she regards me as a god". He then invited me to share their picnic breakfast!

Perhaps womens' liberation is the most important of all the fundamental transformations which are occurring today. Two completely new things are happening to the man-woman relationship. First, women are, for the first time in history, associating with men as colleagues and friends - in every profession, in every activity, even in the armed forces and the astronaut's space-craft. At some deep level of this non-possessive, non-dominant, non-sexual, non-service relationship with women is a profound challenge to the male psyche. A great many important men are emotional adolescents. This new kind of relationship with women is helping them to grow up. And it is having a corresponding effect on women, ridding them of age-old attitudes of dependence and low self-esteem.

In the process of working out this new relationship women may, of course, become domineering (for example, Margaret Thatcher, Britain's first woman Prime Minister from 1979 - 89) and men resentful. When Lady Astor, the first women to become a member of the British House of Commons in 1919, asked young Winston Churchill, in whose social circle she moved, why he never spoke to her in the House, he is said to have replied: "The presence of women in the House of Commons makes me feel as if I were in my bath, and a woman came in, and I had no sponge". It is significant that the Saudi Arabian Government will not allow women to drive cars - an activity which develops threatening qualities of judgement, self-control and initiative.

The second development is that in the modern society, for the first time in history, men and women are expected to "marry for love". When the basis of the relationship was a legal contract, there were dire penalties for breaking it (see Chapter 5). But the new concept means that if love is lacking, one or both partners are felt to have a "right" to break the contract, to separate or divorce and find someone else whom they feel they can love. "Is it a sacrament to tie people up to bite and hate each other?" asked Jawahareal Nehru, India's first Prime Minster, when he introduced India's first secular divorce law in the early fifties. What is "love"? It is not just sexual attraction, not just congenial companionship, but the blending of souls. "They see through each other's eyes". We have already quoted in Chapter 5 Shakespeare's cryptic poem *The Phoenix and the Turtle,* which points to the archetype of this relationship which is at the heart of modern society:

"So they loved, as love in twain
Had the essence but in one;
Two distincts, division none:
Number there in love was slain" . . .

The same theme underlies the apparently fairy-tale story of Mozart's *Magic Flute*. All the heart-aches, the divorces, the sexual violence, the domestic tensions of today represent the turmoil of one of the most powerful developments of modernity. The biological family is being transformed into the spiritual companionship of the sexes. The effect of this transformation on the children of the future is incalculable. The introduction of "family planning", a concept hitherto generally unthought of, is an important adjunct to marrying for love. Children are no longer regarded as the possessions of their parents, to help them in the field or workshop, to care for them in old age, to carry on the ancestral rites. Loving parents are conceiving children in order to enrich the world with new personalities. In 1990 a remarkable document of 54 articles was signed by 61 countries at the United Nations, "The Convention on the Rights of the Child", described as a "Magna Carta" for children. The Convention, which took ten years to draw up, "breaks new ground with [its] holistic approach, which acknowledges that though a child may be adequately nourished (a social right), the right to develop fully is not adequately protected unless the child is also educated (a social and cultural right), allowed to participate in culture and religion (a cultural right), and shielded from such things as arbitrary detention (a civil right) and exploitation at work (a social and economic right). The Convention also recognises the child as an individual, with needs that evolve with age and maturity. Accordingly, it goes beyond existing treaties by seeking to balance the rights of the child with the rights and duties of the parents or others who have responsibility for child survival, development and protection, by giving the child the right to participate in decisions affecting both the present and future" (3).

This entirely new attitude to children is being reinforced by the modern psychologists, who normally regard childhood experience as the key to the problems and potentialities of the adult.

Child development therefore complements psychological development as a key component of "women's' liberation". "If ever the world sees a time when women shall come together purely and simply for the benefit and good of mankind it will be a power such as the world has never known", wrote the Victorian writer Matthew Arnold.

Modern Art

The modern situation has inevitably had an explosive effect upon art. We have seen that art was, as it were, the psychic garment which enfolded the inhabitants of a particular society, embodying its religious cult, its values and ideals. The experience of the Greek temple and its statues was built into the Greek citizen's psyche; the medieval cathedral directed knight and serf to heaven; the Friday service in the Muslim mosque turned the thoughts of all worshippers towards the holy city of Mecca. Traditional artifacts were intentionally expressions of celestial archetypes, and this had a timeless quality. They were standardised; they were largely the collective work of groups; and their ethos was expressed at every level of life, from the vast religious buildings to the smallest articles of clothes or pottery. The great body of traditional art irradiates the psyche of the human race.

Within the past hundred years the context of artistic expression has been transformed in an unprecedented way. First, the concept of Human Rights is eroding the foundations of the traditional public cults; everyone is free to follow any or no cult; so there is no longer a conscious need for collective artistic religious expression. The great traditional schools of art have collapsed - or are collapsing. The artist is expected to follow his personal inspiration in any direction, spiritual or secular, which appeals to him, regardless of the ethos of society. In subject matter, in style, in materials used, all is open. A picture of a can of Campbell's soup is as acceptable as a marvellous portrait. Acid rock music which splits the eardrums and jangles the nerves is as acceptable as the ethereal music of Holst or Tippett. The collapse of the collective art systems has inevitably involved the collapse of the collective value systems.

A profoundly important side effect of the application of Human Rights to art is that, in a sense, "we are now all artists". Modern educational philosophy affirms that children are naturally endowed with some artistic creativity, and that basic education should include opportunities for artistic expression - in painting, music, singing, dancing, drama, poetry writing, and so on. Failure to draw out this potential will inhibit the balanced development of the personality. And in modernised societies there are now multifarious opportunities for any adult to become an artist, part-time or full-time, in clubs. Modern science is making it possible for the ordinary man and woman to have the leisure and the material conditions to be an amateur artist. The result is an incredible outburst of creativity. I myself have nine pictures in my three-room apartment, all painted by friends who are not professional artists.

Secondly, photography (invented in England at the end of the 19th century), and its offshoots, the cinema, television and radio, have liberated art from the need to act as a recorder, through the depicting of people, scenes and events. The artist's function now is to look inwards, and to interpret the outer world in the light of the inner or non-physical world - however this itself may be interpreted (see below). This function was present in all traditional art, and the cult provided the artist with clear guidelines. But the modern artist, in looking inward, has no clear guide lines! He must decide for himself whether "looking inwards" involves seeking God, and if so, in what forms and through what symbols. For he has available to him, not only the forms and symbols of his own traditional cult - Christian, Islamic, Hindu, African, etc, - but those of all cults and creeds which now exist anywhere in the world, and in addition, many of those which have existed anywhere in ages past. Modern photography, modern archaeology and modern communications generally have transformed the artist's field of vision in terms of the inner as well as of the outer worlds. Oriental art, in particular, has linked the artist with new concepts and techniques of meditation and introspection.

This means that, thirdly, modern art is becoming universal. To quote Gaston Diehl, a French art critic: "By exploring his own essence, the artist discovers . . . the manifold riches and virtualities [sic] of the interior life - its complexity, the infinite possibility of its secret impulses and dreams. He thus arrives at the true universality of the living being, by getting rid, once and for all, of the impediments raised up in the past by differences of race, creed or milieu. And thus he makes himself interpreter of human solidarity on the world scale, and this directs it, in turn, towards the idea of a common aesthetic" (4). Sir Herbert Read, the British art critic, makes the same point when he says that, to the Dutch painter Mondrian (1872 - 1944) "art becomes an intuitive means, as exact as mathematics, for representing the fundamental characteristics of the cosmos". "Presumptuous is the artist who does not follow his road through to the end. But chosen are those artists who penetrate to the region of that secret place where primeval power nurtures all evolution", wrote the German artist Paul Klee (1879 - 1940).

But the universe is not simply the planet, nor the cosmos of some 5,000 "fixed stars" discerned by the ancients with the naked eye. "Our epoch has been fated to be bewildered by revelations of immensities of time and space which reason can no longer grasp", writes Gaston Diehl (5). How is the artist to relate his art to the universe of electrons and galaxies, of evolution and relativity and indeterminacy? The pre-occupation of modern artists with theories of light and colour is relevant.

Fourthly, in the modern age, the age of science, the rational faculty is dominant. "Truth" is sought through the process of experiment, measurement, deduction and logic, and much scientific truth has exploded the intuitive "truths" affirmed by the ancients. Nevertheless, humans *are* imaginative as well as rational, and it is through the imagination that qualities such as good and evil, beauty and ugliness, are apprehended. As the traditional public cults collapse, values and ethics have become a personal matter, curbed only by secular, man-made law unrelated to "the Word of God" - or of "the gods". In this critical situation - the most critical in human history - the very survival of the human race depends upon the cultivation of what one might call the "higher imagination" in individuals, so that goodness, beauty and love complement scientific invention and power. Otherwise greed, cruelty and fear may well impel humankind to use nuclear weapons and other technological monstrosities to destroy the world.

At this point modern art and psychology form a crucial partnership. The dark forces which the followers of Freud, Jung and other pioneers of psychology dredge up in "analysis" of their neurotic patients are depicted by many modern artists in their works. Perhaps the most famous of all these works is Picasso's picture *Guernica*, painted in

237

white-hot passion after the Nazis had bombed the defenceless little Basque town of Guernica in Spain on April 28th 1937 as a test of their *Blitzkrieg* tactics. *Guernica* confronts modern man with the need to deal with the violence in his subconscious: a copy of this great picture should hang in the office of every military man who is coolly playing with his colleagues "war games", which are trying to tell his subconscious mind that war is "nothing but" a game.

Since the subconscious is by definition irrational, the psychologists and the artists can perform their mighty task of forcing it up into consciousness without themselves needing to affirm any supra-rational ideals. Freud and Picasso were atheists. But the conscious mind, having confronted the irrational forces, must then acquire the energy to transmute them - to substitute a kindly state of mind for a mind haunted by irrational phobias. Divine power may be needed after all. We are therefore beginning to see both modern art and modern psychology moving into the sphere of the super-conscious: the evocation of the power of the soul, to tune into the celestial archetypes in the spiritual universe, the reservoirs of divine energies. The partnership of art and psychology is thus leading the world towards a universal spirituality which is the essential complement to the universality of science, and in this partnership the feminine plays a crucial integrating role.

Chapter 16

THE EMERGING GLOBAL SPIRITUALITY

Introduction

IN the 20th century a global ethic is emerging, an ethic based on the philosophy of Human Rights - the right of everyone to the conditions for "the full development of the human personality". (see especially articles 25 and 26 of the United Nations Universal Declaration of Human Rights). And this implies, as we said in the Foreword, "Community", relationships based on love.

In Chapter 3 we showed how the traditional religions of the world produced ethical codes, often full of contradictions: containing insights which pointed to the full development of the person, but also pronouncements which encouraged restriction of that development by strict rules controlling human behaviour according to class, caste, function, sex and so on. These ethical codes were supported and enforced by grim sanctions - excommunication, physical punishment, including torture and execution, and the threat of eternal Hell after death.

Today the problem of "ethics" - what is "right or wrong" - emerges into a completely new climate of thought and action. Every modernised society is becoming secular, ending the connection between government and religion, providing legally for religious toleration, making the practice and choice of religion a personal matter. The development of scientific thinking has undermined the revealed authority of traditional ethics. It is embodied for all to see in the incredible achievements of modern technology - it would not be possible to make a list of the inventions of the last 200 years to complement the paragraph-long list of the inventions of 5,000 years in Chapter 10. Concepts of "right" and "wrong" are left to the individual conscience, qualified by secular laws made by secular governments, which can be altered at the will or whim of politicians and their electorates (see Chapter 14). Ethics has become essentially a subjective matter. The fear of Hell is being lifted off the human heart, and replaced by the personal responsibility to formulate one's own ethical principles and to live in accordance with them. The

239

importance of this development cannot be exaggerated. It is the key to the maturation of the human race. But it raises the fundamental question, posed in the Foreword: who is a person? Is he or she an immortal soul, inhabiting a divine universe, or "nothing but" a collection of physical atoms, charges of electricity? Is secularity the last word, or is it a phase leading into a new approach to spirituality which embraces science, which sheds the anachronisms of the traditional religions and reinforces all the ancient precepts which affirm the full development of the human personality in and through love?

There are many signs and symptoms today of religious, spiritual, scientific and social developments which support and develop the ethic of Human Rights.

The Ecumenical Movement

It will be recalled that although other religions have sects, none other has institutions comparable to the organised churches of Christianity. Today there are about 1.5 billion people in the world who are nominally Christians, including 585 million members of the Roman Catholic Church, members of the many Protestant Churches, and the rest members - or, under Communist regimes, ex-members - of the Greek and Russian Orthodox Churches. Now in the ecumenical movement, these churches are beginning to draw together and to stretch out the hand of friendship to other religions. A most important step was taken when, at the Second Vatican Council of 1962-5, summoned by the saintly Pope John XXIII, the Roman Catholic Church finally withdrew the ancient charge of "decide" - killing God - against the Jews, and issued a "decree on Ecumenicism" admitting that the separation of the Christian Churches had involved "sin" on both sides. But the doctrine of Papal Infallibility in matters of faith and morals laid down in the First Vatican Council of 1870 was not revoked, and this made it impossible for the Roman Catholic Church to join the World Council of Churches, founded in 1948 as a "fellowship of Churches which confess the Lord Jesus Christ as God and Saviour according to the Scriptures". The World Council, whose headquarters are in Geneva, brings together some 200 Churches in 90 countries. The Russian, Ukrainian, Rumanian, Bulgarian and Polish Orthodox Churches joined it in 1961 with the official blessing of the Communist governments of their countries. The Christian Churches no longer fight each other - with certain lapses into traditionalism, as between Roman Catholic Croats and Orthodox Serbs, and Protestant and Catholic Irish; they talk to each other, and they work together for social causes. But dogma still prevents them from uniting.

Meanwhile there is a growing dialogue between the world's religions. The basis for this dialogue has been laid in the translation of the scriptures into different languages. The Christian Bible has been translated into more languages than any other book in the world. A benign aspect of 19th century colonialism was the discovery and translation of the texts of the Oriental scriptures by European scholars. These translations flooded into Western Europe and the USA, producing enormous excitement in the minds of influential poets and philosophers such as Goethe, Emerson, Thoreau, Keyserling and Schopenhauer, who prophesied that "the influence of Sanskrit in our time will be no less profound than the renaissance of classical languages in the 15th century" (1). Sir Edwin Arnold's poem about the life of the Buddha, "The Light of Asia", first published in 1879, went through a hundred editions in the USA. A "Parliament of Religions" was held in Chicago in 1893, at which the first Hindu sage to visit the West appeared: Swami Vivekananda, the disciple of a great saint, Sri Ramakrishna (1836-86). "His fascinating face, his noble stature, and gorgeous apparel - red robe and great yellow turban - heightened the effect of this apparition from a legendary world", writes Romain Rolland, his French biographer. "As he pronounced the opening words: 'Sisters and brothers of America!' hundreds rose in their seats and applauded . . . He greeted the youngest of the nations in the name of the most ancient monastic order in the world - the Vedic order of Sannyasins (pilgrims). He presented Hinduism as the mother of religions . . . He quoted from sacred books: 'Whoever comes to Me, through whatever form, I reach him'. 'All men are struggling through paths which in the end lead to Me'. Each of the other orators had spoken of *his* God, the God of *his* sect. He spoke of all their Gods, and embraced them all in the Universal Being" (2). Since 1893 Hindu and Buddhist sages have flooded into the West, not preaching dogma but teaching the practice of meditation and Yoga, of how the ordinary person can develop his or her mind, heart and body himself. For example, in the 1980s I joined a class of elderly housewives in suburban England, many of them practising Christians, to perform with zest the exercises devised by the ancient Rishis (sages) of India 4,000 years ago. We met in the local Borough hall and were partly financed by the Borough Council! Oriental religion is providing the parched modern psyche with methods of cultivating awareness of moral values. At the second Parliament of Religions held in Chicago in 1993, 6,500 people of every possible religion were present, and another 4,000 had to be turned away. The Parliament produced a "Declaration Towards a Global Ethic", (Appendix II). "Hindu India, from the time of Vivekananda's appearance in Chicago, entered the arena of the world religions as a leader, not a pleader", remarks Professor Kraemer, a Dutch theologian. "The Indian world of today, in so far as it finds expression in representative (religious) writers and movements, sounds an unbroken note of victorious self-confidence" (3). The Buddhist sages, particularly those of Japanese Zen Buddhism, have followed in the footsteps of the Hindu Swamis, and since the mid 20th century Buddhism has been asserting itself as a world religion, equipped to meet the spiritual needs of all humankind. The Dalai Lama, Tibet's exiled Buddhist ruler, has said that the practice of loving kindness is ten times more efficacious for spiritual development than any other form of spiritual exercise. The example set by Mohandas Gandhi (1869-1948) in applying Hindu concepts of non-violence *(Karma yoga,* the yoga of action) and love *(ahimsa)* to political struggle has had world-wide repercussions (see below).

The Scientific Study of the Scriptures

Another activity which is laying the basis for global ecumenicism is the application of scientific methods to the study of the scriptures. In the 19th century Protestant scholars in Europe began to examine the authenticity, origin and meaning of the sacred biblical texts in a secular manner. At first there was a cry of outrage from the devout; to subject the words of divine revelation to critical scrutiny was felt to be sacrilege! Only in 1943 did the Vatican officially authorise Roman Catholic scholars to participate in this work. Today it is regarded as the essential basis for all Christian scholarship. And the scholars have found no hard, factual evidence for the actual existence of Abraham, Moses, Jesus or the four authors of the Gospels! Oriental scholars and Jewish Rabbis of the "Reformed" School of Judaism are similarly scrutinising their canon. Only Islamic theologians and "Orthodox" Jewish Rabbis have held back from such critical analysis. "To trace the sources and development of the religious ideas expounded in the *Koran*" is "a question not only meaningless but blasphemous in Muslim eyes", writes Professor Gibb, a British scholar of Islam (4). "The basic elements of Islam remain, for the most part, beyond intellectual challenge in the modern sense . . . There is no such thing as 'higher criticism' of the *Koran*", wrote the Education Editor of the New York Times in 1974 (5). There is, however, a modernist movement, largely led by lay scholars in such intellectual centres as Cairo, Beirut and Karachi. At present most Islamic modernists are on the defensive, either asserting that all the ideas of modernity are embedded in the *Koran,* or else rejecting modernity as Western decadence. Professor Gibb adds that "many modernists, finding the strains of double-mindedness too severe to be borne or the social cost of modernism to the individual too high, end up as ultra-orthodox bigots" (6). At the time of writing a Bangladeshi woman writer, Dr Taslima Nasrin, has had to flee for her life to Sweden for the crime, in the eyes of the Muslim religious leaders, of telling an Indian newspaper that the *Koran* should be "revised thoroughly". (It must be remembered that Western colonialism has had a traumatic impact on the Muslim psyche after centuries of successful Islamic conquest and conversion in the Middle Ages). The scientific scrutiny of the canon therefore presents a profound problem for the billion Muslims in the world. The billion and a half Christians have a problem also. John Hick, a British theologian, sums up the general attitude of Christian theologians. "The point they have mostly reached is a set of variations on the theme that whilst there is salvation within other religions, it is all to be seen as the work of Christ". But he adds that "the gradual facing of the teachings and practices of the other great religions (in the myriad studies and conferences which are taking place today) within the Churches may well bring about as big changes in our way of thinking as did the facing of the fact of biological evolution a century ago" (7).

The Rebirth of Myth

The general effect of the scientific scrutiny of the various scriptures has been to undermine the concept of canon (see Chapter 3). The modern-minded student of comparative religion cannot regard any particular religion as a uniquely divine revelation. This clears the ground for a new vision: to regard the Founders of the various religions as archetypal figures, models, Avatars in Hinduism, incarnations of the celestial Buddha in Buddhism, the "Cosmic Christ" (a concept first put forward by St Paul) to some modern Christians. Everyone is free to draw inspiration from one or more of these archetypes to whom he or she feels attuned. Theology gives way to mysticism; myth is restored to its throne as consisting of great stories setting forth archetypal truths - the search for "the Promised Land"; redemption of evil by love and suffering for others; all-embracing compassion for all living things; the *jihad* or Holy War of Islam as the battle in the psyche between good and evil impulses. For the first time in history a vast reservoir of myths and symbols is being drawn from all the ancient traditions and made available to everybody. Is this reservoir nothing but a collection of subjective fantasies, a palliative for the psychological aridity of modern life, a hotch-potch of themes for the modern artist? Or does it embody spiritual forces which, in Plato's sense, are objectively real? If so, the myths possess in themselves the power to redeem and transform, and he or she who draws them into his soul becomes a redeemer and a transformer. The new mythology is thus not only bringing all the religions together; it is bringing them into their own. It is opening up the channels through which man can gain personal experience of the divine, and then draw on the power of the divine to change the world.

Evolution as a Spiritual Process

Charles Darwin (1809-82) and his successors have proved beyond all doubt the fact of biological evolution from simple to complex organisms. No modern person can accept the literal statements in the Bible and the *Koran* that God created all the natural phenomena in the world in eight days. Less fully proven is the hypothesis that the mechanism of

244

the evolutionary process is that of "natural selection" by blind chance. Darwin admitted that the thought of the eye deeply disturbed him. How could such a complex and purposeful organ develop by blind chance? Aristotle's teleological philosophy - that every organism has its ultimate form inherent in itself - the oak in the acorn, the full grown man or woman in the foetus - cannot be disproved by modern science. (The fact that through genetic engineering the *telos* or end can be changed indicates that there is an end!). Two outstanding thinkers of the West and the East - the French Jesuit priest-palaeontologist Pierre Teilhard de Chardin (1881-1953) and the Hindu sage Sri Aurobindo (1872-1950) have injected the concept of evolution into modern theology. Their essential achievement has been to integrate into the spiritual vision of the universe the concepts of change, development and evolution which are also implicit in the philosophy of Human Rights, and to affirm that the teleological thrust from below is the complement to the pull from above - in Teilhard's terms, from the "Omega Point", in Aurobindo's terms, the "Supreme Consciousness" - that is, in Plato's terms, the celestial Archetypes or Forms which emanate from God. This thinking opens the door to the spiritualisation of the natural world. Through changing the level of their own consciousness humans can "earth" the archetypes (8, 9).

Christianity in Action to Change the World

The great Papal Encyclicals
From 1891 onwards *(Rerum Novarum)*, the Popes have outlined a new social and economic order for the non-Communist world in a series of great Encyclicals. First, they have condemned the capitalist economic regimes as "hard, cruel and relentless in a ghastly measure" *(Quadragesimo Anno,*1931) and asserted that "private property is not an absolute and unconditional right. No one is justified in keeping for his exclusive use what he does not need, when others lack necessities" *(Populorium Progressio,*1967). Expropriation of landed estates is justified in certain circumstances; profit and free competition as key motives for economic enterprise are condemned; planning for development is advocated; social objectives are asserted to be as important as economic growth; basic resources should be pooled; the

"superfluous wealth of the rich countries should be placed at the service of the poor countries" by the establishment of a World Fund, "to be made up in part of money spent on arms", for "every exhausting arms race becomes an intolerable scandal". This means that there must be a world-wide authority capable of exerting authority on the judicial and political plane" - a world government! *(Populorium Progressio)*.

Secondly, the concept of partnership between employees and workers is emphasised; wage earners should participate in ownership, management and profit-sharing; this led to the blessing by Pope John XXIII of the democratic state as the upholder of social order - that is, the West European welfare state, not yet accepted by most Americans *(Mater et Magistra,* 1961 and *Pacem in Terris,* 1963)-(see Chapter 14).

Thirdly, Pope Pius XI in 1931 developed the doctrine of subsidiarity: every task should be performed at its appropriate level, from the village council to global institutions. The nation state is but one level in the ladder. This concept has become incorporated in the philosophy of the European Community.

Fourthly, from 1961 onwards these Papal Encyclicals have reached out, not merely to Roman Catholics or Christians, but to all people everywhere. Pope John Paul II has linked "development" with "peace". "Beyond human and natural bonds", he declared, "there is discerned a new model of the human race which must ultimately inspire our solidarity. This supreme model of unity, which is a reflection of God, is what we Christians mean by communion" *(Sollicitado Socialis,* 1987).

The World Council of Churches has also jumped eagerly into the fray of social and political transformation. It has held many meetings, and issued many reports, on various aspects of the struggle for "a just, participatory and sustainable society". The fact that a growing proportion of its membership is drawn from the developing countries has added great impetus to this urge to promote social transformation.

All these Encyclicals, discussions and resolutions have given Christians their marching orders. A Christian who takes them to heart must perforce act to promote Human Rights, disarmament, the treatment of property as a trust, and the salvation of the natural world for all mankind. This new kind of Christian action demands a commitment to emulate Christ, who cared so deeply for the poor and the afflicted, rather than merely to believe in him as the pledge of personal salvation. How is this commitment being implemented?

Christianity in Action in the West

The fate of the world in the next 50 years hangs largely on the spiritualisation of consciousness in the modernised countries, which must take the lead in solving the problem. Can Christianity achieve this in its own heartland? So far, with one important exception, the Gandhi-inspired Civil Rights movement of Martin Luther King and his followers in the USA, the practical achievements of the Christian Churches in the Western countries have been slight. They have as yet made no major thrust to secure disarmament, to distribute wealth, to halt environmental destruction, to insist on the implementation of the Human Rights in the "Christian" countries of Latin America and South Africa. (In South Africa itself the African Christian clergy there played an outstanding role in ending the system of *Apartheid*).

Western Christianity seems to be paralysed by the prevailing modern schizophrenia. The Herculean task of relating traditional theology to all the modern "disciplines" of the natural and social sciences has turned theologians into professional academics in the university information factories - sixty thousand religious books are published annually in the West. At the same time, an excessive emotionalism, perhaps the psychological counterpart of an excessive intellectualism, is inspiring such phenomena as the charismatic movement, the "underground church", and the evangelical crusades of religious demagogues. The fundamental reason seems to be that Christianity is itself involved in the turmoil of transformation. It has not yet, generally, understood the need to move from theology to mysticism.

Christianity in Action in Latin America

Latin America is the only major region in the developing world in which Christianity is the traditional public cult, and thus the only arena in which it can directly serve as the agent for the leap into modernity. This challenge to act in a revolutionary situation could be crucial for the transformation of Christianity as well as of Latin America.

Latin American politics are, in the second half of this century, sharply polarised between the "Left" and the "Right". Because the continent was colonised 200 years before the advent of the modern age, the "ruling class" is both feudal and alien: white Spanish and Portuguese landlords, in effect feudal barons, still wield virtual powers of life and death over peasants who in many countries are Indians speaking their ancient tongues. Latin America is rapidly becoming industrialised, urbanised and literate. But the modernisation process is occurring in an unhealthy way, gearing development to European and American markets and to the local upper class consumers, and often operated by foreign multinational corporations whose essential aim is to make profits for their foreign investors. The captains of industry are drawn from the feudal class; and so this class, with the support of the military, has essentially monopolised political power since the present countries gained independence from Spain and Portugal in the 19th century. Only in Mexico, Cuba and Nicaragua have there been radical social revolutions - and the Mexican Revolution of 1910 has long since lost the impetus to achieve a real redistribution of wealth. The middle class, the *bourgeoisie,* has developed as a satellite of the feudal class, rather than as its opponent, as in Europe. And so as education and modernisation spread, a revolutionary situation arises, because there is no solid ground on which moderate systems, such as those of European social democracy, can be built. Since 1945, and particularly since 1959 when Cuba became Communist and thus appeared to bring the Soviet menace to the USA's doorstep, American policy has tended to support the "Rightist" dictatorships or regimes with arms and aid in order to prevent the eruption of more "Cubas", even to the extent of "destabilising" an elected Marxist regime in Chile in 1973. To please the Americans, a facade of political democracy and civil rights may be erected; but the crucial economic reform on which a modern society must be based, the equitable distribution of land wealth, is evaded. In Brazil in 1992, there were 154 million people. Of these over 15 million were (and are) very rich and over 100 million very poor.

Since the mid 1970s economic recession and the debt crisis (see Chapter 18), combined with the population explosion, is widening the gulf between rich and poor. There is endemic violence on both sides: guerrillas, kidnappers, torturers, assassins and private armies abound.

The Roman Catholic Church was imported into Latin America by the Spanish and Portuguese conquerors as their moral police force.

This situation, combined with the physical distance from Europe, sealed the majority of the Church leaders off from the transforming currents of modern European thought. Vatican II was a total surprise, challenging them to assimilate in a few months the results of almost 80 years of involvement in modern ideas by the churches in Europe.

In the 60s and 70s the Latin American Church began to awaken to the realities of the Left-Right confrontation and social injustice in Latin America. Fanned by the liberating winds of thought blowing from Vaţican II and by the great Encyclicals, many clergy are beginning to feel that the only viable path for a priest who wishes to emulate Jesus is to join the forces of secular radicalism. The Church is thus trapped into the polarised situation of the secular Latin American world.

The Latin American Church's decisive commitment to action to transform society was made at the Second General Conference of 150 bishops from 24 countries held at Medellin in Colombia in 1968, and opened by Pope Paul VI. The Conference aligned the Church emphatically with the cause of those whose "misery . . . expresses itself as injustice which cries to heaven". It affirmed that the Christian gospel of love implies social justice and personal freedom, and condemned all "oppressors": feudal landlords, foreign and local capitalists and dictatorial rulers who practise "institutionalised violence" and conduct an arms race that "surpasses the limits of reason". It emphasised the importance of *conscientisation* - raising the level of the political and social awareness of the masses. It affirmed that the ignorance of illiterates is an "inhuman servitude", that education at all levels should be of a democratic nature, aimed at developing the student's potential, and that the mass media should be used for educational purposes. It condemned alike the capitalist and communist economic systems, both of which "militate against the dignity of the human person", and asserted that "all men are merely humble stewards of material goods". It advocated peasant ownership of the land combined with co-operatives, and the shifting of industry from the bloated towns to the countryside - measures which radically challenge the feudal landlords. It then proclaimed the vision of the emergence of a "new man". "We are on the threshold of a new epoch in the history of our continent. It appears to be a time full of zeal for full emancipation, of liberation from every form of servitude, of personal maturity and collective integration. In these signs we perceive the first indications of the painful birth of a new civilisation". This new civilisation will be communitarian, based on the active participation of persons in all levels of groups from the informal group celebrating the Eucharist in a private home - 80 per cent in the hands of lay people - to the nation and the continent, and by implication, the world. The Conference called on the church itself to set an example of "poverty". In so doing, it made a vital distinction. "Poverty, as a lack of goods of this world necessary to live worthily with men, is in itself evil". But "spiritual poverty is the attitude of opening up to God", and the person who practises this "values the things of this world" but "does not become attached to them". The Church should, like Christ, assume "poverty as a commitment, through which one assumes voluntarily and lovingly the conditions of the needy of this world in order to bear witness to the evil which it represents and to spiritual liberty in the fact of material goods". Finally, the Pope and the Bishops condemned the use of force and violence as a means of achieving the political, social and economic transformation for which they called. The Catholic Church proclaimed in Medellin the same message which Gandhi had proclaimed in India (see below).

In the Third General Conference of Latin American Bishops, held at Puebla in Mexico in 1979, Pope John Paul II and the Bishops developed the important concept that, as the Pope put it, "there is a social mortgage on all private property". This was explained in the Conference's document: "By the will of the Creator, worldly goods and riches are meant to serve the utility and progress of each and every human being and people. Thus each and every one enjoys a primary, fundamental and absolutely inviolable right to share in the use of these goods, in so far as that is necessary for the *worthy fulfilment of the human person.* All other gifts, including the right of property and free trade, are subordinate to that right".

The clarion call of Medellin and Puebla is being expressed in two ways. At the intellectual level Latin American theologians are formulating the "theology of liberation", substituting the word "liberation" for "development" as the key to the transformation of Latin America - and of the world. "Development" is associated in their minds with capitalist "neo-imperialism", with the "trade-and-aid" policies of the industrialised countries, which they regard as a new form of exploitation and domination. Here, therefore, they join hands with the Marxists: get rid of the oppressors and the capitalist system which impels them to oppress, and all with be well. But then, as religious men, they add that man must also be liberated from his own limitations, such as apathy and ignorance, from his own sin, if he is to become the new man who will make a new world. "Liberation" is linked with "salvation", and salvation with the spiritual evolution of the planet. The theology of liberation seems to be groping towards a philosophy of universal spiritual evolution. "Liberation", "salvation", the maturation of man in order that he may transform his environment, apply to the whole of humankind. As we tune into this theology traditional Roman Catholic attitudes of authoritarianism, paternalism and dogmatism fade into irrelevance. The new thinkers in the Latin American Church are pointing to the vision of universal ethical goals which is crucial to the emergence of the post-modern society.

The second fruit of the "spirit of Medellin" is the call to action. The clerical "progressives" believe that if the Church is to promote the Gospel, it must be fully involved in politics. They are therefore working in political parties, trade unions, peasant leagues and educational institutions to secure Human Rights for the poor and oppressed. All over Latin America they are forming "basic communities" which carry out social, political and spiritual activities - they establish basic health services, they agitate for land reform, they worship together. Their fundamental purpose is the consciousness-raising of the masses, and women are as fully involved as men. They draw spiritual inspiration from the medieval European mystics.

Mysticism and revolutionary action thus complement each other in this revolutionary movement. Some of these clergy find common cause with the Marxists. "As a priest I am not anti-Communist", said Father Camillo Torres of Colombia, who became a folk hero, "because although they may not know it, many of them are true Christians". Torres was expelled from the priesthood for his radical activities, joined the guerrillas, and was killed by the Colombian army in the jungle in 1966. Popes Paul VI and John Paul II, and such committed radicals as Archbishop Helder Camara of Recife in Brazil, exhorted the oppressed to abjure violence. But a number of the radical clergy have come to agree with Camillo Torres that the Christian revolutionary must be prepared to kill as well as be killed. In January 1981 ten Catholic institutions in El Salvador issued a statement saying that, after the murder during 1980 of some 10,000 people, including the liberal Archbishop Oscar Romero and other clergy, by the military forces of the Right, "we are in the situation in which the Church admits the right of legitimate insurrection". It recalled that Pope Paul VI's Encyclical *Populorium Progressio* of 1967 endorses insurrection "in the case of evident and prolonged tyranny that seriously attacks the fundamental rights of the person . . . and the good of the community".

The progressive movement has profoundly split the Latin American Church. Activist clergy are being accused by traditionalists of being Communists, and are being imprisoned, tortured, exiled and murdered by the henchmen of the Right Wing regimes which the traditionalists uphold. In the 1980s the theology of liberation was condemned by Pope John Paul II and the leading Vatican theologians.

This polarisation must surely have a transforming effect on the role of the Church. How can a traditional structure based on the principles of authority, hierarchy and medieval theology support a priesthood committed to the consciousness-raising of the masses and the creation of a new society based on personal self-expression and the participation of all in decision-making? If the Roman Catholic Church in Latin America rises to the challenge to "liberate" Latin Americans from ignorance and oppression, it may also succeed in liberating the whole Church from the shackles of traditionalism.

Christianity in Eastern Europe

What has Communism done to Eastern European Christianity in the period 1917-85? Marxism-Leninism has preached "scientific atheism" on two grounds. The first is philosophical: matter is said to be the basis of all phenomena, including consciousness, so that the religious idea that all things originate in and are permeated by "spirit" or "God" is "scientifically" false. The second is ethical: religion is, according to Marx, "the opiate of the masses", "a powerful weapon helping the exploiter to subdue his victims". "In a society where there is no exploitation religion will completely disappear; it will be unnecessary", and so the un-exploited workers will spontaneously abandon it.

Marx considered religion barely worthy of attention, but Lenin realised its importance as "the main spiritual weapon of the bourgeoisie", and his Soviet successors adopted the same view. "There can be", said Lenin, "nothing more abominable than religion". Since Marxism-Leninism is a dogmatic faith which asserts absolute truth, its believers are fundamentally threatened by any traditional religion which also asserts absolute truth, as well as by the modern humanistic spirit of open-ended inquiry, and by any form of mysticism. Moreover, the perennial claim of all religions that only through union with God can the "new man" be born challenges the basic dogma of the secular Marxist creed: that the collective ownership of the means of production and the elimination of the exploiting classes will themselves produce the new man.

During the Tsarist era the Russian Orthodox Church was the established Church of the land. The majority of the Slav citizens were baptised into it, but the empire was a patchwork of faiths and sects, in most cases based on ethnic factors. In the USSR (population 261 million in 1981) there were estimated in 1980 to be 30 to 40 million practising Orthodox Christians, over 4 million Baptists, 6 million Roman and Uniate (Ukrainian) Catholics, 2 million Jews, 40 million Muslims and half a million Buddhists.

In 1918 the Soviet government formally separated the Russian Orthodox Church from the State. The right of freedom of worship was affirmed in the Constitutions of 1936 and 1977. This meant that religious communities were the only legally permitted non-official groups - a pluralist anomaly in a monolithic society, and thus a constant irritant to the system. This constitutional right was therefore undermined by laws controlling religious sects through a powerful Department of Religious Affairs. Until the advent of Mikhail Gorbachev's leadership in 1985 the Soviet authorities used these laws to persecute religious groups. The measures taken involved: the large-scale closing of churches and of seminaries; the imprisonment, torture and murder of many clergy, often for simply performing their rituals; the refusal to allow Jews to emigrate to Israel; the forcing of the Ukrainian Orthodox Church to sever its ancient ties with Rome and unite with the Russian Orthodox Church; the refusal to publish more than a trickle of religious literature, including the Sacred Books themselves, and to allow any form of religious education; the forced abduction of children of religious parents to be brought up as atheists; and discrimination against religious believers in appointments to all responsible posts.

Meanwhile, there was a massive attempt to inculcate "scientific atheism". The population was deluged with lectures, books and films attacking religion and expounding atheism. In the traditional Muslim Republic of Uzbekistan, no less than 42,000 lectures on this subject were given in the year 1969-70!

The religious policies of the post 1945 communist regimes in Eastern Europe have been essentially the same as those of the USSR, but they have been applied in different contexts and more mildly. The Orthodox Church, the traditional church in Romania, Bulgaria and Serbia, has been sealed off from the West for nearly nine centuries. And so "each tradition (East and West) developed in its own characteristic way, and with the passing of every century, the barrier to understanding grew higher". The Communists therefore confronted, in the Orthodox Church, an institution which had barely been exposed to modern thought. In Hungary, in Czechoslovakia and above all in Poland, however, they have had to deal with the Roman Catholic Church, and in East Germany mainly with the Protestant Lutheran Church, both powerful organisations based in the West and steeped in modern thought. Soviet-type policies were therefore applied in a more moderate way.

The Soviet religious persecution was medieval behaviour, the propagation of scientific atheism a form of fundamentalism. But both must be understood in the light of Russian history. A country which never experienced the Renaissance, the Reformation or the 17th century scientific revolution, remained almost completely stuck in traditional immature attitudes of mind until the Communist Revolution of 1917. The great mass of the people were illiterate peasants who saw no prospect of change in their lives. The half-truth implied in dubbing religion "the opiate of the masses" calls on a person to face the universe as an adult human being, and to master it himself through science. To the millions of peasants and ex-peasants becoming educated under the Communist rule, and rising out of their hovels into the modern world, what a liberation this seemed! But embedded in a thousand years of medieval authoritarianism and superstition is a thousand years of mystical vision of the world of the celestial archetypes (see Chapter 3). What if the saints and angels revealed through the windows of the ancient icons are actually there! If so, scientific atheism may prove to have been the necessary preparation for this deeply mystical people to "see" the archetypes with new eyes, the eyes of people whose minds are stimulated and disciplined by science, and whose hearts are moved by the concern for universal social justice embodied in Marxism. If we accept the Christian myth that suffering purifies and redeems, then it may be that their dark and tragic history has been preparing the Christians of the former USSR to fulfil their true mission for the 21st century: to earth the celestial models of the world community.

There are many signs now of great religious vitality in the former USSR. The first Chairman of the Soviet Godless League said: "Religion is like a nail; the harder you strike it, the deeper it goes". Unregistered sects, both Christian and Muslim, proliferated. Only the USA can rival the USSR in the number and vitality of their religious groups. When the Russian, Ukranian, Romanian, Bulgarian and Polish churches joined the World Council of Churches in 1961 with official blessing, they opened the doors of their ossified structure to the spiritual ferment which is shaking the Western Churches. The Gorbachev - Yeltsin revolution has promised to give real religious freedom to the peoples of East Europe. When this is combined with the longed-for freedom to travel and mix freely throughout the world, the ex-Soviet communists may, in due course, bring a new spiritual inspiration to world affairs.

Hinduism in Action: the Message of Gandhi

Mohandas Gandhi (1869-1948) sought to achieve Human Rights and national freedom in South Africa and India through putting into practice the basic spiritual and ethical teachings of Hinduism. He reactivated a vital ingredient in Hinduism, *Karma yoga,* the yoga of action, by developing what one might call a spiritual strategy which has inspired reformers and revolutionaries around the world. Einstein wrote of him in 1944 that "generations to come may scarcely believe that such a one ever in flesh and blood walked the earth". He drew

255

inspiration from Eastern and Western sources: essentially, the *Bhagavad Gita;* but also the life and teachings of Jesus and the writings of Tolstoy, Thoreau and Ruskin. He was also well educated in British law, which he practised for over 20 years.

Before Gandhi's time, reformers in general saw only two ways of securing their aims: through democratic legal and constitutional systems where these existed, or else through violence. Marxism, as we have seen, specifically endorses the use of force, asserting that "the end justifies the means"; that an immoral means, violence, can achieve a moral end, the rule of love. Gandhi showed modern man that there is a third way, "non-violent passive resistance". This way is based on the principle that every means is its own end, and that if you do the right thing in a spirit of love, you will achieve the right end. "I can say without the slightest hesitation" wrote Gandhi at the end of his autobiography, "that those who say that religion has nothing to do with politics do not know what religion means".

His life long struggle was carried out in two dimensions: he sought to uplift the condition of his fellow countrymen, and, indirectly, of all humanity; and in order to do this, he sought continuously to purify himself. "he was a moral genius who tried to chasten himself first before trying to exert any kind of influence on other people," writes Dr. S. Radhakrishnan, independent India's first President. His autobiography, written in the early 1920s, partly in a British jail, is a candid account of his efforts to tread the spiritual path; it ranges from his discussions with Christian missionaries to his determination to do his own laundry; from his conversations with Viceroys, Indian leaders and prison jailers, to his worries about diet and sex. It reveals how a man who was perhaps the greatest saint of this century worked to fit himself for his life of "consecrated action". Equally he believed that in order to be worthy of independence, India must transform herself. She must shed the caste system - to promote this he renamed the Untouchables *Harijans*, "children of God" - and welcomed them into the ashram in which he lived; she must give women equal rights with men and end such practices as dowries and child marriages; she must achieve harmony between religious sects, in particular Hindus and Muslims: and she must take steps to eliminate the degrading poverty of the masses, partly by encouraging village industries and inculating the dignity of manual labour - Gandhi himself spent two or three hours a day spinning, and encouraged his followers to do likewise. Gandhi was determined that independent India should be a secular, democratic state. To him and the other Indian leaders (including a number of Muslims) the idea of creating the state of Pakistan, based on the particular creed of Islam, was a travesty of true religion and of Human Rights.

Gandhi's life's work was to spiritualise not simply politics but democratic politics. In the traditional societies the ordinary person, living his life according to ancient religious customs and codes, was essentially a-political. When the immature masses are given freedom they try, naturally, to promote their own interests through the new channels which are opened up (see Chapter 14). Gandhi called on the masses to behave as mature spiritual beings: to develop "soul force", *ahimsa,* the power of love which forgives and blesses all men, and put *ahimsa* into practice in *satyagraha* - "firmness in truth", or non-violent passive resistance to laws and practices which violate Human Rights. He thus created a unique kind of political mass movement, based on spiritual ideals, not on religious teachings or on secular political theories. He sought to draw out the full powers of the *satyagrahi's* personality through suffering - for Gandhi agreed with Christians that love necessarily involved suffering. He put into practice the attitude towards poverty which Christians are now asserting: that it is both a terrible evil and a great good. "To a people famished and idle", he wrote, "the only acceptable form in which God can dare appear is work and promise of food as wages". But "civilisation . . . consists not in the multiplication, but in the deliberate and voluntary restriction of wants. This alone promotes real happiness and contentment, and increases capacity for service". He expressed this principle in his own life style. He lived in a hut in an ashram from 1904 until his death in 1948; he wore only a loin cloth and a shawl, and found time in the busy life of a national statesman for such matters as designing latrines for villagers.

When his calls for non-violent action inevitably stirred up outbreaks of violence, Gandhi resorted to another original method: he punished himself, not his followers; he undertook "fasts unto death" to stop the violence. And because he was loved and revered as *Mahatma,* "Great

Soul", usually the violence stopped.

Gandhi's assassination in 1948 by a Hindu fanatic perhaps symbolises the transformation within Hinduism which he initiated. He was a cosmic man. Since his death his ideas and methods have spread across the world, inspiring in particular many African leaders, such as Nelson Mandela, Martin Luther King's Civil Rights Movement in the United States and the Roman Catholic Church's radical movement for social justice in Latin America, and more recently the anti-nuclear-weapons and feminist movements in North America and Western Europe. The film of his life, produced by Sir Richard Attenborough in 1983, has been a world hit because it has an explosive message for all humankind: that the rule of love must be achieved by love, and that to bring it about, those who love God must involve themselves to the hilt in the affairs of men. Thus Gandhi-ism has developed the universalist aspect of Hinduism into a transforming agent in the world of political, economic and social affairs.

The Baha'i Faith

With the spread of religious freedom, education and modern communications, new faiths are springing up. Of these perhaps the most outstanding is the Baha'i Faith. It derives from revelations made to two Iranian prophets in the mid-19th century (one executed by the Muslim priesthood), and claims to be the latest in a series of authoritative revelations descending from Zoroaster, the Buddha, Jesus and Muhammad. In 150 years it has grown from an offshoot of Shi'a Islam into a world religion with almost six million adherents from over 2,200 ethnic groups all over the world, a literature in over 800 languages, a world governing body and 175 national administrative bodies in over 200 territories. It has no clergy and accepts funds only from its registered followers. It has survived opposition from some governments and clergy, notably that of Iran.

The social principles promulgated over a century ago point to the ethics of the modern age: independent investigation into truth; harmony between religion and science; equality of the sexes; universal education; demilitarisation and world peace; world federal government; a world auxiliary language; eradication of poverty; and the abolition of prejudice of all kinds.

The Baha'i International Community has played a prominent part among the Non-Governmental Organisations (NGOs), with accredited status at the United Nations and a number of its Agencies. It contributed to preparations for the Earth, UNCED Summit at Rio de Janiero in 1992 (see Chapter 17), and is represented in the Commission for Sustainable Development set up after Rio. It is also concerned with UN Conferences on population, social development, women and habitat, (see Chapter 18).

There is a resurgent Baha'i Community in the former USSR and its neighbours. Towards the end of the last century there were strong Baha'i groups in the areas adjacent to Persia, and flourishing Communities in Moscow and St Petersburg, but in 1936 the Baha'i Faith was banned by Stalin. Since it is a Baha'i obligation to obey any government, even if antipathetic, in all matters other than relinquishing their Faith, there was no teaching or Baha'i administration until Gorbachev introduced *glasnost* in 1985. By 1994 there were many hundreds of local Baha'i communities and 15 national Spiritual Assemblies in the former Communist countries. Significantly, it is not so much the social teachings of the Baha'i Faith which have attracted these spiritually deprived masses as the writings, prayers and meditations of the founders. The profound social idealism of the Baha'i Faith was embodied in Communism; the Faith adds the spiritual ingredient which Marxism lacks.

The Transformation of Popular Religion

I suggested in Chapter 2 that in traditional societies popular religion was a world-wide phenomenon. Its essential feature was an intuitive awareness that the universe is a cosmopolis, a universal city of humans, gods and spirits, created and pervaded by the Great Spirit, the Supreme Divinity. But the worship of gods and spirits, the attempt to propitiate or exorcise them, produced a religious expression which was often devoid of the transcendental dimension and of the ethical ideals which stem from man's sense of absolute values. Judaism, Christianity and Islam therefore strongly rejected polytheism and animism - although peasants everywhere continued to believe in spirits, gods, devils, witches, saints, goblins, fairies and so on.

Stemming from the belief in spirits, the concept of psychic magnetism pervaded every traditional society. Holy people radiated a heavenly charisma which attracted the gods, while evil people, or those concerned with "unclean" substances, attracted evil spirits.

The main impact of modernity on popular religion has been to destroy it. The thunderous condemnations of idolatry issued from Mount Sinai and the caves of Arabia have been as pinpricks compared to the lethal injections of scientific thinking, technological practice and humanitarian behaviour. The average modern person regards "spirits" as simply a subjective "projection" of the imagination, a fantasy. Archaeologists, anthropologists, psychologists and historians of religion do not condemn the animists, pagans and polytheists as wicked: they simply assume that they were or are deluded.

The backlash of religious fanaticism today is not concerned with popular religion as I have defined it. The disappearance of the negative psychological attitudes embedded in popular religion is surely inevitable. But can it be assumed that the substance of popular religion is equally irrelevant? Is the concept of the universe as a "cosmopolis" of gods and men - a concept which inspired some of the noblest and most sophisticated minds of the Classical world - really nothing but a fantasy? Were all those lovely shrines around which the modern tourists tramp with uncomprehending eyes merely the pathetic expression of "blind superstition"? There are good reasons for replying "No!".

First, the assumption that the spiritual universe does not exist is an unproved hypothesis. Second, if it be a rational hypothesis to assume the existence of a spiritual universe, then the modern mind, which makes the self-expression of the person the central purpose of human life, should regard it as equally rational to assume that the spiritual universe is peopled with persons. Such modern seers as Blake and Swedenborg have insisted that there is nothing vague or abstract about the spiritual states. "As below, so above" as the ancient Gnostics said; the clarity, concreteness, objectivity and individuality which inhere in earthly phenomena is the expression of greater clarity, concreteness, and individuality in heaven.

Third, this latter hypothesis is by modern scientific methods. During the past century, increasing attention has been given to "parapsychology", the scientific investigation of "extra-sensory phenomena" - apparitions, telepathy, communications through mediums, automatic writing, clairvoyance, clairaudience and so on. The first laboratory of parapsychology was established at Duke University in North Carolina by Professor McDougall of Harvard and Professor Rhine in 1931. These researchers and others in post-war USA, Britain and elsewhere, claim that there is overwhelming evidence that humans possess a *psi* capacity, an "extra-sensory non-material element" which enables then to "tune in" to a non-material universe in which discarnate personalities dwell. It is inevitable that much of the experimentation should be of a somewhat trivial nature, since experiences which fill the soul with love and light are not scientifically verifiable - they must be classified as mystical.

Fourth, during the past century, Western psychologists have been unearthing from the "unconscious" psyche, by "clinical" methods, a vast mass of symbolic and allegorical material which indicates that some rational force is imparting coherent messages to the conscious mind through the medium of the unconscious. As noted in Chapter 15, the psychologists tend to assume that this rational force lies within the patient's psyche. But the psychologist's work is confined to studying subjective experience: the origin of that experience - that is, whether it comes from inside or outside the mind - is a matter for the metaphysician. On the face of it, however, it seems more reasonable to suppose - as was universally supposed in olden days - that a person who is receiving hunches, dreams and visions giving him wise advice, is receiving them from a mind other than his own.

Fifth, a similar argument applies to the doctrine of reincarnation, although here we move largely outside the realm of scientific experiment or clinical practice. We have already discussed in Chapter 3 the difficulties which this doctrine presents. It is, in a sense, an ancient version of the assumptions made by modern psychology that all psychological phenomena are subjective - derived from inside the person's own psyche. Just as my own psyche may be warning me in a dream of an impending accident, so my own psyche may be conditioned by my experiences as a priest in ancient Egypt. But how much more simple, how much more logical, how much more marvellous, to believe that I am in profound communion with a separate, objective personality who was, centuries age, a priest in ancient Egypt! And if at times I feel as if I actually were that priest, and experience what he experienced, this is because, when two souls blend in empathy, they become for a time subjectively one - "either was the other's mine", as Shakespeare put it in *The Phoenix and the Turtle*.

This leads us to the subject of the higher spiritualism. A contemporary philosopher, Lawrence Hyde, wrote that: "In the course of the last century Spiritualism has passed through three clearly defined phases. At the beginning the emphasis was laid primarily on the evidence for survival . . . By degrees the desire for instruction from 'the other side' emerged. This phase is now fully developed; all over the world 'guides' and 'teachers' of varying distinction and capacity are imparting their knowledge to seekers after spiritual truth. The great mass of the material . . . is unfortunately commonplace . . . But a certain amount of it is (of a quality) that provides the foundations for a new type of religion, the marks of which are: simplicity . . . optimism . . . widely conceived brotherhood . . . a forward-looking theology (little dependence upon historical revelations . . .), intense interest in the invisible realms of being, and the state of the soul after death . . . (and) concern with the practical applications (psychic and spiritual healing, ministry to the deceased, communion with invisible ministrants, etc). If once the principle be accepted that man can communicate with the Unseen on a whole series of levels, the way is open . . . to association with dwellers on planes of being which have been scarcely touched in the history of the Movement . . . We may contemplate the idea of a sanctified spiritualism, involving the recovery of those spiritual gifts (charisma) which were common in the earliest period of Christianity" (10).

These words were written a few years before the Roman Catholic Church, at the Second Vatican Council of 1962-5, urged the revival and development by both clergy and laity of the "charisms": inspirational speech, prophecy, wise counsel, healing and the bestowal of blessings.

The keynote of the modern age is the urge to develop the creative potential of the individual person. The emergence of the higher spiritualism suggests that increasingly persons will begin to realise consciously that communion with celestial beings is the source of the inspiration which fires their creativity. But if human persons wish to "tune in" to evolved souls in the spiritual cosmopolis they must raise the level of their "vibrations" accordingly. And this involves undertaking, in appropriate ways, the disciplines of the mystical path. Thus the transformation of popular religion will open the door to the mysticism of the future: the spiritual development of the individual person as a member of the cosmopolis of men and gods.

Chapter 17

THE CURRENT WORLD CRISIS

I N order to understand the nature and extent of the current world crisis, we must first look back to the world situation at the end of World War II.

The war caused the death of 55 million Europeans, including at least 20 million Russians. (New researches in Russia are revising the figure upwards). In China, the Japanese invasion which began in 1937 caused the death of some 22 million Chinese. After the surrender of Germany and Italy, the war with Japan was ended by the invention and use of a weapon more sinister than anyone in past ages could have imagined, the nuclear bomb.

By the end of the war in 1945, Europe from the Atlantic to the Urals was shattered, and the large area of eastern China conquered by the Japanese, the other countries of the East Pacific which Japan had occupied, and Japan itself, were equally devastated. The two major world problems, therefore, appeared to be the restoration of the war-shattered economies and the control of this new genie, the nuclear bomb. A third problem quickly came to the fore: the demand for independence of some 75 colonies, most in Africa and Asia, ranging from tiny islands to the mighty India, nearly all acquired by the European powers in the 19th century. In international affairs the period 1945 to 1970 was essentially concerned with dealing with these three problems.

Economic Restoration

The most immediate problem after 1945 was to restore the battered economies of Europe and Asia. A crucial part was played in this enormous task by the United States of America. Japan, under American occupation until 1952, also recovered rapidly with American economic help. China, on the other hand, experienced a Communist revolution in 1949 which cut it off from the "free world". The American Government broke off all contacts with China until President Nixon finally officially recognised the Communist Government's existence and even paid a visit to Beijing in 1972. Thus while Japan rapidly became one of the most prosperous members of the First World, China became one of the poorest members of the Third World.

The Cold War

The second problem after World War II was what to do about the atomic bomb. The biggest bombs dropped in Europe during the war contained 10 tons of chemical high explosive. The two nuclear bombs dropped on Japan by the Americans each contained the equivalent of 12 to 15,000 tons of chemical explosive. In 1952 the Americans successfully tested a hydrogen bomb in the Pacific, with an explosive power of 14 million tons, more than the total explosive power of all the bombs dropped in the six years of World War II. The USA proposed to the USSR that a World Atomic Authority with powers of full control of the manufacture of atomic bombs throughout the world should be set up (the "Baruch Plan"), but Stalin, who had established Communist regimes throughout East Europe, turned down the proposal and the "Cold War" then began. The two "Superpowers", each believing that the other was planning a pre-emptive strike, vied with each other in making ever more sophisticated nuclear bombs and delivery systems. By the time of the Kennedy presidency (1961-3) the Americans believed, wrongly, that the Russians were ahead of them, and American paranoia about the Communist threat almost reached flash-point when Stalin's successor Nikita Khrushchev installed missile bases in Cuba in 1962.

In the use of science for the manufacture and deployment of weapons of mass murder and destruction since 1945 the world has witnessed a phenomenon undreamed of since the days of the bow and arrow, sword and spear, musket and cannon, which were the normal weapons of war until the 19th century. A single nuclear weapon can kill hundreds of thousands of people and the widespread use of chemical and biological weapons could do incalculable harm to the planet. Having let the genie out of the bottle, millions of sane people realise that it must be put back in. But in the 45 years since the invention and use of the atom bomb there has been very little progress in disarmament. By the mid 1980s the five "official" nuclear states - USA, the former USSR, Britain, France and China, together with Israel, - piled up some 70,000 nuclear warheads, of which nearly half are "strategic" - that is, they are not for battlefield use, but could hit a target thousands of miles away. The largest Inter-Continental Ballistic Missiles (ICBMs) now made can travel 8,000 to 15,000 miles an hour and contain the equivalent of several million tons of TNT.

Conventional Weapons

In addition to nuclear weapons, there are now highly sophisticated conventional weapons, such as cluster bombs which burst into fragments inside the human body, and 100 million land mines which explode on touch are buried in the fields, woods and deserts of 62 developing countries where 150 wars have been fought since 1945, killing over 23 million people. World expenditure on arms in the 1980s approached nearly $1 trillion a year. The developing countries have also armed themselves to the teeth (except for Costa Rica, which has no armed forces *and* apparently no enemies!), purchasing highly sophisticated weapons from the eager arms manufacturers and governments of the industrialised countries. By 1990, of the five to seven million people engaged in research and development, around 1.5 million were working in the military sector. And about 30 million people are employed in the world's armed forces.

Arms Control and Disarmament

Over the years, some progress has been made with arms control treaties. Over 20 agreements were negotiated between 1959 and 1993. These include:

(a) A treaty concluded in 1963 to ban nuclear testing in the atmosphere and in the sea. This was signed by the USA, the USSR and Britain. France and China refused to sign it, and France has continued to test nuclear weapons in its Pacific colony, the island of

Moruroa, much to the anger of Australia and New Zealand, who took the matter to the International Court of Justice at The Hague (see Chapter 18).

(b) The Non-Proliferation Treaty (NPT) of 1968 recognises two categories of states: the Nuclear Weapons States (NWSs) which had exploded a nuclear device before 1 January 1967 (USA, USSR, Britain, France and China), and the Non-Nuclear Weapons States (NNWSs). (China and France did not sign the treaty until 1992). Under the Treaty the NWSs undertake to reduce their nuclear arsenals and to help the NNWSs to develop peaceful nuclear technology in return for the latter's commitment not to develop nuclear weapons. By 1994 165 states had signed the Treaty. It is monitored by the International Atomic Energy Agency in Vienna. Twenty-five years from its entry into force a conference to decide the future of the NPT will be held in 1995.

Until the advent of Gorbachev as ruler of USSR in 1985 the NWSs had not reduced their nuclear stockpiles. Britain, for example, is increasing its nuclear submarine warheads from 192 to 384 - the latter the equivalent of 4,000 Hiroshimas. This refusal to carry out nuclear disarmament has given a number of NNWSs their cue secretly to work on the construction of nuclear arsenals. Israel, India, Pakistan and South Africa are known or strongly suspected to have or have had nuclear capability, though South Africa says it has destroyed its warheads, and Africa should become a Nuclear-Weapon-Free-Zone in 1995. Brazil and Argentina have also halted nuclear weapon development. Iraq, a signatory to the NPT, has clearly breached it, as may have North Korea. Iran, Libya and Syria are suspected of an interest in nuclear capability, but are more likely to acquire this by obtaining plutonium on the black market - a sinister possibility opened up by the economic collapse of the former Soviet Union. Each time the experts render nuclear warheads harmless, they bring plutonium back into circulation. The thousands of unpaid or unemployed technicians who worked or work in the former USSR's vast military establishment are desperate for money and for the "good life" which the embrace of capitalism is supposed to bring. Packages of radioactive plutonium used for nuclear bombs - one speck in a person's lung can cause cancer - are turning up in Germany in trucks and trains from Moscow. The shady characters in Germany who are buying them may be the agents of the shady governments, fanatics and terrorists who now haunt the world.

Of the new republics emerging from the former Soviet Union, Kazakhstan, Belarus, and, very recently, Ukraine where there are large Russian nuclear bases, are returning the missiles to Russia and have joined the NPT. A far stronger international control system, combined with genuine nuclear disarmament by the NWSs - see below - will be needed to prevent the proliferation of nuclear weapons in the 21st century.

(c) After years of discussion the USA and the USSR signed a treaty in 1987 providing for the global elimination of American and Soviet ground-based missiles (ballistic and Cruise) of intermediate range. A total of some 2,200 missiles were eliminated - but not their warheads, which are simply in storage. To some British women it had a special emotional significance, since it represented the successful end of a 6 year long women's vigil outside the American cruise missile air base at Greenham Common in Berkshire, England, to which women had come to make their protest from all over the world.

(d) This Treaty was followed by the START negotiations, launched in 1985, which propose the elimination of all land-based inter-continental missiles by both countries, in two stages, by 2003. The Russians are even talking of an earlier date if the Americans will pay for the destruction of some of their missiles! This again raises the question of the need for international supervision of the huge task of eliminating the weapons of mass destruction, and converting the vast military-industrial complexes in both countries to peaceful uses.

(e) At the time of writing, the United Nations' Committee on Disarmament at Geneva is negotiating treaties for a Comprehensive Ban on nuclear testing everywhere, and an end to the production of fissile material that could be used for bomb-making.

(f) The Conventional Arms Treaty (CFE), imposing strict limits on conventional forces in Europe, was signed by 22 countries in 1990.

(g) Several treaties have been signed forbidding military activities in Antarctica, Space and the Seabed.

(h) Chemical and biological weapons are almost as sinister as nuclear weapons, but much less widely discussed. A Convention outlawing the stockpiling and use of biological weapons, though still permitting research (allegedly for defensive purposes), was agreed in 1972. But the advent of modern biotechology has made it easy to bypass the provisions of this Convention, which must be revised and strengthened.

The use of chemical weapons in World War I led to the conclusion of the Geneva Protocol of 1925, which banned the use of poison gas in war. More than 120 countries have signed it. But the Protocol did not prohibit the development, production or stockpiling of such weapons. The USA and the USSR have huge stockpiles, and some 30 countries have made or can make them - only a basic chemical industry is required. Chemical defoliation was carried out by the USA in the Vietnam War, devastating millions of acres of land in Vietnam and Cambodia. Chemical weapons were used by Saddam Hussein, ruler of Iraq, in the Iraq-Iran war of 1980-88, and against Iraqi Kurdish rebels in 1986. The sudden end of the Gulf War of January to March 1992 was probably at least partly due to the fact that an American soldier would only survive for five minutes inside his anti-chemical warfare suit in a chemical attack in the hot desert summer. After 21 years of negotiation, therefore, a Chemical Weapons Convention was signed in 1993, which will enter into force when 65 states have ratified it. It prohibits the development, production and stockpiling of chemical weapons, and demands the destruction of all existing stockpiles. Highly lethal chemical weapons are particularly difficult to destroy; the USA is using far-off Johnston Island in the Pacific as a dump for its discarded material. The aim is to complete the destruction of all these weapons between 1995 and 2005. An Organisation for the Prohibition of Chemical Weapons, consisting of all parties to the Treaty, will be established at The Hague in The Netherlands to implement its terms.

The Third World

De-colonisation
All the colonies of the major European states in Asia and Africa were eventually given their independence, some with a good grace, as in the British withdrawal from India, some only after bloody wars, as in the French attempt to retain Algeria, which cost a million Algerian lives, over 10 per cent of the population, and the Portuguese attempt to retain

Angola and Mozambique. Two major legacies of colonialism were a psychological sense of cultural and political inferiority, compounded by the practical fact that with partial exceptions, such as that of India, the colonial powers failed to prepare their colonies for independence. They maintained law and order, but were not concerned with "development", either economic or social. When Zaire, the former Belgian Congo, gained independence in 1960, there were about a dozen Congolese graduates, and no Congolese doctor, engineer or lawyer. When Tanzania gained independence from Britain in 1961, there were a hundred native graduates in a population of 10 million. The legacy of unplanned de-colonisation contributed to the recent tragedy in Rwanda.

A witch-hunt of "Communists" began in the USA in the 1950s, and brutal military dictatorships, which fostered American interests, were supported and armed by the USA and its West European allies around the world. Thus the terms "First World" - the USA and its allies and friends in West Europe (of which France and Britain were armed with smaller nuclear forces), Japan, Australia, New Zealand and Canada; "Second World" - the USSR and its "satellite" states in East Europe; and "Third World" - the remainder of Africa, Asia and Latin America, came into use. Since the Gorbachev revolution of 1985 ended the Cold War these terms have become out of date. United Nations' thinking and literature distinguishes between two categories of country in the context of the world crisis: "industrialised", which includes the former USSR, now the Commonwealth of Independent States, and "developing", the former Third World. (Sometimes "North" and "South" are used - terms which are slightly less precise). Communist China, whose position in the Second World was equivocal, now comes firmly into the category of developing countries: in 1991 China's *per caput* income was $370, Japan's $26,900.

Development Aid : Use and Misuse

Apart from China and a few small non-European countries which established Communist regimes, such as North Korea, the First World did not, during this period, neglect the Third World. The policy of "aid to the developing countries" was initiated by President Truman in his "Four Point" programme of 1950-53, offering aid in the form of technical assistance. The United Nations and the multifarious bodies connected with it (see Chapter 18) began to give various forms of aid. The European Community, formed in 1950, also set up an institutionalised system of aid to the former colonies of its member states. At the suggestion of President Kennedy, the United Nations General Assembly pronounced the 1960s the "Development Decade" and set targets of 5 per cent growth for the developing countries and one per cent transfer of national income as aid by the industrialised countries. Later this target was fixed at 0.7 per cent of G.D.P. as governmental aid. The concept that the industrial countries should help the developing countries was born. But the general attitude of the rich countries, like the attitude of many rich Americans to the poor in their own country, was that "aid" was, like "welfare", a form of charity. The programmes would be wound up as soon as the developing countries had established their industrial infrastructure and could stand on their own feet in the modern world. The idea that humanity is a community whose members all have a *right* to share its resources had not dawned on the minds of most of the leading politicians and businessmen, obsessed with the philosophy of competition and the desire to promote their own national "growth" (see Chapter 14). Salving their consciences with "aid", these obsessions blinded their eyes to the fact that the conflicts which have afflicted the developing countries since 1945 are partly the psychological expression of the tensions arising from the sudden jump from traditionalism, via colonialism, to modernity, and partly to the fact that "aid" is failing to cure the miseries of poverty. In fact, these conflicts have been fuelled by the eagerness of the industrialised countries to increase their own wealth by exporting sophisticated conventional weapons to the developing countries.

At the present time (1994) the gulf between the three-quarters of the world's population of 5.5 billion people who live in the developing countries and the quarter who live in the industrialised countries may be summed up by the following figures: the industrialised countries possess 80 per cent of the world's income, eat 50 percent of its food, produce 90 per cent of its manufactured goods, and consume 70 per cent of its energy, 75 per cent of its minerals and 85 per cent of its wood. They control 84 per cent of the world's trade (70 per cent through their multinational companies), and they also control the vital information and communications industries. They do 95 per cent of the world's research - only 6 to 7 per cent of the world's scientists and engineers work in the developing countries. Meanwhile in these poor countries 2 billion people lack electricity and use what wood is left after their forests have been cut down for export, for cooking and heating. Nearly 2 billion lack clean water and over 2 billion have no adequate sanitation - the two biggest causes of disease after malnutrition. One billion have worms in their bodies. Over one billion are "marginalised", living in "absolute poverty", half a billion are unemployed or grossly under-employed. A third are under 15 years old. "Aid" has become a mockery, not only because, compared with the United Nations' aid target of 0.7 per cent GDP, about 0.3 per cent is being given; but also because the developing countries are paying about two and a half times as much money as they receive in "aid" to service debt charges of some $160 billion to the industrialised countries.

The Changing World

The question of converting the world's vast military industrial complexes from war to peace production will be discussed below and in Chapter 18. Already the phrase "the peace dividend" is in the air. Meanwhile, a range of major new problems for humankind and the world we live in have come to notice in recent years. They transcend national boundaries, threatening both industrialised and developing worlds, and are not amenable to solutions by old fashioned diplomacy or military force.

Environmental Threats

The Greenhouse Effect
The "Greenhouse Effect" is the term now applied to the threat of the sudden heating up of the earth's atmosphere through the excessive discharge into it of certain gases. These gases create a blanket which lets the sun's rays through to the earth, but traps some of the heat that would otherwise be radiated back into space. The most important of these is carbon dioxide. Some 50 per cent of this comes from the burning of fossil fuels, coal and oil; and the other 50 per cent from

272

burning down the tropical forests - partly because burning releases carbon dioxide, and partly because the leaves of the trees absorb it. In Europe one 100-year-old beech tree purifies the air content of 800 homes annually. Chloroflurocarbons (CFCs, see below) account for a further 15 to 20 per cent of the greenhouse effect; each molecule of these gases traps as much heat as 15,000 molecules of carbon dioxide. The other greenhouse gases include nitrous oxide given off by fertilisers, and methane emanating from rubbish tips, paddy fields, and eructations from cattle. Many scientists now believe that these gases have warmed the earth by 0.5 degrees Celsius over the last 100 years and that if this process continues unchecked the temperature could rise another 1.5 to 4.5 °C before 2050.

This is beyond civilised man's experience. The world has not been as much as three degrees warmer than today since the end of the last ice age 10,000 years ago, and the rate of rise will be greater than any experienced since then. The increase will not be uniform; there will be greater extremes of both heat and rainfall, with more frequent gales in the temperate zones and tropical storms in the low latitudes. Sea levels will rise, probably by about a metre in the next hundred years or so, covering some low-lying oceanic islands such as the Maldives, and, in conjunction with typhoons, making large areas of, for example, Bangladesh uninhabitable. Changes of rainfall pattern may make some rice-growing areas and the US grain belt arid, though crop growth may be promoted in parts of Russia. Overall, there is a real fear that food production will fall just when it must increase to feed the rising population (see below) whose presence will further contribute to global warming. Infectious diseases may increase their range; malaria, for example, could return to Britain.

How likely is all this? From measurements at observatories in Hawaii there is no doubt that the amount of carbon dioxide in the atmosphere has increased since the start of the Industrial Revolution, and is projected to double by the year 2060. This should produce a rather greater rise in temperature than that observed so far, but sulphur dioxide aerosols from fossil fuel burning may have counteracted some of the rise. The eight warmest years on record have all been since 1980.

Some projections are more apocalyptic. If the permafrost in north

Canada and Siberia should melt extensively the methane and carbon dioxide freed could produce a runaway greenhouse effect sufficient to melt in turn the Greenland and Antarctic icecaps. This would cause a far greater rise in sea level, widespread flooding, and many millions of environmental refugees. But the surface temperature of the ice caps is many degrees below zero and this fear may therefore be exaggerated.

Overall there is nevertheless real cause for concern and a need for a positive response before global warming has gone too far. The key actions needed are greatly to reduce consumption of fossil fuels and to halt deforestation.

Ozone Depletion

A small amount of the three-atom form of oxygen, "ozone", in the stratosphere limits the amount of solar ultraviolet radiation reaching the Earth's surface. Unchecked, ultraviolet radiation would seriously affect the plant plankton which is the basis of the ocean's food web and so drastically reduce fish stocks. It also affects the growth of land vegetation, including food crops. In animals, including humans, it depresses the immune system and causes skin cancers and cataracts. A one per cent reduction in stratospheric ozone leads to a two per cent increase in ultraviolet radiation at ground level.

Reduction in stratospheric ozone over the Antarctic was first discovered by British scientists in 1985. This has progressed since then and has been complemented by a similar reduction over the Arctic which is also progressing. According to scientists, ozone depletion is caused by certain gases called chlorofluorocarbons (CFCs) and halons, which are released into the atmosphere by the use of refrigerators, hamburger cartons, paint and hair sprays, and fire extinguishers. These gases rise into the stratosphere where they liberate chlorine, one atom of which can destroy 100,000 molecules of ozone. CFCs also act as greenhouse gases (see above).

The main producer of CFCs is the giant Du Pont chemical corporation in the USA, which controls 25 per cent of the world market. In 1987 the USA made 90 per cent of the world's total production of CFCs and consumed one third of it. China has plans for a refrigerator in every home, and India for a massive expansion of refrigeration. Fortunately Du Pont has pioneered the production of an alternative

274

chemical which is ozone harmless, but is more expensive and is also a greenhouse gas.

The industrial countries negotiated the first environment treaty in Vienna in 1986. The Montreal Protocol to this Treaty of 1987 commits its signatories to phase out CFCs by 2000. In order to secure the adherence of India, China and other developing countries the industiral countries have set up a fund of $240 million to help them to buy the more expensive chemicals. But this sum is far too small. Nevertheless, as Norman Myers, the distinguished environmentalist, points out, the Protocol represents a new atmosphere in North-South relations. China and India have been pressing ahead with the production of CFC plants. Observation of their own commitments will not save the industrial countries from pollution by the developing countries. The North is beginning to discover that only by co-operation with the South can it protect its own interests (1).

Loss of Biodiversity
We do not know how many species of animals and plants currently share the earth with us; estimates vary from 10 to 30 million (2). What *is* clear is that, largely as a result of human activity and population growth, the numbers are falling fast. Again, accurate estimates of how many species are being lost are impossible; many of them are rare and local, for example in a small area of rain forest - the ecosystem which is both the most diverse and the most threatened. But an informed guess would be that two to three million species could disappear in the next century (3). Apart from their intrinsic value, the gene bank of these species represents an irreplaceable resource for agriculture and medicine (4).

Population Issues

The Population Explosion
In September 1994, in Cairo, the United Nations held its third global population conference. The first was held in Bucharest in 1974, the second in Mexico City in 1984. Eighteen thousand government delegates, representatives of Non-Governmental Organisations and journalists assembled in Cairo, a third of them women. The conference

endorsed a 20-year "Programme of Action" drafted by the United Nations. This, though, is not binding on the countries concerned - each participant, as a sovereign state, is free to interpret and implement its recommendations as it sees fit. United Nations' Secretary-General Boutros Boutros-Ghali told the conference that, according to United Nations' projections, the world's population, estimated at 5.6 billion in 1994, is expected to increase to between 7.9 and 11.5 billion by the year 2050 - when the babies of today are middle-aged. The difference between these figures represents the difference between the "high" and "low" scenarios worked out by the experts (5). The high scenario estimates that the world population will treble to 15 billion by the year 2075 and reach over 25 billion by 2150. The medium scenario, the most often quoted, forecasts stabilisation of the world population at about 10 to 11 billion by the year 2050. The low scenario estimates that the population will peak at about 8 billion by the year 2050 and then decline to below 5 billion by 2150. The medium scenario shows the industrialised world's population remaining stable at about one billion. The major increases will be in Africa and Asia, despite the efforts of China and India, where population control measures, however crude, have been in hand for some time.

Has the world the "carrying capacity" for population increases of this order? Has it the capacity to give the nine tenths of the world's population - 9 billion - who will be living in the developing countries in 2050 a standard of living adequate to the lives of human dignity called for in the Universal Declaration of Human Rights? To stabilise the world's population at its present level is one of the most crucial problems facing the world today. "If current population and consumption trends continue, science and technology may not be able to prevent either irreversible degradation of the environment or continued poverty for much of the world", stated the Presidents of the US National Academy of Sciences and the Royal Society of London in 1992 (6).

The Conference showed a significant change of perspective from the attitudes which prevailed in Bucharest and Mexico. In Bucharest in 1974, the developing countries told the industrial countries that "development is the best contraceptive" implying "give us more help for development". The latter, led by the USA, pressed instead for family planning programmes - which would cost them less. But "the relationship between population growth and economic development is not a negative one", James Buckley, head of the US delegation, told the surprised Cairo conferees (7). By 1994 the US government had shaken off the shackles of the anti-abortion lobby and had come to agree with the great majority of delegates from North and South, including some from Roman Catholic and Muslim countries (Saudi Arabia, Sudan, Iraq and Lebanon did not attend) that population control is crucial to the elimination of poverty and economic development. The new factor in Cairo was the emphasis on the right of women to control their own bodies, through the provision of "full access to family planning and reproductive health centres", as the Programme says, and to have meaningful work outside the home - to be "empowered". And this involves education; the Programme provides that all girls should be in school by the year 2000. The Vatican argued vainly against abortion. The Programme laid down that $17 billion should be provided to finance reproductive health programmes by the year 2000, rising to $21.7 billion in 2015. Two-thirds of the total sum is to be provided by the developing countries (8).

"Never before in history have women been able to sit in somewhat equal positions with men to accomplish a major enterprise in ethical thinking", said a leading American Catholic theologian. "The call for a shift in power between the genders is the main event at this conference. The high moral quality comes from the presence of women" (9).

AIDS

AIDS is a disease which is caused by the Human Immune-Deficiency Virus, which is transmitted from one person to another through contact with body fluid. Often years after infection, the virus leads to AIDS and death. The present situation is described as follows in the United Nations' Human Development Report 1994: "The cumulative number of HIV infected people world-wide is now around 15 million, with more than 12.5 million in developing countries - 9 million in sub-Saharan Africa, 1.5 million in Latin America and 2 million in Asia. Most HIV-infected people live in urban areas, and 70 per cent are in the prime reproductive ages of 20-40 years. One million are children. In the United States AIDS is now the prime cause of death for men aged 25-

44, and the fourth most important for women in that age group. The cumulative direct and indirect costs of HIV and AIDS in the 1980s has been estimated conservatively at 240 billion dollars.

Future projections are alarming. By 2000, the number of HIV infected people is expected to rise to between 30 and 40 million - 13 million of them women. By that time, the epidemic could have left more than nine million African children as orphans. The geographical distribution of HIV and AIDS is changing. In the mid-1980s the epidemic was well established in North America and Africa, but by the year 2000 most of the new infections will be in Asia. In Thailand today there are an estimated 500,000 HIV infected people, and in India, more than a million. The global cost - direct and indirect - of HIV and AIDS by 2000 could be 500 billion a year - equivalent to more than 2 per cent of global GNP" (10). Nevertheless, even in the worst affected African countries, the AIDS epidemic will not have a major impact on population growth even if it continues uncontrolled.

A drug, AZT, has been made which can retard the disease, but the British firm which makes it, Burroughs Wellcome, sells it at prices which health care resources in the developing countries cannot afford, while making huge profits (11).

The spread of AIDS can be controlled by public health measures, such as education in the avoidance of indiscriminate and uncontrolled sex, with the free availability and use of barrier contraceptives, scrupulous testing of blood and blood products for transfusion or injection, and effective action against intravenous drug abuse. The behaviour of the virus has made the development of vaccines difficult, but preliminary trials under the aegis of the World Health Organisation are now beginning.

Refugees and Displaced Persons
The combination of rising population, loss of agricultural land (see below), poverty, drought and war has forced many people to leave their homes as the only alternative to starvation. At least 35 million people from the South have migrated north in the past thirty years, and a further million join them every year. Another million or so are working overseas on contracts for fixed periods. There are 15 to 30 million illegal international migrants. In the developing countries today, there

are nearly 20 million internally displaced people and about 27 million refugees world-wide. Control of international migration is an economic, not an administrative, issue. It needs co-operation that integrates foreign assistance, trade liberalisation, technology transfers and more generous labour legislation.

Such is the present situation. Further climate change could increase the flow of refugees, and, if the seas start to rise through global warming, tens or hundreds of millions will have to leave low-lying coastal lands.

Food and Agriculture

If everyone is to have an adequate diet, defined as 2,500 calories for men, 2,000 for women and 1,500 for old people and children, the world's present population's food consumption must increase by 30 per cent. Given the unavoidable rise in population, by the end of the century world food production must increase by 70 per cent, and by the year 2050 by 330 per cent. Expert opinion is very uncertain if this can be done. At present, agricultural research is declining in both industrialised and developing countries. It has been estimated by the United Nations' Food and Agriculture Organisation (FAO) that by the end of the century the gap between supply and demand will be of the order of 30 million tons, a deficit of 25%, and by the year 2050 this will have increased to 50%. Land available for food production can probably only be increased by about 15 per cent. The world's food supply therefore depends essentially on increasing yields by about 250 per cent. This might involve:

(a) Increasing the use of nitrogen fertilisers by 460%, which in turn involves using 500 million tons of oil equivalent energy, 10% of the total current world consumption of energy. In the longer term, however, excessive use of nitrogen fertilisers damages the soil, pollutes water supplies with nitrates which may cause cancer, and gives off nitrous oxide which is a greenhouse gas. Modern fertilisers are expensive, so cannot be used by peasant farmers, and can thus increase inequity in land ownership.

(b) Destroying pests; but many of the pesticides currently used are poisons and contaminate the food chain.

(c) Providing irrigation; but recently built large dams, in Egypt, Brazil, China and elsewhere, are producing critical ecological hazards, and salinisation of irrigation systems.

(d) Producing improved crop strains; genetic breeding is presently reducing the genetic basis of major food crops to a dangerously narrow level. The newer strains are also expensive and beyond the resources of small farmers.

The permanent effects of the Green Revolution, which now affects a third of the world's cropland, are uncertain. While it enabled growth in grain production to keep ahead of growth in human numbers from 1950-84, productivity is now levelling off and is projected to fall in the future (12). Meanwhile, current policies are severely reducing the possibility of even maintaining many existing animal and vegetable food supplies. Half the world's wetlands, which cover 6% of the earth's surface, and which are now recognised as a valuable source of sustainable animal and vegetable food, have been lost during this century, through drainage, pollution, over-fishing and irrigation.

The tropical rain forests, which it is estimated could produce 20 times as much nourishing food as at present, have since 1900 been reduced by 40%, partly to provide firewood for 2 billion people in the developing countries, partly to provide cropland (some for cash crops and beef exports to the developed world), and partly for commercial exports of wood to the industrialised countries, a trade which has increased by a factor of 16 in the past 30 years. Due to the thin soil, where nutrients are normally rapidly recycled, deforestation causes irreversible soil degradation. Unless deforestation is arrested, much of the South East Asian and West African forests will have disappeared by the year 2000, and those of Latin America reduced by a further 40%; and all tropical forests will have disappeared in 85 years.

Desertification is caused by over-cultivation, over-grazing, bad irrigation and deforestation. At present rates of desertification a third of the world's cropland will disappear by the end of the century. Severe water shortages are predicted for 30 countries in Africa and Asia within 15 years as a result of over-use and climate change.

Large areas of cropland are devoted, in developing and in industrialised countries, to cash crops which are of no nutritional value, such as coffee, tea, cotton, tobacco, drug crops and sugar and sorghum to produce ethanol to take the place of petroleum as a fuel.

In the Western industrialised countries 70% of total grain consumption is fed to livestock. Grain converted to meat loses over 75% of its calories and over 65% of its protein. Ten pounds of grain produce one pound of meat. Physiologists assert that in general the human body does not need meat for good health. Nevertheless, there are some environments, such as Welsh and Scottish hills and in Australia and New Zealand, which can be used for animal-rearing but are unsuitable for growing crop plants.

Fish yields are declining, due to over-fishing and pollution, and the effects of climate change and ozone depletion could worsen this trend.

The combination of these factors confirms that we are rapidly approaching the carrying capacity of the planet for the human species. Experts differ as to the number of human beings that the Earth can feed, but they all agree that the higher figures quoted above for the possible rise in population are far above this number. If these levels are reached many millions will die of starvation.

Agonising Choices for Energy

The world is poised on the threshold of a completely new energy era. The age of fossil-fuel energy, which made the industrialisation of the North possible, is coming to an end. Oil will be exhausted in 30 to 50 years, natural gas in 200 years and coal in 300 years at present rates of use. As already noted, the use of these resources threatens the climate. If coal and oil have to be rejected, alternative sources of energy are fission nuclear power or various technologies, still largely underdeveloped, for harnessing the power of the sun, wind and waves and recycling hydrogen. And while for the industrial countries it is a question of changing the technologies needed to meet the energy needs of a generally adequate lifestyle, for the billions in the developing countries it is largely a question of developing modern technology from scratch. The matter is urgent, for as we have seen, the wood supplies on which 2 billion people have depended are either used up or must be conserved. China, which has large reserves of coal, and India, which has smaller reserves, are pushing ahead with industrialising on the basis of coal. But should the developing world jump straight into the post-fossil-fuel age? If so, should it opt for fission nuclear energy or are there alternatives?

Fission Nuclear Energy

The dangers of fission nuclear energy have been much discussed. It produces radioactive plutonium which can be used for nuclear weapons. Much of the radioactive waste produced is so dangerous that no satisfactory way has been found to store it or to decommission the equally lethal reactors themselves after their active life of about 30 years. Since the near disaster at Three Mile Island in the USA and the disaster at Chernobyl in the Ukraine, there has been increasing resistance to the nuclear option, but the Club of Rome recently advised, "with the greatest reluctance, that it should be kept open as being probably less dangerous than the combustion of oil and coal" (13). But what would this option involve? In 1990, 424 nuclear reactors, which had cost about $200 billion, - all but 16 in the industrialised countries - were supplying 17 per cent of the world's electricity. It has been calculated that to meet a doubled or trebled demand, allowing for the population increase and the development needs of the poor countries, several thousand reactors would have to be built. The plutonium these produce could be used for nuclear weapons, and there is no solution in view to the problem of disposing of nuclear waste (14).

Fusion Nuclear Energy

"Fusion", the fusion of light atoms to release energy, is the process which powers the sun and the stars; and it has now been applied by mankind in the hydrogen bomb, which is a thousand times more potent than the atomic fission bomb. But the technology for harnessing this mighty force for peaceful purposes has not yet been mastered. If it could be, it has been estimated that a fusion reactor could produce 2000 Mw of electricity continuously, using only one ton of fuel per annum - deuterium derived from hydrogen in water, and therefore in unlimited supply. Research into the development of fusion energy has been carried out in the USA, the ex-Soviet Union, the European Community, China and Japan for 30 years, working in collaboration. In Britain and USA experts have high hopes of success by the end of the second half of the next century. The capital cost of a fusion reactor is likely to be roughly equivalent to that of a fission fast breeder reactor. And they would have no military importance. Their "giantism" might be turned to good account by building them to supply energy to regions rather than countries. But it is too soon to say whether fusion energy is a realistic long-term energy option.

Hydrogen Gas

Hydrogen can be burnt as we now burn coal, oil or natural gas. The basic arguments for substituting hydrogen for other fuels are that it is non-polluting, and can cause no atmospheric imbalance, such as the greenhouse effect. It only forms water, the substance from which it came. Its separation from and recombination with oxygen form a closed cycle which can be a safe and efficient source of energy for as many aeons as the sun shines on the earth.

Christopher Flavin, of the Worldwatch Institute in Washington, concludes that "The road to a sustainable energy is a long one, but a key gap may soon be crossed; a picture of a new energy economy is beginning to emerge, one that may bridge the political divisions that have stymied progress so far. The solar-hydrogen economy is compellingly simple in design, economically practical, and ecologically necessary. Moreover, it does not require radical scientific break-through or the discovery of any entirely new resources. This vision of the possible may finally spark an energy evolution. If so, the pace of change could surprise us all" (15).

Renewables

One way in which the coming energy crisis is being met is by applying modern technology to the development of traditional renewables: hydro, wind, tidal and geothermal power and biomass. Novel modes of directly collecting solar heat for small-scale heating and lighting and other domestic uses and the generation of electricity through photo-voltaic cells (electric batteries) charged by the Sun and small electric generators is making fairly rapid progress in both industrial and developing countries. For example, the ever-resourceful Chinese have built some 90,000 small-scale hydro-units, which together produce the amount of electricity which would be produced by six nuclear power stations. The Chinese invention of small biogas plants for farmers, in which methane gas is produced from dung and human faeces, with the residue used for fertiliser, has been adopted in 46 countries. Metal windmills are dotting the great open spaces of California and are planned for the wind-swept mountains and islands of northern Britain. Plans are in hand to harness the tides around the coasts of Britain and France, and Brazil is running a quarter of its cars on ethanol produced from sugar-cane.

Energy Conservation

Research, so far inadequate, is going on in the industrial countries into technologies for saving energy at the domestic and local levels. The energy-conserving housing of Canada and Sweden could be modelled throughout the temperate and cold zones of the world, and cars must become more energy efficient. Integrated public transport policies both save energy and reduce pollution in city centres. In the USA, the State of California has introduced legislation requiring 2% of cars to be electric-powered by 2000. Other American states may follow suit. In developing countries, energy-efficient stoves could greatly reduce the rate at which wood is being burnt.

Energy and Communications

The development of small-scale, self generating electricity in the developing countries is prompting the communications revolution. In many countries there is now a TV in every village, operated by photo-voltaic cells. Ghanaian farmer Kwabena Nten lives with his two wives, eight full-time workers and some 23 children in a homestead 300 miles from the capital, Accra. There is no electricity; there are no shops nor market. But he starts his day at 6 a.m. by listening to the radio news. The studios of Radio for Peace International of the campus of the United Nations' University for Peace in Costa Rica broadcast to 50 countries. The United Nations' Development Programme and the World Bank have carried out an Energy Sector Assessment Programme which is helping many developing countries to establish realistic energy strategies for the billions who still live rural lives.

A World Energy Policy

This brief survey of the world energy situation indicates that there is

284

an overriding need for a world energy policy, which will combine micro and macro production of benign forms of energy at levels suited both to the basic and creative needs of all human beings.

It is extraordinary that no United Nations Specialised Agency for energy exists, comparable to the 15 which are concerned with economic and social matters. The only international energy body related to the United Nations is the International Atomic Energy Agency in Vienna, with 112 member states, whose task is to promote the development of peaceful nuclear energy throughout the world, and to ensure that no country, apart from the five recognised nuclear powers, is using its reactors for military purposes. It has no powers of enforcement. New technology could transform the world's energy situation and thereby the world's economy, providing the basis for "sustainable development". Meanwhile each of the 185 member states of the United Nations formulates its own national energy policy without reference to any regional or world strategy.

Minerals

Minerals are of central importance in modern technology. For instance, chromium and manganese as well as iron are essential for the production of steel; and copper and aluminium (of which bauxite is the raw material) for electricity. In World War II the USA placed nearly 300 minerals on its short supply list. To maintain its current life-style the USA consumes 40,000 pounds of minerals per head a year; the developing countries' consumption is, of course, a fraction of this figure. The world's mineral deposits, which can now be accurately surveyed by earth satellites equipped with remote sensory devices, are concentrated in four regions: that of the former USSR (the largest deposits); North America; Australia; and southern Africa. Global consumption of minerals has been increasing by about 90% a decade, and the point has been reached when the exhaustion of certain key minerals within the next 50 to 100 years is in sight. This applies in particular to industrial diamonds, gold, silver, tin, zinc, nickel, copper, lead, antimony, cadmium and molybdenum. Already copper is being extracted from deposits containing only 0.5% ore. The exploitation of the large mineral deposits in Antarctica, which would, in the opinion of some scientists, spell ecological disaster, is now forbidden by international treaty. In 1969 the US National Academy of Sciences called for international action to explore, conserve and manage the world's mineral resources in the common interest, and advocated planned international research. The Law of the Sea Treaty of 1982, now ratified, has declared the minerals of the deep ocean floor - nodules of manganese, copper, cobalt and nickel - to be "the common heritage of mankind", over which no state should have sovereign rights, to be explored and exploited by an "international regime to be established ... for the benefit of mankind as a whole, taking into particular consideration the interests and needs of the developing countries" (see Chapter 18). If such global policies are not pursued, the strong will be tempted to grab what they can from the weak and the weak to use their resources to blackmail the strong.

But the situation may be helped by new technology, which is creating a variety of new materials, giving the designer a very wide choice. Availability of raw materials need no longer be the critical issue, since there are many alternatives. The distinction between the material and the production of an object made from it is often vanishing; the material is "designed" for that particular application, together with the object to be produced, in a combined process.

The UNCED Conference at Rio

After the Stockholm Conference on the Environment of 1972, and the publication in 1987 of the Brundtland Report which put forward the key concept of "sustainable development" (16), awareness of the environmental threat began to spread among ordinary people in the industrial countries. This led to the United Nations' Conference on Environment and Development (UNCED), held in Rio de Janeiro in 1992 - the first United Nations' conference on a special topic to be held at the Summit level. One hundred and twenty heads of state attended - President Bush of the USA with great reluctance - as well as representatives of 58 other states. UNCED concentrated on four problems:

(a) The danger of "global warming". A Convention on reducing carbon dioxide emissions by 12 to 15 per cent by the year 2000 was signed, but only as a general statement of intent, awaiting Protocols providing for action. President Bush brushed aside the advice of the majority of the scientists and listened to the businessmen who asserted that the dangers were not fully proven. Yet if nothing is done soon, China, possessing one sixth of the world's coal stocks, is likely to forge ahead with coal-based industrialisation and "wreck the climate for everyone". The Convention entered into force in March 1994 and by August 1994 had been ratified by 93 states.

(b) A Convention on biodiversity, aimed at protecting the gene bank in developing countries from exploitation by the industrial countries, was signed, but the USA abstained, largely because it felt that the USA's biotechnology industry would be compromised. Later, the Clinton administration endorsed the Convention.

(c) A draft Convention on the protection of the tropical forests was not signed because of the opposition of India and Malaysia to interference with their national sovereignty.

(d) Draft Conventions on dealing with desertification and conservation of ocean fish stocks were shelved.

Documents setting out 27 Principles ("Agenda 21") and 40 specific targets for planning environmental policy in the 21st century were approved. Thus many essential problems have been identified and guidelines for the international community have been established. But who is to carry these policies forward? This will be discussed in Chapter 18. The vital problem which emerged at UNCED was that of funding sustainable development in the developing countries. UNCED's Preparatory Commissions estimated the cost of implementing Agenda 21 at $125 billion in annual flows from rich to poor. All that UNCED achieved was a vague commitment by the rich to consider reaching the 0.7 per cent of GDP aid target of annual flows from rich to poor set by the United Nations (see above). The general level in 1993 was 0.3 per cent. President Bush summed up the attitude of these countries when he remarked, as he left, that "the time of the open cheque book is over".

Population control, arms control, refugees, debt problems (see Chapter 18), clean water supplies and the question of building up buffer stocks, were other topics which, according to Mrs Gro Brundtland, the Prime Minister of Norway, received inadequate attention. Nor was there discussion of two crucial facts: that the world's armed forces are the single largest polluter on earth; and that sustainable development involves "limits to growth" for the industrialised countries.

The Peace Dividend

Norman Myers gives a short list of some of the possibilities that could be achieved if part of the $900 billion a year (almost $3 billion daily) outlay on the military were used for humane and environmental purposes (17). These include: $40 billion a year to boost developing-world agriculture sufficiently to prevent starvation; $36 billion a year to provide safe water and sanitation for the third of the world's population which lacks them; $12 billion a year to reverse desertification; $3 billion a year to provide contraception for all couples who desire it; $2.2 billion a year for a global immunisation programme and eradication of malaria; $2 billion a year for the Tropical Forest Action Programme - less than two month's arms spending so far! Eight times as much - $120 billion a year - is spent on development of new weapons as on research into new forms of energy.

Conclusion

As we survey the emerging problems of today against the background of the world situation described at the start of this Chapter, it becomes clear that the world is entering a completely new era. Politically, the world is composed of states pursuing power politics. Economically, business firms, large and small, are competing with each other for "profitability in world markets", and in so doing are exploiting the availability of cheap labour in the North and the South. "Aid" to poor countries is a declining charitable hand out, and is outweighed by a burden of debt twice its amount. Nuclear weapons are still stockpiled, although in reduced numbers, and could fall into the hands of poor states which nourish bitter grievances. Sophisticated non-nuclear weapons are being eagerly sold by the industrial countries to these poor states. The violence, corruption, decadence and proliferation of local but terrible wars in the developing world are symptoms of the frustration and suffering of the billions caught up in this mesh of problems which they do not understand, and far less have the power to control. But now certain situations, in particular the climate threat and the energy crisis, give them some power of clout. They can pursue economic policies which would be disastrous for the industrial countries. The only way forward must involve a global commitment to planning and sharing the earth's resources, to social policies based on "Basic Needs First", to the abolition of nuclear weapons and the drastic reduction of the production and sale of conventional weapons to those needed for police purposes, national and international. A large majority of the scientists and researchers in the world must be enlisted to work on these problems; and their work could be financed by the "peace dividend", the money saved by disarmament.

Chapter 18

THE FOUNDATION OF WORLD COMMUNITY

Introduction

THE ongoing world crisis outlined in Chapter 17 is stark. *Unless* urgent action is taken, there are likely to be major disasters within the next 30 years or so. Common-sense suggests that this action must rest on six principles. (i) *sharing;* (ii) *planning* on the basis of agreed priority needs; (iii) *conservation* of basic resources; (iv) *"conversion "* of assets from military to civilian production which, of course, involves disarmament; (v) all these policies should be carried out in a *participatory,* not an authoritarian mode, through democratic legal systems and through the "community" process; (vi) in accordance with the principles of "subsidiarity" they should be implemented at every le*vel of organisation:* global, regional, national, provincial and local (see Chapter 14). The implementation of these six principles will involve the transformation of the world society into a community based on "Liberty, Equality and Fraternity", on the full implementation of Human Rights. There is no other way.

A survey of the world scene shows that the foundations of the world community are being laid – a process which started essentially after World War II, less than 50 years ago. The basic building blocks of the pyramidal structure which is emerging are, of course, the nation states, since it is in them that sovereignty essentially resides in international law (see Chapter 13). But in the last 50 years there has been an extraordinary thrust – beyond the nation state into regional and global bodies, and within the nation state into local bodies.

The Function of the United Nations

At the apex of the emerging world community is the United Nations, established in 1945. Its functions, set out in its Charter, are:

(a) To save succeeding generations from "the scourge of war" by "uniting our strength to maintain international peace and security";

(b) To promote "human rights and fundamental freedoms for all without distinction as to race, sex, language or religion"; and

(c) "To employ international machinery for the promotion of the economic and social advancement of all peoples".

The creation in 1919 of the League of Nations to carry out the first of these functions represented an extraordinary leap forward in human affairs. The age-old attitude that fighting is a glorious human activity and that the warrior is a superior human being was rejected as both immature and immoral, and the principle of "collective security" was affirmed, the principle that each should automatically be responsible for the security of all, within a framework of the rule of law. The League of Nations, with the International Court of Justice as its adjunct, was set up to resolve disputes and conflicts. Since almost all of Africa and much of Asia was colonised, and since the USA refused to join it, the League's membership was restricted essentially to the countries of Europe (including the USSR) and Latin America; it was universal in theory but not in fact.

Out of the terrible experience of World War II the United Nations was born. Another extraordinary leap forward in human affairs was taken. For the League's function was essentially negative: to prevent the sovereign states from fighting each other. The United Nations' two new functions are essentially positive: to create a better world for humankind. They involve it in almost every aspect of human life, and they take it beyond the rule of law, and thus by implication beyond the sovereign state, into the moral realm of world community. The membership of the United Nations is now almost universal: 185 states in September 1994. The only state which refuses to join is Switzerland. The United Nations represents almost all of the 5.5 billion inhabitants of the Earth.

The Structure of the United Nations

The main organs of the United Nations are the General Assembly, the Security Council, the Economic and Social Council, and the International Court of Justice. In addition, the United Nations' has a "family" of "Specialised Agencies", with their own constitutions and funds, such as the World Health Organisation (WHO), the Food and Agricultural Organisation (FAO), the World Bank, the International Monetary Fund (IMF), and bodies supported by voluntary contributions, such as UNICEF (the United Nations International Children's Emergency Fund), and the United Nations High Commission For Refugees (UNHCR). Altogether the "family" has 31 members; the only significant matter which they do not collectively cover is energy (see Appendix III).

The International Labour Organisation (ILO) is unique in that it is composed not only of representatives of governments but also of employers and trade unions, who all participate in decision-making. It has adopted a record of 174 Conventions about labour conditions (of which Britain has ratified 66), and it won the Nobel Peace Prize in 1969.

The General Assembly of the UN represents the 185 member states as such. (The latest member to join is the tiny Pacific island of Palau). South Africa, having at last accepted the principles of Human Rights, has been re-admitted to the fold. Each member, however big or wealthy, however small or poor, has one vote. Its resolutions are passed by a two-thirds majority, but they are non-binding, for this would involve a surrender of state sovereignty. The United Nations is therefore undemocratic in that, in defiance of its own philosophy of Human Rights, its parliamentary body does not control its own executive organs.

The Security Council, composed of 15 states, has "primary" responsibility for the maintenance of international peace and security on behalf of the whole United Nations. Its decisions *are* binding – member states are committed by virtue of their membership to carrying them out – even if they have not participated in them. The Charter gives the Security Council "teeth" to enforce its decisions: the right to impose economic and/or military sanctions on a misbehaving state, and to create and use a United Nations' armed force – an international police force – for peacekeeping. The composition of the Security Council reflects the realities of political power when the United Nations was set up in 1945. The five great powers of that date, USA, USSR, China, Britain and France, have permanent seats with the right of veto; the ten other states are elected by the General Assembly for two year periods. The veto was cast 279 times between 1945 and 1985, mainly by the Communist USSR, making the Security Council largely ineffective. Between 1985, when Mikhail Gorbachev came to power in the USSR and announced that his country's policy would now be to disarm and to co-operate with the USA and all other states in working for peace and progress through the United Nations, and 1994 (the time of writing) there have been onlt two vetoes. The Security Council passed 650 Resolutions between 1945 and 1990; between 1990 and mid-1994 it has passed over 800.

The Economic and Social Council consists of 54 states elected by the General Council for a term of three years. It links the work of the Specialised Agencies to the General Assembly, to which it is responsible. Unlike the Security Council, it does not have the power to act on behalf of the General Assembly. In 1992 a Sustainable Development Commission of 52 member states was set up under the Economic and Social Council to implement the policies agreed at UNCED, the Rio Summit Conference on Environment and Development.

The International Court of Justice, set up in 1919 as an adjunct to the League of Nations, consists of 15 judges elected by the General Assembly and the Security Council. It hears cases submitted to it by governments, and then takes binding decisions. So far it has been a weak body, since not many states make use of it. When Nicaragua sued the USA in the Court for mining its harbours, the USA, which had agreed in principle to accept the Court's findings, refused to comply.

The Chief Administrative Officer of the United Nations is the Secretary-General, chosen by the General Assembly on the recommendation of the Security Council, which thus has a veto on his nomination.

The Achievements of the United Nations System

On the face of it the United Nations has not achieved much in the 49 years of its existence. The major global problems outlined in Chapter 17 are becoming ever more acute. The United Nations has been unable to halt the apparent slide towards cataclysm. Its outer surface inevitably reflects the tensions and quarrels of its 185 member states. Yet under the surface new and little published developments are laying the foundations of world community.

Disarmament
The United Nations has had very limited success in carrying out its first, and what most people regard as its most important, function. The system of collective security provided for in its Charter has not worked. This system was based on the expectation that the five permanent member states of the Security Council would co-operate to maintain world peace. Instead, they have armed themselves with over 50,000 nuclear weapons, directed essentially against each other, and held the whole world hostage in a balance of terror. They have growled at each other for forty years in the Cold War, hotting it up from time to time by fighting the long-drawn-out wars in Vietnam and Afghanistan, invading Hungary, Egypt, Czechoslovakia, Grenada and Panama, and intervening less obviously in about half of the 120 or so third world conflicts since 1945. And they have stuffed the developing countries with highly sophisticated conventional arms.

In 1978 the United Nations affirmed its central responsibility for disarmament by holding its First Special Session on Disarmament, as a result of which it set up a 40-state Committee on Disarmament as the main international forum for negotiations. But in practice the superpowers have largely bypassed this forum and negotiated themselves a series of limited arms control treaties (see Chapter 17).

Today there are faint signs of a new dawn. First, there was the emergence on the world scene of a Soviet leader who proposed that the USSR should lead the world into disarmament through the United Nations, involving total nuclear disarmament, and major disarmament of conventional weapons. Secondly, the General Assembly of the United Nations, in a special session held in 1987 on Disarmament and

294

Development, affirmed for the first time that "security" lies not only in "defence" against an "enemy", but also in eliminating the misery of under-development. The implication of this new linkage of security to development is that *security* demands the transfer of resources by the rich countries from arms to "aid"! Third, "conversion" of industry from war to peace production, an essential corollary to disarmament, has now been put on the United Nations' agenda. The Thorsson Report of 1981 on Disarmament and Development pointed out that conversion can be painless, avoiding economic dislocation, if it is *planned* and carried out over a period of about ten years. A General Assembly Resolution of 1981 called on all countries with arms industries to initiate conversion plans. Hitherto, Sweden has been the only country to respond to this call. In the 1980s the subject of economic conversion was taboo in the USA. Now there is a new mood in that country. President Clinton has agreed to provide $20 billion to fund conversion, though the Republican control of Congress resulting from the elections of November 1994 may set back this programme.

The United Nations' Charter provides, in Chapter VII, that the Security Council may use armed force or impose non-military sanctions "to maintain or restore international peace and security." These clauses have been invoked, as we shall see below, but at immense cost in military lives, civilian suffering and material destruction. As early as 1948 the need became apparent for something different, "peacekeeping" and conciliation. In the Third World, independence was being granted by the former colonial powers, new boundaries were being drawn, civil, tribal or territorial wars were erupting on a massive scale, sometimes in the wake of outside intervention (for example, the American invasion of Vietnam (1964-75) which killed 50,000 American and two million Vietnamese, maiming another four million; the French colonial war in Algeria (1954-62) which killed a million Algerians; South Africa's support of rebel forces in Mozambique and Angola; Cuba's support of anti-rebel forces in Angola and Namibia; and Morocco's intervention in Western Sahara), and where in many cases attempts were being made to hold the first free and fair elections a new country had ever known. United Nations' peace-keepers have patrolled disputed frontiers in Kashmir (since 1948), the Middle East (since 1956), Cyprus (since 1963), the former Yugoslavia (since 1993 with 20,000 troops),

295

holding the fort while the political leaders argue interminably about their rights. In their distinctive blue berets and white army trucks, armed only with side-arms for self-defence, they have guarded refugee camps, helped to organise the relief supplies for civilian victims of war poured in by the large number of Western charities, and co-operated with another vital UN institution, the UN High Commission for Refugees (UNHCR), which in 1992 was caring for some 27 million refugees and 20 million "displaced persons" i.e. people in their own countries who have lost their homes.

In certain countries, such as the former Belgian Congo, where 20,000 UN military and civilian peace keepers, contributed by 35 countries, spent four years (1960-64) suppressing army mutiny, and establishing law and order and essential services in the vast new country of Zaire, the UN force UNCONGO was granted authority by the Security Council to use force when necessary to perform its functions. The whole operation cost $400 million. Another outstanding United Nations' success was its organisation and supervision of the independence of Namibia, a territory in South West Africa rich in material wealth. Namibia, which had been a German colony from 1884 to 1918, was then given as a League of Nations "Mandate" (in practice, colony) to South Africa, which refused to accept the United Nations' Security Council's declaration of independence in 1966, and ruled the territory on the basis of *apartheid*. Civil war between Blacks and Whites, the former supported by Angola and Cuba, ensued until finally, in 1989, the United Nations secured South Africa's withdrawal and sent a peace-keeping force to monitor democratic, non-racial elections, and help the drafting of Namibia's first constitution. Namibia's first President, the independence leader Sam Nujoma, was sworn in by the United Nations' Secretary-General – unofficially, and perhaps unconsciously, acting as King or President of the World! The United Nations has also carried out a somewhat similar operation in Cambodia, rescuing it in 1991 from a decade of civil war and war with Vietnam, and organising free elections, for which there was an almost 90 per cent turn-out. Perhaps the United Nations' most dramatic success has lain in South Africa's elections of April 1994, when for the first time South Africa's Black majority were given the vote. Although some angry, rich and well-armed Whites could have wrecked the great change which they had

296

been resisting for decades, the combination of nearly 3000 international observers to cover 9000 voting places, with Nelson Mandela's extraordinary moral authority and the desire of the South African Whites to rejoin the international community and end the economic sanctions imposed on the country, ensured that all went off peacefully.

Cyprus, a British colony from 1878 until 1961, subsided after independence into civil war between its Greek majority and its Turkish minority. This situation was compounded when Turkey invaded and occupied a third of the island in 1974. In 1964 the United Nations Secretary-General sent in a 7,000-strong peace-keeping force to act as a buffer between the two communities, which is still there in 1994.

On the two occasions on which the three Western permanent members of the Security Council, the United States, Britain and France, have fought a war under the fig-leaf of the United Nations' flag (the Korean War from 1950-3 and the Gulf War of 1990-1) they were motivated essentially more by their own interests than by United Nations' principles. The possibility that the only realistic solution for apparently intractable racial, tribal and cultural problems such as those of Bosnia, Somalia, Rwanda and perhaps Kashmir would be a period as a United Nations' protectorate, may now be on the horizon. These conflicts also show that if men (almost never women) are sufficiently strongly motivated to kill one another, and are armed to do so, it is difficult or impossible to stop them, and unfair to blame the UN for failing to make peace. In the long run peace depends more on to removing poverty and ignorance than on international police action.

In April 1994 there were almost 70,000 United Nations' personnel drawn from 66 countries (many of them in the Third World) engaged in 18 peace-keeping operations around the world (1). Many others have been wound up, having performed their tasks – or in some cases failed. A total of 528,000 military police and civilian personnel had served under the flag of the United Nations up to January 1992; the total cost of the operations over 10 years is estimated at $8.3 billion, as compared with world expenditure on arms of nearly one trillion dollars a year between 1987 and 1994. Nevertheless, the peace-keeping operations constitute the beginning of the policing of world affairs. If United Nations' peace-keeping is to be effective in an increasingly chaotic world, the *ad hoc* forces must be expanded into a permanent police force and directed by the "Military Staff Committee" or permanent Headquarters provided for in Chapter VII of the Charter, and properly financed. At present countries which contribute forces and relief materials pay for these themselves – and of course many are in arrears. At the end of this Chapter we shall note proposals for the proper financing of an effective United Nations' Police Force. The alternatives are surely unacceptable: increasing world-wide chaos, or the assumption by the United States of the role of Policeman of the World.

Preventive Diplomacy

Nevertheless, the need to send in UN peace keepers or peacemakers is a confession of failure. The most constructive alternative is preventive diplomacy. This involves confidence-building measures to prevent disputes arising, to prevent existing disputes escalating into conflict and limiting the spread of conflict. It requires fact-finding through early warning systems. This could include existing UN staff, a network of human rights commissioners or non-governmental organisations. Modern electronic communication technology (the Information Superhighway) will also be vital here, for example, by satellite monitoring, either through existing organisations, commercial satellites or by the UN acquiring its own satellite network. Successful preventive diplomacy is, of course, far less expensive than the options needed if it fails or is not attempted. This is one of the reasons why it should be tried early.

In the light of information provided by these means, the Secretary-General, perhaps directly or perhaps through the Security Council, should be empowered to send fact-finding missions. As has already occurred, he himself can act as a personal mediator. There are many other lower-level ways in which mediation can occur at a more local level, and a network for initiating or activating these is needed. Certain groups such as Buddhists and Quakers are particularly skilled in this form of mediation; they prefer to use the term "peacemaking" for this activity rather than non-aggressive military intervention.

Sanctions

Sanctions are another alternative to military intervention. As shown

298

in South Africa and Southern Rhodesia before it became Zimbabwe, sanctions can contribute to ending unjust regimes and situations, though only slowly, and armed conflict is likely to continue in the time they take to work. As seen in Iraq and the former Yugoslavia, sanctions can, and do, harm the general population affected, and they should always exclude food, medical supplies and humanitarian aid. Difficult decisions may have to be made between allowing conflict to persist while sanctions take effect, as in South Africa, or resorting to armed action. In the Gulf, estimates were that sanctions would take at least a year to work; insufficient time was allowed before armed intervention.

Action by neighbouring states and other less legitimate parties can undermine the effectiveness of sanctions; for example, oil continued to reach Southern Rhodesia through South Africa for a considerable time after the former's Unilateral Declaration of Independence, and arms smuggling has undoubtedly occurred in former Yugoslavia. How far, and by what means can the net of enforcement be extended in such circumstances?

"Proper Soldiering "
We noted in Chapter 7 how fighting and wars were going on all through the 5,000 years of the history of civilisations (in the plural). In this century some 109 million men have been killed in war, compared to 19 million in the 19th century. Twenty-three million have been killed in conflicts since 1945. In 1900, 90 per cent of war casualties were military combatants; today, 90 per cent are civilians. Many of the post-1945 wars are traditional wars of aggression and greed, taking place in the developing countries. But at the same time, and particularly in the industrialised countries, there has been a subtle shift to the concept of "defence" against an enemy". Perhaps the most significant aspect of the peaceful collapse of Communism in East Europe in 1989-90 was the sudden disappearance of the enemy! To watch President Gorbachev touring West Europe and USA holding out the hand of friendship and receiving an immediate warm response, to hear two of his senior advisers joke to an audience in Copenhagen about the American "enemy complex", while they affirmed that the USSR was determined to co-operate with the Western powers in the United Nations, was an extraordinary experience. The "enemy" had become a psychological

delusion, the reality was the friend! And, as the enemy complex fades, there will be a greater demand to use the "peace dividend" for friendly purposes.

One practical way of turning enemies into friends and implementing the peace dividend is the idea that some at least of the 30 million young men in the world's armed forces should be assigned to environmental security activities. The Indian Army has already pioneered this policy on a wide scale; and 22 other countries, including USA, Britain, France, Germany and Italy, have set their armed forces on this path. One can envisage that the time may soon come when the United Nations' Commission for Sustainable Development will have at its disposal a large corps of trained military environmentalists drawn from the national armed forces, helping to turn battle-fields into gardens and enemies into friends (2).

Controlling Conventional Arms
The arms trade, with its huge pay-off in profits and jobs, is the fuel which makes the hideous war massacres possible. The curbing and even ending of this trade should be a top priority of disarmament. Between 1969 and 1988 the USSR exported $236 billion worth of arms, the USA $149 billion, and France, Britain and West Germany $84 billion (3). In 1992 the United Nations made a start by setting up a Register of Conventional Arms, to which all member states are required to report data on the transfer of seven categories of offensive conventional weapons "considered most de-stabilising". But it does not include local production and procurement, and it excludes certain vital categories, such as bombs, small arms and ground-to-air-missiles. By 1994, 80 countries, including all exporters except South Africa, had submitted data. But 60 per cent of importers have refused to report, including Saudi Arabia, Kuwait, Iran, Syria, Taiwan and Thailand. There is clear evidence that the British and American Governments have conived in illegal arms deals with Iraq and Iran respectively. Britain is bribing Malaysia and Indonesia (which invaded the former Portuguese colony of East Timor in 1975, and has killed a third of the East Timorese population – 200,000 people – who were demanding independence) with aid for environmentally unsound projects – a big dam and a power station respectively – in order to gain contracts worth

$2 million each for supplying large quantities of arms to these countries. Meanwhile British aid for Tanzania, the world's second poorest country with no military aspirations, remains at an all-time low! So much for Human Rights! (4). It is of vital importance, therefore, that the Register of conventional arms be strengthened and extended. The International Association of Lawyers Against Nuclear Arms (IALANA) and the World Order Models Project (WOMP) have recently drafted a Convention on the Monitoring and Reduction of Arms Stockpiling, Production and Transfers. This would establish an Agency under the auspices of the UN to supervise a ten-year three-stage programme which would eventually result in the banning of all arms transfers and the reduction of arms to no more than those needed for territorial defence. Under the Convention disputes would be referred to the International Court of Justice.

The Development of International Law
The United Nations and its Specialised Agencies have laid the foundations for a system of international law. They have promoted some 20,000 treaties on every kind of topic, ranging from the Law of the Sea Treaty (see below) to the Human Rights Conventions, to treaties concerning the conditions of workers on land and sea. This new body of international law is developing in many directions. A United Nations' "Code of Conduct" for the multinational corporations, which produce 30 per cent of the world's GNP, carry 70 per cent of the world's trade, and do most of the world's research – 95 per cent of which is carried out in the industrialised countries – may lay the basis for international commercial law. But at present (1994) the Secretary-General has closed down the department concerned and brought this vital project to a stand-still.

A system of international criminal law is emerging. The "Rules of War" which forbid the infliction of suffering on innocent civilians, prisoners of war or wounded combatants, have been formulated in a series of international Conventions since the beginning of the century, including a Convention banning the crime of genocide (1948). They have now been supplemented by two new and revolutionary categories of crime: the crime of waging aggressive war; and the crime of *not* disobeying an order to commit a war crime. These two categories,

301

known as the "Nuremberg Principles" because they were laid down at the Nuremberg Trials of the Nazi leaders in 1945-6, were unanimously endorsed by the General Assembly and have thus become international law. The United Nations has drafted an International Criminal Code, which deals with terrorism and torture as well as war crimes and the Nuremberg Principles. It is setting up an International Criminal Court to enforce the Code.

According to Dr. Benjamin Ferencz, a former American Prosecutor at the Nuremberg Trials, "The Security Council already has legal authority to create organs needed to do its job. On issues threatening world peace it can compel parties to accept decisions of the International Court of Justice. As illustrated by the new International Criminal Court for Yugoslavia, the Council can – in very short order – also create a permanent international criminal tribunal to hold personally accountable all those who flout the laws of peace and humanity "(5). Dr. Ferencz was referring to a Court of eleven judges recently set up at The Hague, which is collecting evidence to try Yugoslavians accused of crimes such as massacre, torture and rape. In November 1994 the Vice President of Rwanda in Central Africa, where a hideous civil war is raging, announced that they would co-operate with a United Nations' Genocide Tribunal which is being set up to investigate the killing of a million Rwandans of one tribe by another.

The two United Nations' Covenants of Human Rights outlined in Chapter 12 add a further dimension to international law. Their enforcement is monitored by a United Nations' Commission of 43 states. Under an "Optional Protocol" to the Covenant of Civil and Political Rights, which has been signed by 61 states, signatory states will permit their citizens to petition the Commission direct if they think that their Human Rights are being violated. This is an affirmation of the principle that the person counts *as such,* and not simply as the citizen of a state. The developing international law of Human Rights challenges the provision in the United Nations' Charter (Article 2) which forbids the United Nations to intervene "in matters which are essentially within the domestic jurisdiction of any state". It also challenges the right of self-determination of *peoples* laid down in the two Covenants (see Chapter 12). Until 1994 the only United Nations' institution for dealing with violations of Human Rights was a Committee of 33 national

302

representatives which met in Geneva once a year. In 1993 the General Assembly voted unanimously to establish the post of Permanent High Commissioner for Human Rights. The Western nations wanted him to have enforcement rights, and Italy proposed a United Nations' Court of Human Rights similar to that of the Council of Europe, to which individuals could appeal over the heads of their governments (see below). But China said no!

There is a growing sense in the world today that Human Rights everywhere are everybody's business, as the mass media make everyone aware of what other *persons,* far and near, are suffering. This must inevitably create an impetus to strengthen the system of international law which implements and protects Human Rights.

Promotion of Economic, Social and Environmental Development
The ground work for world planning has been laid. The international organisations have collected a vast amount of information in almost every field, carried out extensive surveys and held innumerable conferences. Population censuses, for example, which were unthought of in a large part of the world before 1945, are now made regularly in all countries, often with United Nations' help. A vast world coverage of expertise is developing. And the computer is making it possible to organise the facts collected in a myriad ways. The data and the tools for world planning now exist – an entirely new development since 1945.

From the early 1970s the United Nations has issued a series of major reports which have projected knowledge of the world's main problems from the confines of offices, laboratories and filing cabinets into the public arena. Huge conferences of officials and experts, watched over by hordes of unofficial groups (non-governmental organisations – NGOs – see below) have been held on the Environment, Food, Health, Habitations, Population, Women's' Rights, Disarmament, and the relationship of Disarmament to Development. A series of reports produced for the United Nations by international commissions of distinguished persons, culminating in the UNCED conference described in Chapter 17, have provided blue-prints for the longer-term planetary future. Add to these conferences and reports various outline plans and strategies drawn up by the Specialised Agencies for food, employment, health and the conservation of the environment, and the

International Labour Organisation's criteria of "Basic Needs" - and the terms of reference are in place, the groundwork accomplished, for a mighty thrust forward into the era of global planning, based on the *needs*, not wants, of the human race.

The United Nations has launched the *beginnings of the world welfare state,* the structure for *sharing the world's resources.* The idea that rich countries should "aid" poor countries is new in history. The concept of "aid to developing countries" launched by President Truman in 1949 as a charitable hand-out to enable these countries to become "self-sustaining" by the end of the century has been described in Chapter 17. As we have seen, this hope has not been fulfilled. The developing countries' economies "grew" at a reasonable rate – about 5 per cent – in the 1960s and early 1970s; but since the mid 1980s their growth rate has slowed down, and by 1994 many of them are experiencing a negative growth rate – sliding into a morass of debt (the total debt of the developing countries grew from $100 billion in 1970 to over $1,500 billion in 1992), famine, hunger and despair. This backward movement is the result of a combination of factors: the enormous oil price hike launched in 1973; the consequent flood of "petro-dollars", which have been loaned by Western banks to the leaders of gullible or greedy developing countries at exorbitant interest rates; the collapse of the world prices of the commodities which the developing countries export; the rise of the drug culture; the plunder of natural resources, such as the tropical rain forests, by the multinational companies or local bosses for short term gain, causing ecological disasters which lead to famines; and the failure of the rich countries to meet more than about 50 per cent of their aid target. (The Communist world gave, overall, very little aid). As a result, by the early 1990s the poor countries are sending to the rich about 50 per cent more in interest payments than they are receiving in aid. The concept of *Partners in Development* which launched the Second Development Decade has faded. The hope of co-operation has been superseded by the reality of confrontation between "North" and "South".

The Brandt Report *North-South: A Programme for Survival* of 1980 foresaw that "aid" in the form of *ad hoc,* short term charitable handouts was an inadequate and inappropriate means of promoting development. It called for a real world welfare state, based on a form of world income tax, to be levied essentially on international trade, especially the arms trade. "Military expenditure and arms export might be one element entering into a new principle for international taxation for development purposes. A tax on arms trade should be at a higher rate than that on other trade" (6). The same proposal, for an international welfare state financed by a tax on the arms trade, was made by Pope Paul VI in his Encyclical *Populorum Progressio* of 1967.

It is no wonder that the rich countries have shuddered away from the leap forward involved in expanding short-term, *ad hoc* aid into a permanent world welfare state. For by the early 1990s it is clear that the world welfare state itself cannot be an *ad hoc* structure. It will have to be part of a wider leap forward into a "New International Economic Order", involving the construction of a world financial and trading system, managing world resources and the emerging world market to meet basic needs, transferring technology from rich to poor countries, and moving from competition to co-operation. A tentative beginning was made in creating such an International Economic Order after the war, with the establishment of the General Agreement on Tariffs and Trade (GATT) to liberalise trade, the World Bank to make loans – mostly at market rates – to developing countries, and the International Monetary Fund (IMF) to stabilise world currencies. But now protectionism is setting in again; the IMF and the World Bank have failed to solve the debt crisis, and the austerity measures which they demand in return for their help are fomenting revolution in some developing countries. In the economic sphere the stark alternative is emerging: slide back into chaos, or leap forward into community. The danger signals are embodies in the proposed new trade regime of GATT.

The new GATT trade agreement bodes ill for the development of world community. GATT, an international negotiating body, succeeded between 1947 and 1979 in reducing the average tariff rates from 40 to 5 per cent on some 80,000 items. Its 109 member states accounts for 90 per cent of world trade. In 1994, after eight years of negotiations in Uruguay, GATT concluded a new kind of agreement. For the first time agriculture and textiles – the latter constituting a third of developing countries' exports – have been included in its scope, opening Western markets to their cheap exports but encouraging Western manufacturers to flood these countries with types of manufactured goods and technology which they should be developing for themselves. GATT has now been extended to services – finance, banking, patent rights (TRIPPS) and intellectual property rights (TRIMS). To give one example, under the new GATT Agreement, it would be possible for an official of a multinational corporation to slink into a field in Africa or Asia, pick a plant, analyse its genetic potential for food, seeds or medicine in a laboratory of Europe or America, and then patent the result, so that the country in which it grew cannot use its own plants for development.

GATT had no headquarters; its members met from time to time to negotiate. Now a new body, the World Trade Organisation (WTO) has been set up in Geneva in January 1995 to direct an organisation which is likely to be, essentially, a servant for the Western-based multinational corporations.

The dominance of the North is also apparent in the work of the IMF and the World Bank. Articles 57, 63 and 64 of the UN Charter give the Economic and Social Council control of the Specialised Agencies, but the Agencies seem in effect autonomous – and their policies those of the major Western governments. If problems such as the debt crisis and sustainable appropriate development in the South are to be resolved, the contribution of the Agencies should be reviewed and they should be placed under direct UN control through the General Assembly and the Economic and Social Council, or perhaps through a new Economic Security Council with effective enforcement powers.

The principle that basic "commons" are a trust, to be administered collectively on behalf of the whole community, has been embodied by the United Nations in the *Law of the Sea Convention*. Hitherto the oceans, which cover 70 per cent of the earth's surface, have "belonged" to no-one; until the middle of this century "territorial waters" were regarded in international law as extending only three miles beyond a country's coastline. Since 1945 the realisation that the oceans contain large quantities of oil, fish and minerals, and the development of modern technology for exploiting these resources, has raised for the first time the idea of dividing up the oceans as a source of wealth. In 1970 the General Assembly of the United Nations made a historic Declaration, proposed by the Government of Malta, affirming that the contents of the oceans are *"the common heritage of mankind"*, and that *"no state should be claim sovereign rights over any part thereof"*. An International Seabed Authority should explore and exploit these resources "for the *benefit of mankind as a whole, taking into particular consideration the interests and needs of the developing countries"*. This Declaration has two fundamental implications. The first is the explicit departure from the modern idea that the ownership of private property is a fundamental human right (as asserted in Article 17 of the Universal Declaration of Human Rights – see Chapter 13), and the reintroduction, in a secular form, of the traditional concept of property as a sacred trust of the community. The second is the idea of introducing *ab initio,* in this area so far untouched by the long fingers of the nation state, an international authority with real executive powers.

From 1972 to 1982 a Law of the Sea Conference, attended by 155 states, spent ten years drafting the Convention. But set on by the wolves of national sovereignty and the lions of big business, the noble principle of "the common heritage of mankind" has been emasculated. The Convention provides that all coastal states should have national sovereignty over an "economic zone" extending two hundred miles beyond their shores. Since most of the underwater oil and gas, estimated to be worth at least $30 trillion, is in the continental shelf under this zone, this will give a number of states, both rich and poor, a bonanza in oil as well as in fish (ten states get half the oil), while about a third of the world's nations, most of them very poor, will be excluded from this part of the "common heritage". The deep seas beyond the two hundred mile limit abound in "nodules" of nickel, copper, cobalt and manganese. The Convention sets up an International Seabed Authority to administer the mining of these nodules on the principle of international revenue-sharing. The mining will be carried out on an equal basis by private and national state-owned companies, and by an operating organ of the Seabed Authority, to be called "The Enterprise". Some people consider this Treaty to be the biggest step forward in the creation of a system of world law and order since the founding of the United Nations. But the "common heritage" principle conflicts with the free enterprise philosophy, based on the concept of the absolute right to private property. So when the Treaty was presented for signature in 1982, while 159 states signed it, the USA, Britain, Germany and some other western states refused to do so. On

November 16th 1993, Guyana became the 60th state to ratify the Convention, which therefore came into force a year later. Non-signatories (including Britain, USA and Germany) will then be outside the law if they start to mine minerals on their own – and they are the countries which possess the necessary technology.

The major purpose of the Law of the Sea Treaty is to establish an orderly regime for shipping by regulating by law the rights of passage through territorial waters, narrow straits and sea lane passages such as those of the Philippines and Indonesia. The interest of the Americans and other Western states, who opposed the Treaty because of the Common Heritage principle, is reviving because of the need for a legal regime for the rights of passage. Led by the United Nations' Secretary-General and senior American officials, plans are afoot (in 1994) to amend the sea bed mining provisions so that legal mining can start.

There is talk of extending the Common Heritage concept to the global commons which are still owned by no-one, viz, the rest of the resources in the deep oceans, and the contents of outer space, which is becoming more crowded. The concept is already the basis for the 1979 Moon Treaty, which requires states to establish a joint management system "to govern the exploitation of the natural resources of the moon, as such exploitation is about to become feasible". Another significant decision has been embodied in an international treaty of 1991 which declares the Antarctic a "World Park", protecting its exquisite environment and forbidding exploitation of its vast natural resources.

Regional Organisations

Eleven major inter-governmental regional organisations have been established, in South East Asia, Africa, Latin America and the Caribbean (the Organisation of American States includes the USA), the Arab world, and West Europe (see Appendix III). These bodies, founded by the governments of the region, are complemented by United Nations' regional Economic Commissions. There are also certain inter-regional bodies, such as the Commonwealth, the North Atlantic Treaty Organisation (NATO), the Organisation for Economic Co-operation and Development (OECD), the Organisation of Petroleum Exporting Countries (OPEC), and the Organisation for Security and Co-operation in Europe, which includes East and West Europe. Since two West European organisations provide a model for the restructuring of the United Nations, we must discuss them in some detail.

Federalism in West Europe
"Europe" has never been a political entity since the days of the Roman Empire, except for the short periods of Napoleon's and Hitler's domination. After World War II there was a deep desire in Western Europe to construct a new moral and political order which should make war between Europeans impossible. Unofficial groups sprang up at every level to work to *faire l'Europe* – "create Europe". Many Europeans felt that a federal Europe offered the only constructive solution to the problem of Germany. There were economic motives: many believed that only through international action could slumps be avoided and trade expanded. A measure of collective economic planning was a condition of American Marshall Aid for European reconstruction. And a technological revolution was revealing the possibilities of mass production and marketing. Unification also seemed important for defence against the Communist threat from the East. Finally, after the War the United States consistently used its influence to promote a United States of Europe, partly as a bastion for its own defence against the Soviet Union, and partly because it agreed with the "Europeans" that federation would prevent a recurrence of the European wars in which America had been reluctantly involved.

The Council of Europe
As the European Movement gathered force in the late 1940s, it was faced with a fundamental question of principle: should the United States of Europe be a *confederation,* an association of sovereign nation states, like the United Nations; or should it be a *federation,* involving a specific surrender of sovereignty to federal organs of government, on the model of the United States of America? The countries of West Europe split into two camps on this issue. West Germany, France, Italy and the Benelux countries (Belgium, the Netherlands and Luxembourg) were in favour of federation. Britain, the Scandinavian countries and other smaller states wished to see Europe develop on confederal lines. As a result, ten states set up the Council of Europe in

May 1949. The Council is composed of a parliamentary body called the "Consultative Assembly", and a Committee of Ministers. Membership is open to all countries which "accept the principles of the rule of law, and of human rights and fundamental freedoms". This provision disqualified the Communist States, and Spain and Portugal until their dictatorships ended in the mid 1970s. It obliged Greece and Turkey to withdraw when they established military dictatorships in the late 1970s. In 1995 the Council haas 33 members, including the former Communist states of central Europe – Hungary, Poland, the Czech Republic, Slovakia and Slovenia. In practice, its sphere of action (see below) has been largely usurped by the European Community except in the field of Human Rights.

Its Consultative Assembly is the first international parliamentary body set up in modern times. It consisted, in 1994, of 210 Members of Parliament chosen from among their own members by the parliaments of the member states. It is creating a body of European law, embodied in several hundred Conventions and Agreements, which supplement national laws. The most important of these agreements are the European Convention on Human Rights (1953) and the European Social Charter (1965). If Britain decides to have a written constitution, as is likely, these two Conventions will be written into it.

The Council of Europe has set up a unique body, the European Court of Human Rights, to deal with violations of its Human Rights Conventions. It is the only court in the world to which individual citizens can appeal over the heads of their governments on human rights matters. All member states except Greece, Cyprus, Malta and Turkey have accepted this procedure, and agree to regard the Court's verdict as final and binding. Although such appeals may take six years to be heard, the number is rapidly increasing – the majority of the cases being those brought by British citizens against the British Government. The quiet success of the European Court provides a precedent for a United Nations' Court of Human Rights.

The European Community / Union
The failure of their effort to make the Council of Europe into a supranational body led the "Europeans" to take a new initiative, producing *a new kind of federalism,* which we may call incremental or

310

functional federalism. It involved adopting a step-by-step approach in the less sensitive sectors of public life, those of economic and social affairs.

On 9 May 1950 the French Foreign Minister, Robert Schuman, issued to the astonished world the famous "Schuman Declaration". He proposed placing the whole Franco-German coal and steel output under a common authority, open to the participation of the other countries of Europe, providing a basis for economic development *"as a first step in the federation of Europe which would make any war between France and Germany not only unthinkable but materially impossible".*

The Treaty of Paris of April 1951, signed by France, West Germany, Italy, Belgium, the Netherlands and Luxembourg set up the European Coal and Steel Community. This body was so successful that in the Treaty of Rome of 1957 the Six created two more "Communities": the European Economic Community, which became known as the Common Market, and Euratom, to deal with peaceful nuclear energy. In 1967 the three Communities were merged into the European Community, whose headquarters are in Brussels, but which also functions partly in Luxembourg and partly in Strasbourg, where it uses the Council of Europe's Assembly Chamber.

There is no other international body in the world called a "Community". The 40 or so international bodies are all "Organisations" or "Associations" – words which imply impersonal mechanisms, while "Community" resonates the sense of brotherhood, of unity-in-diversity, of organic growth. The European Community is the first truly supranational body in the modern world, involving a real, though as yet limited, surrender of national sovereignty. The constitution of the Community, which is embodied in the Treaties of Paris and Rome, provides that the Community should gradually *develop* its functions and its powers as well as expand its membership. The Community is thus an evolving, not a static, body.

Membership: Britain, Denmark and Ireland joined the Community in 1973, and Greece in 1981. By 1986, with the accession of Spain and Portugal, membership had doubled to 12 states. Sweden, Finland and Austria joined in January 1995, but the Norwegians voted by a narrow majority to keep out. Turkey applied to join in 1987, but is not yet considered to fulfil the essential conditions for membership

– the practise of democracy and Human Rights. The admission of the Czech Republic, Hungary, Poland, Slovakia, Bulgaria and Romania is in the offing.

Functions: The Community's functions have so far been confined to economic and social matters, stretching into environmental and monetary affairs. The Single European Act of 1986 removed all trade barriers between the member states and enabled the Single Market to come into full operation in 1992. The Maastricht Treaty of 1993 provides for the development of the Community into a monetary union, with a single currency, the ecu, to be introduced before the end of the century, and for a European Social Chapter setting out workers' rights. (Britain and Denmark opted out of endorsing this Chapter). A single currency implies a single Bank and a single Ministry of Finance – but while there is to be a European Central Bank, a Ministry of Finance has not been written into the treaty. It also provides that the member states should develop "a common foreign and security policy" and should "co-operate" on "justice and home affairs". These fields still lie outside the Community's legal functions, so they are described as "wings" of the *"European Union"*. The "Union" thus points towards the further federal development of the "Community".

Structure and powers: The *executive power* of the Community is vested partly in a *Council of Ministers* representing the national governments of the member states, and partly in a *Commission* of 20 Commissioners appointed by the member governments – two each by the larger states and one each by the smaller – for five year tenures. The Governments also choose the President of the Commission. Each Commissioner has a specific portfolio – transport, agriculture, energy, foreign affairs, finance, etc. – so that each is an embryo minister of a European administration. The Commission submits policy proposals to the Council of Ministers, and takes decisions and formulates regulations itself on lesser matters. It has its own regular budget, independent of national contributions, derived mainly from customs duties and levies, and from a proportion – up to one per cent – of the VAT tax levied by all member states. The partnership between the Commission and the Council of Ministers is intended to ensure that the Commission's "Community" approach is harmonised with the national policies which the Ministers represent. In practice, of course, this system has resulted in many delays and deadlocks.

Under the Treaty of Rome the Council of Ministers' decisions had to be unanimous. The Single European Act introduced weighted voting for many matters, the number of votes being allotted to the countries according to the size of their populations. Unanimity is only required for decisions such as appointments to the Commission and the Court of Justice (see below), accession of new states, and the defence, foreign, home and justice policies which still lie outside the scope of the Community. The Council of Ministers, the supreme executive organ, meets behind closed doors and is not openly accountable to the Community's own Parliament, far less to the public. This is called "the democratic deficit".

The third partner in the Community system is the European Parliament. Its 626 members are directly elected (since 1979) by the citizens of all the Community countries, for 5 years. They sit in party groups, ranging from Communists to Conservatives, thus forming embryonic European parties. The Parliament has the right to adopt or reject the Commission's budget as a whole, to dismiss the Commission by a two-thirds majority, to be consulted about Community legislation, and, since the Maastricht Treaty of 1993, to reject, in some fields of legislation, a measure approved by the Council of Ministers. It is beginning to be a "co-legislator" with the Council. It also approves the appointments of a new Commission and accession of new member states. Thus the "democratic deficit" is being gradually reduced.

Finally, a European Court of Justice, composed of 15 judges, interprets the three treaties which established the Community, and hears cases involving individuals, firms, governments, the Commission and the Council of Ministers. Community law applies directly to individuals and corporations, and the Court can fine Governments which fail to comply with its rulings. A body of European case law is being created.

The Court's judgements overrule those of national courts. And once adopted, Community law cannot be amended or revoked by any national parliament. In voluntarily joining the Community, a state implicitly agrees to adjust its national law to the Community's evolving legal system. Enforcement powers are not needed. This is indeed incremental federalism!

The Community has now reached the point where it is being looked at as a model for other regions. It has an Association with 65 African, Caribbean and Pacific states, former colonies of members, which is institutionalised in an Executive Council of Ministers of the 15 and the 65, and a similar parliamentary body; they confer, in these bodies, about trade and aid as equal partners. And through this Association, as well as by other means, understanding of the Community's complex and subtle structure is spreading to the developing world. World federalism could develop in an incremental way as a Community of Communities.

International Regionalism Outside Europe
Today *regionalism* – the urge to perform certain tasks at the regional level – is stirring in the most unexpected areas of acute political division. For example, in 1986 seven countries of the Indian sub-continent, with a combined population of a billion people, formed the South East Asian Association for Regional Co-operation (SEAARC), which launched an Integrated Programme of Action in the fields of agriculture, rural development, metrology, telecommunications, scientific and technological co-operation, health and population, transport and civil aviation, and arts, sport and culture! In November 1994, Israel was invited to a conference in Morocco to discuss with Arab states the interlocking economic problems, such as the sharing of river waters, which beset their region. A beginning was made in putting regional before national interests. The potential development of regionalism in Africa is also of great significance, particularly since South Africa has turned from a white foe into a black – or multicoloured – friend. The Organisation of African Unity was founded in 1963, its headquarters in Addis Ababa, will the long-term aim of developing an African Military Command and an African Common Market. In June 1994 Nelson Mandela confirmed this aim, to which South Africa can bring not only its great natural wealth but also a modern industrial infrastructure and technological expertise which exist nowhere else on the continent. A small beginning was made in regional co-operation when the Economic Community of 16 West African States (ECOWAS) attempted to mediate in a civil war which broke out in Liberia in 1990, and sent in a Military Observer Group (ECOMOG) and troops. In

1993 the United Nations sent some 500 military observers and other staff to co-operate with ECOMOG – the first ever regional peace-keeping mission to co-operate with the United Nations (7).

Grass Roots Activity

All the activities which take place at the global, regional and national level depend, in the last resort, on what the ordinary people do. Groups at this level are of two kinds: official organs of local government, which are normally part of the constitutional structure of the state; and spontaneous "grass roots" groups. In the developed countries the state and local governments are normally well equipped to provide the services which the citizens require to enable them to enjoy their Human Rights. The creative energy released in a society based on Human Rights can therefore freely express itself in a myriad groups or clubs formed for personal development – in religion, sport, hobbies and so on. The great number of groups sprouting up to promote humanitarian causes bears witness to humankind's innate fraternal feelings. And since fraternal love cannot but embrace the whole of humanity, many of these groups are perforce international in scope. Two hundred groups were present at the San Francisco Conference which drew up the UN charter. Today, there are some 7,000 peace groups in the United States alone. Such groups are now officially called Non-Governmental Organisations (NGOs) – an expression invented by the United Nations, whose Charter authorises its Economic and Social Council to establish relations with them. An NGO is generally defined as a private non-profit-making body with an international structure (8).

Neither NGOs nor private local clubs existed – or exist – in Communist countries. The most astonishing phenomenon, however, has been the upsurge of NGOs in the non-Communist developing countries, with the exception of the Arab world. These NGOs emerging in Africa, Asia and Latin America seem often to be an alternative rather than a supplement, as in the West, to the local government. They express the spontaneous demands of the peasants in the villages and urban slums for their Human Rights. A team organised by the Club of Rome (a liberal Western "think-tank") visited 93 rural projects in 19 countries in all three continents in 1983-5. Their basic conclusion was that "the increasing number of NGOs is evidence of the fact that the villagers feel that nothing will come of their lives if they fail to take the initiative to improve their living conditions". They found that while "most associations affirm their apolitical character", all were committed to "the ideology of Human Rights"! (9). A United Nations' Report of 1987 estimated that some 2,000 NGOs in the West are linked to some 6,000 NGOs in the developing countries. Western NGOs have coaxed many Third World NGOs into existence, either directly by "aiding" development projects with funds, equipment and advice, or indirectly by instilling into the region the modern concepts of banking, cultivation, co-operation and so on. The Club of Rome's Report estimates that some 100 million rural villagers have benefited from "NGO sponsored development work" – still only a fraction of the 2 billion inhabitants of Third World villages. The key words used to describe what the Club calls "the Barefoot Revolution" are: "people-orientated"; "consciousness-raising"; "empowerment"; and "self-reliance"; and the projects involve "small-scale enterprises", and "participation in decision-making" in the context of "sustainable development" – the theme of the Brundtland Report (see Chapter 17). In parts of Asia and Latin America the peasants are being impelled to organise themselves by the conversion of farm lands from traditional food crops to cash crops for export, and the consequent tendency of big landlords to push them off their tiny plots to make way for the lucrative "agrobis" with the West – the population of the urban slums is increasing at an annual rate of over 10 per cent (10).

These NGOs involve people at the bottom, and peasant women are at the bottom of the bottom. It is not surprising, therefore, that the NGOs are providing a forum for the "empowerment" of women, who do on an average more work than men, yet world-wide receive only one per cent of the world's income and own less than one per cent of its property. Because of the migration of men to the cities and mines to seek work, women head 15 to 20 per cent of the households in Africa, the Middle East and Latin America (11). For the first time women are playing a major part in leading a vast modern revolution.

Here are three examples of barefoot revolutionary activities.

The "Green Belt Movement" was founded in 1977 in Kenya by a young woman, Wangari Maathai, a university lecturer and the wife of a Member of Parliament. It involves the community planting of "green belts" of trees round human settlements. It aims to plant 15 million trees and thus save Kenya's wood supply from being used up in 30 to 40 years. The movement is organised by women, supported by the United Nations' Environment Programme (whose headquarters are in Nairobi), and the National Council of Women of Kenya, an umbrella organisation for urban and rural women's groups; funded in part by the Voluntary Fund of the UN Decade for Women and promoted by a mass media campaign. Within a decade 1,000 public Green Belts had been created. The movement deliberately aims at developing a positive image of women and involving children and disabled people in the tree planting process. All are encouraged to co-operate for the good of all, including the natural world. How can the government, the farmers or the companies cut down trees while such a movement is flourishing?

A second example comes from Ahmedabad in North West India. In 1971 a group of women cart pullers founded the Self Employment Womens' Association (SEWA) to escape the grip of male money-lenders and merchants, and to support their families – since nearly half had been deserted by their husbands. This trade union of 20,000 poor, illiterate women, market vendors, head carriers, cart pullers, weavers, fuel and waste paper collectors, shellers of cotton pods and peanuts (with their teeth), stone-breakers and street sweepers, then organised their own bank, which in 10 years built up a working capital of $800,000. When the town authorities tried to turn them out of the market place, they successfully went on strike, invoking Gandhi's teaching of *satyragraha* – non-violent action.

A third example is the 150,000 "basic communities", comprising some 3 million people, which have been created in Brazil at the instigation of the Roman Catholic Church. These groups carry out social, political and spiritual activities. They establish basic health services, they promote land reform, they worship together, meeting in private homes. Their fundamental purpose is the "consciousness-raising" of the masses; and women are as much involved as men. Such "basic communities" are in fact springing up all over Latin America (see Chapter 16).

The Club of Rome's report ends on an ominous note. "The barefoot revolution is at present unallied to political or ideological forces, but it could easily change into a political movement or be taken over by extremist political forces. The final outcome of this struggle will depend on the solutions to the problems of poverty and exploitation addressed in this study, and on the speed with which the agents of development can mobilise" (12).

Recent Russian experience may also have something to offer the West – a sense of community in the workplace whose roots go far back into Russian history. Western industry and trade, which tend to treat persons as "things", to be used, exploited and then thrown aside as "redundant", can learn from this source.

A workers' collective is an integral part of every Russian state enterprise. It includes every employee, from blue-collar workers to top management, who all perceive themselves as equals and entitled to participate in enterprise decision making – a process very different from that of Western corporations. Russian collective or communitarian values originate in the medieval village, where survival, in the face of brutally adverse climatic and economic conditions and geographical isolation, depended upon extraordinary group cohesion and discipline. By necessity, the group took priority over the individual.

These adverse conditions also made centralism essential to the viability of the state. The "deep structures" of these seemingly contradictory centralist and grassroots elements are at the root of the behaviour that comes naturally to the Russians.

The workers' collective traditions embodied in the state enterprise is being revitalised. There is an array of "fringe benefits" – housing, health care, education and recreation, that bind members together. The workers' collectives have influenced Russia's form of privatisation, enabling workers and managers to wind up owning a majority of shares in most state enterprises. Today this influence presses the government to continue subsidies to enable the enterprises to avoid the dreaded condition of social exclusion we call "unemployment" – this may account for the persistence of unemployment at very moderate levels even after three years of Yeltsin's reforms (13).

A World Language

In Chapters 2, 12 and 13 we have discussed the language situation of

318

the world – some 3-5,000 distinct languages, several thousand more dialects and 50 alphabets. The rapid progress of world unification through communications technology; involvement in common interests and problems at every level, from the village to the United Nations; the general acceptance of the global ethic of Human Rights; the proliferation of international organisations at both the governmental and non-governmental levels; and the rapid spread of literacy are some of the factors which are making it urgent to develop a universal language and script. The United Nations uses five languages and the European Community nine – each member state is entitled to speak in meetings and to have all official documents translated into its own language. When the Nordic states, the Central European states and Turkey join the Community its language situation will become absurd!

There are weighty reasons for rejecting the promotion of a single universal language at the expense of the existing Babel of 3,000 languages. For a language expresses a cultural identity, just as an individual's voice intonation and handwriting express his or her personal identity. Moreover, many ancient languages, such as Egyptian, Sanskrit, Hebrew, Chinese and Arabic were regarded as having a magical or sacred quality. People like the Celts of Ireland, Scotland and Brittany, the Basques of Spain (whose language is unique), the Quechas of Peru, the Maoris of Aotearoa (New Zealand) are determined to keep their ancient tongues alive.

The most likely development, therefore, is that by general agreement every one will learn a single second language in addition to their mother tongue. There are two obvious candidates for the world language of the future. The first is English. At present it is spoken by less than 10 per cent of the world's population; but it is the almost universal language of science and technology, themselves universal in nature, and it is the language in which most important conferences, official and unofficial, are held. With 14 national languages and scripts, the Indian Parliament in Delhi debates in English. The other alternative is Esperanto, a language invented by a Polish scholar, Dr. Zamenhof, in the late 19th century, inspired by "homaranismo", his core belief in the unity of humankind. Using the Latin script, based on roots drawn from nine European languages and phonetic in spelling, it is four to ten times as simple to learn as any national language. In China and

319

Japan it is becoming increasingly popular. Perhaps its greatest attraction is that it is non-racial, non-national, and not identified with any ancient memories or psychological reflexes from the "collective unconscious". In an Esperanto-speaking world, no-one would need to feel culturally inferior because they did not speak English, French, Spanish, Arabic or Russian! A world language would appear on the scene just at the crucial point in history when the world is becoming unified!

A third possibility would be to develop Esperanto – or any other suitable language which may be invented in the near future – as the general world language, while retaining English (preferably with the spelling reformed, as advocated by Bernard Shaw) as the language for intellectual use by the politicians, administrators, scholars, scientists, technicians, air traffic controllers, European Community officials, and so on. This would have the advantage of avoiding the translation of the millions of books and academic papers which are necessary for the intellectual – who are pushing the future of the planet along – but are of no interest to the vast majority of ordinary people who are involved in humble but essential work.

Conclusion: Reform of the United Nations

Chapter 17 outlined the current world crisis and quoted the solemn warnings of leading experts on the need for drastic and urgent action to avert world catastrophe. In this Chapter we have described the existing international structures which are in place to deal with the crisis. It is obvious that they are fundamentally inadequate. Major changes must be made very soon. Much discussion of United Nations' reform is taking place, but most of it assumes that the sovereign state must remain the basis of the world order – a principle strongly affirmed by the present Secretary-General, Boutros Boutros-Ghali (14). This may be "realistic", but it is not in line with the ethos of the modern age, the ethic of Human Rights. The time has come to implement the global spiritual ethic which is emerging (see Chapter 16) and offer a model for the structures which must be built on the present foundations.

In the final analysis, these aims and goals are clear-cut:

(i) *The General Assembly,* of the United Nations must be

democratised, based ultimately on "one person one vote" for all inhabitants of the planet. The system of basing voting rights on states which vary dramatically in population and size must in due course be abolished. Two main proposals for General Assembly reform have been put forward. One is for weighted voting, for which there are various schemes. Harold Stassen, the only statesman still living who, as a representative of President Truman, signed the United Nations' Charter, has proposed that the number of votes per state should range, in terms of total population, annual GNP and annual per caput production, from 1000 for the ten major states to one for the smallest. A proposal much discussed by the Association of World Federalists in America is "the Binding Triad": The General Assembly would make binding decisions (which it cannot at present) by resolutions which receive concurrent majority votes based on three factors: (a) one nation one vote; (b) population; and (c) contributions to the UN budget. But it has been pointed out that "the danger of arguing for amending the Charter with a voting system factoring in wealth may escape the affluent at any one point in time, but the economic histories of the oil-producing developing countries point to it. Tomorrow, 'wealth' might be water" (15).

Two main proposals are under discussion for some sort of Second Chamber which would infuse into the nation-state run General Assembly the democratic element implied in the preamble to the Charter: *"We the Peoples of the United Nations"*. The first is for a "United Nations' Parliamentary Assembly" representing the parliaments of the member states. This idea is drawn from the model of the two international parliamentary bodies in Western Europe – see above. If the model of the European Union's parliament were followed, the UN's Second Chamber might in due course be directly elected and gradually gain control over or complement the General Assembly, which might become a chamber representing states, as in the USA (16). One problem with this proposal is that not all states are democratic and have genuinely elected parliaments. Yet half to three quarters of the world's population are, in 1994, living under relatively democratic and pluralistic regimes. In 1993 elections were held in 45 countries – and we have seen above how anxious are the citizens of many developing countries to vote and to engage the United Nations to monitor their elections. If we reject the participation of China, whose population is a fifth of the human race, a World Parliament of representatives of elected parliaments seems a viable proposition. As with the Parliament of the Council of Europe, dictatorship might be a disqualification for voting.

The other proposal is for an NGO World Council related to the United Nations, consisting of representatives of Regional Councils, which in turn would have representatives from National NGO Councils in member nations. These would be linked to General Assemblies in New York and possibly Geneva, which would include representatives of topical or special interest NGOs – for example, those which participate in United Nations' Conferences and their Preparatory Commissions (Prepcoms). This involvement would create a mechanism for peoples' participation in the United Nations. The NGOs are thus preparing, the way for *"We, the Peoples"*, the "world citizenry" to make the United Nations a transnational, rather than what it is at present, an inter-state organisation.

(ii) *The Security Council.* If the United Nations is to become democratic, its chief executive body, the Security Council, and its Secretary-General, who is a sort of prime minister, must be made accountable to an elected Assembly, as in the British Constitution, or directly to the world electorate, as in the American Constitution. (As we have seen in Chapter 14, these are the two modern models for democracy). At present only the Security Council's decisions are binding on members; the General Assembly can merely recommend. It may take a little time (but time is short) to alter this channel of responsibility. Meanwhile the restructuring of the Security Council seems to be regarded by most world leaders as the most urgent reform needed for the UN. Some have proposed the addition of Germany and Japan as permanent members; others have added major states in other regions, such as Brazil, Nigeria and India. Many have advocated the abolition of the veto. The most creative proposal is, surely, that the Security Council should represent regional Communities, thus embodying the principle of subsidiarity – a World Community organised in a hierarchy of Communities. One Community is already operating supranationally; others exist in embryo, and such a reform would encourage them to develop. The second crucial reform, not at present discussed by governments, is to make the Security Council democratically responsible to the General Assembly. This may also take time, as the experience of the European Union shows. The Secretary-General, or the leader of the majority party or grouping, would then become Prime Minister or Chief Eecutive of the world.

(iii) *The Commision for Sustainable Development (CSD)* set up under the Economic and Social Council (ECOSOC) by the United Nations Conference on Environment and Development at Rio de Janeiro in 1992 (see Chapter 17) should become a complementary body to the Security Council: it should have powers to take binding decisions on all matters dealing with development and environment. Its powers should, moreover, be widened to include the issue of unsustainable consumption – "Basic Needs First" – in order that the finite resources of the planet may be equally shared.

(iv) *The International Court of Justice* must be empowered to take decisions of principle which are binding on all its members. For example, the World Health Organisation and the UN General Assembly have asked it for a ruling that the use, or threat of use, of nuclear weapons is illegal in international law. It must be able to take the initiative in indicting states and individuals for violating international law, to hear appeals from individuals and corporations as well as from states (as does the European Community's Court), and to enforce its decisions, which should take precedence, as do those of the European Community, over national law. The ICJ will be complemented by the planned International Criminal Court and a Court of Human Rights.

(v) The United Nations must create the proposed permanent *United Nations' Police Force* discussed above, to enforce law as well as to monitor and mediate.

(vi) A proposal put forward by two senior ex-United Nations' officials, Sir Brian Urquhart and Erskine Childers, that *all the United Nations' Specialised Agencies should be located in New York* (not a single one is there) should be adopted. They could then become the embryonic Ministries of a World Government (17). They should be supplemented by new Agencies dealing with energy, transport and appropriate technology.

(vii) *Funding of the United Nations.* Total UN expenditure for 1992 has been estimated at $10.5 billion, constituting less than $3 or £2 for every human being in the world. This would maintain Britons on alcoholic beverages for about 15 weeks (18). Governmental arms expenditure constituted about $150 per human being.In 1993 the Secretary-General reported that unpaid contributions had accumulated over the years to over $2 billion. Only 47 states had paid their regular annual contributions and almost two thirds of the total outstanding was owed by the United States ($834 million) and the Russian Federation ($598 million) (19).

A major reform must therefore be to endow the United Nations with reliable independent sources of finance, so that it does not have to rely on the contributions of the national governments. Various suggestions have been made. Nobel Peace Prize winner Oscar Arias, former Prime Minister of Costa Rica, has proposed a Global Demilititarisation fund financed from the peace dividend (see above), which would be used to finance disarmament, demobilisation, retraining and re-education of military personnel for civilian life, and also for conversion to peace projects. A Nobel Prize winner for economics, James Tobin, proposes a tax on international currency transactions, estimated to run in 1994 at $1 trillion a day, which should be underpinned by a permanent single currency. Other possibilities are a carbon tax, which would be easy to collect and environmentally friendly, and also a world tax on the arms trade, as suggested as long ago as 1980 in the Brandt Report (see above).

(viii) The General Assembly and the World Executive Authority should be empowered to declare certain resources "the Common Heritage of Humankind" and to set up Resource Management Commissions, which would develop and distribute these resources in accordance with the International Labour Organisation's principle of "Basic Needs First". (The Transnational Corporations, with their vast international expertise, could be agents of this system).

(ix) Esperanto and English should be the languages used in the General Assembly and by the United Nations generally.

If the United Nations could be restructured on these lines, the nation state would gradually subside into its relevant place in helping to implement the principles of global housekeeping, sharing, planning, conservation and conversion, in the emerging World Community.

AFTERWORD

THE PERSON IN THE UNIVERSE

WE have noted in Chapter 3 certain central principles in the traditional view of the universe. First, matter is the embodiment of spirit. Second, matter is in some mode endowed with personality, through which spirit expresses itself. Third, the concept of level, gradation, degree is fundamental to the structure of the universe; as the soul unfolds its inherent powers, it ascends through "levels" which are both states of consciousness and locations of the stars. Finally, love enfolds and guides all things, and love is embodied in persons, celestial and mortal.

But - this coherent and sublime vision of the structure of the universe had one fatal flaw: it was not in accord with the facts of the objective physical phenomena!

What is modern man's picture of the universe at the end of the 20th century? With the aid of telescopes, cameras, computers, satellites and other modern inventions, his vision can now penetrate to distances of a billion light years - one light year is 5.9 trillion miles, or 9.5 trillion kilometres. The new Hubble telescope now circling the Earth may enhance this vision several times. Through this exploration, and using the crucial tool of mathematics, he has discovered the following situation.

The earth is one of nine planets which circle round our sun. Our sun is an insignificant star in the vast galaxy of the Milky Way, which contains an estimated 100 billion stars spread out over a distance of 100,000 light years. And there are billions of other galaxies, some containing over a trillion stars. Some objects at the far reaches of the universe, quasars, are as bright as a trillion suns. This unimaginably huge number of stars is stretched out over an unimaginably huge area. Distances of ten to twenty billion light years are characteristic of our universe. Nor are the stars "fixed", as the Ancients believed. The individual stars rotate on their axes; and the space containing the galaxies is expanding, so that they appear to be moving away from us at ever increasing speeds the further away they are. Yet nine-tenths or more of the material of the universe may be in a form invisible to us.

What happened to achieve this extraordinary transformation of the view of the universe from the unchanging faith of millennia to the ever-expanding factual knowledge of today? As we have seen in Chapter 10, the turning point came with the work of certain mathematicians and astronomers in 17th century Europe, aided by the invention of the telescope. Their calculations and observations provided empirical proof that the motions of the stars are determined by the laws of Nature. Gradually, and not without much huffing and puffing by Christian traditionalists, it was accepted that if the laws of Nature conflict with the edicts of religious revelation, it is the laws of Nature which are right. Not only the Roman Catholic Church and Martin Luther, but even John Wesley, in the 18th century, found it difficult to accept the rejection of Biblical authority involved in believing that the earth goes round the sun; while Darwin's theory of evolution, which shattered faith in the calculation from *Genesis* that the world was created by God in 4004 B.C., provoked a cry of rage which still reverberates today.

The major casualty of the scientific revolution of the 17th century was God. At first He was simply withdrawn, as it were, from active service, becoming for Newton and other God-fearing scientists the Great Watchmaker who sets the machine of Nature into motion. It was then inevitable that He should fade out of the picture. And the withdrawal of God has meant, of course, the fading out of the traditional idea that the universe is peopled with gods and goddesses, angels and archangels, fairies, demons and devils, endowing material phenomena with moral and aesthetic *qualities,* embodied in spiritual energies flowing between personalities. Science has *depersonalised* the physical universe, and in so doing, deprived it of the force affirmed so powerfully by the ancient philosophers and poets, from Plato and Jesus Christ to Dante: *love!*

The withdrawal of God from the scene has been accompanied by the collapse of the concept of eternity. We have seen that the Ancients believed, not only that the spiritual universe is eternal, but that the spiritual attribute of eternity is manifested in the light and motion of the stars. Newton held that space and time are "absolutes", "without relation to anything external". This view has been shattered by the combined impact of the two great 20th century discoveries; that the whole universe is changing and evolving in time; and that all material phenomena are "relative" to each other, and to the conscious mind which is observing them, in a single space-time continuum. There appears to be only one unchanging factor in the physical universe: the speed of light - 186,000 miles a second.

The scientific method is based essentially on dissection and analysis, *reducing* matter to its component parts, and then putting them together in a *mechanistic* model in which the whole is simply the sum of the parts. So amazing have been the results of "reductionist" scientific thinking that it now profoundly conditions every aspect of modern society. One might say that the scientific way of looking at the universe has hypnotised the modern mind.

If the universe is "nothing but" physical matter, or energy - since matter is energy - what is its purpose, and what is the purpose of our human lives in it? Here are the reactions of two leading astronomers to the challenge presented by their own discoveries. Fred Hoyle, the British astronomer, writes: "It seems to me that religion is but a desperate attempt to find an escape from the truly dreadful situation in which we find ourselves. Here we are in this wholly fantastic Universe with scarcely a clue as to whether our existence has any real significance. No wonder that many people feel the need for some belief that gives them a sense of security, and no wonder that they become very angry with people like me who say that this security is illusory. But I do not like the situation any better than they do . . . Perhaps the most majestic feature of our whole existence is that while our intelligences are powerful enough to penetrate deeply into the evolution of this quite incredible universe, we still have not the smallest clue to our own fate" (1).

A British mathematician, Professor John Taylor, echoes Fred Hoyle: "The problem is that even if the universe is energy, why is it here at all? The only answer I can give is that there is no reason at all, no purpose, nothing. The universe just is, as energy" (2).

It can surely be by no chance that the historical emergence of the idea that *the person* should develop his creative potential has been accompanied by the incredible development of theoretical and applied science and by the discovery, in particular, of the scientific facts of biological and stellar evolution. Concepts of political, economic and social change, development, growth, evolution and dynamism are replacing fixed and immutable attitudes. The idea of creating a new man and of building a better world is fundamental to the modern age. And science has placed in this free person's hands the tools with which to transform or destroy the world. Modern man is called upon to steer the evolutionary process himself! What are his goals? What are the models which he envisions? There are no more important questions in the world today.

This brings us back to the question of what personhood is. Modern reductionist thought is tempted to explain a human as "nothing but" a "naked ape" or a superior rat. In this case all his spiritual aspirations and his ethical standards, including his capacity to love, are nothing but the reflexes of the chemicals in his glands. All values are relative, all ideals meaningless - as an important school of modern philosophy asserts. The alternative is to postulate that the core of the unique person is an immortal soul, created by God, and endowed in heaven with an inherent knowledge of "truth". "As above, so below", as the Ancients said. Experience indicates that a person has three major faculties, Mind, Heart and Will - the ability to think, feel and act. The fate of the world depends on balancing the development of the mind, so powerfully promoted by science, with the development of the heart - the capacity to expedience the higher emotions, the capacity to love.

And this brings us to the question of mortality. All the traditional religions, with the qualified exception of Judaism and Theravada Buddhism, believe that the individual person survives death in some mode, and all mystical traditions affirm a gradual unfolding of the soul's potential, whether or not through reincarnation in a physical body. Modern society gives an entirely new significance to the evolution of personhood in earthly life, a significance undreamed of in traditional society, and then proceeds, in many cases, to deny the possibility of its further development after death! It is rather odd that just when the phenomenon of personhood is exploding on earth, persons should describe the enormous universe which they are discovering as nothing but a meaningless mass of energy!

The survival of the essential person after death could therefore be regarded as the corollary to the doctrine of Human Rights. In affirming this doctrine modern man is, unconsciously, affirming the immortality of the souls, incarnate and discarnate, in what Martin Luther King called "cosmic companionship". The more evolved, who dwell in "higher" states of being, bless and inspire those struggling "on earth" with whom their souls resonate. Spiritual empathy extends vertically into heaven as well as horizontally across the earth. The barriers of time are shattered.

Now let us look at the situation from the philosophical angle. "It is through our consciousness that we contemplate and comprehend the universe", writes the British astronomer Sir Bernard Lovell (3). The most important statement of Descartes, the 17th century philosopher who summed up the philosophic implications of the scientific revolution, was *"cogito, ego sum"* - "I think, therefore I am". This tremendous affirmation of the integrity of the human mind can be regarded as the corollary to the tremendous affirmation, made in the 20th century, of the integrity of the vast universe. Does the universe exist objectively apart from our own consciousness which is observing it? If we reject reductionism, which asserts that consciousness is an expression of matter, do we reach the opposite position, that matter is an expression of consciousness? This is the view asserted by Oriental religion throughout the centuries: consciousness is present in all phenomena at different levels and in different modes. The Sanskrit word *maya* applied to the material world does not mean "illusion", as is often asserted in the West, but rather "appearance". My chair appears to be made of hard wood; but on another level of perception it is made of protons, neutrons and electrons. The physical sun is an "appearance" for the spiritual Sun, declared the Pharaoh Akhenaten in 1379 B.C. In the end, truth emerges from a union between subject and object, observer and observed, the human consciousness and the vast universe. The mystery of love - two are one and one is two - is the fundamental factor!

Twentieth century science has already made a departure from the mechanistic outlook introduced by Newtonian physics and embodied in the philosophy of Descartes. For in the macroworld of the galaxies and in the microworld of subatomic particles the Newtonian laws of nature do not apply. In the modern view of the cosmos, Newton's theory of gravitation has been incorporated into Einstein's General Theory of Relativity. On the smallest scale, the phenomena are governed by the quantum theory, in which Heisenberg's Uncertainty Principle is fundamental; it is impossible, for example, to know both the position and the velocity of a particle precisely at the same time. Yet it is already clear, on the one hand that the properties of the minutest building blocks of matter govern the behaviour of the universe at large, but on the other hand that these two basic theories of twentieth century physics are incompatible with one another. So scientists are now searching for a still more fundamental theory which would unify the two - truly a Theory of Everything.

But even in the everyday world between the atom and the cosmos there are limits to our knowledge. The advent of supercomputers has enabled other scientists to study immensely complex systems such as the weather, and it appears that these too are ultimately unpredictable - a butterfly flapping its wings in the rain forests of Brazil may affect the weather thousands of miles away in Europe. Similar phenomena of complexity and chaos may describe - but not prescribe - the behaviour of human societies, the global economy, and the most complex object we know of in the universe, our own brain. Particularly interesting effects occur on the edge between complex but organised systems and chaos, when a system reaches a critical degree of complexity - as, perhaps, in evolution when the brain first exceeded a certain number of nerve cells or interactions between them. It is not surprising that neither the individual human brain nor human societies are always rational. But scientists such as Nobel-Prize-winner Murray Gell-Mann believe that general laws relating to these phenomena may nevertheless be discovered in the next few years (4).

Randomness and indeterminacy are, then, basic phenomena, and so also are interdependence, order and harmony! Time and space form one continuum, as does the observer and the objects observed. Already in the 1930s the astronomer Sir James Jeans was moved to exclaim that the universe begins to look like a great Mind. Can there be a Mind without a Heart? And the Mind united to the Heart finds expression in Personhood. The dreadful nothingness described by the astronomers quoted above turns into joy and glory beyond measure!

In the doctrine that the universe is full of persons, united by love, therefore lies the solution to our central human problem: how to envision the goals for the evolution of our planet. These goals are the archetypes or models projected by celestial minds, revealed to us through the profound blending of souls through love. "Blessed are the pure in heart, for they shall see God." This remark by Jesus Christ may be regarded as the key to the future of the world.

APPENDIX I

UNIVERSAL DECLARATION OF HUMAN RIGHTS

ON DECEMBER 10, 1948, the General Assembly of the United Nations adopted and proclaimed the Universal Declaration of Human Rights, the full text of which appears in the following pages. Following this historic act, the Assembly called upon all Member countries to publicise the text of the Declaration and "to cause it to be disseminated, displayed, read and expounded principally in schools and other educational institutions, without distinction based on the political status of countries or territories."

PREAMBLE

Whereas recognition of inherent dignity and of the equal and inalienable rights of all members of the human family is the foundation of freedom, justice and peace in the world,

Whereas disregard and contempt for human rights have resulted in barbarous acts which have outraged the conscience of mankind, and the advent of a world in which human beings shall enjoy freedom of speech and belief and freedom from fear and want has been proclaimed as the highest aspiration of the common people,

Whereas it is essential, if man is not to be compelled to have recourse, as a last resort, to rebellion against tyranny and oppression, that human rights should be protected by the rule of law,

Whereas it is essential to promote the development of friendly relations between nations,

Whereas the peoples of the United Nations have in the Charter reaffirmed their faith in fundamental human rights, in the dignity and worth of the human person and in the equal rights of men and women and have determined to promote social progress and better standards of life in larger freedom,

Whereas Member States have pledged themselves to achieve, in co-operation with the United Nations, the promotion of universal respect for and observance of human rights and fundamental freedoms,

Whereas a common understanding of these rights and freedoms is of the greatest importance for the full realisation of this pledge,

Now, Therefore,

THE GENERAL ASSEMBLY

proclaims

THIS UNIVERSAL DECLARATION OF HUMAN RIGHTS as a common standard of achievement for all peoples and all nations, to the end that every individual and every organ of society, keeping this Declaration constantly in mind, shall strive by teaching and education to promote respect for these rights and freedoms and by progressive measures, national and international, to secure their universal and effective recognition and observance, both among the peoples of Member States themselves and among the peoples of territories under their jurisdiction.

Article 1. All human beings are born free and equal in dignity and rights. They are endowed with reason and conscience and should act towards one another in a spirit of brotherhood.

Article 2. Everyone is entitled to all the rights and freedoms set forth in this Declaration, without distinction of any kind, such as race, colour, sex, language, religion, political or other opinion, national or social origin, property, birth or other status.

Furthermore, no distinction shall be made on the basis of the political, jurisdictional or international status of the country or territory to which a person belongs, whether it be independent, trust, non-self-governing or under any other limitation of sovereignty.

Article 3. Everyone has the right to life, liberty and security of person.

Article 4. No one shall be held in slavery or servitude; slavery and the slave trade shall be prohibited in all their forms.

Article 5. No one shall be subjected to torture or to cruel, inhuman or degrading treatment or punishment.

Article 6. Everyone has the right to recognition everywhere as a person before the law.

Article 7. All are equal before the law and are entitled without any discrimination to equal protection of the law. All are entitled to equal protection against any discrimination in violation of this Declaration and against any incitement to such discrimination.

Article 8. Everyone has the right to an effective remedy by the competent national tribunals for acts violating the fundamental rights granted him by the constitution or by law.

Article 9. No one shall be subjected to arbitrary arrest, detention or exile.

Article 10. Everyone is entitled in full equality to a fair and public hearing by an independent and impartial tribunal, in the determination of his rights and obligations and of any criminal charge against him.

Article 11. (1) Everyone charged with a penal offence has the right to be presumed innocent until proved guilty according to law in a public trial at which he has had all the guarantees necessary for his defence. (2) No one shall be held guilty of any penal offence on account of any act or omission which did not constitute a penal offence, under national or international law, at the time when it was committed. Nor shall a heavier penalty be imposed than the one that was applicable at the time the penal offence was committed.

Article 12. No one shall be subjected to arbitrary interference with his privacy, family, home or correspondence, nor to attacks upon his honour and reputation. Everyone has the right to the protection of the law against such interference or attacks.

Article 13. (1) Everyone has the right to freedom of movement and residence within the borders of each state. (2) Everyone has the right to leave any country, including his own, and to return to his country.

Article 14. (1) Everyone has the right to seek and to enjoy in other countries asylum from persecution. (2) This right may not be invoked in the case of prosecutions genuinely arising from non-political crimes or from acts contrary to the purposes and principles of the United Nations.

Article 15. (1) Everyone has the right to a nationality. (2) No one shall be arbitrarily deprived of his nationality nor denied the right to change his nationality.

Article 16. (1) Men and women of full age, without any limitation due to race, nationality or religion, have the right to marry and to found a family. They are entitled to equal rights as to marriage, during marriage and at its dissolution. (2) Marriage shall be entered into only with the free and full consent of the intending spouses. (3) The family is the natural and fundamental group unit of society and is entitled to protection by society and the State.

Article 17. (1) Everyone has the right to own property alone as well as in association with others. (2) No one shall be arbitrarily deprived of his property.

Article 18. Everyone has the right to freedom of thought, conscience and religion; this right includes freedom to change his religion or belief, and freedom, either alone or in community with others and in public or private, to manifest his religion or belief in teaching, practice, worship and observance.

Article 19. Everyone has the right to freedom of opinion and expression; this right includes freedom to hold opinions without interference and to seek, receive and impart information and ideas through any media and regardless of frontiers.

Article 20. (1) Everyone has the right to freedom of peaceful assembly and association. (2) No one may be compelled to belong to an association.

Article 21. (1) Everyone has the right to take part in the government of his country, directly or through freely chosen representatives. (2) Everyone has the right of equal access to public service in his country. (3) The will of the people shall be the basis of the authority of government; this will shall be expressed in periodic and genuine elections which shall be by universal and equal suffrage and shall be held by secret vote or by equivalent free voting procedures.

Article 22. Everyone, as a member of society, has the right to social security and is entitled to realisation, through national effort and international co-operation and in accordance with the organisation and resources of each State, of the economic, social and cultural rights indispensable for his dignity and the free development of his personality.

Article 23. (1) Everyone has the right to work, to free choice of employment, to just and favourable conditions of work and to protection against unemployment. (2) Everyone, without any discrimination, has the right to equal pay for equal work. (3) Everyone who works has the right to just and favourable remuneration ensuring for himself and his family an existence worthy of human dignity, and supplemented, if necessary, by other means of social protection. (4) Everyone has the right to form and to form trade unions for the protection of his interests.

Article 24. Everyone has the right to rest and leisure, including reasonable limitation of working hours and periodic holidays with pay.

Article 25. (1) Everyone has the right to a standard of living adequate for the health and well-being of himself and of his family, including food, clothing, housing and medical care and necessary social services, and the right to security in the event of unemployment, sickness, disability, widowhood, old age or other lack of livelihood in circumstances beyond his control. (2) Motherhood and childhood are entitled to special care and assistance. All children, whether born in or out of wedlock, shall enjoy the same social protection.

Article 26. (1) Everyone has the right to education. Education shall be free, at least in the elementary and fundamental stages. Elementary education shall be compulsory. Technical and professional education shall be made generally available and higher education shall be equally accessible to all on the basis of merit. (2) Education shall be directed to the full development of the human personality and to the strengthening of respect for human rights and fundamental freedoms. It shall promote understanding, tolerance and friendship among all nations, racial or religious groups, and shall further the activities of the United Nations for the maintenance of peace. (3) Parents have a prior right to choose the kind of education that shall be given to their children.

Article 27. (1) Everyone has the right freely to participate in the cultural life of the community, to enjoy the arts and to share in scientific advancement and its benefits. (2) Everyone has the right to the protection of the moral and material interests resulting from any scientific, literary or artistic production of which he is the author.

Article 28. Everyone is entitled to a social and international order in which the rights and freedoms set forth in this Declaration can be fully realised.

Article 29. (1) Everyone has duties to the community in which alone the free and full development of his personality is possible. (2) In the exercise of his rights and freedoms, everyone shall be subject only to such limitations as are determined by law solely for the purpose of securing due recognition and respect for the rights and freedoms of others and of meeting the just requirements of morality, public order and the general welfare in a democratic society. (3) These rights and freedoms may in no case be exercised contrary to the purposes and principles of the United Nations.

Article 30. Nothing in this Declaration may be interpreted as implying for any State, group or person any right to engage in any activity or to perform any act aimed at the destruction of any of the rights and freedoms set forth herein.

THE PRINCIPLES
OF A
GLOBAL ETHIC

PARLIAMENT OF THE WORLD'S RELIGIONS
(Chicago, USA, 1993)

Declaration Toward a Global Ethic

THE following Declaration was discussed at the centenary celebration Sarva-Dharma-Sammelana held at Bangalore in August 1993. It was further discussed and then signed by religious leaders and launched at the Parliament of the World's Religions. The Declaration, together with an accompanying statement on 'The Principles of a Global Ethic' was launched at the closing session of the Parliament on Saturday, September 4th, following an address by H. H. the Dalai Lama.

---

*The text entitled 'Introduction' was produced by an Editorial Committee of the 'Council' of the Parliament of the World's Religions in Chicago on the basis of the Declaration composed in Tübingen (here headed 'Principles'). It was meant to serve as a brief summary of the Declaration for publicity purposes. At the same time it was intended to be read aloud in public. So this text was read out publicly at the solem concluding plenary on 4 September 1993 in Grant Park, Chicago: a number of passages were greeted with spontaneous applause by the audience of thousands.

EARTH CANNOT BE CHANGED FOR THE BETTER UNLESS THE CONSCIOUSNESS OF INDIVIDUALS IS CHANGED FIRST

THE world is in agony. The agony is so pervasive and urgent that we are compelled to name its manifestations so that the depth of this pain may be made clear.

PEACE eludes us...the planet is being destroyed...neighbours live in fear...women and men are estranged from each other...children die!

This is abhorrent!

WE condemn the abuses of Earth's ecosystem.

WE condemn the poverty that stifles life's potential; the hunger that weakens the human body; the economic disparities that threaten so many families with ruin.

WE condemn the social disarray of the nations; the disregard for justice which pushes citizens to the margin; the anarchy overtaking our communities; and the insane death of children from violence. In particular we condemn aggression and hatred in the name of religion.

But this agony need not be.

IT need not be because the basis for an ethic already exists. This ethic offers the possibility of a better individual and global order, and leads individuals away from despair and societies away from chaos.

WE are women and men who have embraced the precepts and and practices of the world's religions.

WE affirm that a common set of core values is found in the teachings of the religions and that these form the basis of a global ethic.

WE affirm that this truth is already known, but yet to be lived in heart and action.

WE affirm that there is an irrevocable, unconditional norm for all areas of life, for families and communities, for races, nations and religions. There already exist ancient guidelines for human behaviour which are found in the teachings of the religions of the world and which are the conditions for a sustainable world order.

We Declare:

WE are interdependent. Each of us depends on the well-being of the whole, and so we have respect for the community of living beings, for people, animals, and plants, and for the preservation of Earth, the air, water and soil.

WE take individual responsibility for all we do. All our decisions, actions and failures to act have consequences.

WE must treat others as we wish others to treat us. We make a commitment to respect life and dignity, individuality and diversity, so that every person is treated humanely, without exception. We must have patience and acceptance. We must be able to forgive, learning from the past but never allowing ourselves to be enslaved by memories of hate. Opening our hearts to one another, we must sink our narrow differences for the cause of the world community, practising a culture of solidarity and relatedness.

WE consider humankind our family. We must strive to be kind and generous. We must not live for ourselves alone, but should also serve others, never forgetting the children, the aged, the poor, the suffering, the disabled, the refugees and the lonely. No person should ever be considered or treated as a second-class citizen, or be exploited in any way whatsoever. There should be equal partnership between men and women. We must not commit any kind of sexual immorality. We must put behind us all forms of domination or abuse.

We commit ourselves to a culture of non-violence, respect, justice and peace. We shall not oppress, injure, torture or kill other human beings, forsaking violence as a means of settling differences.

We must strive for a just social and economic order, in which everyone has an equal chance to reach full potential as a human being. We must speak and act truthfully and with compassion, dealing fairly with all, and avoiding prejudice and hatred. We must not steal. We must move beyond the dominance of greed for power, prestige, money and consumption to make a just and peaceful world.

Earth cannot be changed for the better unless the consciousness of individuals is changed first. We pledge to increase our awareness by disciplining our minds, by meditation, by prayer, by positive thinking. Without risk and a readiness to sacrifice there can be no fundamental change in our situation. Therefore we commit ourselves to this global ethic, to understanding one another, and to socially-beneficial, peace-fostering and nature-friendly ways of life.

APPENDIX III

INTERNATIONAL ORGANISATIONS

I – THE UNITED NATIONS "FAMILY"

1. Bodies which are a part of the UN, but supported by voluntary contributions from governments, NGO and individuals and not out of the UN's regular budget:

UN Centre for Human Settlements (Habitat), Nairobi;

UNICEF, New York;

United Nations' Conference on Trade and Development (UNCTAD), Geneva;

United Nations' Development Programme (UNDP), New York;

United Nations' Disaster Relief Office (UNDRO), Geneva;

United Nations' Environment Programme (UNEP), Nairobi;

United Nations' Fund for Population Activities (UNFPA), New York;

United Nations' High Commission for Refugees (UNHCR), Geneva;

United Nations' Institute for Training and Research (UNITAR), New York;

United Nations' International Training and Research Institute for the Advancement of Women (INSTRAW), Dominican Republic;

United Nations' Relief and Work Agency for the Palestinian Refugees (UNWRA), Vienna;

United Nations' University, Tokyo;

World Food Council (WFC) and World Food Programme (WFP), Rome.

TOTAL: 14.

2. United Nations' Specialised Agencies, which have their own constitutions, membership and financing, but are linked to the UN:

UN Food and Agriculture Organisation (FAO), Rome;

International Bank for Reconstruction and Development and International Development Association, which together constitute the World Bank, Washington;

International Monetary Fund, Washington;

International Finance Corporation, an affiliate of the World Bank, Washington;

International Civil Aviation Association (ICAO), Montreal;

International Fund for Agricultural Development (IFAD), Rome;

International Labour Organisation (ILO), Geneva;

International Maritime Organisation (IMO), London;

International Telecommunications Union (ITU), Geneva;

United Nations' Education, Science and Cultural Organisation (UNESCO), Paris;

United Nations' Industrial Development Organisation (UNIDO), Vienna;

International Postal Union, Berne;

World Health Organisation (WHO), Geneva;

World Intellectual Property Organisation (WIPO), Geneva;

World Meterological Organisation (WMO), Geneva.

TOTAL: 15.

II – RELATED ORGANISATIONS WHICH ARE NOT PART OF THE UN "FAMILY"

International Atomic Energy Agency, (IAEA) Vienna.

World Trade Organisation (WTO), formerly General Agreement on Tariffs and Trade (GATT), Geneva.

III – INTERGOVERNMENTAL REGIONAL ORGANISATIONS

United Nations' Economic Commissions for: Europe (East and West);

Latin America and the Caribbean;

Asia and the Pacific;

Western Asia; and Africa.

Association of South East Asian Nations (ASEAN): 1967. Brunei, Indonesia, Malaysia, Philippines, Singapore and Thailand.

Origination of African Unity (OAU): 1963. 60 African States.

Organisation of American States (OAS): 1990. 32 states including USA but not Canada.

Caribbean Community (CARICOM): 1973. 13 states (not Cuba).

South Pacific Forum: New Zealand, Australia and 9 island states.

Council of Europe: 1949. 33 West European states, including Turkey.

European Union: (formerly **Community**) 1951. 15 West European states.

League of Arab States: 1945.

Organisation of Petroleum exporting Countries (OPEC): 1960. Arab oil-producing states plus Ecuador, Gabon, Indonesia, Nigeria and Venezuela. 13 members.

South Asian Association for Regional Co-operation (SAARC): 1986. Bangladesh, Bhutan, India, Maldives, Nepal, Pakistan and Sri Lanka.

The Commonwealth: A loose association or club of about 70 countries, some as big as India, some tiny islands, which were at one time British colonies. They are linked by their acceptance of the British monarch as Head of the Commonwealth.

The North Atlantic Treaty Organisation (NATO): 1949. A
military alliance of a number of West European countries, plus
USA and Canada, with an International Supreme Headquarters,
set up to deal with the "Soviet threat".

Organisation for Security and Co-operation in Europe
(formerly **Conference on**) (OSCE), 1975, 53 countries, including
USA and Russia, discuss co-operation on Human Rights, security,
economics, science and technology.

References

Chapter 1
THE DISCOVERY OF THE PAST

1. H.V.F. Winstone, *Uncovering the Ancient World* (London: Constable, 1985), p.20.

2. Colin Renfrew, "The Emergence of Civilisation" in *The Penguin Encyclopaedia of Ancient Civilisations,* edited by Arthur Cotterell (Harmonsworth: Penguin, 1980), p.12.

3. Colin Renfrew, op.cit., p.15.

4. Colin Renfrew, op.cit., p.14.

5. Colin Renfrew and Paul Bahn, *Archaelogy: Theories, Methods and Practice* (London: Thames and Hudson, 1991), p.370.

Chapter 2
LANGUAGES AND SCRIPTS

1. *The Alphabet Throughout the Ages and in all Lands* (London: Staples Press, 1953), p.18.

2. Ibid., p.35.

Chapter 3
RELIGION

1. J.D. North, *Chaucer's Universe* (Oxford: Clarendon Press, 1988), p.37.

2. Richard Cavendish, *King Arthur and the Grail* (London Paladin Books, 1985), p.188.

3. Jacques Soustelle, *The Daily Life of the Aztecs* (Harmondsworth: Penguin, 1964), p.110.

4. I.F. Tingay and J. Badcock, *These Were the Romans* (Amersham: Hulton Educational Publications, 1985), p.51.

5. John Romer, *Romer's Egypt: A New Light on the Civilisation of Ancient Egypt)* London: Michael Joseph-Rainbird, 1982), p.13.

6. Munemoto Yanagi *et al, Byzantium* (Secaucus: N.J., Chartwell Books, 1978), p.11.

7. Christine Hobson, *Exploring the World of the Pharaohs* (London: Thames and Hudson, 1987), pp.22-37.

8. Nigel Davies, *The Ancient Kingdoms of Mexico* (Harmondsworth: Penguin, 1982), pp.22-32.

9. Karl Ludvig Reichelt, *Religion in Chinese Garment* (London: Lutterworth Press, 1951), pp.45-6.

10. Karel Capek, *President Masaryk Tells his Story* (London: Allen and Unwin, 1936), pp.212-3.

11. Gershom R. Cohen, "The Talmudic Age", in *Great Ages and Ideas of the Jewish People,* edited by Leo W. Schwarz (New York: Random House, 1956), p.175.

12. Elaine Pagels, *The Gnostic Gospels* (Harmondsworth: Penguin, 1979).

13. *The International Standard Bible Encyclopaedia* (Grand Rapids, Michigan: William B. Eedman's Publishing Co., 1979-88), p.606.

14. Roland Bainton, *The Penguin History of Christianity* Vol. 2, (Harmondsworth: Penguin, 1967), pp.51-2.

15. Bertrand Russell, *A History of Western Philosophy* (London: Allen and Unwin, 1946), p.592.

16. A.J. Arberry, *Sufism* (London: Allen and Unwin, 1950), p.60.

17. F.M. Cornford, *Before and After Socrates* (Cambridge: Cambridge University Press, 1932), p.37.

18. J.M. Plumley, "The Religion of Ancient Egypt", in *The Penguin Encyclopaedia of Ancient Civilisations,* edited by Arthur Cotterell (Harmondsworth: Penguin, 1980), p.69.

19. J. Burnet, "Philosophy", in *The Legacy of Greece,* edited by R.W. Livingstone (Oxford: Clarendon Press, 1951), p.85.

20. F.M. Cornford, op.cit., p.103.

21. Abraham S. Halkin, "The Judaic-Islamic Age", in *Great Ages and Ideas of the Jewish People,* edited by Leo W. Schwarz (New York: Random House, 1956), p.245.

22. Wilfred Cantwell-Smith, *Islam in Modern History* (New York: New American Library, 1957), p.77.

23. Ernest Barker, "The Conception of Empire", in *The Legacy of Rome,* edited by Cyril Bailey (Oxford: Oxford University Press, 1951), p.55.

Chapter 4
GOVERNMENT AND SOCIETY:
KINGSHIP AND CLASS

1. "Coronation", in *Royal Encyclopaedia* (London: Macmillan, 1991),pp.122-4.

2. Carmen Blacker, "The Shinza or God-seat in the *Daijosai* - Throne, Bed or Incubation Couch", *Japanese Journal of Religious Studies* 1990, pp.179-97.

3. A.L. Basham, *The Wonder that was India,* Vol. 1 (London: Sidgwick and Jackson, 1969), pp.32-4.

4. John Romer, *Ancient Lives* (London: Weidenfeld and Nicholson, 1984), p.4.

5. Michael Loewe, *The Pride that was China* (London: Sidgwick and Jackson. 1990), p.123.

6. Philip Rawson, *Indian Asia* (Oxford: Phaidon Press, 1977), pp.78-9.

7. René Guerdan, *Byzantium, Its Triumph and Tragedy* (London: Allen and Unwin, 1956), pp.20-26.

8. "Feudalism", *Encyclopaedia Britannica,* Vol. 4 (Chicago, 1992), p.755.

9. G.G. Coulton, *Medieval Panorama,* Vol. I (London: Collins-Fontana, 1961), p.260.

10. Derk Bodde, *China's Cultural Tradition* (New York: Rinehart, 1957), p.54.

11. Lin Yutang, *The Gay Genius: The Life and Times of Su Tungpo* (London: Heinemann, 1948), pp.34-5.

12. T.G.H. James, *Pharaoh's People: Scenes from Life in Imperial Egypt* (London: Bodley Head, 1984), pp.116-7.

13. John K. Fairbank, "The Nature of Chinese Society", in *Imperial China: The Decline of the Last Dynasty and The Origins of Modern China - The 18th and 19th Centuries,* edited by Franz Schurmann and Orville Schell (New York: Random House, 1967), p.37.

14. Carlo Levi, *Christ Stopped at Eboli* (London: Cassell, 1948), pp.116-7.

15. Virginia Cowles, *The Romanovs* (London: Collins, 1971), p.95.

16. R.H. Barrow, *The Romans* (Harmondsworth: Penguin, 1953), pp.209, 216.

17. Robert N. Bellah, "Beyond Belief", in *Essays on Religion in a Post-Traditional World* (New York: Harper and Row, 1970), p.155.

18. H.A.L. Fisher, *A History of Europe*, Vol. 1 (London: Fontana, 1968), p.317.

19. Marius B. Jansen, *Japan and its World: Two Centuries of Change* (New York: Princeton University Press, 1980).

20. Edwin O. Reischauer, *Japan: The Story of a Nation* (New York: Alfred A. Knopf, 1970), p.123.

Chapter 5
WOMEN

1. Alan K. Bowman, *Egypt After the Pharaohs* (London: British Museum Publications, 1986), p.134.

2. *The Guardian*, 2 April 1991.

3. G.M. Trevelyan, *Illustrated English Social History*, Vol. 1 (Longmans, 1942), p.64

4. *New York Times*, 31 December, 1977.

5. Robert Flacelière, *Daily Life in Greece at the Time of Pericles* (London: Weidenfeld and Nicholson, 1965), p.55.

6. Ibid., p.56.

7. Ibid., p.67.

8. Leonard Cottrell, *Life Under the Pharaohs* (London: Pan Books, 1960), pp.54-70.

9. Ibid., pp.77-8.

10. William and Charlotte Wiser, *Behind Mud Walls, 1930-60* (Berkeley and Los Angeles, University of California Press, 1963), pp.73, 85.

11. Jack Belden, *China Shakes the World* (New York: Harper and Row, 1949), pp.310-12. Quoted in Derk Bodde, *China's Cultural Tradition,* (New York: Rinehart, 1957), p.48.

12. Oswyn Murray, "Life and Society in Classical Greece", in *The Oxford History of the Classical World,* edited by John Boardman, Jasper Griffin and Oswyn Murray (Oxford: Oxford University Press, 1986), p.215.

13. Ananda K. Coomaraswsamy, *Buddha and the Gospel of Buddhism* (New York: Harper and Row, 1964), p.164.

14. G.M. Trevelyan, op.cit., pp.61-2.

Chapter 6
SLAVERY

1. Oswyn Murray, "Life and Society in Classical Greece", in *The Oxford History of the Classical World,* edited by John Boardman, Jasper Griffin and Oswyn Murray (Oxford: Oxford University Press, 1992), p.223.

2. C.I.F. Tingay and J. Badcock, *These were the Romans* (Amersham: Hulton Education Publications, 1985), p.128.

3. Oswyn Murray, op.cit.

4. Robert Flacelière, *Daily Life in Greece at the Time of Pericles* (London: Weidenfeld and Nicholson, 1985), p.52.

5. Alan K. Bowman, *Egypt after the Pharaohs* (London: British Museum Publications, 1986), p.152.

6. Iris Origo, *The Merchant of Prato* (Harmondsworth: Penguin, 1963), pp.99-100.

7. Basil Davidson, *The Africans: An Entry into Cultural History* (Harmondsworth: Penguin, 1973), pp.245-6.

8. Bruce Catton, *The Penguin Book of the American Civil War* (Harmondsworth: Penguin, 1960), p.9.

9. UNESCO, *The Birthright of Man* (New York: UNIPUB, 1969), p.845.

10. John Matthews, "Roman Life and Society", in *The Oxford History of the Classical World,* edited by John Boardman, Jasper Griffin and Oswyn Murray (Oxford: Oxford University Press, 1992), p.769.

11. "Slavery", *Encyclopaedia Britannica,* Vol. 27 (Chicago, 1992), pp.285-98.

12. Henry Chadwick, "Envoi: On Taking Leave of Antiquity" in *The Oxford History of the Classical World,* edited by John Boardman, Jasper Griffin and Oswyn Murray (Oxford: Oxford University Press, 1992), p.824.

13. R.B. Nye and J.E. Morpurgo, *The Birth of the USA,* Vol. 1 (Harmondsworth: Penguin, 1964), pp.76-7.

Chapter 7
FIGHTING AND WAR

1. Allan Massie, "Theodosius I (The Great)", in *A Hundred Great Lives of Antiquity,* edited by John Canning (London: Methuen, 1985), p.244.

2. Allan Massie, "Hannibal", in *A Hundred Great Lives of Antiquity,* edited by John Canning (London: Methuen, 1985), p.156.

3. David Howarth, *A Near Run Thing: The Day of Waterloo.* (London: Collins, 1986), pp.198, 205, 210.

4. Martin Windrow, *The Medieval Knight* (London: Franklin Watts, 1985), p.28.

5. H.A.L. Fisher, *A History of Europe,* Vol. 1 (London: Fontana, 1968), pp.617-8, 635-6.

6. G.C. Coulton, *Medieval Panorama,* Vol. II (London: Fontana, 1961), p.150.

7. J.G. Bennett, *The Masters of Wisdom* (London: Turnstone Books, 1977), p.142.

8. John A. Boyle, "Mongols", in *Colliers Encyclopaedia,* Vol. 16 (New York: Macmillan, 1983), p.455C.

9. B.H. Warmington, *Carthage* (Harmondsworth: Penguin, 1960), pp.249-55.

10. James Parkes, *A History of the Jewish People* (Harmondsworth: Penguin, 1967), pp.34-9.

11. John A. Boyle, op.cit.

12. Michael Wood, *In Search of the Dark Ages* (London: B.B.C., 1981), p.234.

13. Oliver Taplin, "Homer", in *The Oxford History of the Classical World,* edited by John Boardman, Jasper Griffin and Oswyn Murray (Oxford: Oxford University Press, 1992), p.58.

14. Leslie Alcock, *Arthur's Britain* (London: Allen Lane, 1971), p.57.

15. Richard Stoneman, "Aeschylus", in *A Hundred Great Lives of Antiquity,* edited by John Canning (London: Methuen, 1985), p.253.

16. J.G. Bennett, op.cit., p.56.

17. C.M. Bowra, *The Greek Experience* (London: Weidenfeld and Nicholson, 1957), p.23.

18. David Howarth, op.cit., p.65.

19. Jawaharlal Nehru, *The Discovery of India* (Bombay: Asia Publishing House, 1966), pp.88-9.

20. Michael Loewe, *The Pride That Was China* (London: Sidgwick and Jackson, 1990), p.138.

21. John K. Fairbank, *The United States and China* (Cambridge, Mass.: Harvard University Press, 1948), p.57.

22. Derk Bodde, *China's Cultural Tradition* (New York: Rinehart, 1957), p.60.

23. G.C. Coulton, op.cit., p.273.

24. Donald Soper, "St. Paul", in *A Hundred Great Lives of Antiquity,* edited by John Canning (London: Methuen, 1985), p.518.

25. Gabriel le Bras, "Canon Law", in *The Legacy of the Middle Ages,* edited by C.G. Crump and E.F. Jacob (Oxford: Oxford University Press, 1951), p.342.

26. George Trevelyan, *The Deeper Symbolism in Heraldry,* Wrekin Trust lecture no. 37 (Hereford: Wrekin Trust, 1972).

27. Richard Cavendish, *King Arthur and the Grail* (London: Paladin Books, 1985), p.60.

Chapter 8
EDUCATION

1. Georges Contenau, *Everyday Life in Babylon and Assyria* (London: Edward Arnold, 1954), pp.188-9.

2. T.G.H. James, *Pharaoh's People: Scenes of Life in Imperial Egypt* (London: Bodley Head, 1984), p.150.

3. Jacques Soustelle, *The Daily Life of the Aztecs* (Harmondsworth: Penguin, 1964), pp.176, 179.

4. Franz Schurmann and Orville Schell, "The Humanist Ethos of Traditional China" in Imperial China: The Decline of the Last Dynasty and The Origins of Modern China – The 18th and 19th Centuries (New York: Random House, 1967), p.9.

5. Michael Loewe, *Imperial China* (New York: Praeger, 1969), p.193.

6. Ibid., p.142.

7. Edwin O. Reischauer, *Japan: The Story of a Nation* (New York: Alfred A. Knopf, 1970), p.103.

8. Robert Flacelière, *Daily Life in Greece at the Time of Pericles* (London: Weidenfeld and Nicholson, 1965), pp.102-3.

9. Joint Association of Classical Teachers, *The World of Athens: An Introduction to Classical Athenian Culture* (Cambridge: Cambridge University Press, 1984), p.287.

10. Oswyn Murray, "Life and Society in Classical Greece", in *The Oxford History of the Classical World,* edited by John Boardman, Jasper Griffin and Oswyn Murray (Oxford: Oxford University Press, 1986), p.228.

11. Spiros Photinos, *Olympia: Complete Guide* (Athens: Olympic Publications, 1989), p.18.

12. Ibid, p.11.

13. Robert Flacelière, op.cit., pp.204-8.

14. Hugh Last, "Family and Social Life" in *The Legacy of Rome,* edited by Cyril Bailey (Oxford: Oxford University Press, 1951), pp.213, 217.

15. Colin Wells, *The Roman Empire* (London: Fontana, 1988), pp.272-8.

16. René Guerdan, *Byzantium, its Triumph and Tragedy* (London: Allen and Unwin, 1956), p.69.

17. Alfred Guillaume, *Islam* (Harmonsworth: Penguin, 1954), p.74.

18. H.A.R. Gibb, *Mohammedanism: An Historical Survey* (Oxford: Oxford University Press, 1953), pp.96-7.

19. Alfred Guillaume, "Philosophy and Theology" in *The Legacy of Islam,* edited by Thomas Arnold and Alfred Guillaume (Oxford: Oxford University Press, 1943), p.241.

20. H.A.R. Gibb, op.cit., p.139.

21. H.A.R. Gibb, op.cit., pp.145-6.

22. G.G. Coulton, *Medieval Panorama,* Vol. II, (London: Fontana, 1961), pp.7-9.

23. G.G. Coulton, *Medieval Panorama,* Vol. I, (London: Fontana, 1961), p.260.

24. G.G. Coulton, *Medieval Panorama,* Vol. II, (London: Fontana, 1961), pp.13, 11.

25. Denys Hay, *Europe in the 14th and 15th Centuries* (London: Longmans, 1989), pp.361, 363.

26. Charlotte Waterlow and Archibald Evan, *Europe 1945 to 1970* (London: Methuen, 1973), p.87.

Chapter 9
COMMUNICATIONS

1. G.M. Trevelyan, *Illustrated British Social History,* Vol. 4 (London: Longmans, 1952), p.71.

2. James Wellard, *The Search for Lost Cities* (London: Constable, 1980), p.71.

3. C.I.F. Tingay and J. Badcock, *These were the Romans* (Amersham: Hulton Education Publications, 1985), p.48.

4. Michael Loewe, *Imperial China* (New York: Praeger, 1969), p.216.

5. Evan Hadingham, *Lines to the Mountain Gods: Nazca and the Mysteries of Peru* (London: Harrap, 1987), p.226.

6. H.V. Martin, *In the Steps of St. Paul* (London: Rich and Cowan, 1936), p.336.

7. Derek St. Clair Stannard, personal communication.

8. Esther Warner, *Trial by Sasswood* (Harmondsworth: Penguin, 1995), pp.64-5.

9. Lin Yutang, *The Gay Genius: The Life and Times of Su Tungpo* (London: Heinemann, 1948), pp.40-47.

Chapter 10
SCIENCE

1. Joseph Needham, *The Grand Titration: Science and Society in East and West* (London: Allen and Unwin, 1969), p.14.

2. "The History of Science", *Encyclopaedia Britannica,* Vol. 27 (Chicago: 1992), p.32.

3. Joseph Needham, op.cit., p.16.

4. Georges Contenau, *Everyday Life in Babylon and Assyria* (London: Edward Arnold, 1954), p.225.

5. Walter Eugene Clark, in *The Legacy of India,* edited by G.T. Garratt (Oxford: Clarendon Press, 1938), p.347.

6. Oscar Paz, *The New York Review of Books,* 6 December 1990.

7. Brian M. Fagan, *Kingdoms of Gold, Kingdoms of Jade: The Americas before Columbus* (London: Thames and Hudson, 1991), p.162.

8. Serge Sauneron, *The Priests of Ancient Egypt* (New York: Grove Press, 1960), p.66.

9. A.L. Basham, *The Wonder that was India* (London: Sidgwick and Jackson, 1969), p.490.

10. Jawaharlal Nehru, *The Discovery of India* (Bombay: Asia Publishing House, 1966), p.227.

11. A.L. Basham, op.cit., p.496.

12. Joseph Needham, op.cit., pp.416-7.

13. Michael Loewe, *The Pride that was China* (London: Sidgwick and Jackson, 1990), p.240.

14. Joseph Needham, op.cit., p.44.

15. Joseph Needham, op.cit., p.21.

16. H.V.F. Winstone, *Uncovering the Ancient World* (London: Constable, 1985), p.126.

17. J.M. Dubbey, *The Development of Modern Mathematics* (London: Butterworth, 1970), p.9.

18. H.V.F. Winstone, op.cit.

19. Joseph Needham, op.cit., p.150.

20. Walter Eugene Clark, op.cit., pp.355-6.

21. Joseph Needham, Quoted in *Chinese Medicine, the Web that has no Weaver,* by Ted J. Kaptchuk (London: Rider, 1983), p.35.

22. Louise Morgan, Introduction to Shrimant Pratinidi, "Surya Namaskars", in *The Ten-Point Way to Health* (London: J.M. Dent and Sons, 1951), pp.7-8.

23. Nancy Treharne, personal communication.

24. Benjamin Farrington, *Greek Science* (Harmondsworth: Penguin, 1953), p.37-9.

25. Ibid, p.59.

26. Charles Singer, "Biology", in *The Legacy of Greece,* edited by R.W. Livingstone (Oxford: Clarendon Press, 1951), p.175.

27. Charles Singer, "Medicine", in *The Legacy of Greece,* edited by R.W. Livingstone (Oxford: Clarendon Press, 1951), pp.203-5.

28. Max Mayerhof, in *The Legacy of Islam,* edited by Thomas Arnold and Alfred Guillaume (Oxford: Oxford University Press, 1943), p.322.

29. Ibid, pp.329-30.

30. Bertrand Russell, *History of Western Philosophy* (London: Allen and Unwin, 1947), p.446.

31. Ibid, p.442.

32. G.G. Coulton, *Medieval Panorama,* Vol. II (London: Collins 1961), p.60.

Chapter 11
ART

1. T.R. Harris, *Egyptian Art* (London: Spring Books, 1966), p.22.

2. Philip Rawson, *Indian Asia* (Oxford: Phaidon Press, 1977), pp.130-2.

3. Titus Burchardt, *The Art of Islam* (Westerham: World of Islam Publishing Co., 1976), p.29.

4. Philip Rawson, op.cit., p.27.

5. Alan K. Bowman, *Egypt After the Pharoahs* (London: British Museum Publications, 1986), p.175.

6. Derk Bodde, *China's Cultural Tradition* (New York: Rinehart, 1957), p.32.

7. Lin Yutang, *The Gay Genius: the Life and Times of Su Tungpo* (London: Heinemann, 1948), pp.248-9.

8. Edwin O. Reischauer, *Japan: The Story of a Nation* (London: New York: Alfred A. Knopf, 1970), pp.70-71.

9. Peter Conrad, "The Last Emperor", *The Observer Magazine,* 30 December 1990, pp.34-7, 39.

10. Wim Swann, *The Gothic Cathedral* (London: Ferndale Press, 1981), p.14.

11. Evan Hadingham, *Lines to the Mountain Gods: Nazca and the Mysteries of Peru* (London: Harrap, 1987), p.118.

12. J.M. Plumley, "The Religion of Ancient Egypt", in *The Penguin Encyclopaedia of Ancient Civilisations,* edited by Arthur Cotterell (Harmondsworth: Penguin, 1980), p.70.

13. Titus Burchardt, op.cit.

14. Ernst Benz, *The Eastern Orthodox Church: Its Thought and Life* (New York: Doubleday, 1963), pp.6-18.

15. G. Gardner, Introduction to Dante, *The Divine Comedy* (London: J.M. Dent, 1948), p.xv.

16. Sydney Waterlow, personal communication.

17. Kenneth Clark, *Civilisation: A Personal View* (London: John Murray, 1970), p.305.

18. Ibid., p.243.

Chapter 12
AFRICA

1. Thomas Packenham, *The Scramble for Africa: 1876-1912* (London: Weidenfeld and Nicholson, 1991), p.xv.

2. Basil Davidson, *The Africans: An Entry into Cultural History* (Harmondsworth: Penguin, 1973), p.28.

3. John Mbiti, *African Religions and Philosophy* (New York: Doubleday, 1970), p.318.

4. Paul Bohannan and Philip Curtin, *Africa and Africans* (New York: Natural History Press, 1971), pp.252-5.

5. John Mbiti, op.cit., pp.19-31.

6. Basil Davidson, op.cit., p.32.

7. Gabriel M. Setiloane, *African Theology: An Introduction* (Johannesburg: Khateville, 1986), pp.49-50.

8. Ibid., pp.17-20.

9. Steven Allford, "Witch Doctor", *Link* (Godalming Churches, Surrey, December 1990), p.18.

10. John Mbiti, op.cit., p.171.

11. Edwin W. Smith, *Knowing the African* (London: Lutterworth Press, 1946), pp.101-2.

12. Geoffry Parrinder, *Religion in Africa* (Harmondsworth: Penguin, 1969), p.28.

13. J. Spencer Trimingham, *The Influence of Islam upon Africa* (London: Longman, 1980), p.46.

14. Ibid., p.68.

15. Ibid., p.119.

16. Ibid., pp.133, 137.

17. John Mbiti, op.cit., p.268.

18. James H. Vaughan, "Social and Political Organisation in Traditional Society", in *Africa,* edited by Phyllis Martin and Patrick O'Meara (Bloomington, Indiana: Indiana University Press, 1977), pp.178-9.

19. Mervyn Claxton, *Culture and Development* (Paris: UNESCO, 1994), pp.13-14.

20. John Lamphear, "Two Basic Scenes in African History: Migration and State Formation", in *Africa,* edited by Phyllis Martin and Patrick O'Meara (Bloomington, Indiana: Indiana University Press, 1977), pp.92-3.

21. Edwin W. Smith, op.cit., p.118.

Chapter 13
THE PHILOSOPHY OF HUMAN RIGHTS

1. "Income Tax", in *The Hutchinson Softback Encyclopaedia* (London: Hutchinson, 1991), p.417.

2. "Income Tax", in *The Concord Desk Encyclopaedia,* Vol.II (New York: Concord Reference Books, 1982), p.621.

Chapter 14
THE IMPLEMENTATION OF HUMAN RIGHTS

1. John Kenneth Galbraith, *The World Economy since the Wars: A Personal View* (London: Sinclair Stevenson, 1994), p.47.

2. Charlotte Waterlow and Archibald Evans, *Europe 1945-1970* (London: Methuen, 1973), pp.234-5.

3. United Nations Development Programme, *Human Development Report 1994* (Oxford: Oxford University Press, 1994), p.26.

4. John Kenneth Galbraith, op.cit., p.241.

5. Donella H. Meadows, Dennis L. Meadows, Jorgen Randers and William W. Behrens III, *The Limits to Growth: A Report for the Club of Rome's Project on the Predicament of Mankind* (London: Pan, 1974).

6. E.F. Schumacher, *Small is Beautiful: A Study of Economics as if People Mattered* (London: Blond & Briggs, 1973).

7. Mikhail Gorbachev, *Perestroika: New Thinking for our Country and the World* (London: Collins, 1987), pp.30-5.

8. United Nations Development Programme, op.cit., p.207.

9. Ibid., p.48.

Chapter 15
THE ERUPTION OF THE IMAGINATION: PSYCHOLOGY, FEMINISM AND ART.

1. Geraldine Foster, *Yoga and Western Psychology* (Oxford: Oxford University Press, 1934).

2. Lyn Owen, *Weekly Guardian*, 16 May 1976.

3. United Nations' Centre for Human Rights, *Information Kit on the UN Convention on the Right of the Child* (New York: United Nations, 1990).

4. Gaston Diehl, *The Moderns: A Treasury of Painting Throughout the World* (New York: Crown Publishers, 1961), p.22.

5. Ibid., p.8.

Chapter 16
THE EMERGING GLOBAL SPIRITUALITY

1. Hendrik Kraemer, *World Cultures and World Religions: The Coming Dialogue* (Philadelphia: Westminster Press, 1960), p.233.

2. Romain Rolland, *The Life of Vivekananda and the Universal Gospel* (Calcutta: Advita Ashram, 1965), pp.36-8.

3. Hendrick Kraemer, op.cit., p.152.

4. H.A.R. Gibb, *Mohammedanism* (Oxford: Oxford University Press, 1953), p.37.

5. Edward B. Fiske, *New York Times*, 18 September 1974, p.12.

6. H.A.R. Gibb, *Modern Trends in Islam* (Chicago: University of Chicago Press, 1947), p.119.

7. John Hick, *The Centre of Christianity* (New York: Harper and Row, 1978), p.71.

8. Beatrice Bruteau, *Evolution Towards Divinity: Teilhard de Chardin and the Hindu Traditions* (Wheaton, Ill.: Theosophical Publishing House, 1974).

9. Satprem, *Sri Aurobindo or the Adventure of Consciousness* (Pondicherry: Sri Aurobindo Ashram, 1968).

10. Lawrence Hyde, unpublished manuscript.

Chapter 17
THE CURRENT WORLD CRISIS

1. Norman Myers, *Ultimate Security: The Environment Basis of Political Stability* (London: W.W. Norton, 1993), p.170.

2. Ibid., p.179.

3. Edward O. Wilson, *The Diversity of Life* (London: Allen Lane, 1992), p.280.

4. Ibid., pp.283-99.

5. United Nations Information Centre for the UK and Ireland, *News Summary* NS/26/90, 8 September 1994.

6. Royal Society of London / US National Academy of Sciences, *Population Growth, Resource Consumption and a Sustainable World* (London: 1992), p.1.

7. *Christian Science Monitor,* 8 September 1994.

8. *Financial Times,* 14 September 1994.

9. *Observer,* 11 September 1994.

10. United Nations Development Programme, *Human Development Report 1994* (Oxford: Oxford University Press, 1994), p.28.

11. Pratap Rughani, "Love in a Plague of Hatred", *New Internationalist,* 1993, no.250, December 1993, p.7.

12. Lester R. Brown, "Facing Food Insecurity", in *State of the World 1994,* edited by Lester R. Brown *et al* (London: Earthscan, 1994), pp.177-97.

13. Club of Rome, *The First Global Revolution* (London: Simon and Schuster, 1991), p.117.

14. World Commission on Environment and Development, *Our Common Future,* (The Brundtland Report) (Oxford, Oxford University Press, 1987), pp.181-9.

15. Christopher Flavin,"Building a Bridge to Sustainable Energy", in *State of the World 1992,* edited by Lester R. Brown *et al* (London: Earthscan, 1992), p.45.

16. World Commission on Environment and Development, op.cit., pp.8-9.

17. Norman Myers, op.cit., pp.219-21.

Chapter 18
THE FOUNDATION OF WORLD COMMUNITY

1. *United Nations Peacekeepers,* (New York: United Nations Department of Public Information, 1994).

2. Michael Harbottle, *What is Proper Soldiering?* (Chipping Norton: Centre for International Peacebuilding, 1991).

3. Ruth L. Sivard, *World Military and Social Expenditures, 1991* (Washington D.C.: World Priorities, 1991), p.17.

4. United Nations Development Programme, *Human Development Report, 1994* (Oxford: Oxford University Press, 1994), p.56.

5. Benjamin B. Ferencz, "Making the United Nations Work", *INFORM* (Goshen, Indiana: Journal of the Fourth Freedom Forum, No. 15, Fall 1994), p.14.

6. Independent Commission on International Development Issues, *North South: A Programme for Survival,* (The Brandt Report) (London: Pan, 1980), p.284.

7. *United Nations Peacekeeping,* op.cit., pp.136-45.

8. Bertrand Schneider, *The Barefoot Revolution: A Report to the Club of Rome* (London: Intermediate Technology Publications, 1998), p.77.

9. Ibid., p.84.

10. Ibid., p.71.

11. Irene Dankelman and Joan Davidson, *Women and Environment in the Third World* (London: Earthscan, 1988), pp.5, 16.

12. Bertrand Schneider, op.cit., p.237.

13. Paul Lawrence and Charalambos Vlachoutsicos, personal communication.

14. Boutros Boutros-Ghali, *An Agenda for Peace* (New York: United Nations, 1992), p.17.

15. Erskine Childers and Brian Urquhart, *Renewing the United Nations System* (Uppsala: Dag Hammarskjold Foundation, 1994), p.125.

16. Erskine Childers, "A UN for All Our Children", in *Challenges to the United Nations: Building a Safer World* (London: C.I.I.R., 1994), p.205.

17. Erskine Childers and Brian Urquhart, op.cit., pp.189-90.

18. Erskine Childers, "The United Nations System", in *Challenges to the United Nations: Building a Safer World* (London: C.I.I.R., 1994), pp.24-5.

19. Erskine Childers and Brian Urquhart, op.cit., pp.148-9.

AFTERWORD

1. Fred Hoyle, *The Nature of the Universe* (Oxford: Blackwell, 1950), pp.115, 118.

2. John Taylor, "Matter Beyond the End of its Tether", in *Cosmology Now,* edited by Laurie John (London: BBC, 1973), p.166.

3. Francis Graham-Smith and Bernard Lovell, *Pathways to the Universe* (Cambridge: Cambridge University Press, 1988), p.225.

4. Murray Gell-Mann, *The Quark and the Jaguar* (London: Little, Brown, 1994).

Bibliography

Alcock, Leslie, *Arthur's Britain* (London: Allen Lane, 1971).

Arberry, A.J., *Surfism* (London: Allen and Unwin, 1950).

Arnold, Thomas and Guillaume, Alfred, *The Legacy of Islam* (Oxford: Oxford University Press, 1943).

Baily, Cyril (ed.), *The Legacy of Rome* (Oxford: Oxford University Press, 1951).

Bainton, Roland, *The Penguin History of Christianity,* Vol.2, (Harmondsworth: Penguin, 1967).

Basham, A.L., *The Wonder that was India,* Vol.1 (London: Sidgwick and Jackson, 1969).

Barrow, R.H., *The Romans* (Harmondsworth: Penguin, 1953).

Bellah, Robert N., *Essays on Religion in a Post-Traditional World* (New York: Harper and Row, 1970).

Bennett, J.G., *The Masters of Wisdom* (London: Turnstone Books, 1977).

Benz, Ernst, *The Eastern Orthodox Church: Its Thought and Life* (New York: Doubleday, 1963).

Boardman, John, Griffin, Jasper, and Murray, Oswyn (eds.) *The Oxford History of the Classical World* (Oxford: Oxford University Press, 1986).

Bodde, Derk, *China's Cultural Tradition* (New York: Rinehart, 1957).

Bohannan, Paul and Curtin, Philip, *Africa and Africans* (New York: Natural History Press, 1971).

Boutros-Ghali, Boutros, *An Agenda for Peace* (New York: United Nations, 1992).

Bowman, Alan K., *Egypt After the Pharaohs* (London: British Museum Publications, 1986).

Bowra, C.M., *The Greek Experience* (London: Weidenfeld and Nicholson, 1957).

Brown, Lester R. (ed.), *State of the World 1994* (London: Earthscan, 1994).

Bruteau, Beatrice, *Evolution Towards Divinity: Teilhard de Chardin and the Hindu Traditions* (Wheaton,Ill.: Theosophical Publishing House, 1974).

Burchardt, Titus, *The Art of Islam* (Westerham: World of Islam Publishing Co., 1976).

Canning, John (ed.), *A Hundred Great Lives of Antiquity* (London: Methuen, 1985).

Cantwell-Smith, Wilfred, *Islam in Modern History* (New York: New American Library, 1957).

Capek, Karel, *President Masaryk Tells his Story* (London: Allen and Unwin, 1936).

Catton, Bruce, *The Penguin Book of the American Civil War* (Harmondsworth: Penguin, 1960).

Cavendish, Richard, *King Arthur and the Grail* (London: Paladin Books, 1985).

Childers, Erskine (ed.) *Challenges to the United Nations: Building a Safer World* (London: C.I.I.R., 1994).

Childers, Erskine and Urquhart, Brian, *Renewing the United Nations System* (Uppsala: Dag Hammarskjold Foundation, 1994).

Clark, Kenneth, *Civilisation: A Personal View* (London: John Murray, 1970).

Claxton, Mervyn, *Culture and Development* (Paris: UNESCO, 1994).

Club of Rome, *The First Global Revolution* (London: Simon and Schuster, 1991).

Colliers Encyclopaedia (New York: Macmillan, 1983).

Contenau, Georges, *Everyday Life in Babylon and Assyria* (London: Edward Arnold, 1954).

Coomaraswsamy, Ananda K., *Buddha and the Gospel of Buddhism* (New York: Harper and Row, 1964).

Cornford, F.M., *Before and After Socrates* (Cambridge: Cambridge University Press, 1932).

Cotterell, Arthur (ed.) *Penguin Encyclopaedia of Ancient Civilisations,* (Harmondsworth: Penguin, 1980).

Cottrell, Leonard, *Life Under the Pharaohs* (London: Pan Books, 1960).

Coulton, G.G., *Medieval Panorama,* Vols.I and II (London: Collins Fontana, 1961).

Cowles, Virginia, *The Romanovs* (London: Collins, 1971).

Crump, C.G. and Jacob, E.F., *The Legacy of the Middle Ages* (Oxford: Oxford University Press, 1951).

Dankelman, Irene and Davidson, Joan, *Women and Environment in the Third World* (London: Earthscan, 1988).

Dante, *The Divine Comedy* (London: J.M. Dent, 1948).

Davies, Nigel, *The Ancient Kingdoms of Mexico* (Harmondsworth: Penguin, 1982).

Davison, Basil, *The Africans: An Entry into Cultural History* (Harmondsworth: Penguin, 1973).

Diehl, Gaston, *The Moderns: A Treasury of Painting Throughout the World*(New York: Crown Publishers, 1961).

Dubbey, J.M., *The Development of Modern Mathematics* (London: Butterworth, 1970).

Fagan, Brian M., *Kingdoms of Gold, Kingdoms of Jade: The Americas before Columbus* (London: Thames and Hudson, 1991).

Fairbank, John K., *The United States and China* (Cambridge: Mass.: Harvard University Press, 1948).

Encyclopaedia Britannica (Chicago, 1992).

Fisher, H.A.L., *A History of Europe,* Vol.I (London: Fontana, 1968).

Flacelière, Robert, *Daily Life in Greece at the Time of Pericles* (London: Weidenfeld and Nicholson, 1965).

Galbraith, John Kenneth, *The World Ecomony since the Wars: A Personal View:* London: Sinclair Stevenson, 1994).

Foster, Geraldine, *Yoga and Western Psychology* (Oxford: Oxford University Press, 1934).

Gell-Mann, Murray, *The Quark and the Jaguar* (London: Little, Brown, 1994).

Gibb, H.A.R., *Modern Trends in Islam* (Chicago: University of Chicago Press, 1947).

Gibb, H.A.R., *Mohammedanism: An Historical Survey* (Oxford: Oxford University Press, 1953).

Gorbachev, Mikhail, *Perestroika: New Thinking for our Country and the World* (London: Collins, 1987).

Graham-Smth, Francis and Lovell, Bernard, *Pathways to the Universe* (Cambridge: Cambridge University Press, 1988).

Guerdan, René, *Byzantium, Its Triumph and Tragedy* (London: Allen and Unwin, 1956).

Guillaume, Alfred, *Islam* (Harmondsworth: Penguin, 1954).

Hadingham, Evan, *Lines to the Mountain Gods: Nazca and the Mysteries of Peru* (London: Harrap, 1987).

Harbottle, Michael, *What is Proper Soldiering?* (Chipping Norton: Centre for International Peacebuilding, 1991).

Harris, T.R., *Egyptian Art* (London: Spring Books, 1966).

Hay, Denys, *Europe in the 14th and 15th Centuries* (London: Longmans, 1989).

Hick, John, *The Centre of Christianity* (New York: Harper and Row, 1978).

Hobson, Christine, *Exploring the World of the Pharaohs* (London: Thames and Hudson, 1987).

Howarth, David, *A Near Run Thing: The Day of Waterloo* (London: Collins, 1986).

Hoyle, Fred, *The Nature of the Universe* (Oxford: Blackwell, 1950).

Independent Commission on International Development Issues, *North-South: A Programme for Survival,* (The Brandt Report) (London: Pan, 1980).

James. T.G.H., *Pharaoh's People: Scenes from Life in Imperial Egypt* (London: Bodley Head, 1984).

Jansen, Marius B., *Japan and its World: Two Centuries of Change* (New York: Princeton University Press, 1980).

Joint Association of Classical Teachers, *The World of Athens: An Introduction to Classical Culture* (Cambridge: Cambridge University Press, 1984).

Kaptchuk, Ted J., *Chinese Medicine, The Web that has no Weaver* (London: Rider, 1983).

Kraemer, Hendrik, *World Cultures and World Religions: The Coming Dialogue* (Philadelphia: Westminster Press, 1960).

Levi, Carlo, *Christ Stopped at Eboli* (London: Cassell, 1948).

Livingstone, R.W. (ed.), *The Legacy of Greece* (Oxford: Clarendon Press, 1951).

Loewe, Michael, *Imperial China* (New York: Praeger, 1969).

Loewe, Michael, *The Pride that was China* (London: Sidwick and Jackson, 1990).

Martin, H.V., *In the Steps of St. Paul* (London: Rich and Cowan, 1936).

Martin, Phyllis and O'Meara, Patrick (eds.) *Africa* (Bloomimgton Indiana: Indiana University Press, 1977).

Mbiti, John, *African Religions and Philosophy* (New York: Doubleday, 1970).

Meadows, Donella H., Meadows, Dennis L., Randers, Jorgen and Behrens, William W. III, *The Limits of Growth: A Report for the Club of Rome's Project on the Predicament of Mankind* (London: Pan, 1974).

Myers, Norman, *Ultimate Security: The Environmental Basis of Political Stability* (London: W.W. Norton, 1993).

Needham, Joseph, *The Grand Titration: Science and Society in East and West* (London: Allen and Unwin, 1969).

Nehru, Jawaharlal, *The Discovery of India* (Bombay: Asia Publishing House, 1966).

North, J.D., *Chaucer's Universe* (Oxford: Oxford University Press, 1988).

Nye, R.B. and Morpurgo, J.E., *The Birth of the USA*, Vol.I (Harmondsworth: Penguin, 1964).

Origo, Iris, *The Merchant of Prato* (Harmondsworth: Penguin, 1963).

Packenham, Thomas, *The Scramble for Africa: 1876-1912* (London: Weidenfeld and Nicholson, 1991).

Pagels, Elaine, *The Gnostic Gospels* (Harmondsworth: Penguin, 1979).

Parkes, James, *A History of the Jewish People* (Harmondsworth: Penguin, 1967).

Parrinder, Geoffrey, *Religion in Africa* (Harmondsworth: Penguin, 1969).

Pratinidi, Shrimant, *The Ten-Point Way to Health* (London: J.M. Dent and Sons, 1951).

Photinos, Spiros, *Olympia: Complete Guide* (Athens: Olympic Publications, 1989).

Rawson, Philip, *Indian Asia* (Oxford: Oxford University Press, 1977).

Reichelt, Karl Ludvig, *Religion in Chinese Garment* (London: Lutterworth Press, 1951).

Reischauer, Edwin, O., *Japan: The Story of a Nation* (New York: Alfred A. Knopf, 1970).

Renfrew, Colin and Bahn, Paul, *Archaeology: Theories, Methods and Practice* (London: Thames and Hudson, 1991).

Rolland, Romain, *The Life of Vivekananda and the Universal Gospel* (Calcutta: Advita Ashram, 1965).

Romer, John, *Romer's Egypt: A New Light on the Civilisation of Ancient Egypt* (London: Michael Joseph-Rainbird, 1982).

Romer, John, *Ancient Lives* (London: Weidenfeld and Nicholson, 1984).

Royal Encyclopaedia (London: Macmillan, 1991).

Royal Society of London / U.S. National Academy of Sciences, *Population Growth, Resource Consumption and a Sustainable World* (London: 1992).

Russell, Bertrand, *A History of Western Philosophy* (London: Allen and Unwin, 1946).

Sauneron, Serge, *The Priests of Ancient Egypt* (New York: Grove Press, 1960).

Satprem, *Sri Aurobindo or the Adventure of Consciousness* (Pondicherry: Sri Aurobindo Ashram, 1968).

Schneider, Bertrand, *The Barefoot Revolution: A Report to the Club of Rome* (London: Intermediate Technology Publications, 1988).

Schumacher, E.F., *Small is Beautiful: A Study of Economics as if People Mattered* (London: Blond & Briggs, 1973).

Schurmann, Franz and Schell, Orville (eds.) *Imperial China: The Decline of the Last Dynasty and The Origins of Modern China – The 18th and 19th Centuries* (New York: Random House, 1967).

Schwarz, Leo W. (ed.) *Great Ages and Ideas of the Jewish People,* (New York: Ramdom House, 1956).

Setiloane, Gabriel M., *African Theology: An Introduction* (Johannesburg: Skateville, 1986).

Sivard, Ruth L., *World Military and Social Expenditures 1991* (Washington D.C.,: World Priorities, 1991).

Soustelle, Jacques, *The Daily Life of the Aztecs* (Harmdonsworth: Penguin, 1964).

Smith, Edwin W., *Knowing the African* (London: Lutterworth Press, 1946).

Swann, Wim, *The Gothic Cathedral* (London: Ferndale Press, 1981).

The Alphabet throughout the Ages and in all Lands (London: Staples Press, 1953).

The Concord Desk Encyclopaedia, Vol.II (New York: Concord Reference Books, 1982), p.621.

The Hutchinson Softback Encyclopaedia (London: Hutchinson, 1991) p.417.

The International Stanard Bible Encyclopaedia (Grand Rapids, Michigan: William B. Eedman's Publishing Co., 1979-88).

Tingay, I.F. and Badcock, J., *These Were the Romans* (Amersham: Hulton Educational Publications, 1985).

Trevelyan, G.M., *Illustrated English Social History*, Vol.1 and 4 (Longmans, 1942).

Trimingham, J. Spencer, *The Influence of Islam upon Africa* (London: Longman, 1980).

UNESCO, *The Birthright of Man* (New York: UNIPUB, 1969).

United Nations Centre for Human Rights, *Information Kit on the UN Convention on the Right of a Child* (New York: United Nations, 1990).

United Nations Development Programme, *Human Development Report 1994* (Oxford: Oxford University Press, 1994).

United Nations Peacekeeping (New York: United Nations Department of Public Information, 1994).

Warmington, B.H., *Carthage* (Harmondsworth: Penguin, 1960).

Warner, Esther, *Trial by Sasswood* (Harmondsworth: Penguin, 1955).

Waterlow, Charlotte and Evans, Archibald, *Europe 1945 to 1970* (London: Methuen, 1973).

Wellard, James, *The Search for Lost Cities* (London Constable, 1980).

Wells, Colin, *The Roman Empire* (London: Fontana, 1988).

Wilson, Edward O., *The Diversity of Life* (London: Allen Lane, 1992).

Windrow, Martin, *The Medieval Knight* (London: Franklin Watts, 1985).

Winstone, H.V.F., *Uncovering the Ancient World* (London: Constable, 1985).

Wiser, William and Charlotte, *Behind Mud Walls, 1930-60)* (Berkeley and Los Angeles, University of California Press, 1963).

Wood, Michael, *In Search of the Dark Ages* (London: B.B.C., 1981).

World Commission on Environment and Development, *Our Common Future,* (The Brundtland Report) (Oxford: Oxford University Press, 1987).

Yanagi, Munemoto, *et al, Byzantium* (Secaucus N.J.: Chartwell Books, 1978).

Yutang, Lin, *The Gay Genius: The Life and Times of Su Tungpo* (London: Heineman, 1948).

Index